Shojo Beat

YMOUS
NOISE

Ryoko Fukuyama

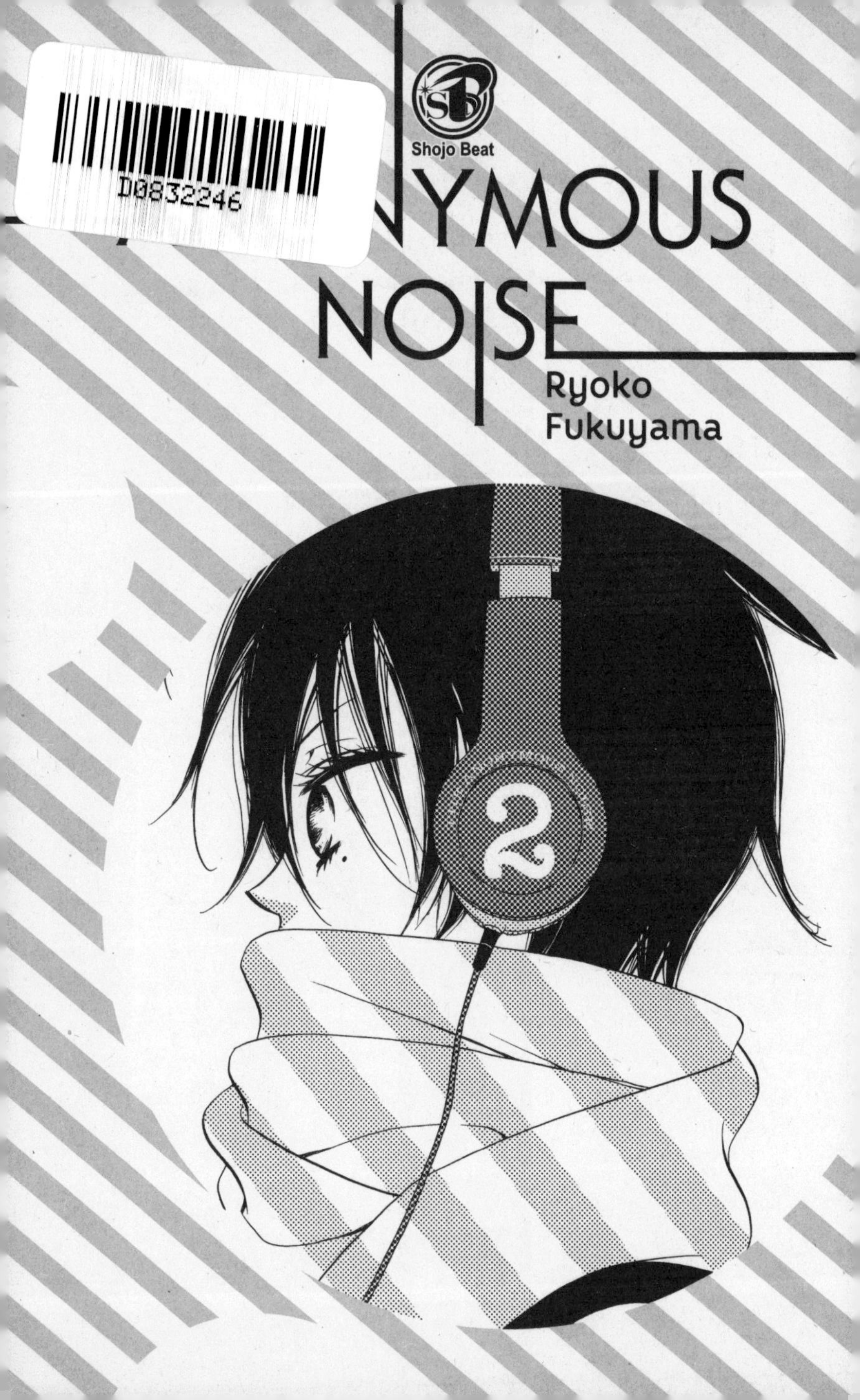
2

Anonymous
Noise
Volume 2

CONTENTS

Characters

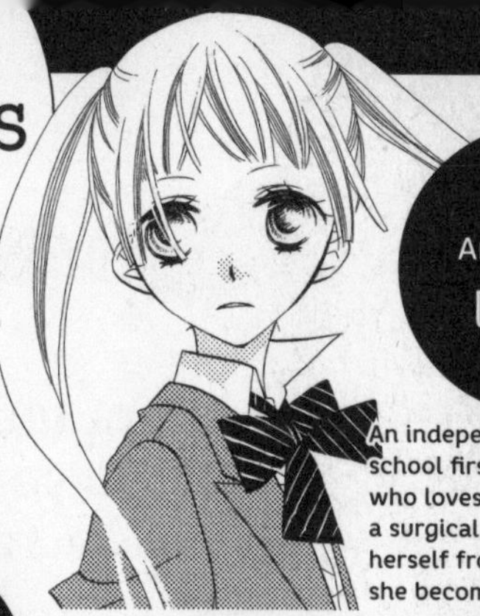

Nino Arisugawa
[Nino]

An independent-minded high school first-year student who loves to sing. She wears a surgical mask to stop herself from screaming when she becomes emotional.

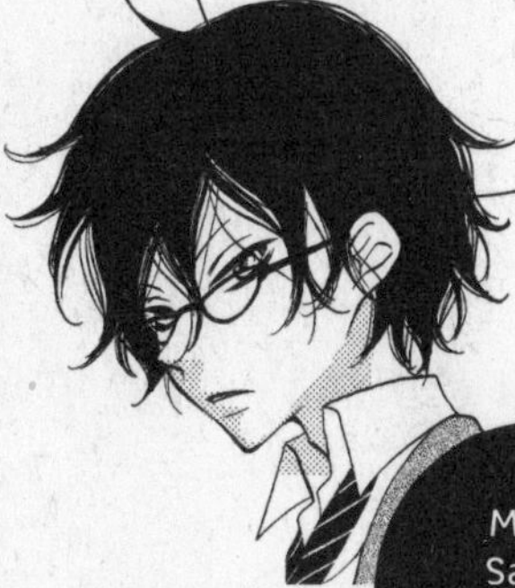

Momo Sakaki
[Momo]

A childhood friend of Nino's who loves bad puns. He attends the same high school as Nino and Yuzu, and he seems to compose music too.

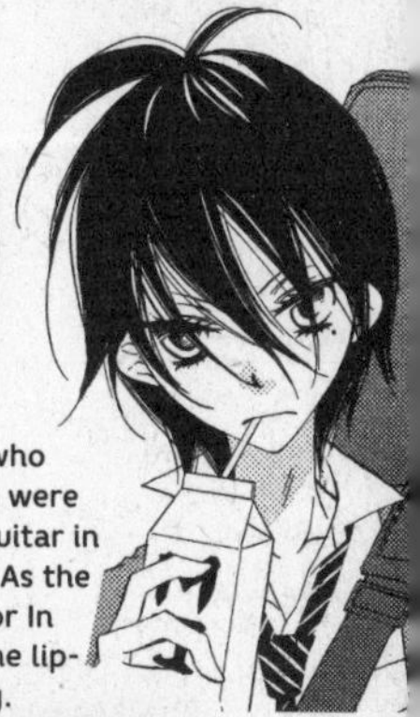

Kanade Yuzuriha
[Yuzu]

A young composer who met Nino when they were children. He plays guitar in the Pop Music Club. As the fake front woman for In No Hurry to Shout, he lip-synchs while in drag.

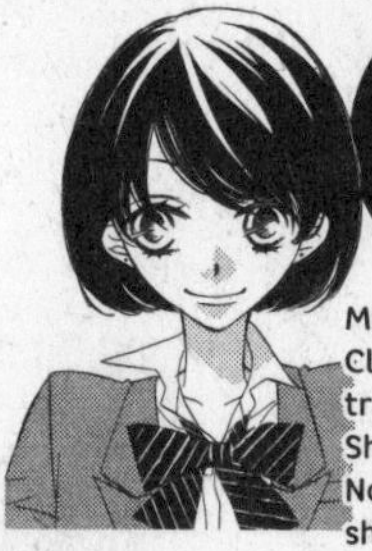

Miou Suguri

Miou sings in the Pop Music Club and does the vocal tracks for In No Hurry to Shout. However, when In No Hurry performs live, she plays the role of the guitarist, "Cheshire."

in NO hurry to shout;

In No Hurry to Shout

A popular rock band whose members hide their identities with masks and eye patches.
Vocals: Alice
Guitar: Cheshire
Bass: Queen
Drums: Hatter

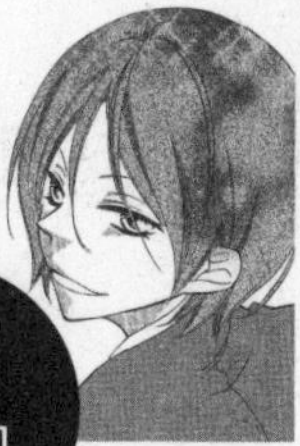

Ayumi Kurose
[Kuro]

Kuro plays the drums in the Pop Music Club and is "Hatter" in In No Hurry.

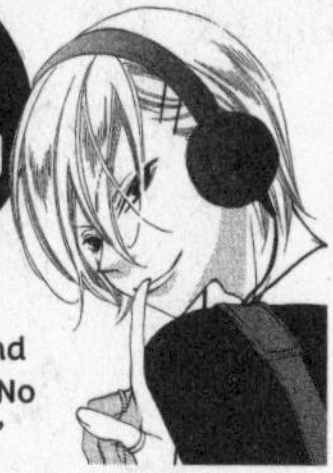

Yoshito Haruno
[Haruyoshi]

President of the Pop Music Club and the bassist for In No Hurry as "Queen."

Story

★ Music-loving Nino was abandoned twice in her youth—first by her girlhood crush Momo and then by the young composer Yuzu. Believing both their promises that they would find her again through her voice, Nino keeps singing. Later, in high school, she reunites with Yuzu.

★ Nino successfully fills in for the missing Miou during a Pop Music Club concert. But even performing together doesn't help resolve the conflicting feelings that Yuzu and Nino have. And now Miou has asked that Nino replace her in In No Hurry to Shout!

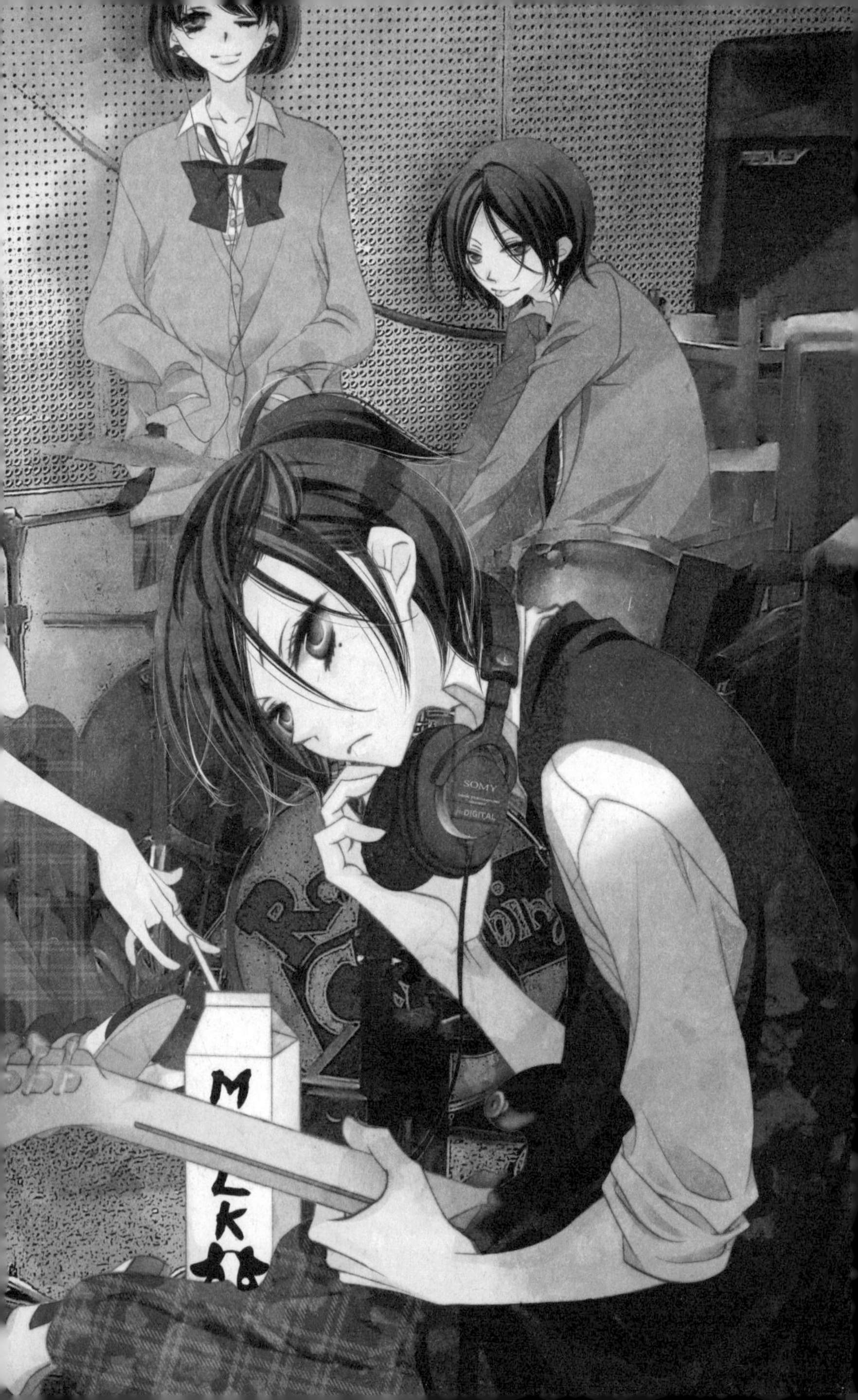
SOMY
DIGITAL
M
L
K

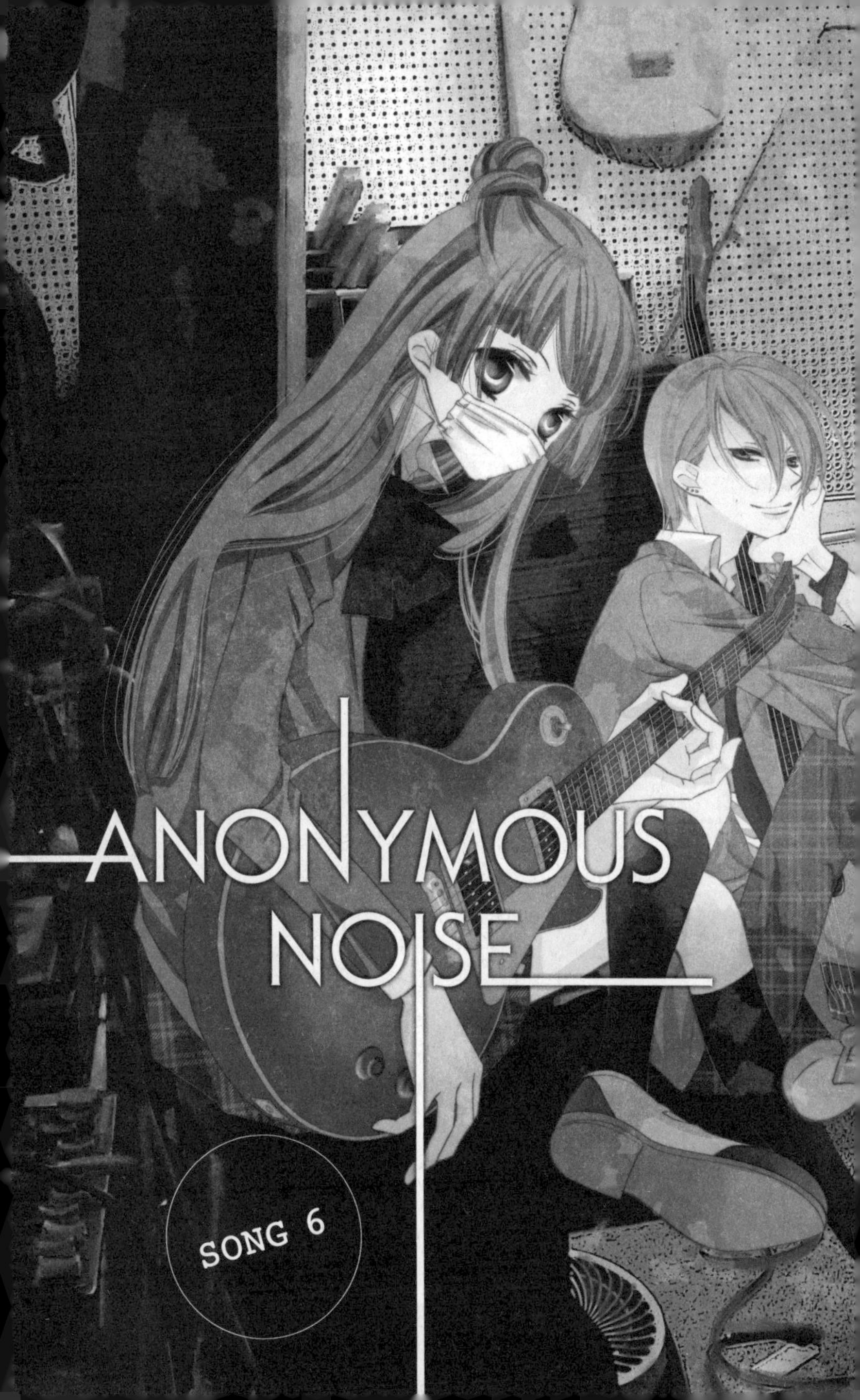
ANONYMOUS
NOISE
SONG 6

THE HEART-POUNDING EPIC SAGA OF **YUZU AND HIS MILK** EPISODE 2

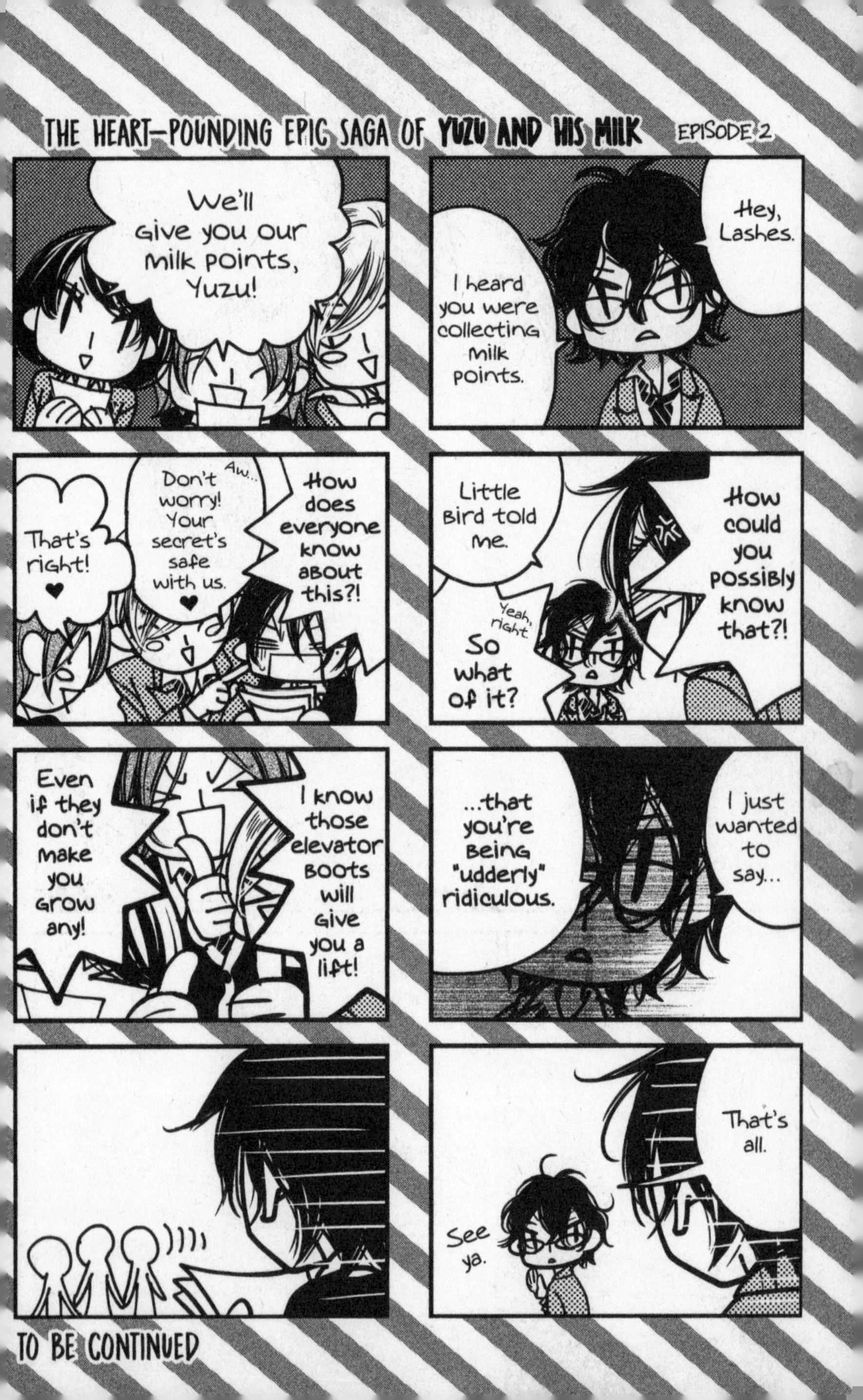
Hey, Lashes.
I heard you were collecting milk points.
We'll give you our milk points, Yuzu!
How could you possibly know that?!
Little Bird told me.
Yeah, right.
So what of it?
How does everyone know about this?!
Aw...
Don't worry! Your secret's safe with us. ♥
That's right! ♥
I just wanted to say...
...that you're being "udderly" ridiculous.
I know those elevator boots will give you a lift!
Even if they don't make you grow any!
That's all.
See ya.

TO BE CONTINUED

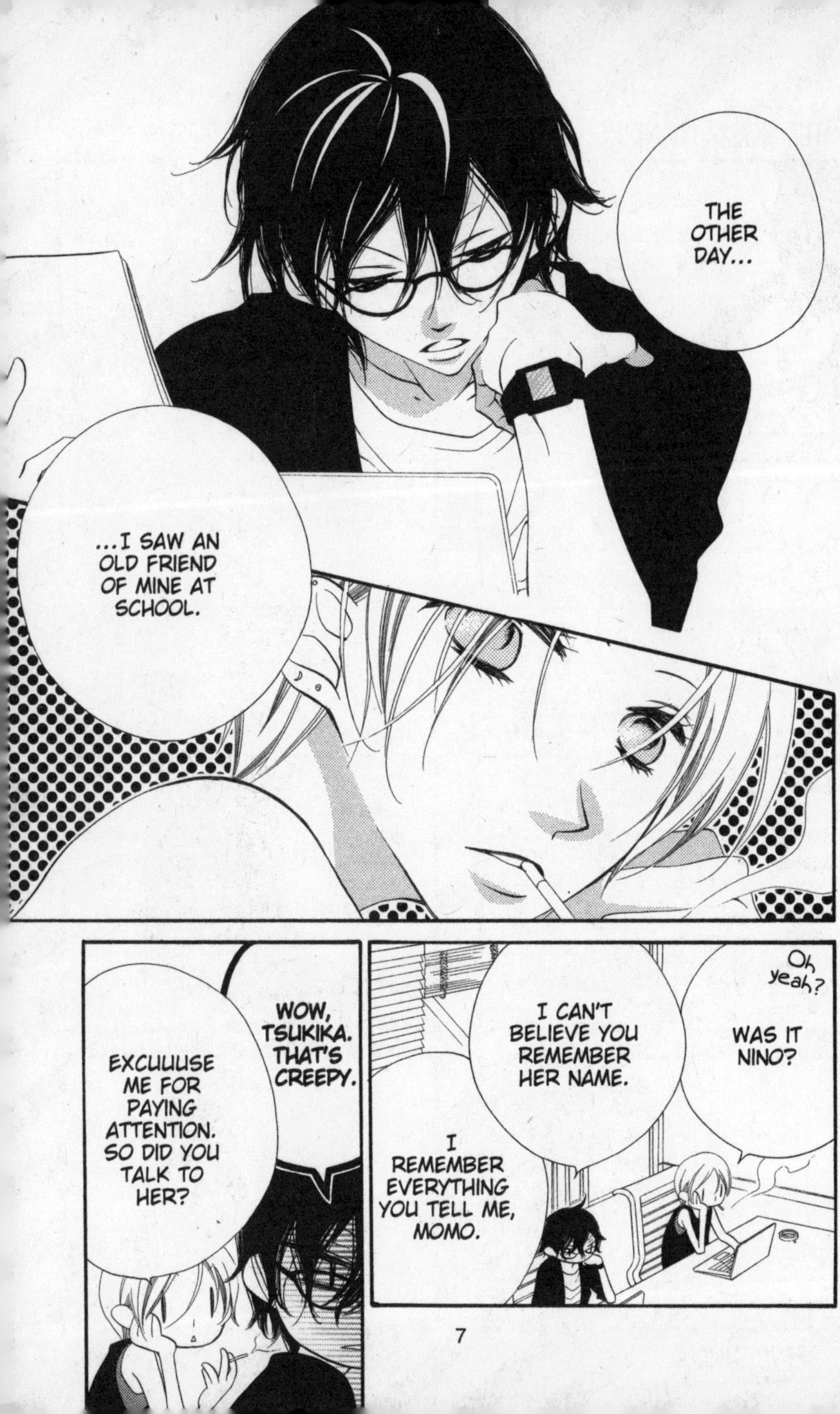
THE OTHER DAY...
...I SAW AN OLD FRIEND OF MINE AT SCHOOL.
Oh yeah?
WAS IT NINO?
I CAN'T BELIEVE YOU REMEMBER HER NAME.
I REMEMBER EVERYTHING YOU TELL ME, MOMO.
WOW, TSUKIKA. THAT'S CREEPY.
EXCUUUSE ME FOR PAYING ATTENTION. SO DID YOU TALK TO HER?

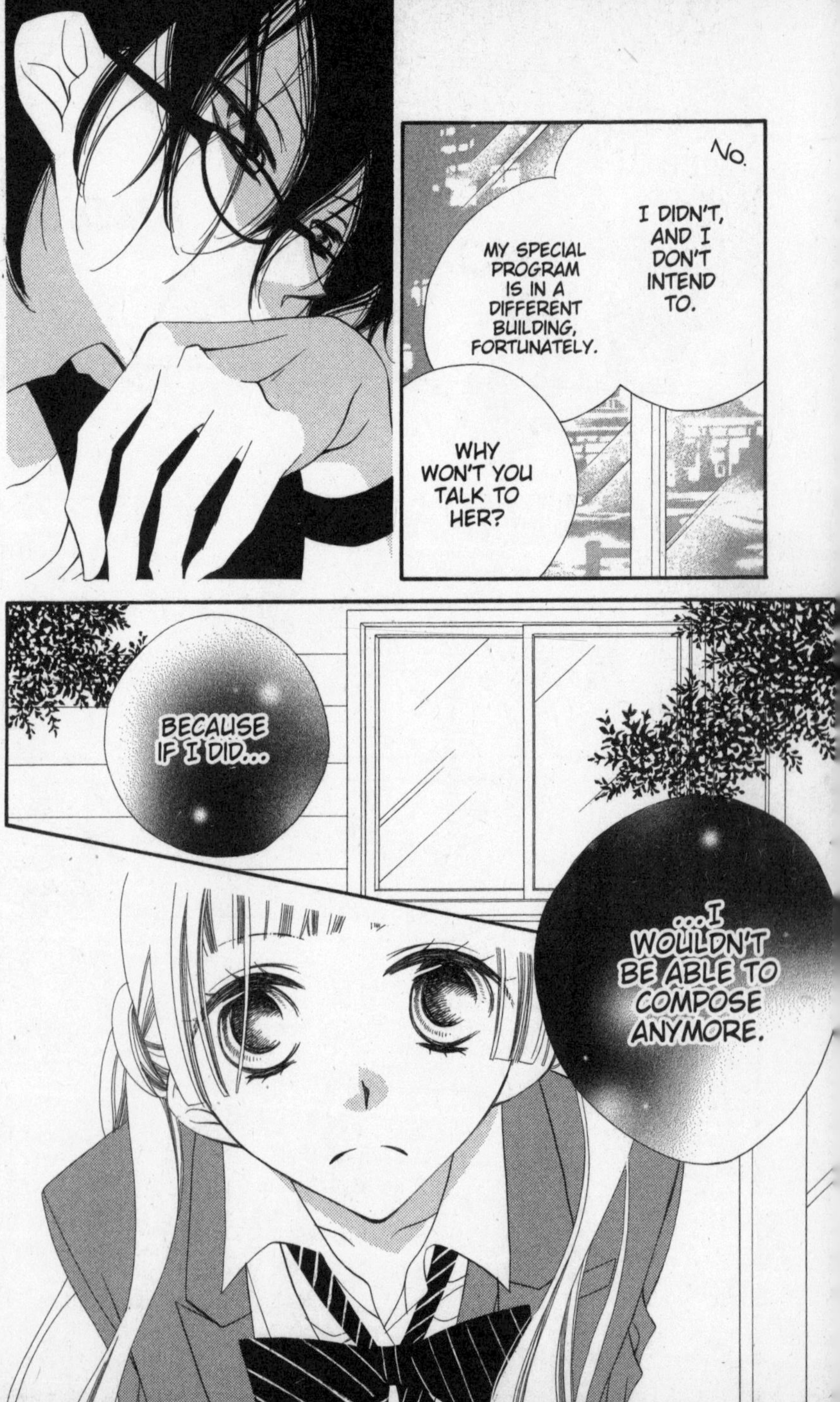
No.
I DIDN'T, AND I DON'T INTEND TO.
MY SPECIAL PROGRAM IS IN A DIFFERENT BUILDING, FORTUNATELY.
WHY WON'T YOU TALK TO HER?
BECAUSE IF I DID...
...I WOULDN'T BE ABLE TO COMPOSE ANYMORE.

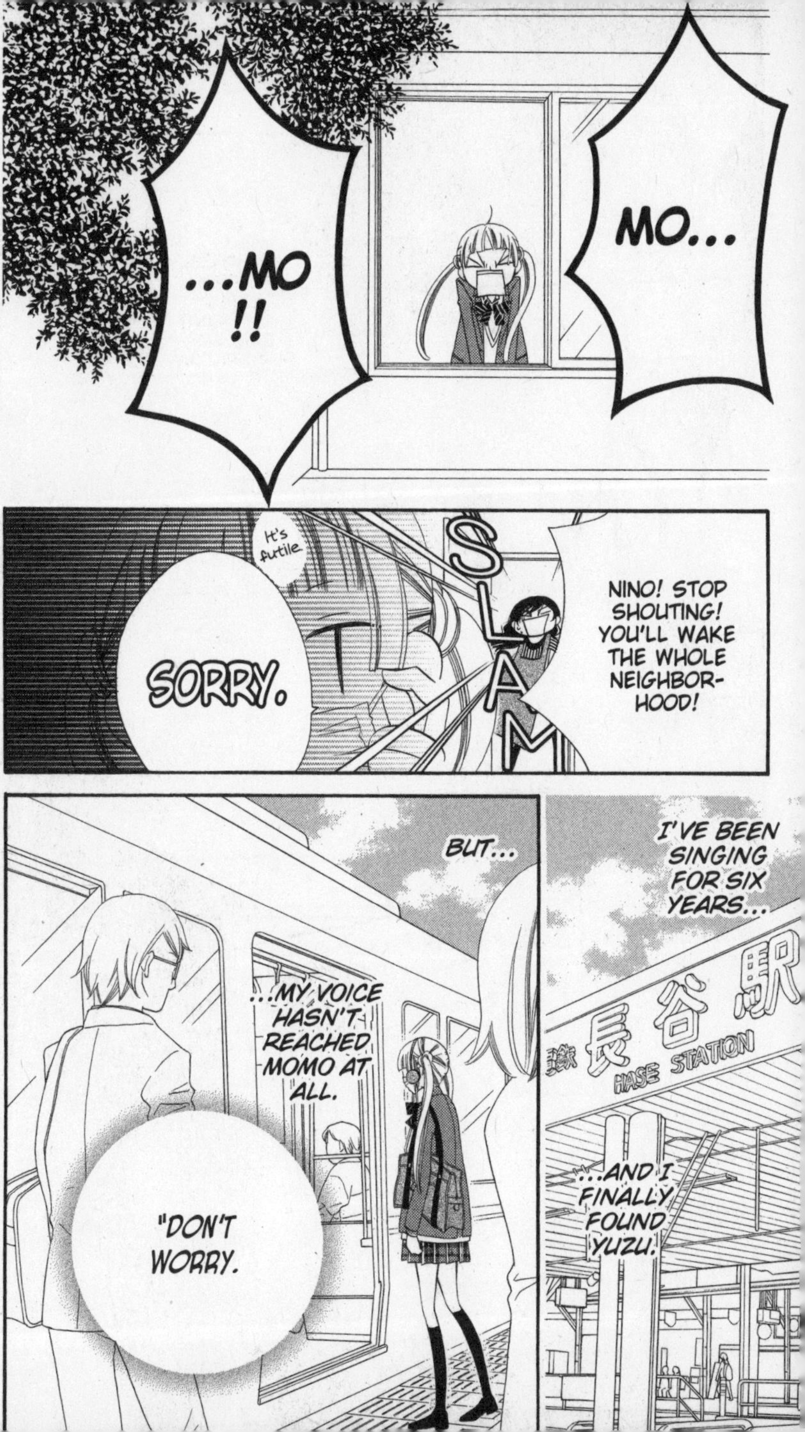
MO...
...MO !!
NINO! STOP SHOUTING! YOU'LL WAKE THE WHOLE NEIGHBOR-HOOD!
SLAM
It's futile
SORRY.
I'VE BEEN SINGING FOR SIX YEARS...
長谷駅
HASE STATION
...AND I FINALLY FOUND YUZU.
BUT...
...MY VOICE HASN'T REACHED MOMO AT ALL.
"DON'T WORRY.

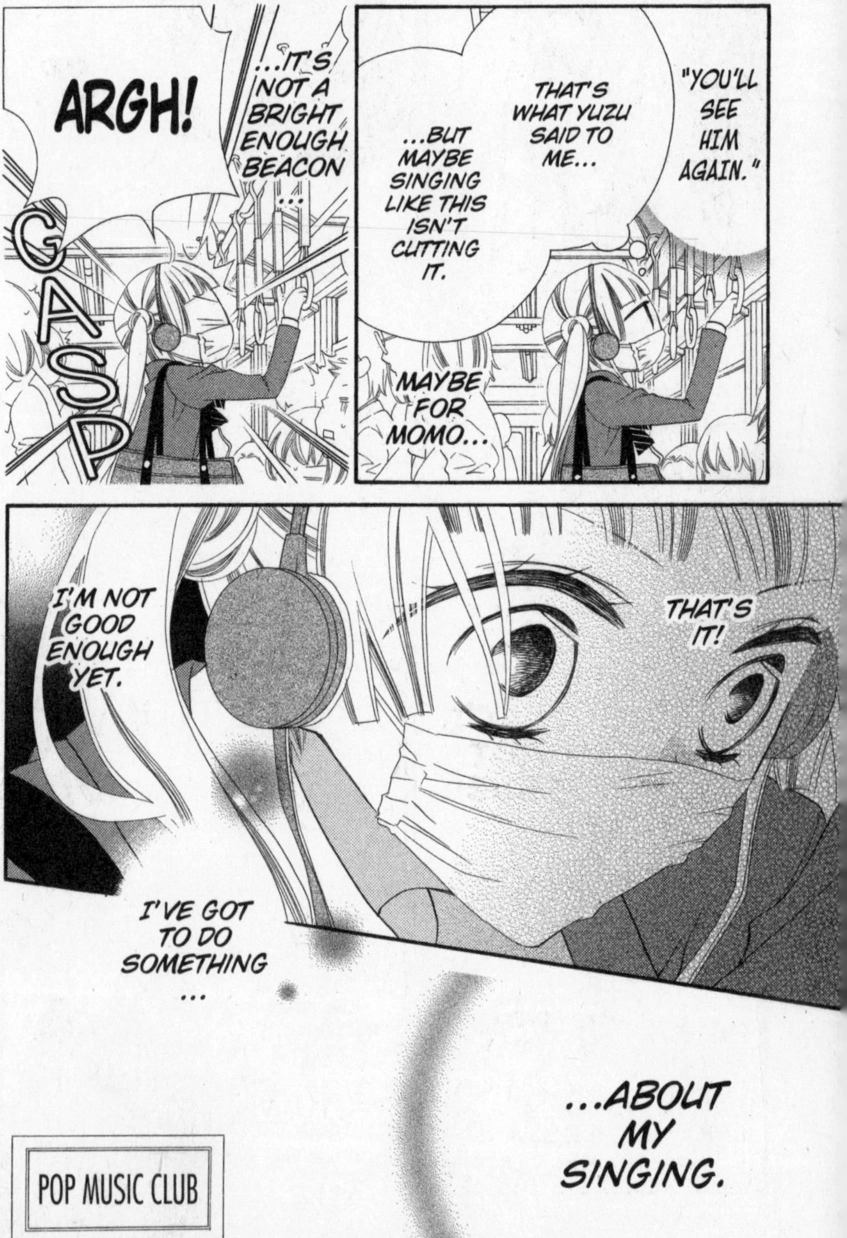

"YOU'LL SEE HIM AGAIN."
THAT'S WHAT YUZU SAID TO ME...
...BUT MAYBE SINGING LIKE THIS ISN'T CUTTING IT.
MAYBE FOR MOMO...
...IT'S NOT A BRIGHT ENOUGH BEACON...
ARGH!
GASP
THAT'S IT!
I'M NOT GOOD ENOUGH YET.
I'VE GOT TO DO SOMETHING...
...ABOUT MY SINGING.
POP MUSIC CLUB

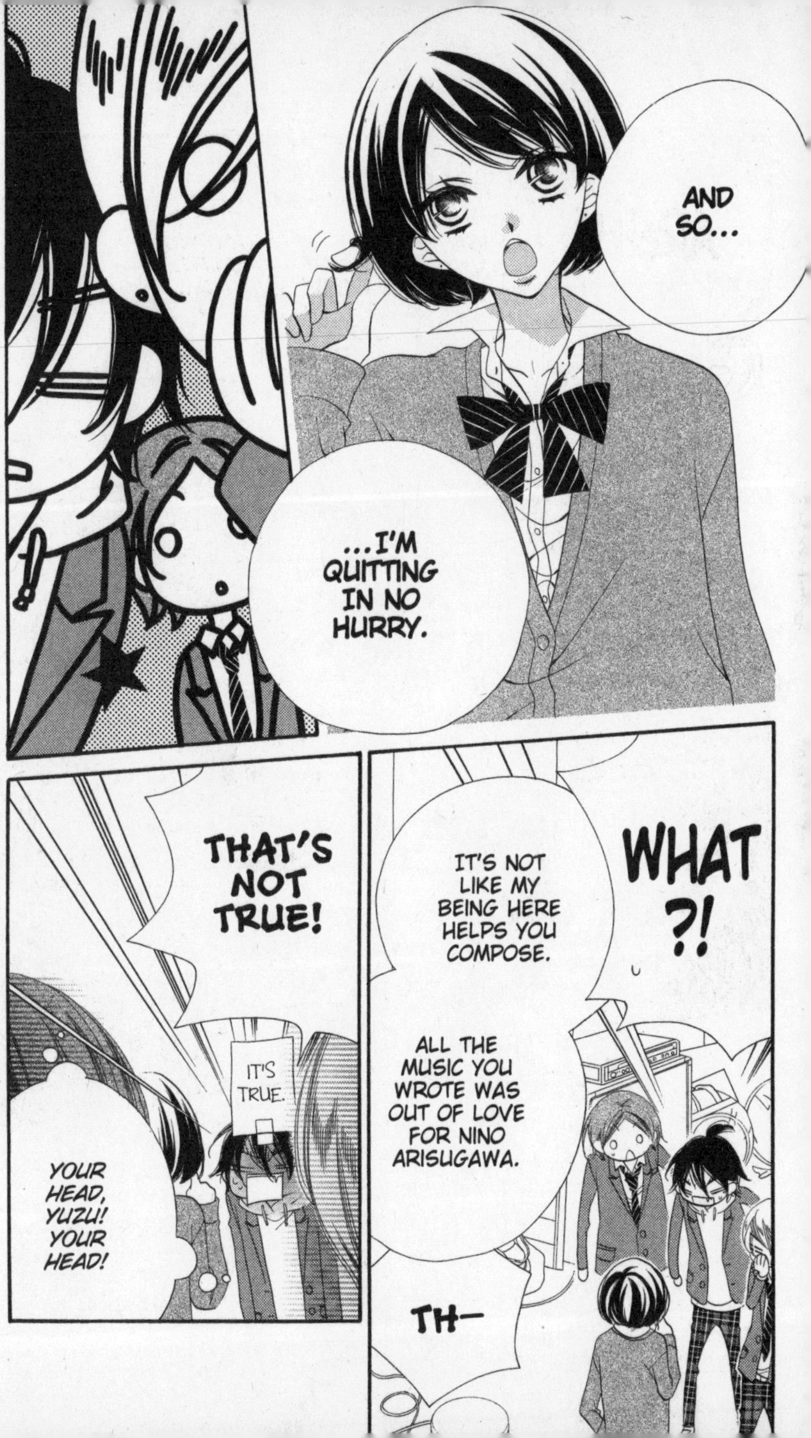
AND SO...
...I'M QUITTING IN NO HURRY.
WHAT?!
IT'S NOT LIKE MY BEING HERE HELPS YOU COMPOSE.
ALL THE MUSIC YOU WROTE WAS OUT OF LOVE FOR NINO ARISUGAWA.
TH—
THAT'S NOT TRUE!
IT'S TRUE.
YOUR HEAD, YUZU! YOUR HEAD!

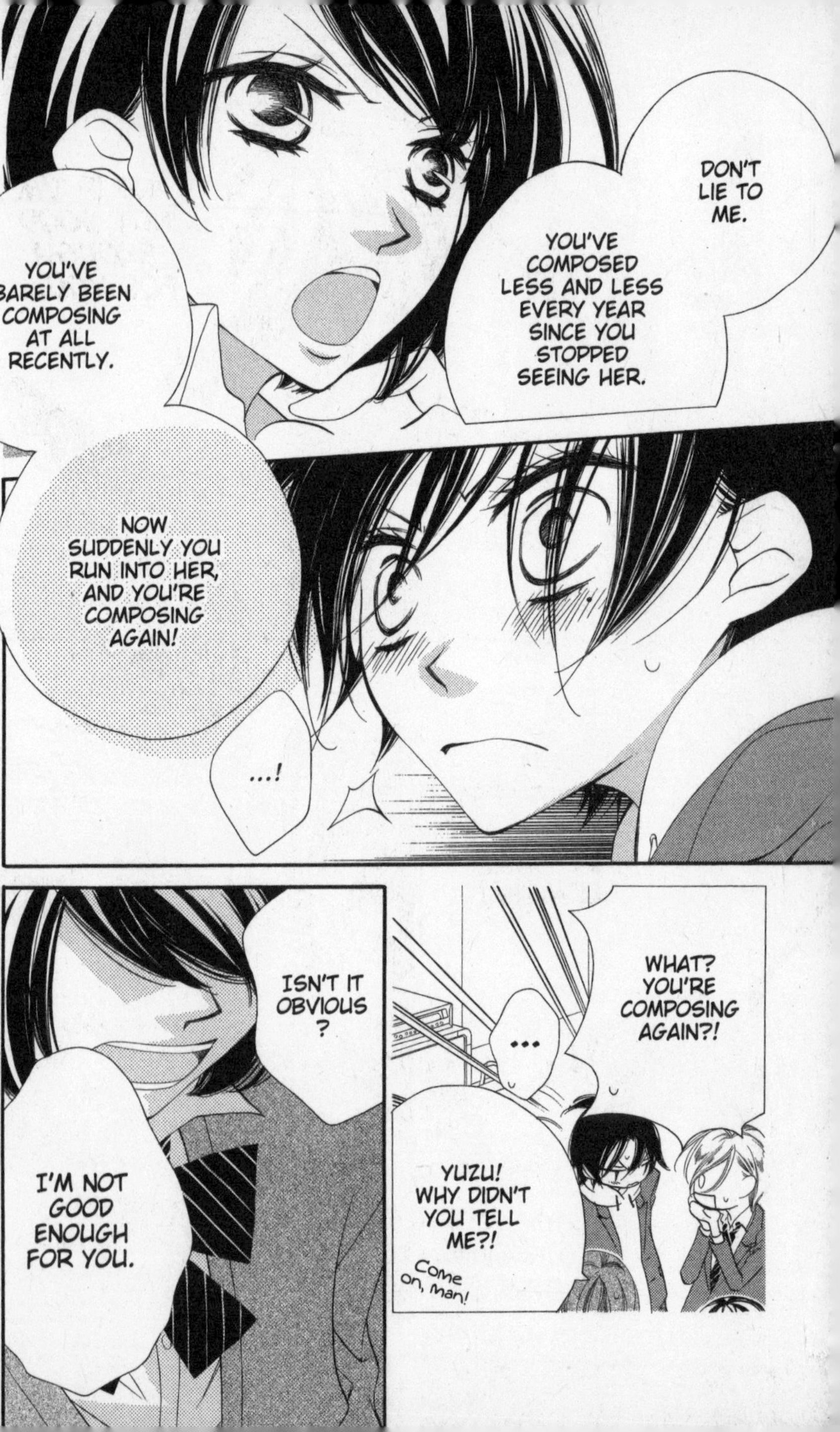
DON'T LIE TO ME.
YOU'VE COMPOSED LESS AND LESS EVERY YEAR SINCE YOU STOPPED SEEING HER.
YOU'VE BARELY BEEN COMPOSING AT ALL RECENTLY.
NOW SUDDENLY YOU RUN INTO HER, AND YOU'RE COMPOSING AGAIN!
...!
WHAT? YOU'RE COMPOSING AGAIN?!
...
YUZU! WHY DIDN'T YOU TELL ME?!
Come on, man!
ISN'T IT OBVIOUS?
I'M NOT GOOD ENOUGH FOR YOU.

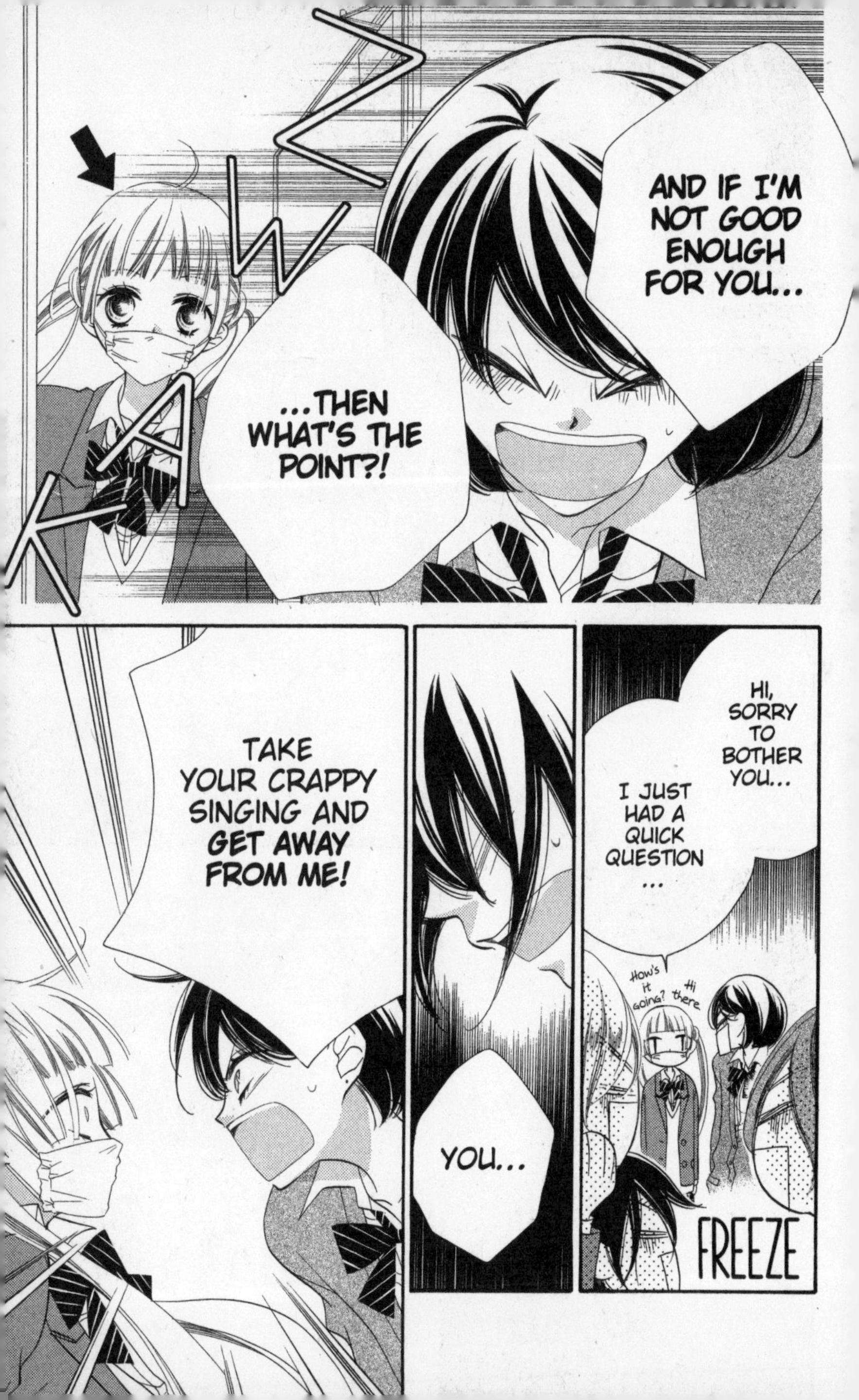
AND IF I'M NOT GOOD ENOUGH FOR YOU...
...THEN WHAT'S THE POINT?!
KAW
HI, SORRY TO BOTHER YOU...
I JUST HAD A QUICK QUESTION ...
How's it going?
Hi there
FREEZE
YOU...
TAKE YOUR CRAPPY SINGING AND GET AWAY FROM ME!

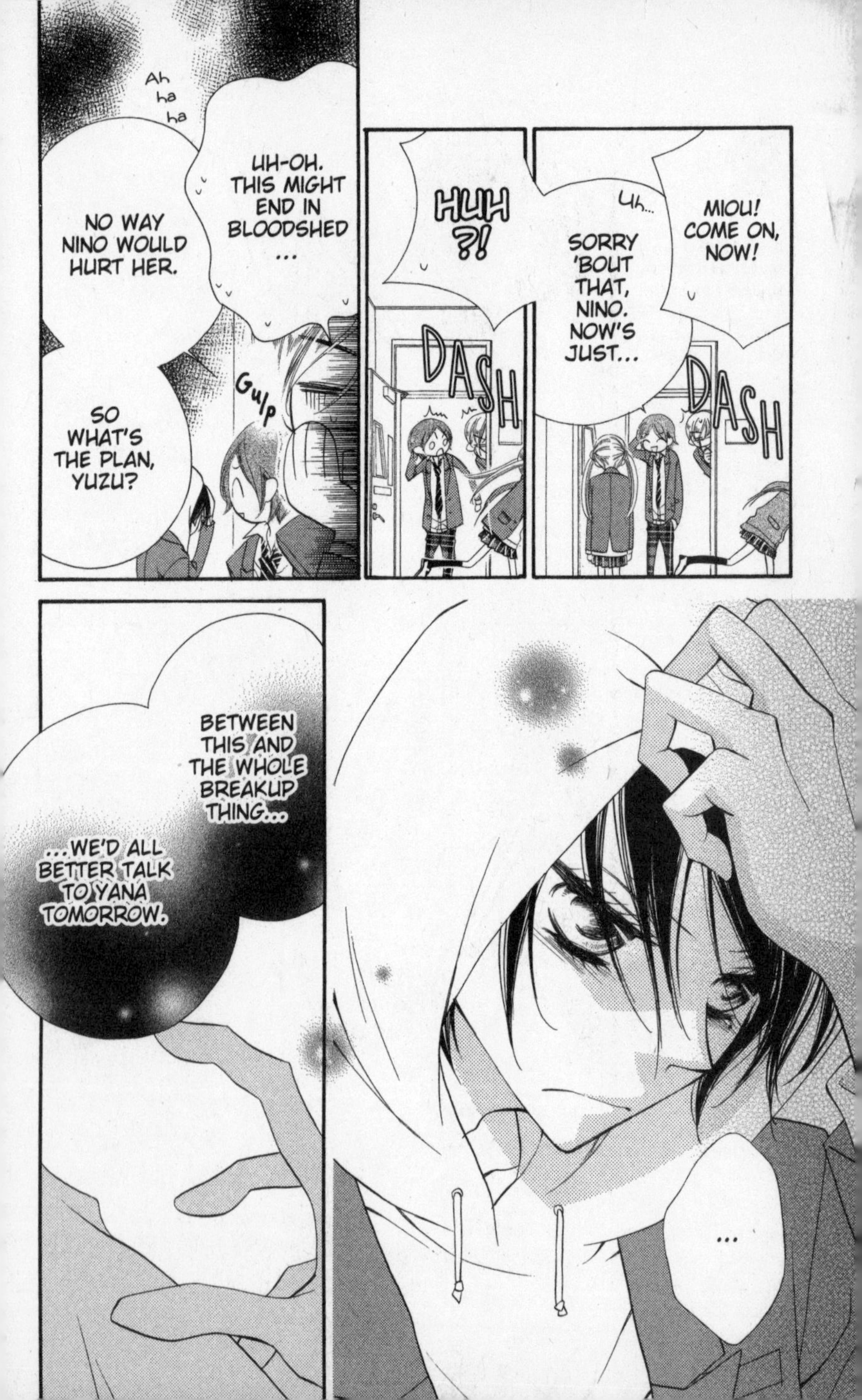
MIOU! COME ON, NOW!
Uh...
SORRY 'BOUT THAT, NINO. NOW'S JUST...
DASH
HUH ?!
DASH
UH-OH. THIS MIGHT END IN BLOODSHED ...
Ah ha ha
NO WAY NINO WOULD HURT HER.
Gulp
SO WHAT'S THE PLAN, YUZU?
...
BETWEEN THIS AND THE WHOLE BREAKUP THING...
...WE'D ALL BETTER TALK TO YANA TOMORROW.

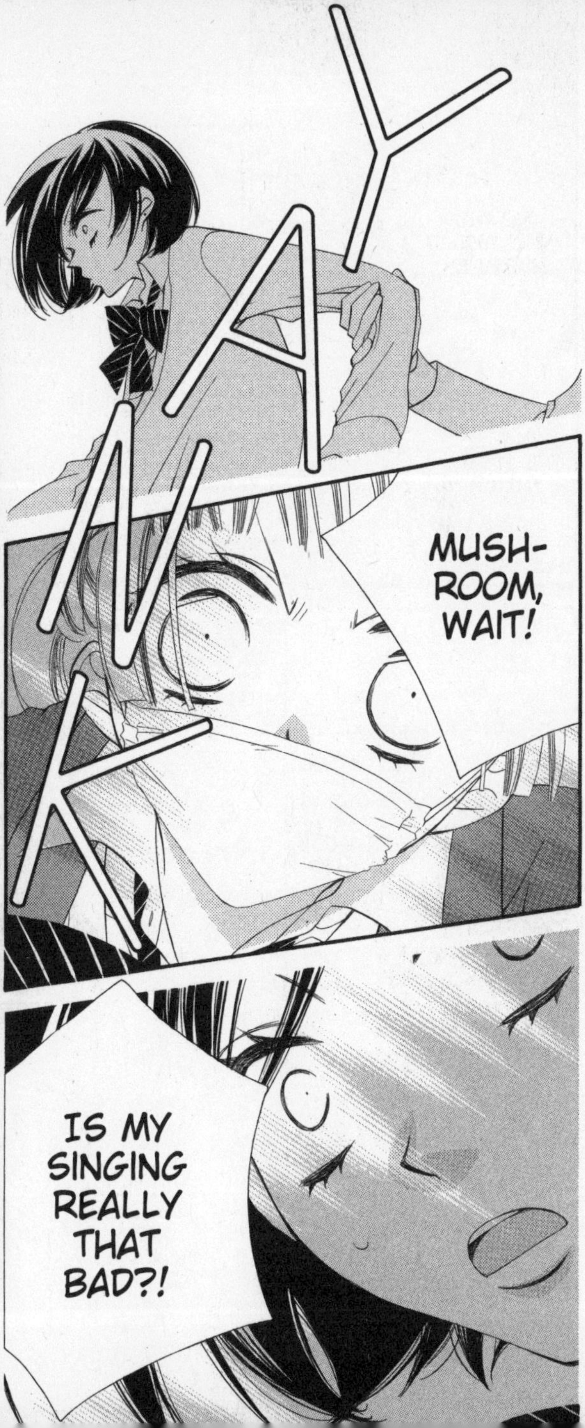
YANK
MUSH-ROOM, WAIT!
IS MY SINGING REALLY THAT BAD?!

1

It's a pleasure to meet you! I'm Ryoko Fukuyama.

Thank you so much for buying Anonymous Noise volume 2! I'm so incredibly happy!

The cover character for this volume is Yuzu. I had intended for it to be a close-up like the art of Nino on the first printing of volume 1, but I just couldn't get a close-up that I liked.

WHAT? WHY ?!

So I went with a wider view, and that was perfect. The only problem is that you can't see how short Yuzu is.

I'M NOT SHORT! I'M 5'1"!

OH...

—RIGHT.

Anyway, I'm so glad you're enjoying Anonymous Noise volume 2.

HERE'S A FROG PLAYING GUITAR.

NICE TO MEET YOU!

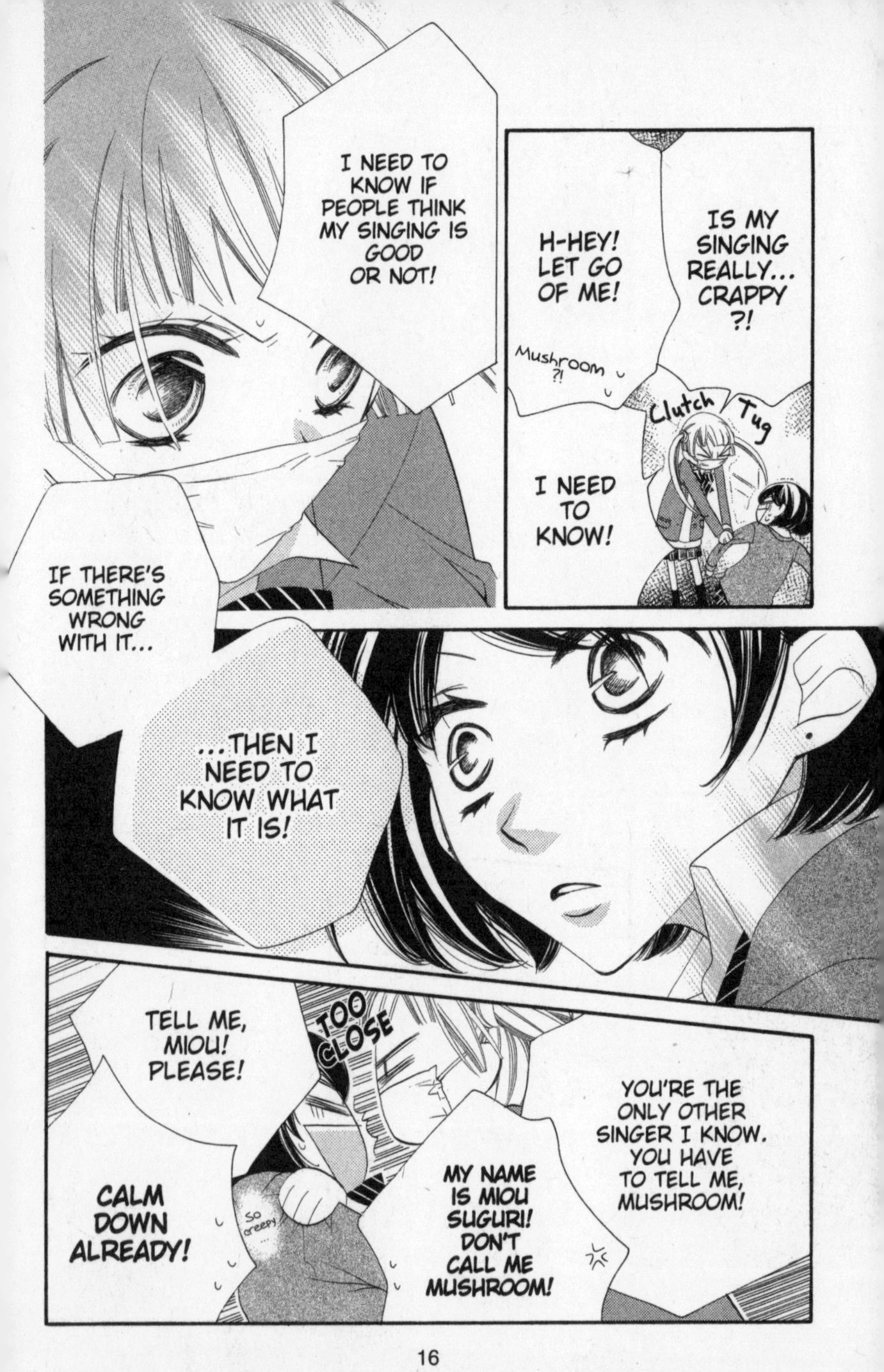
IS MY SINGING REALLY... CRAPPY?!
H-HEY! LET GO OF ME!
Mushroom ?!
Clutch
Tug
I NEED TO KNOW!
I NEED TO KNOW IF PEOPLE THINK MY SINGING IS GOOD OR NOT!
IF THERE'S SOMETHING WRONG WITH IT...
...THEN I NEED TO KNOW WHAT IT IS!
YOU'RE THE ONLY OTHER SINGER I KNOW. YOU HAVE TO TELL ME, MUSHROOM!
MY NAME IS MIOU SUGURI! DON'T CALL ME MUSHROOM!
TOO CLOSE
TELL ME, MIOU! PLEASE!
So creepy...
CALM DOWN ALREADY!

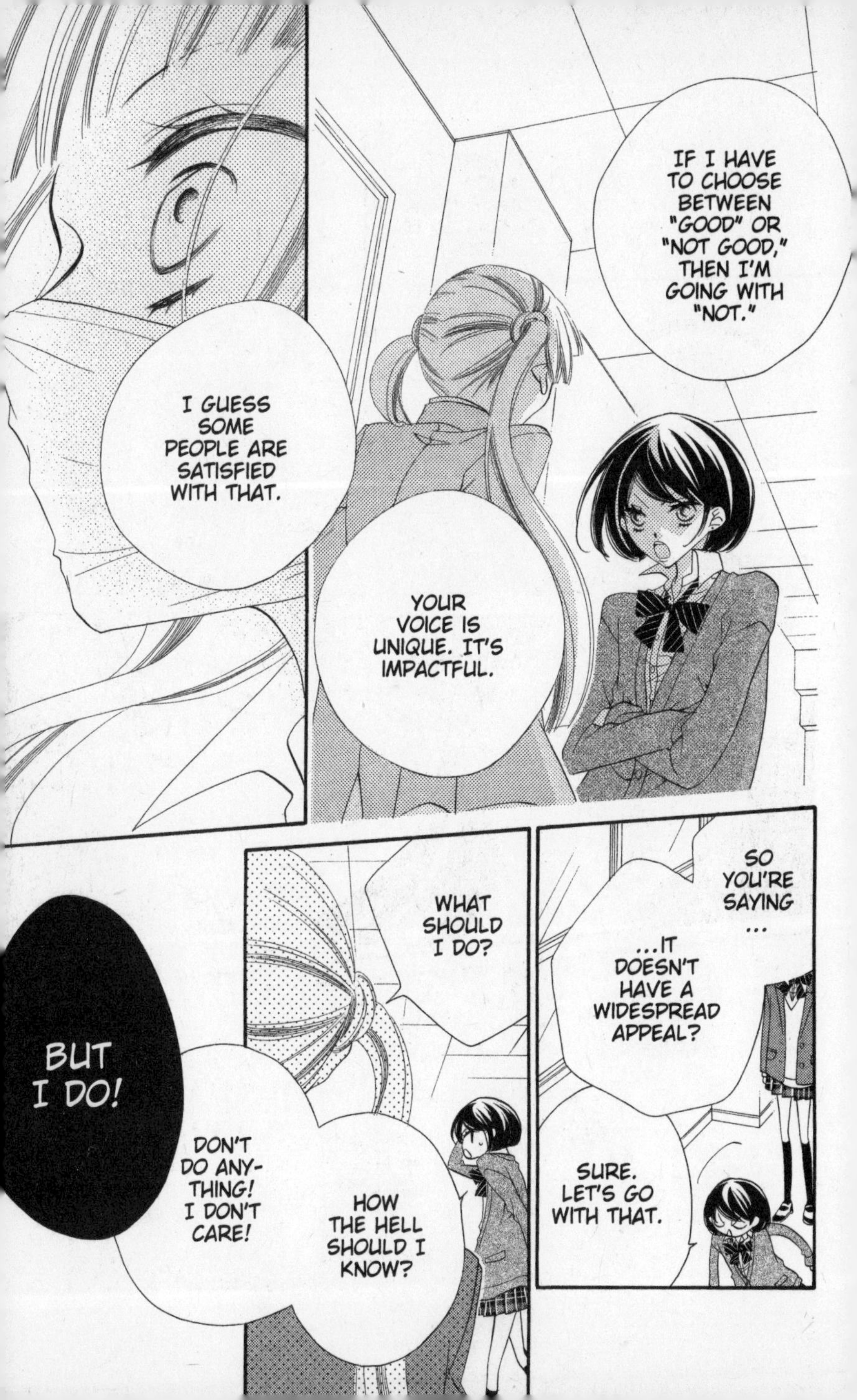

IF I HAVE TO CHOOSE BETWEEN "GOOD" OR "NOT GOOD," THEN I'M GOING WITH "NOT."
YOUR VOICE IS UNIQUE. IT'S IMPACTFUL.
I GUESS SOME PEOPLE ARE SATISFIED WITH THAT.
SO YOU'RE SAYING...
...IT DOESN'T HAVE A WIDESPREAD APPEAL?
SURE. LET'S GO WITH THAT.
WHAT SHOULD I DO?
HOW THE HELL SHOULD I KNOW?
DON'T DO ANY-THING! I DON'T CARE!
BUT I DO!

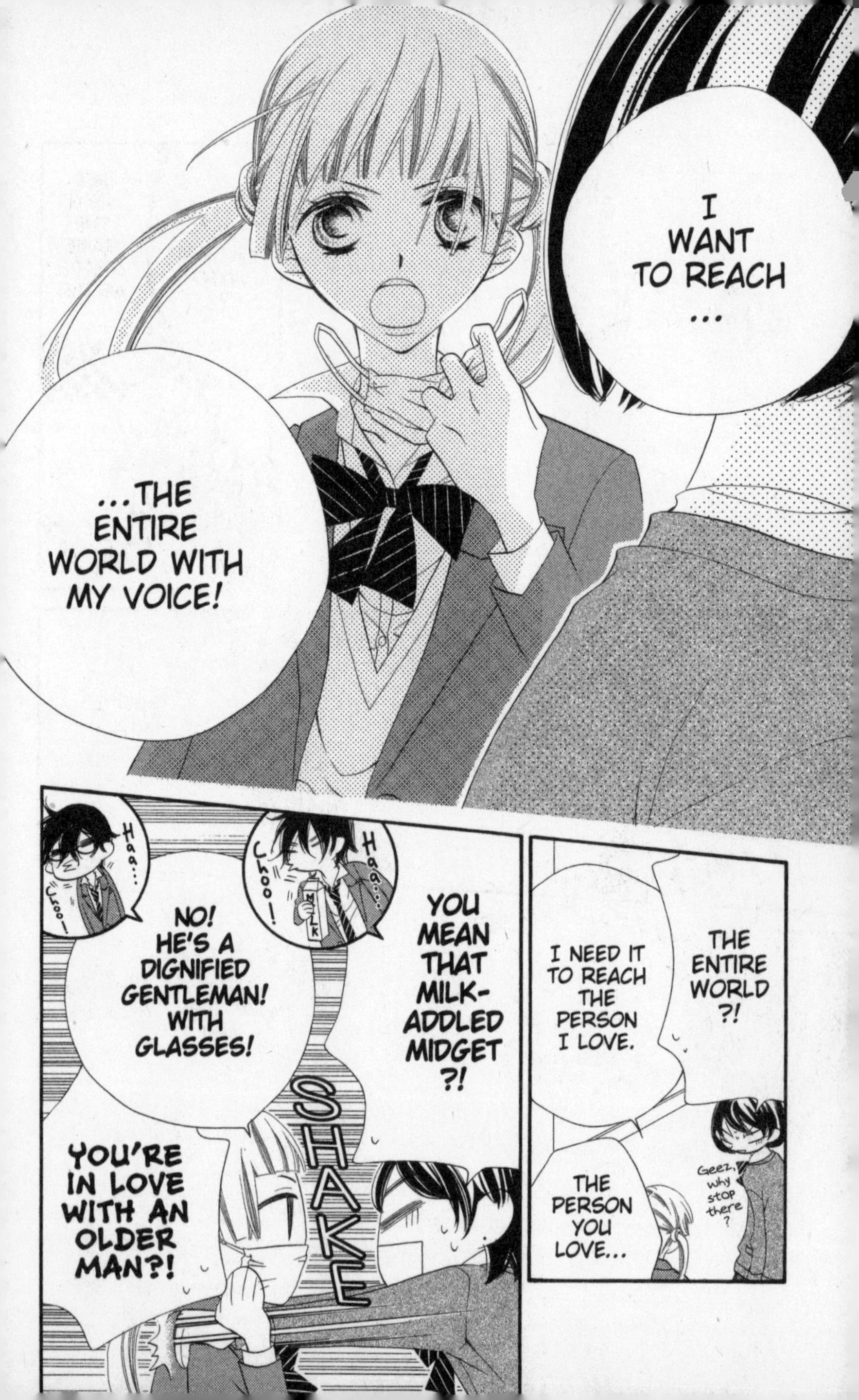
I WANT TO REACH ...
...THE ENTIRE WORLD WITH MY VOICE!
THE ENTIRE WORLD ?!
I NEED IT TO REACH THE PERSON I LOVE.
Geez, why stop there?
THE PERSON YOU LOVE...
YOU MEAN THAT MILK-ADDLED MIDGET ?!
Haa... Choo!
MILK
Haa... Choo!
NO! HE'S A DIGNIFIED GENTLEMAN! WITH GLASSES!
SHAKE
YOU'RE IN LOVE WITH AN OLDER MAN?!

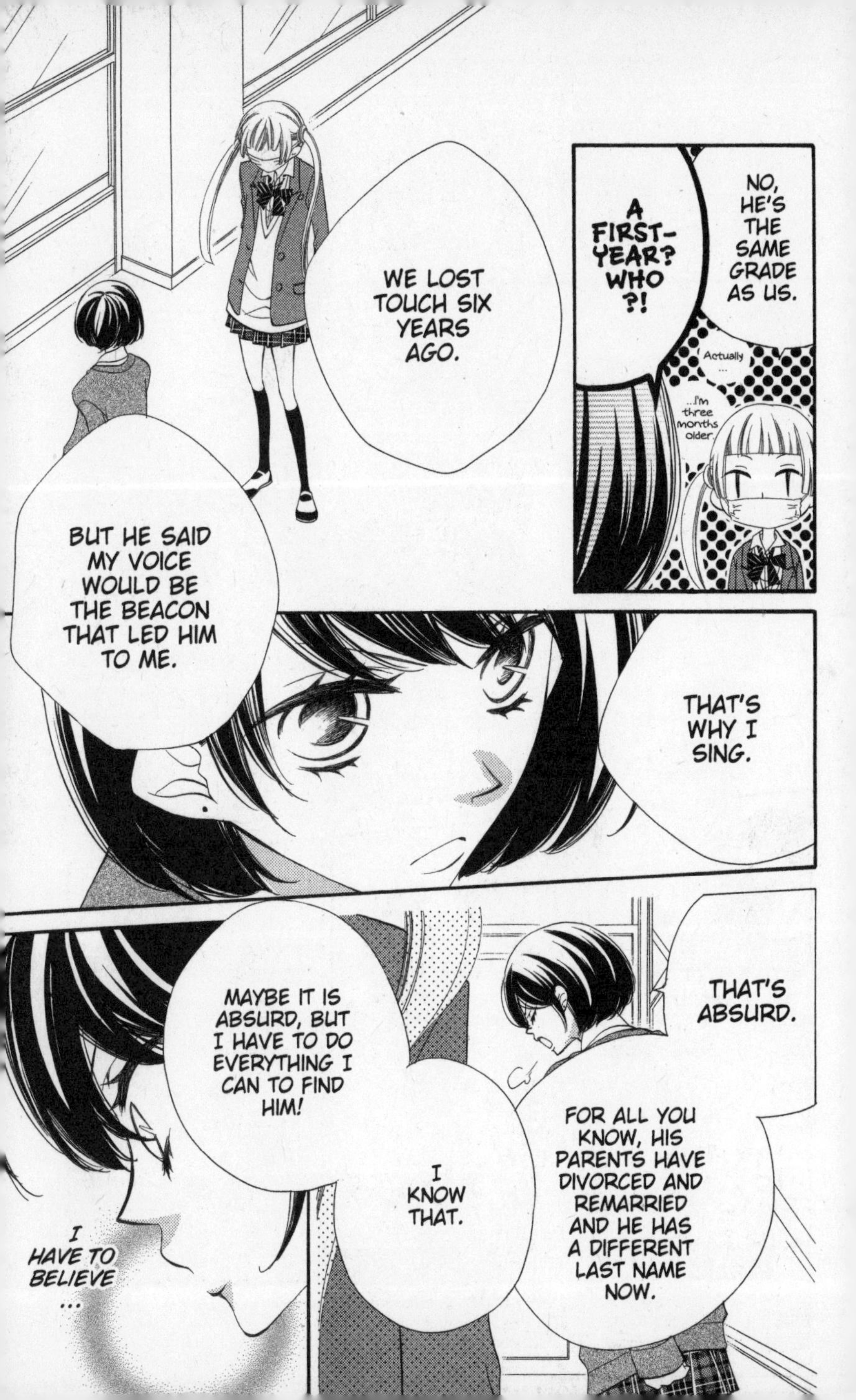
A FIRST-YEAR? WHO?!
NO, HE'S THE SAME GRADE AS US.
Actually...
...I'm three months older.
WE LOST TOUCH SIX YEARS AGO.
BUT HE SAID MY VOICE WOULD BE THE BEACON THAT LED HIM TO ME.
THAT'S WHY I SING.
THAT'S ABSURD.
FOR ALL YOU KNOW, HIS PARENTS HAVE DIVORCED AND REMARRIED AND HE HAS A DIFFERENT LAST NAME NOW.
I KNOW THAT.
MAYBE IT IS ABSURD, BUT I HAVE TO DO EVERYTHING I CAN TO FIND HIM!
I HAVE TO BELIEVE...

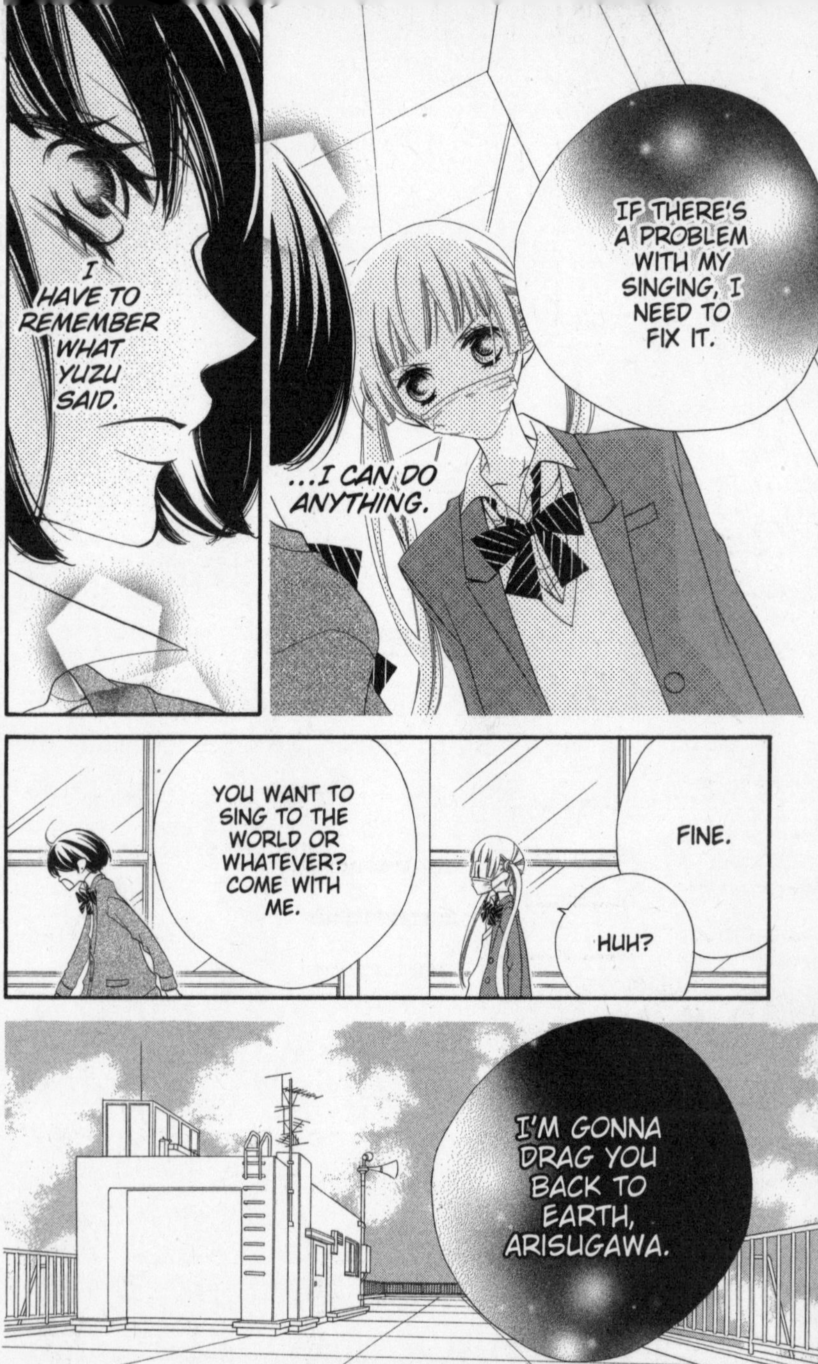
IF THERE'S A PROBLEM WITH MY SINGING, I NEED TO FIX IT.
...I CAN DO ANYTHING.
I HAVE TO REMEMBER WHAT YUZU SAID.
FINE.
HUH?
YOU WANT TO SING TO THE WORLD OR WHATEVER? COME WITH ME.
I'M GONNA DRAG YOU BACK TO EARTH, ARISUGAWA.

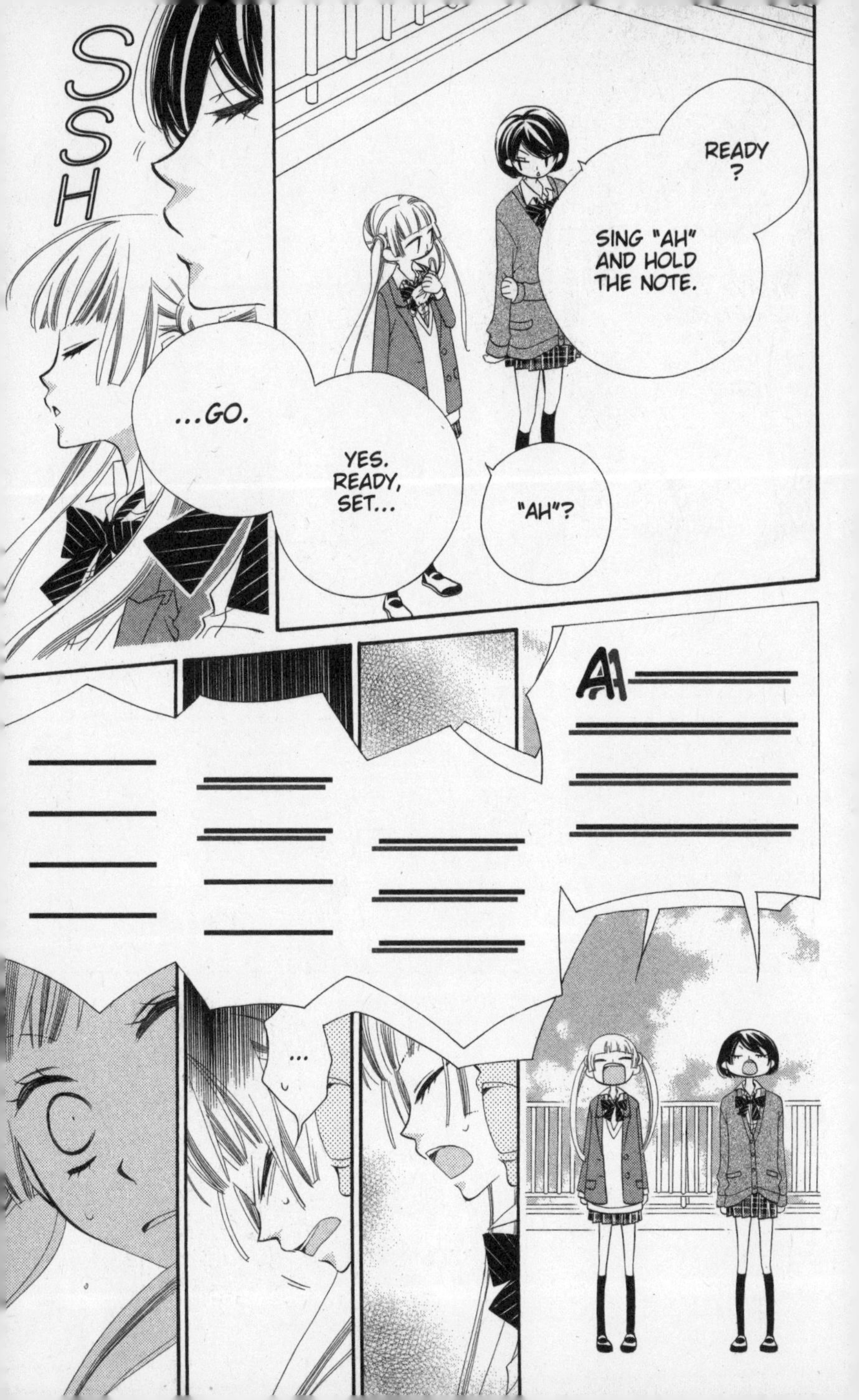
READY ?
SING "AH" AND HOLD THE NOTE.
"AH"?
YES. READY, SET...
...GO.
SSH
AH———
...

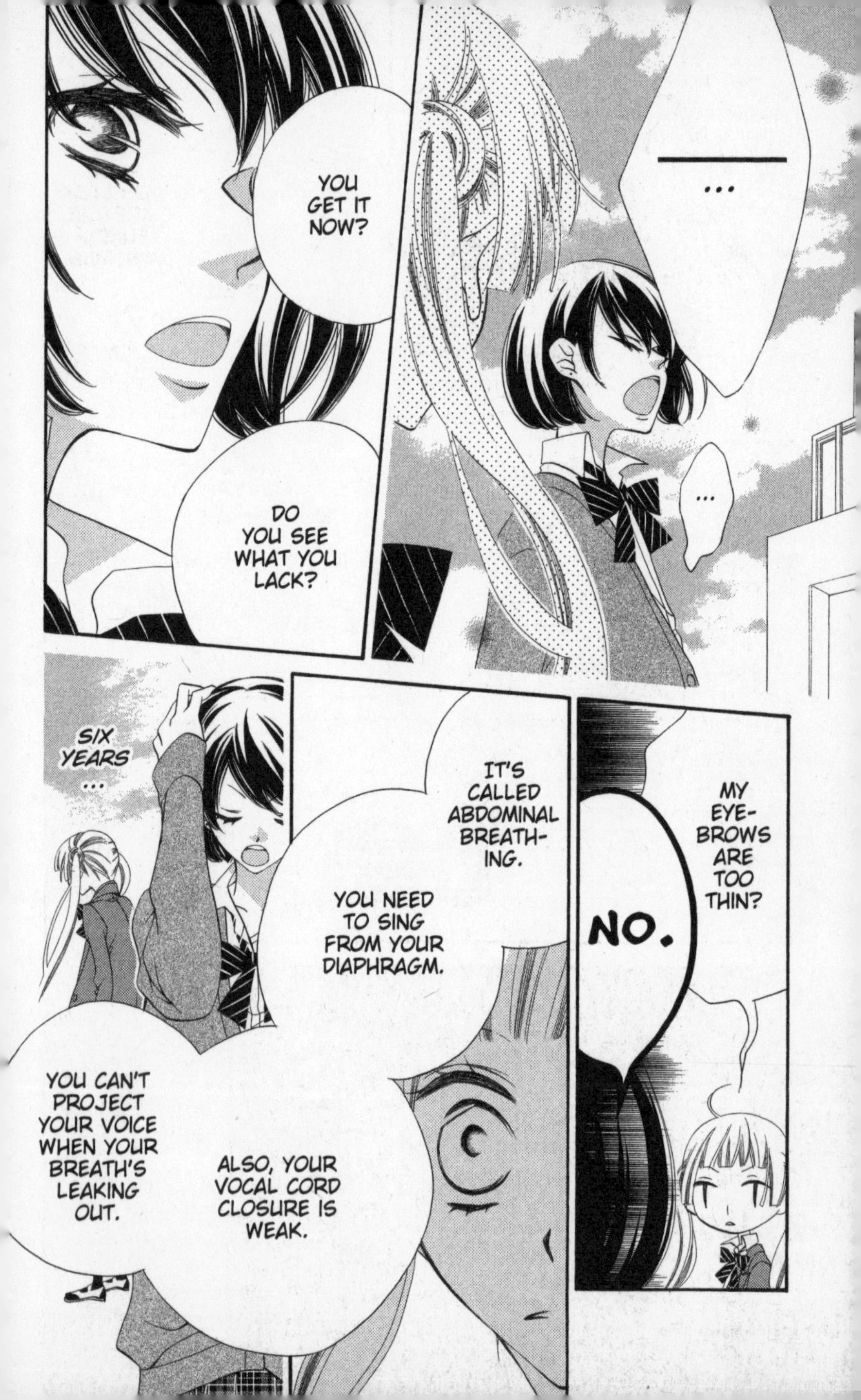
———...
...
YOU GET IT NOW?
DO YOU SEE WHAT YOU LACK?
MY EYE-BROWS ARE TOO THIN?
NO.
IT'S CALLED ABDOMINAL BREATH-ING.
YOU NEED TO SING FROM YOUR DIAPHRAGM.
SIX YEARS...
YOU CAN'T PROJECT YOUR VOICE WHEN YOUR BREATH'S LEAKING OUT.
ALSO, YOUR VOCAL CORD CLOSURE IS WEAK.

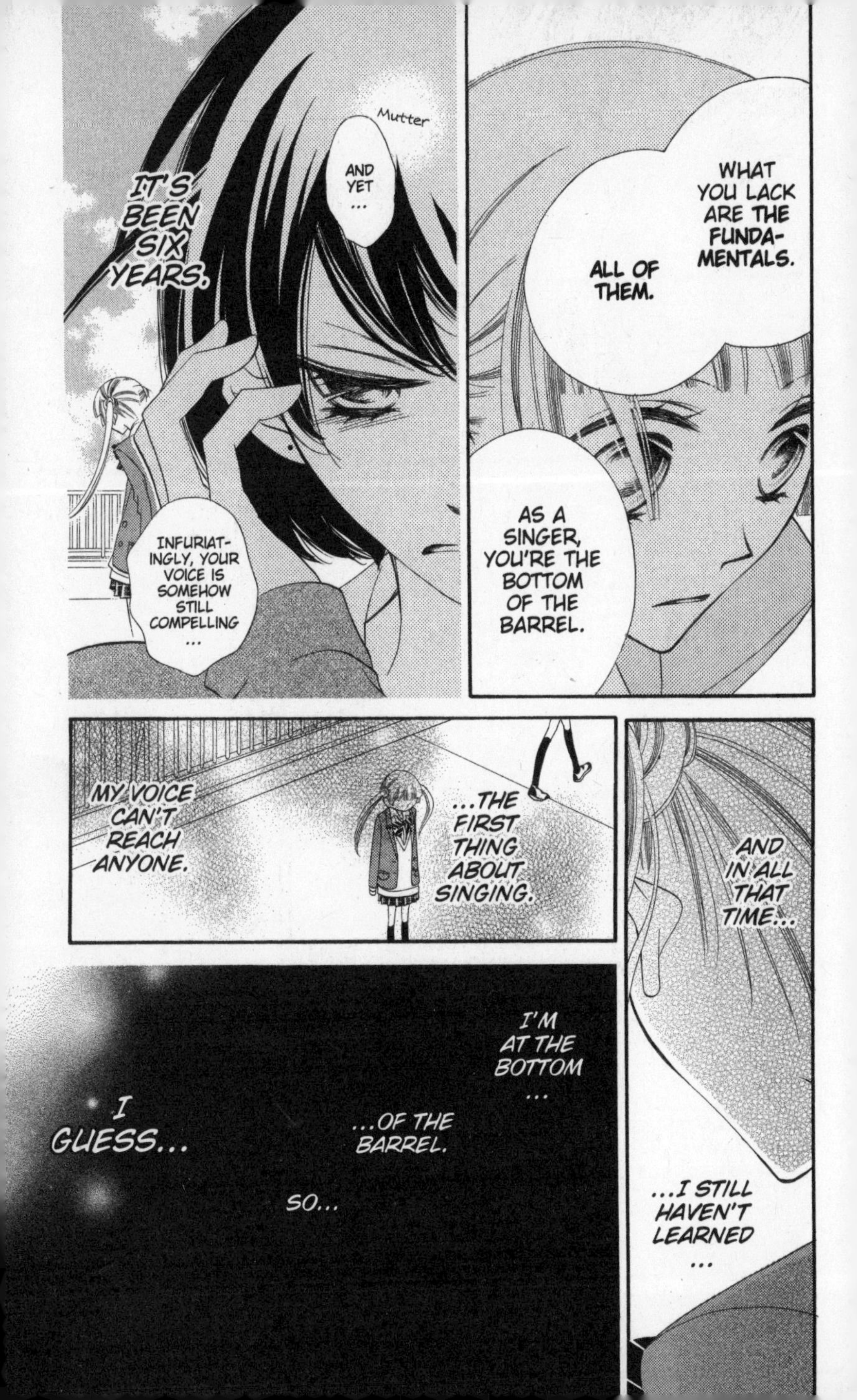
WHAT YOU LACK ARE THE FUNDA- MENTALS.
ALL OF THEM.
AS A SINGER, YOU'RE THE BOTTOM OF THE BARREL.
Mutter
AND YET ...
IT'S BEEN SIX YEARS.
INFURIAT- INGLY, YOUR VOICE IS SOMEHOW STILL COMPELLING ...
AND IN ALL THAT TIME...
...I STILL HAVEN'T LEARNED ...
...THE FIRST THING ABOUT SINGING.
MY VOICE CAN'T REACH ANYONE.
I'M AT THE BOTTOM ...
...OF THE BARREL.
SO...
I GUESS...

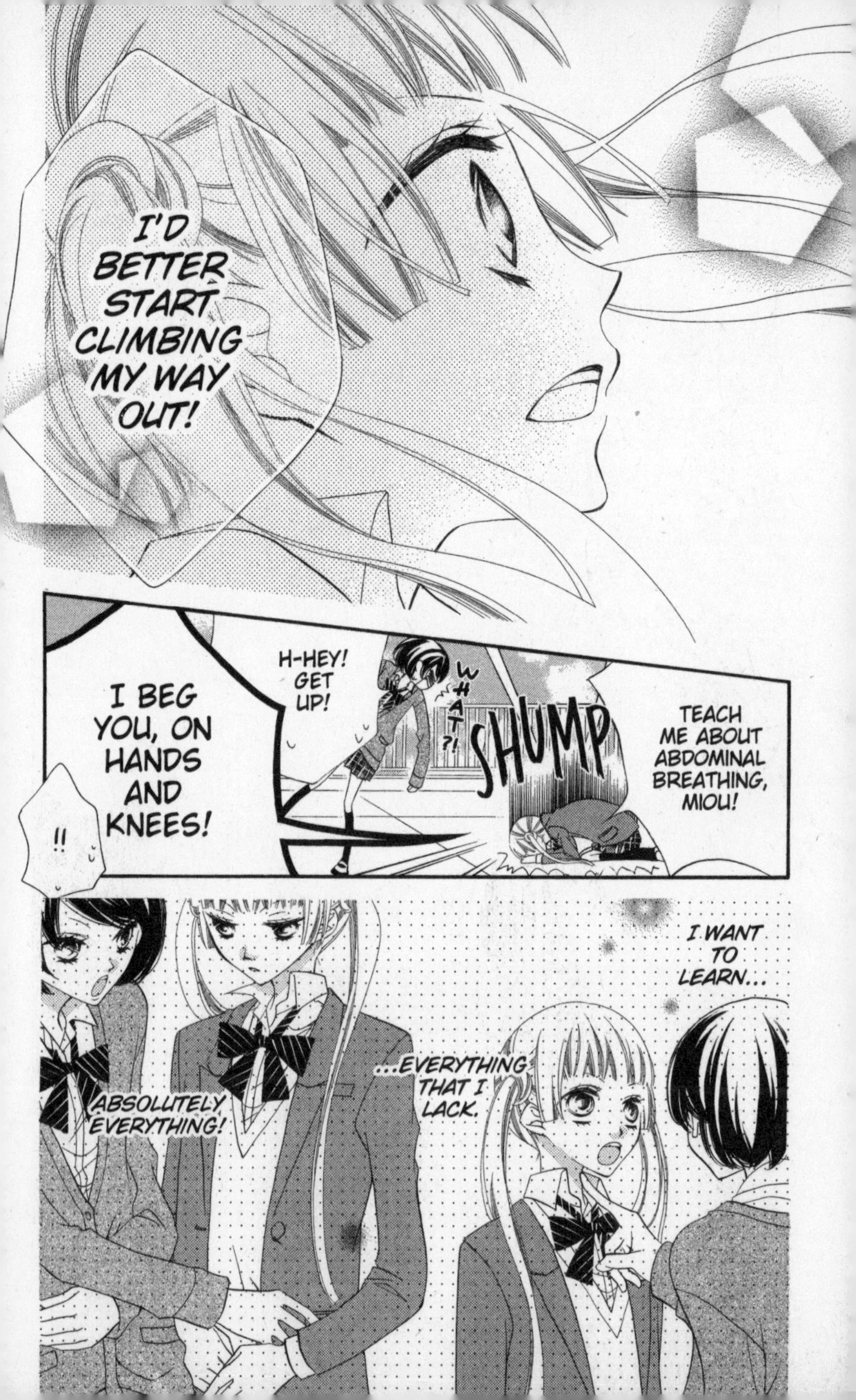
I'D BETTER START CLIMBING MY WAY OUT!
TEACH ME ABOUT ABDOMINAL BREATHING, MIOU!
SHUMP
WHAT?!
H-HEY! GET UP!
I BEG YOU, ON HANDS AND KNEES!
!!
I WANT TO LEARN...
...EVERYTHING THAT I LACK.
ABSOLUTELY EVERYTHING!

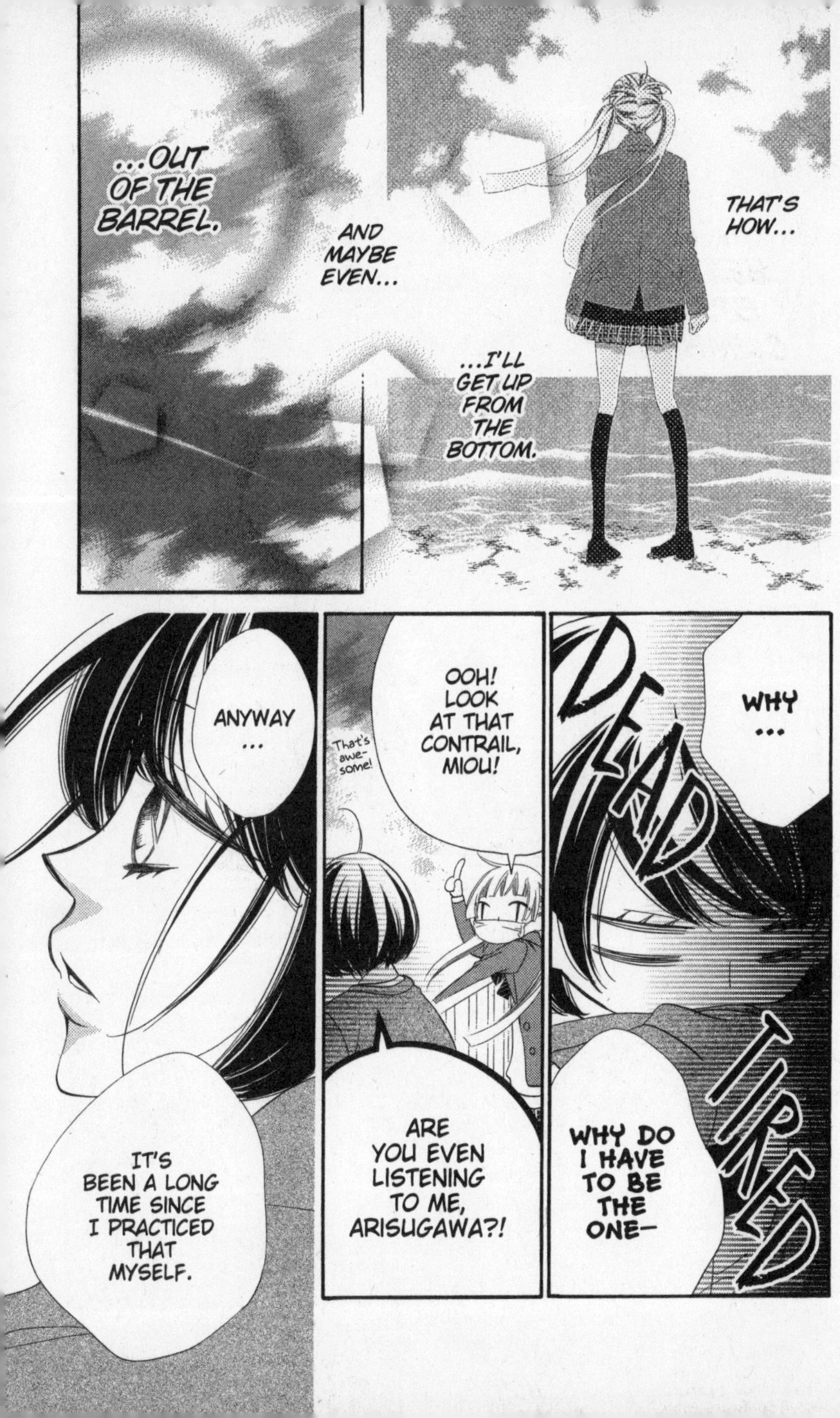
THAT'S HOW...
...I'LL GET UP FROM THE BOTTOM.
AND MAYBE EVEN...
...OUT OF THE BARREL.
WHY...
DEAD TIRED
WHY DO I HAVE TO BE THE ONE—
OOH! LOOK AT THAT CONTRAIL, MIOU!
That's awesome!
ARE YOU EVEN LISTENING TO ME, ARISUGAWA?!
ANYWAY...
IT'S BEEN A LONG TIME SINCE I PRACTICED THAT MYSELF.

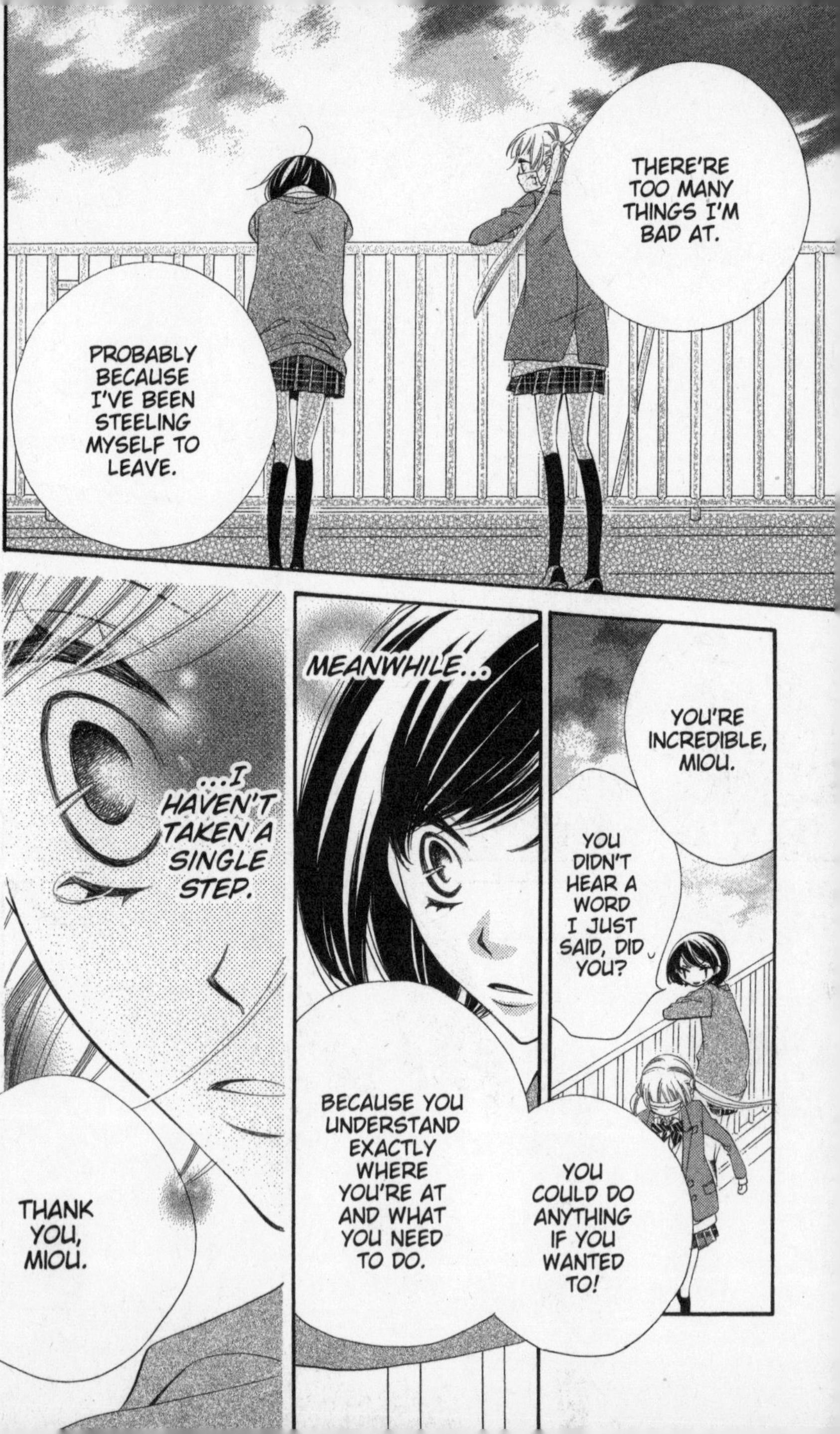
THERE'RE TOO MANY THINGS I'M BAD AT.
PROBABLY BECAUSE I'VE BEEN STEELING MYSELF TO LEAVE.
YOU'RE INCREDIBLE, MIOU.
YOU DIDN'T HEAR A WORD I JUST SAID, DID YOU?
YOU COULD DO ANYTHING IF YOU WANTED TO!
MEANWHILE...
BECAUSE YOU UNDERSTAND EXACTLY WHERE YOU'RE AT AND WHAT YOU NEED TO DO.
...I HAVEN'T TAKEN A SINGLE STEP.
THANK YOU, MIOU.

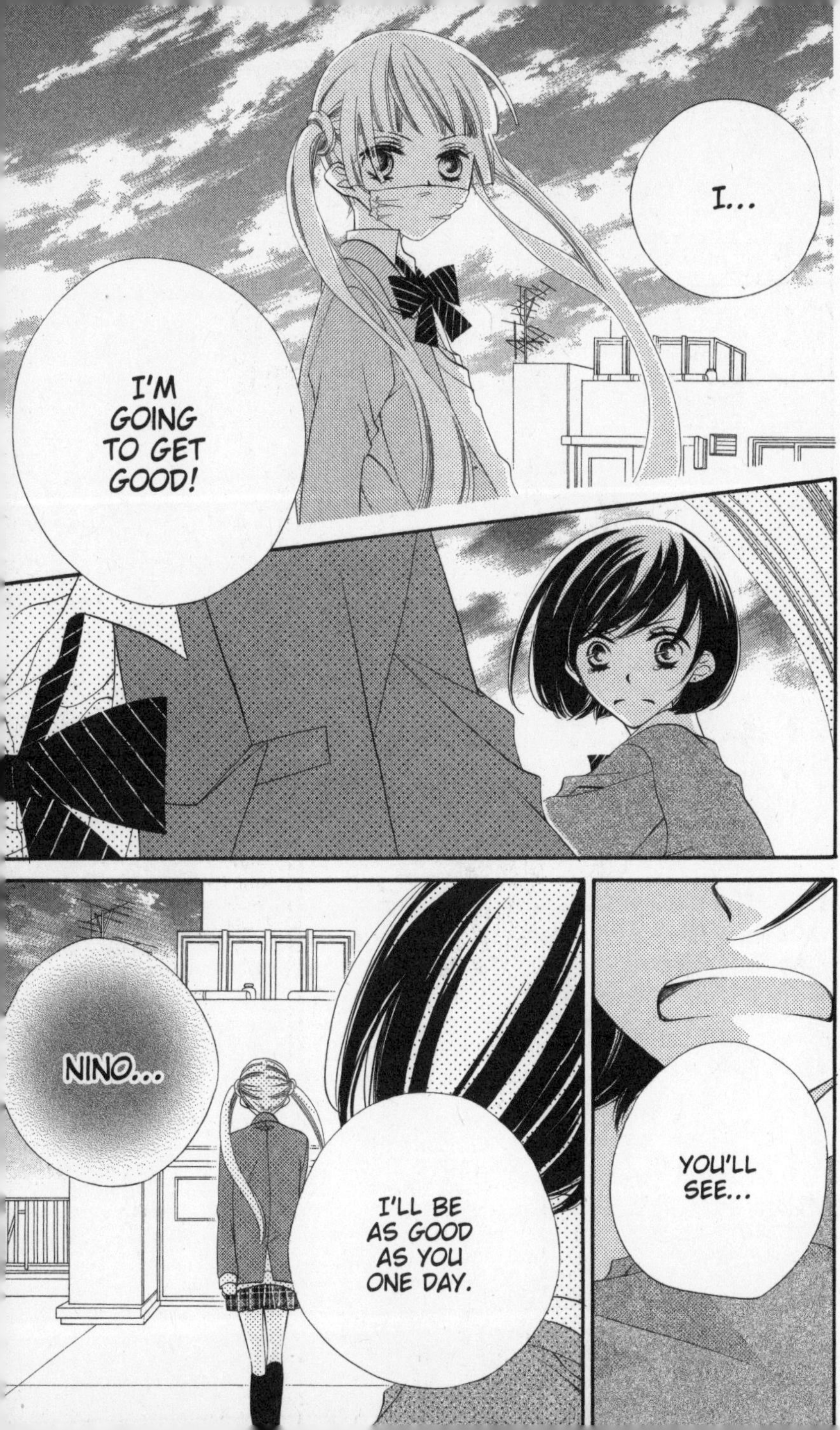
I...
I'M GOING TO GET GOOD!
YOU'LL SEE...
I'LL BE AS GOOD AS YOU ONE DAY.
NINO...

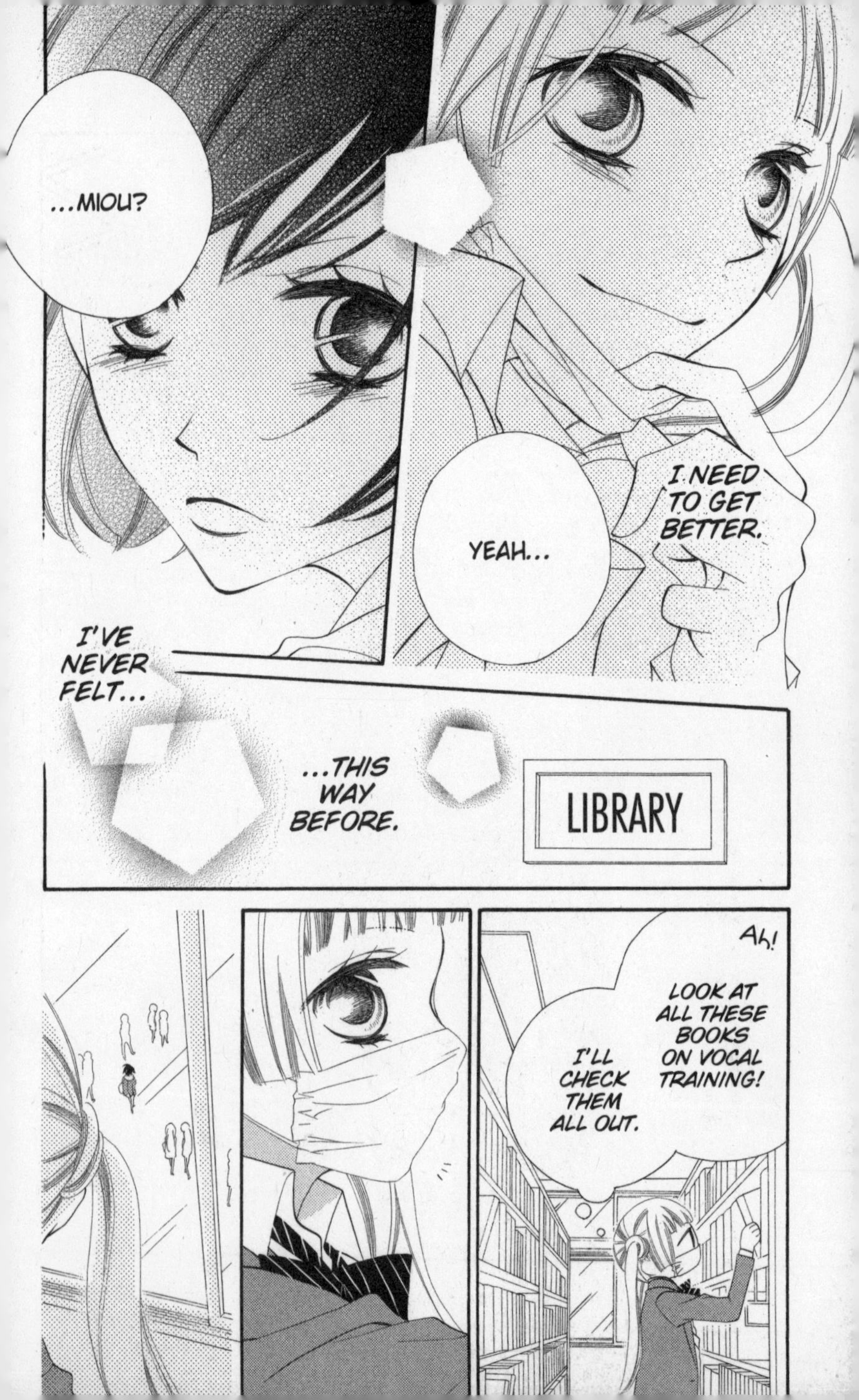
I NEED TO GET BETTER.
YEAH...
...MIOU?
I'VE NEVER FELT...
...THIS WAY BEFORE.
LIBRARY
Ah!
LOOK AT ALL THESE BOOKS ON VOCAL TRAINING!
I'LL CHECK THEM ALL OUT.

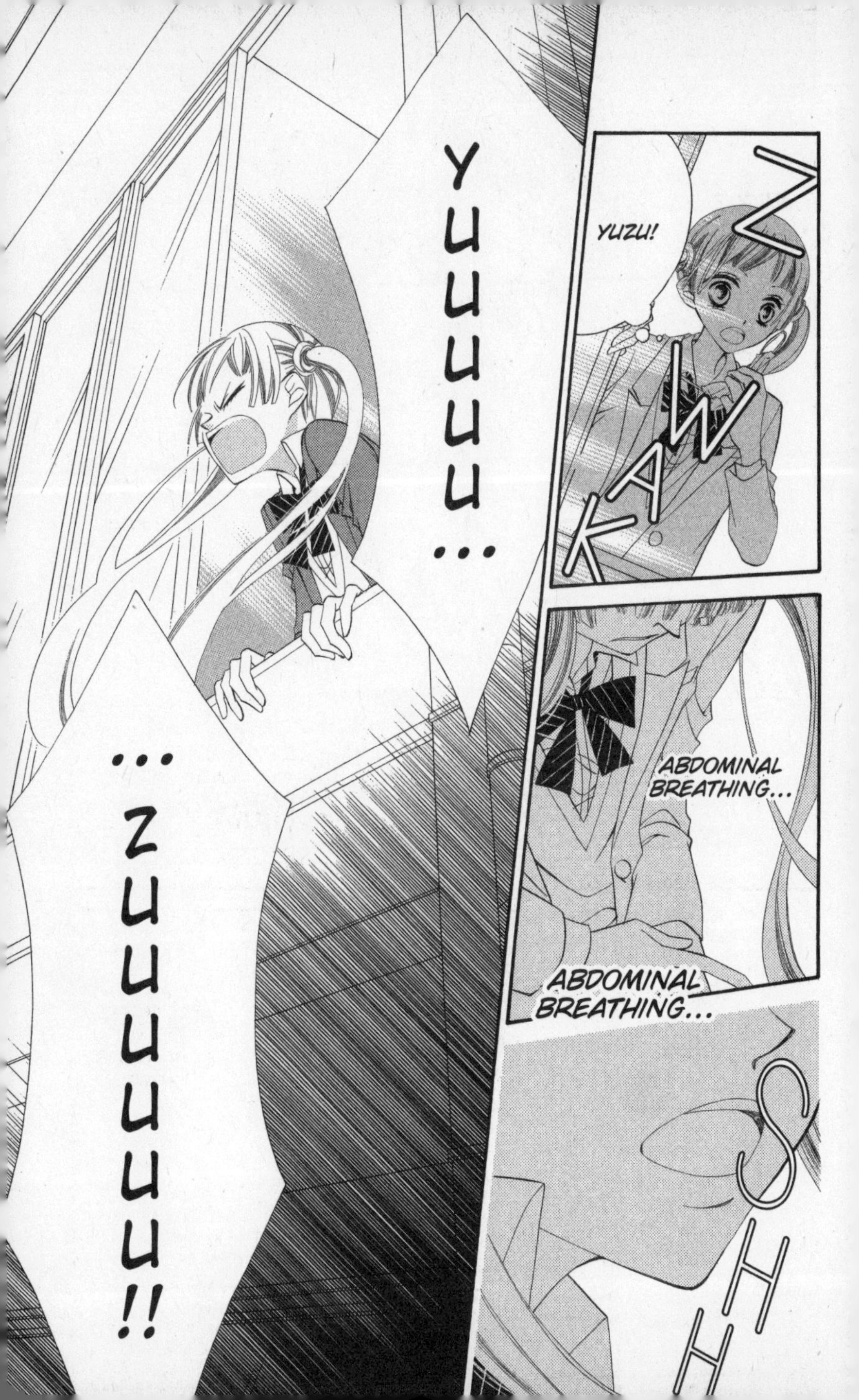
YUZU!
KAWA
ABDOMINAL BREATHING...
ABDOMINAL BREATHING...
SHH
YUUUUU...
...ZUUUUUU!!

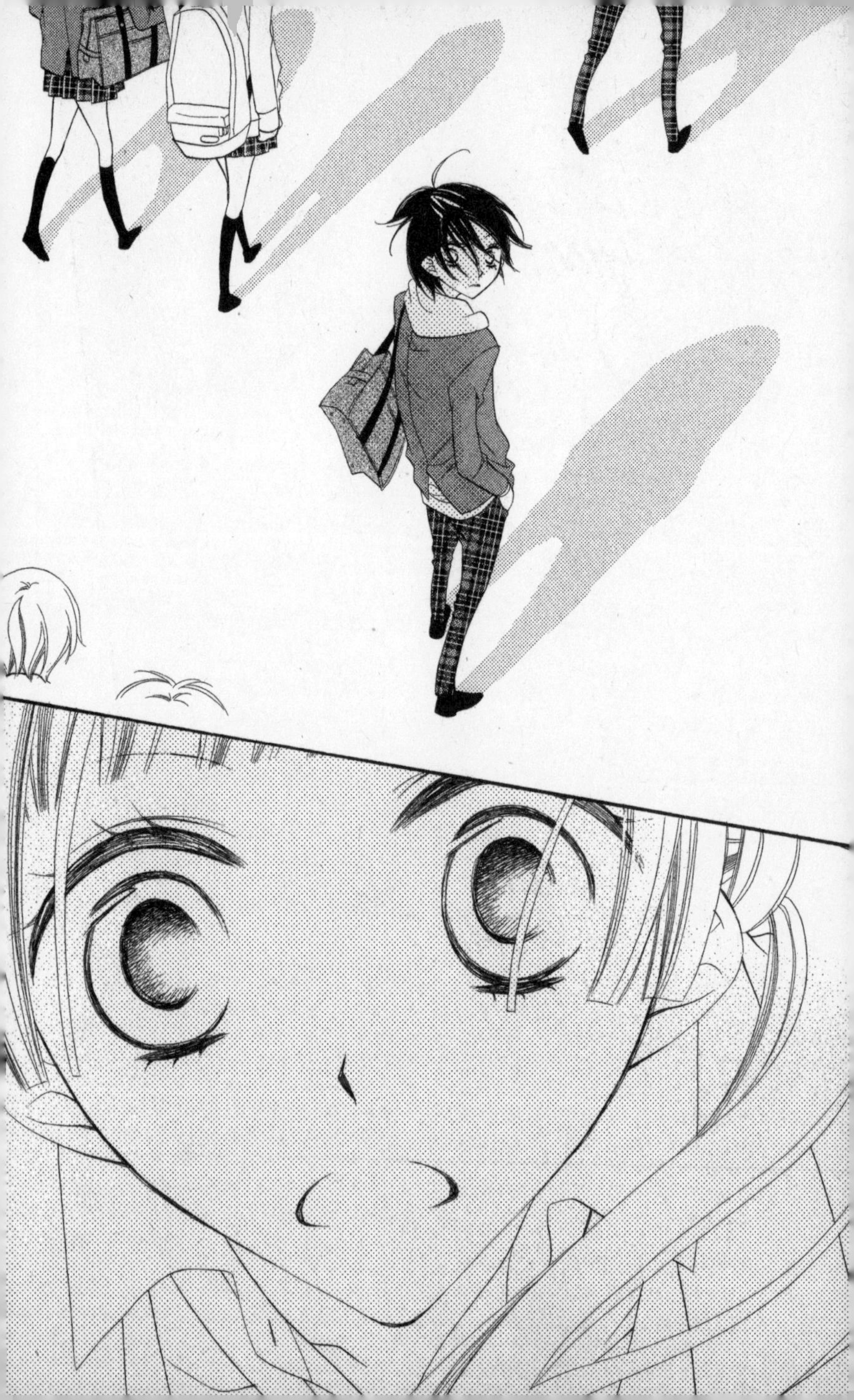

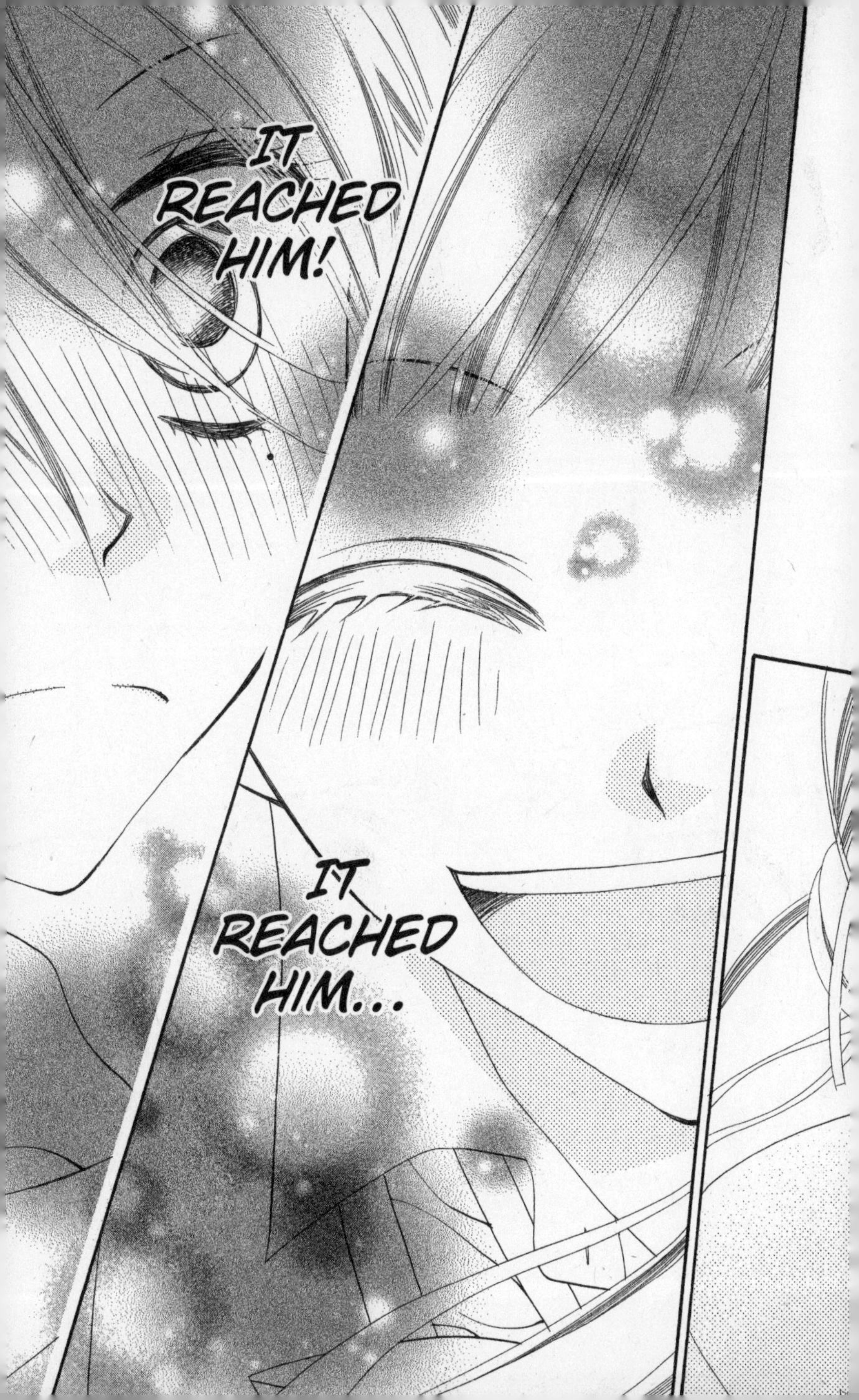
IT REACHED HIM...
IT REACHED HIM!

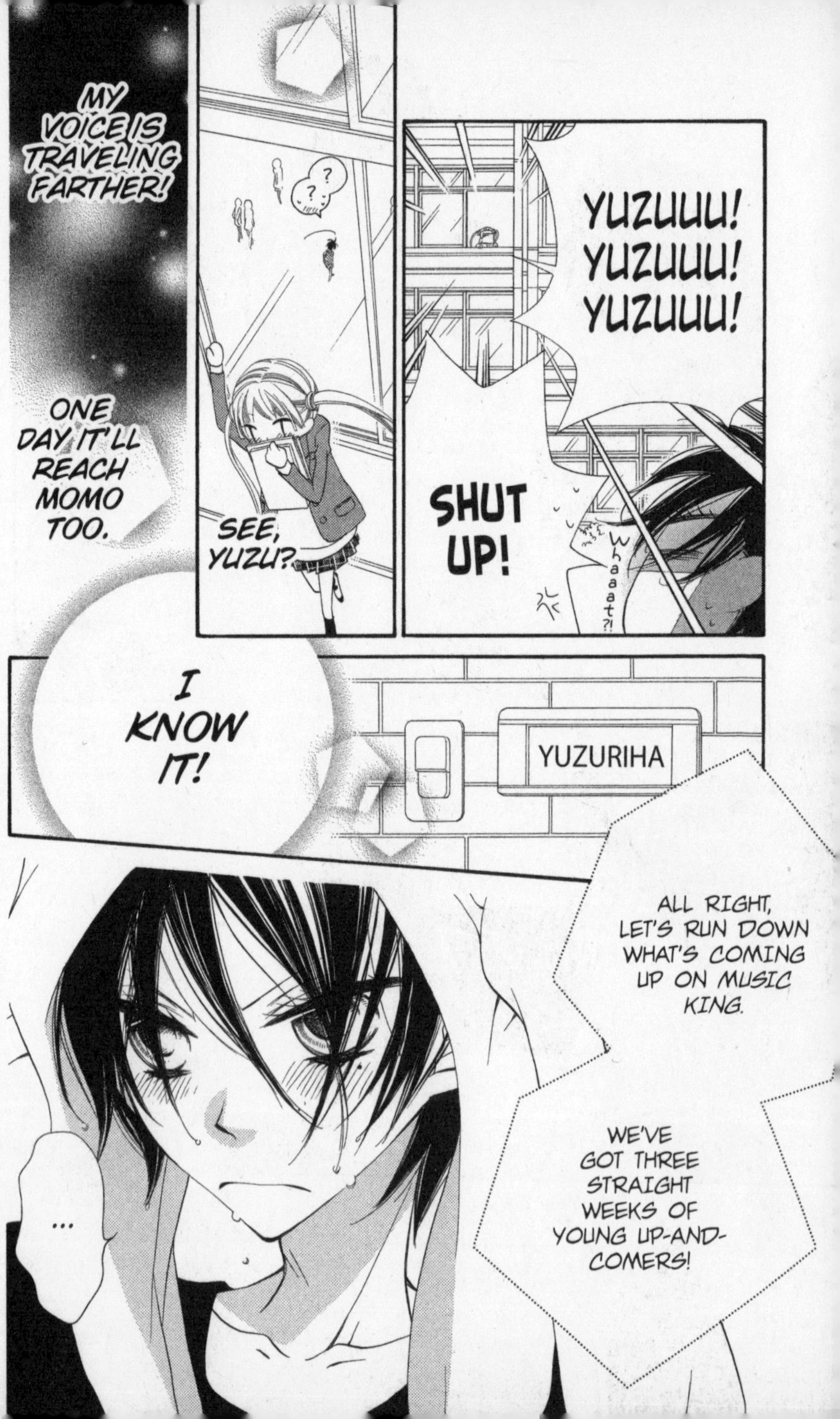
YUZUUU! YUZUUU! YUZUUU!
SHUT UP!
Whaaat?!
?
??
SEE, YUZU?
MY VOICE IS TRAVELING FARTHER!
ONE DAY IT'LL REACH MOMO TOO.
YUZURIHA
I KNOW IT!
ALL RIGHT, LET'S RUN DOWN WHAT'S COMING UP ON MUSIC KING.
WE'VE GOT THREE STRAIGHT WEEKS OF YOUNG UP-AND-COMERS!
...

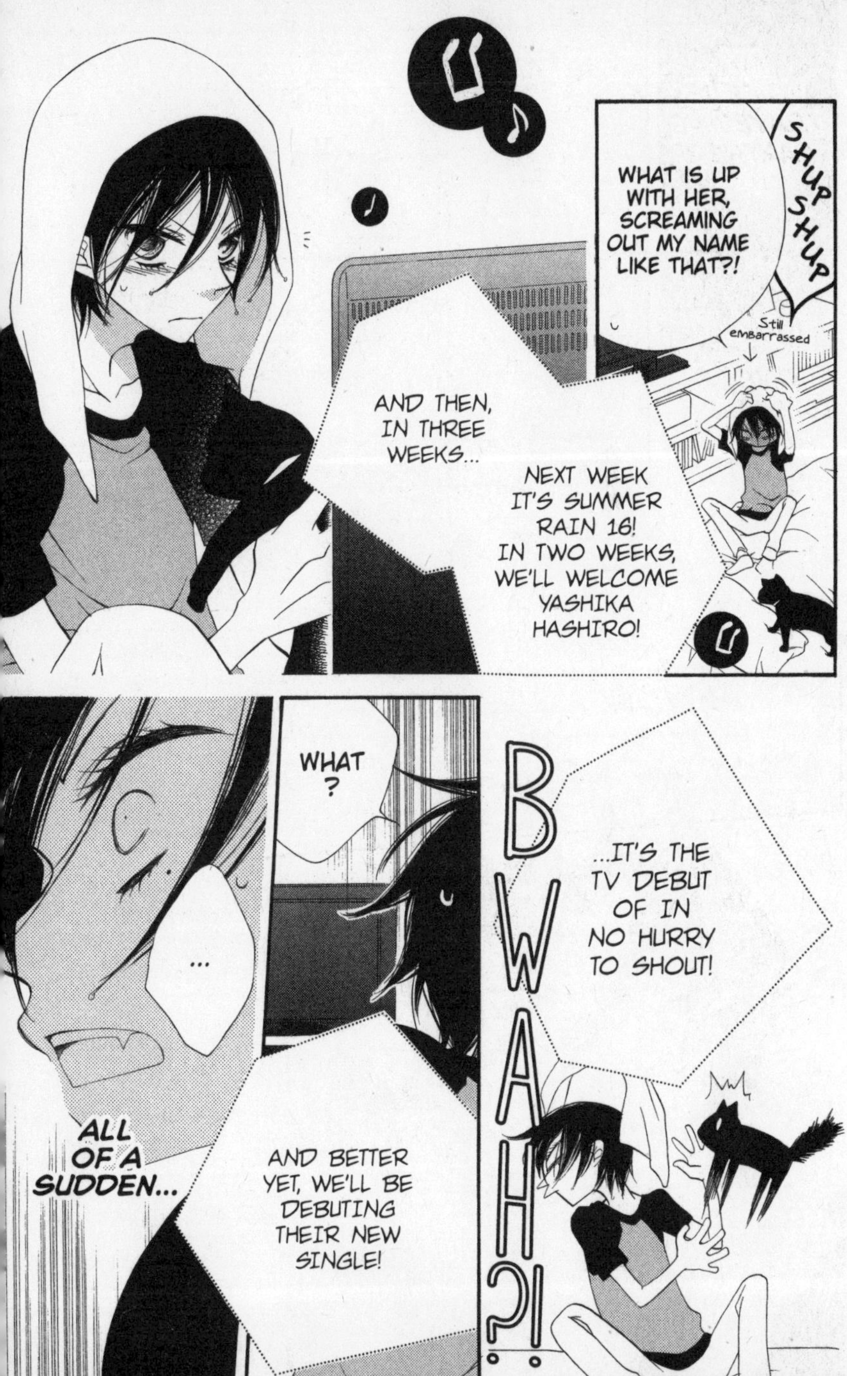
SHUP SHUP
WHAT IS UP WITH HER, SCREAMING OUT MY NAME LIKE THAT?!
Still embarrassed
NEXT WEEK IT'S SUMMER RAIN 16! IN TWO WEEKS, WE'LL WELCOME YASHIKA HASHIRO!
AND THEN, IN THREE WEEKS...
BWAH?!
...IT'S THE TV DEBUT OF IN NO HURRY TO SHOUT!
WHAT?
...
ALL OF A SUDDEN...
AND BETTER YET, WE'LL BE DEBUTING THEIR NEW SINGLE!

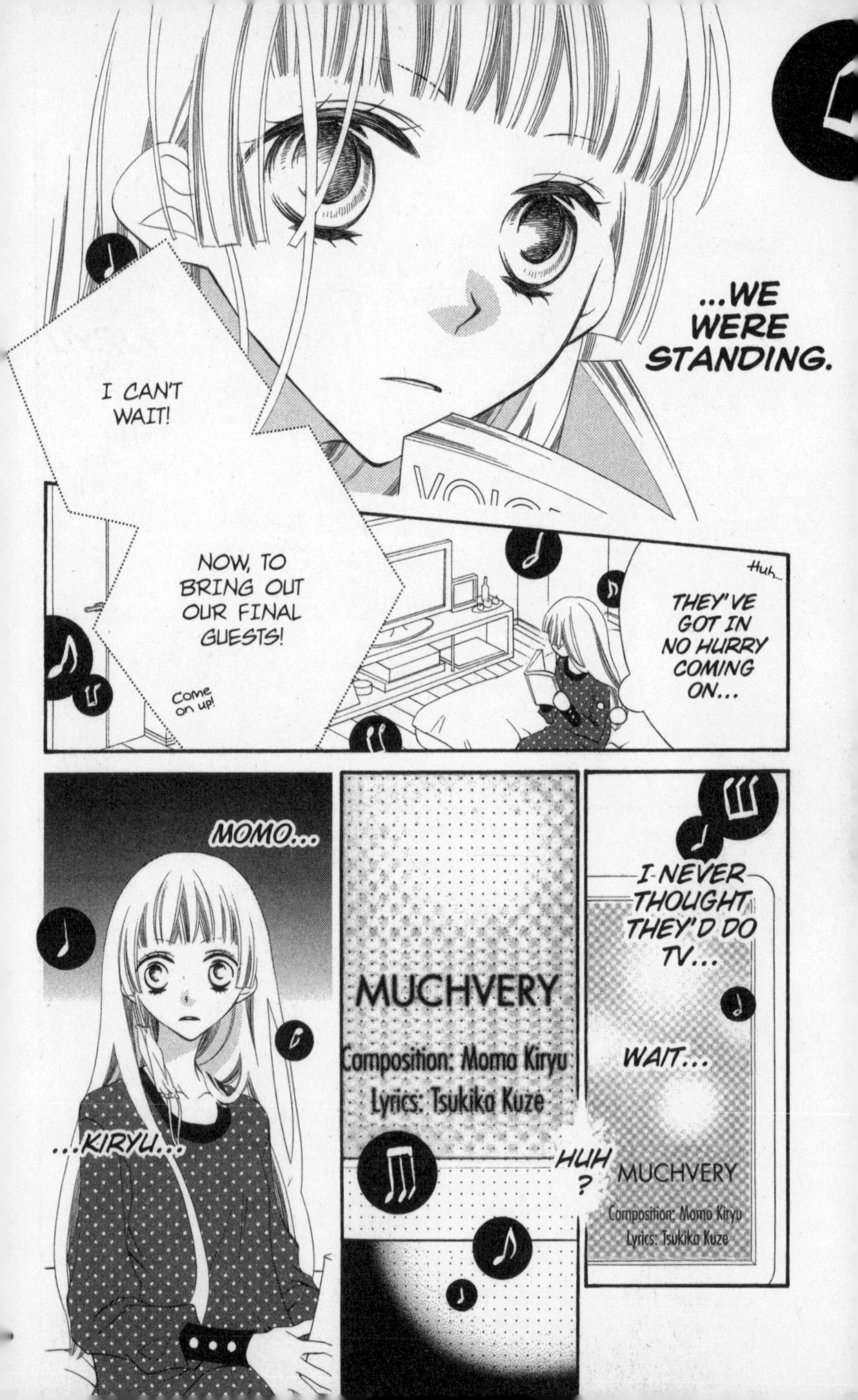
...WE WERE STANDING.
I CAN'T WAIT!
Huh...
THEY'VE GOT IN NO HURRY COMING ON...
NOW, TO BRING OUT OUR FINAL GUESTS!
Come on up!
I-NEVER THOUGHT THEY'D DO TV...
WAIT...
MUCHVERY
Composition: Momo Kiryu
Lyrics: Tsukika Kuze
HUH?
MUCHVERY
Composition: Momo Kiryu
Lyrics: Tsukika Kuze
MOMO...
...KIRYU...

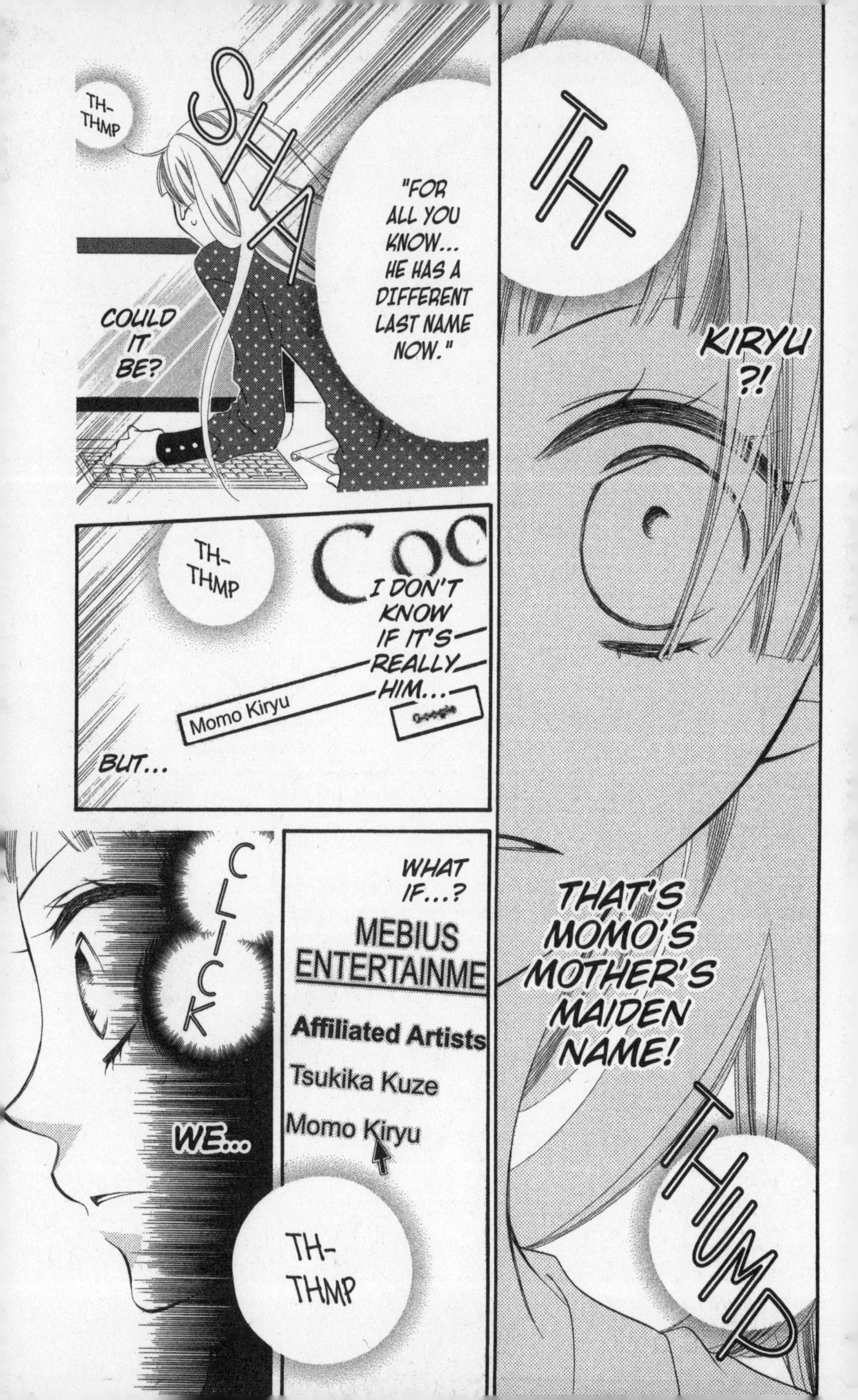
TH-
KIRYU ?!
THAT'S MOMO'S MOTHER'S MAIDEN NAME!
THUMP
TH-THMP
SHA
"FOR ALL YOU KNOW... HE HAS A DIFFERENT LAST NAME NOW."
COULD IT BE?
TH-THMP
I DON'T KNOW IF IT'S REALLY HIM...
Momo Kiryu
BUT...
WHAT IF...?
MEBIUS ENTERTAINME
Affiliated Artists
Tsukika Kuze
Momo Kiryu
TH-THMP
CLICK
WE...

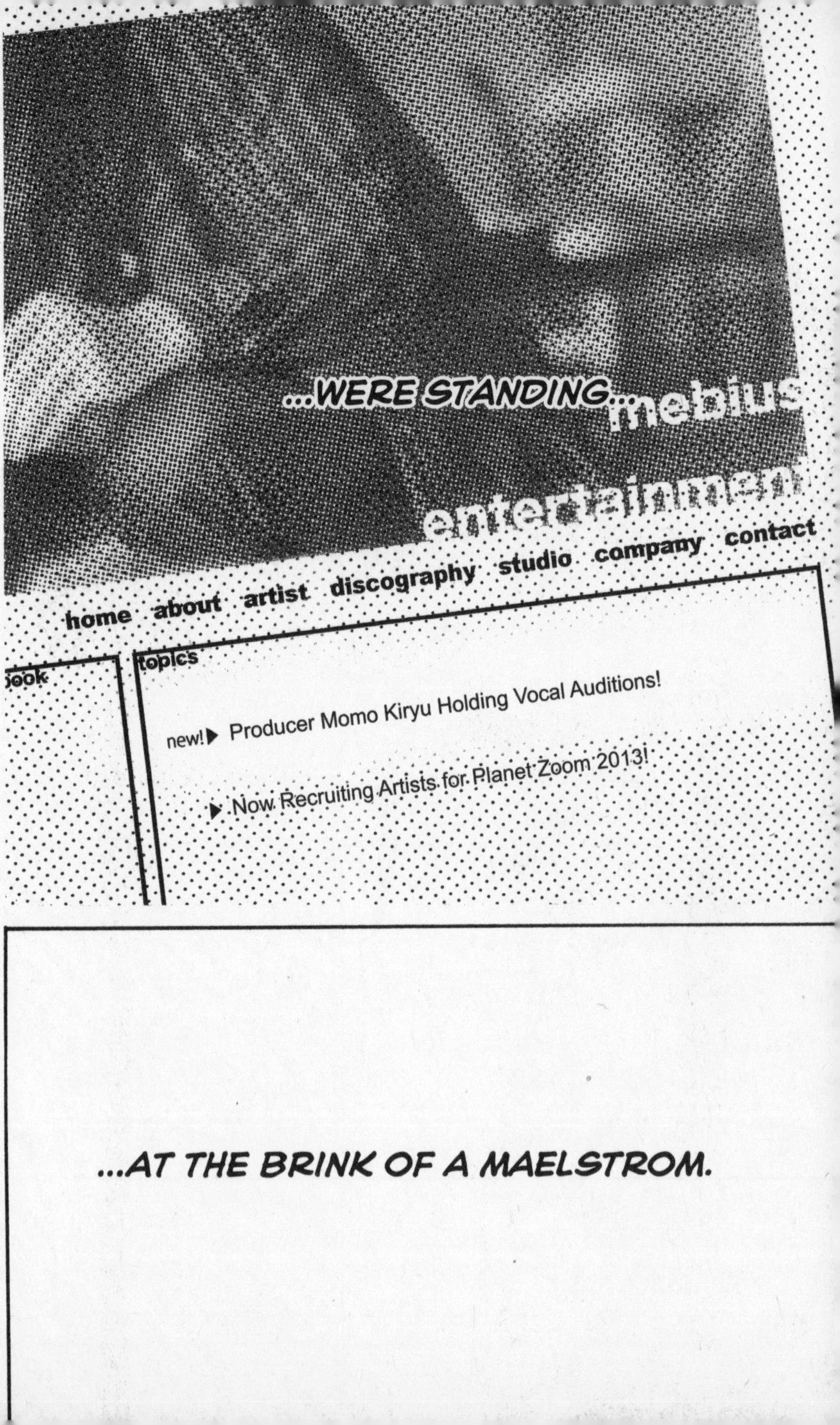
...WERE STANDING...
mebius
home about artist discography studio company contact
topics
new! ▶ Producer Momo Kiryu Holding Vocal Auditions!
▶ Now Recruiting Artists for Planet Zoom 2013!
...AT THE BRINK OF A MAELSTROM.

SONG 7

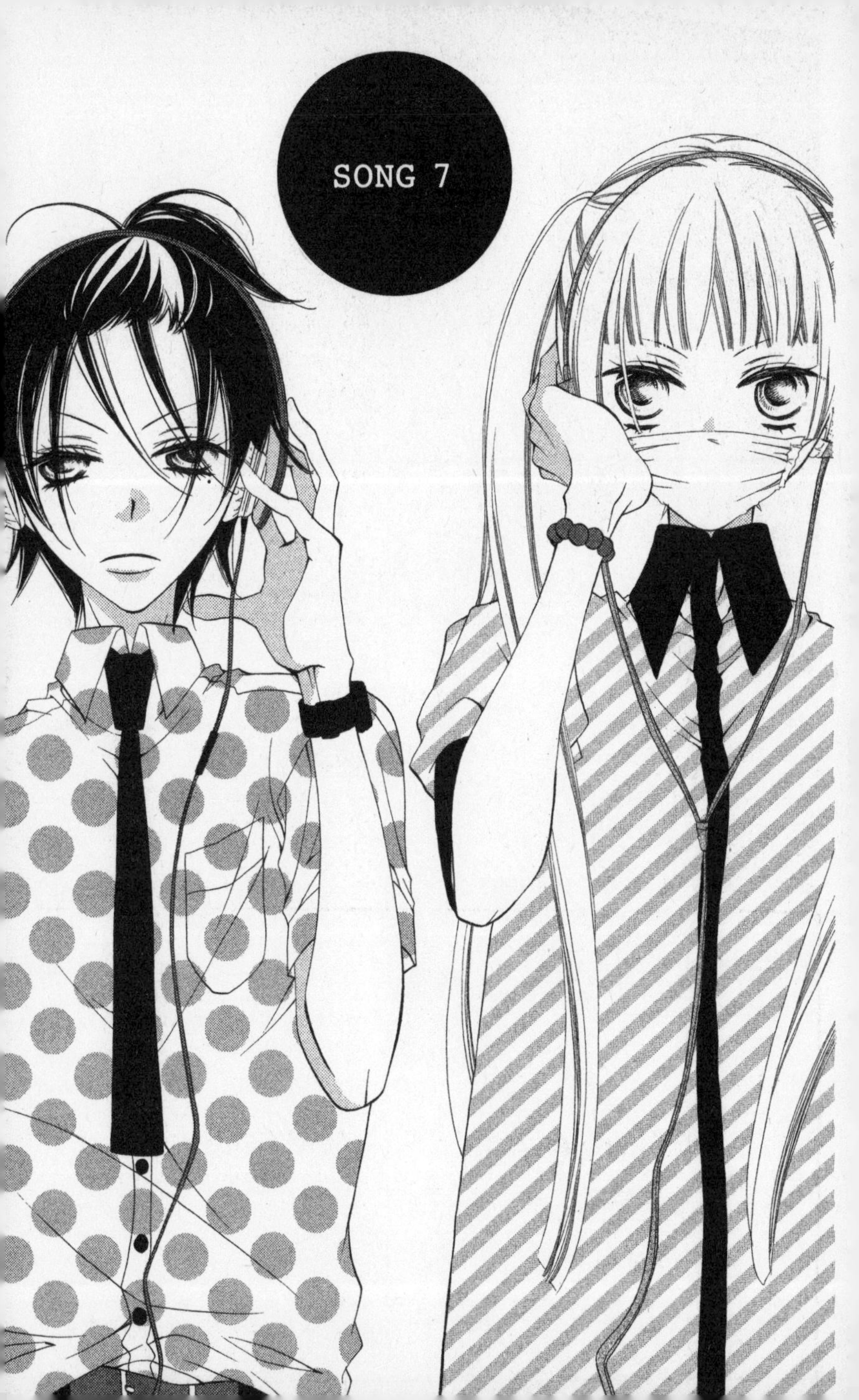

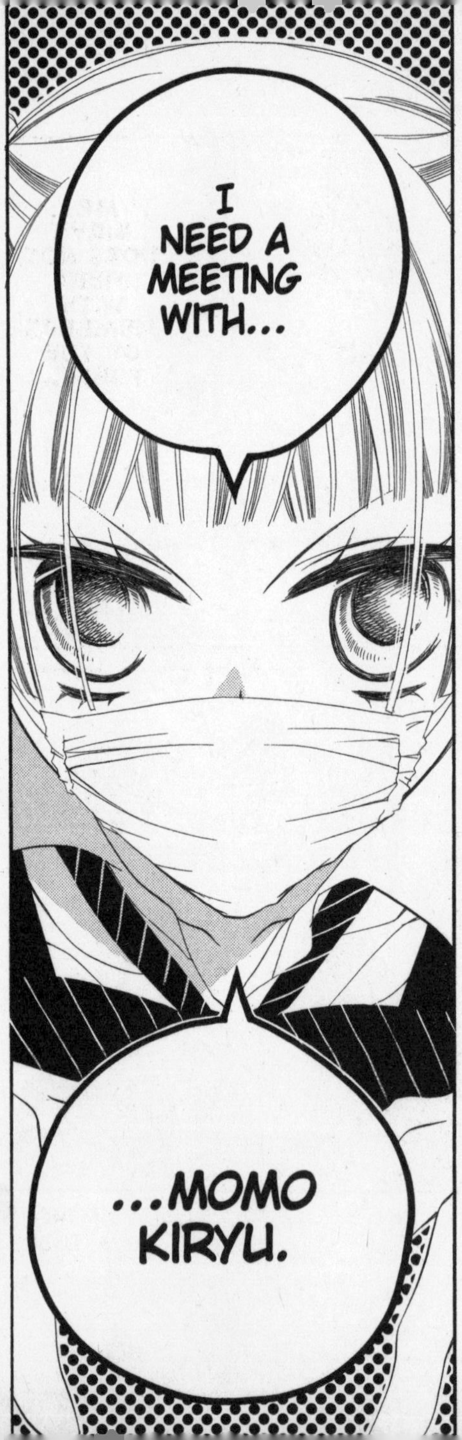
I NEED A MEETING WITH...
...MOMO KIRYU.

MOMO KIRYU

Background Information

Genre: J-Pop
Occupation: Composer
Studio: Mebius Entertainment

Momo Kiryu is a Japanese music composer. His blood type is AB. He writes music for BABY, an idol group. His third single for BABY, titled "Baby Baby," earned the band entry into NHK's prestigious televised New Year's Eve "Kohaku" concert. Momo Kiryu is male but is often mistaken for female due to his name.

No photographs or additional biographical information has been released.

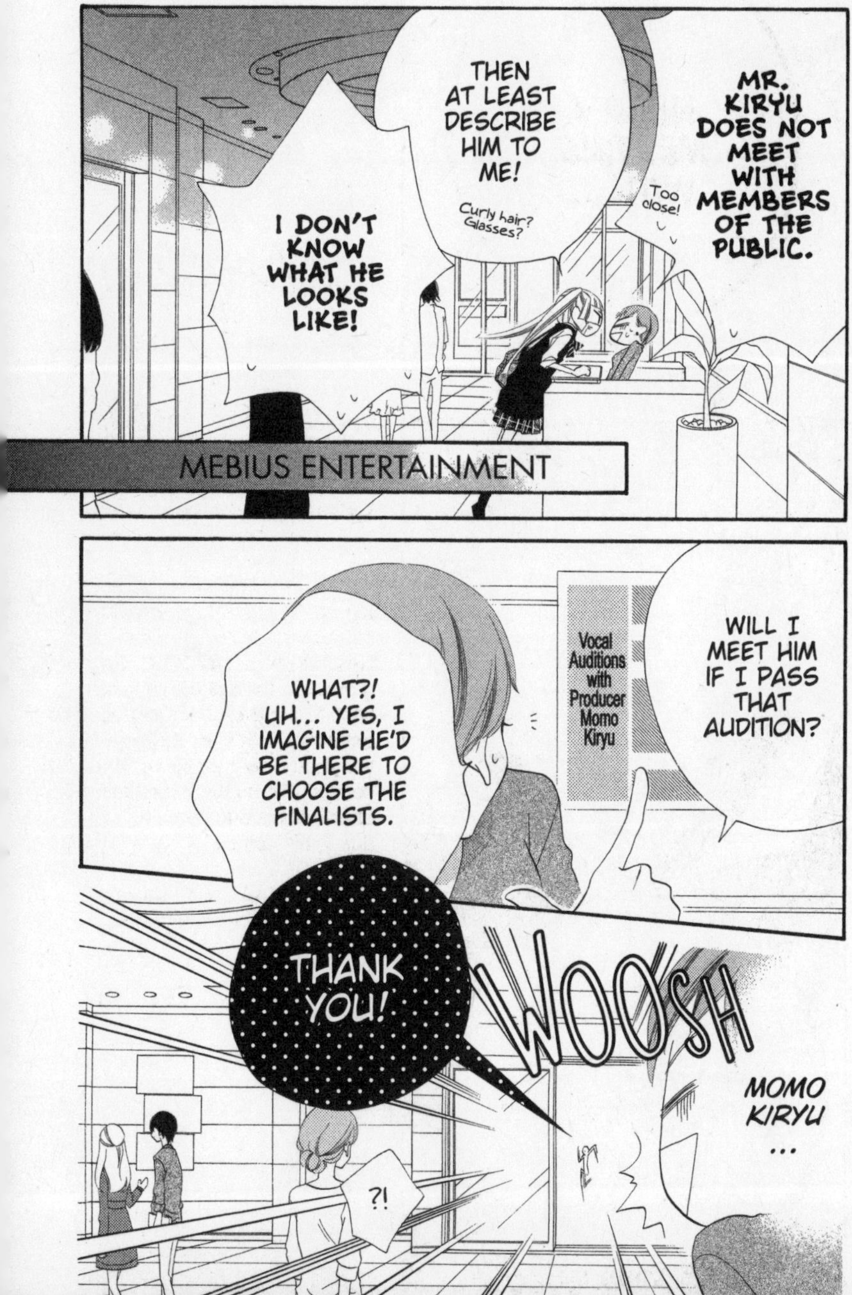
MR. KIRYU DOES NOT MEET WITH MEMBERS OF THE PUBLIC.
Too close!
THEN AT LEAST DESCRIBE HIM TO ME!
Curly hair? Glasses?
I DON'T KNOW WHAT HE LOOKS LIKE!
MEBIUS ENTERTAINMENT
WILL I MEET HIM IF I PASS THAT AUDITION?
Vocal Auditions with Producer Momo Kiryu
WHAT?! UH... YES, I IMAGINE HE'D BE THERE TO CHOOSE THE FINALISTS.
MOMO KIRYU ...
WOOSH
THANK YOU!
?!

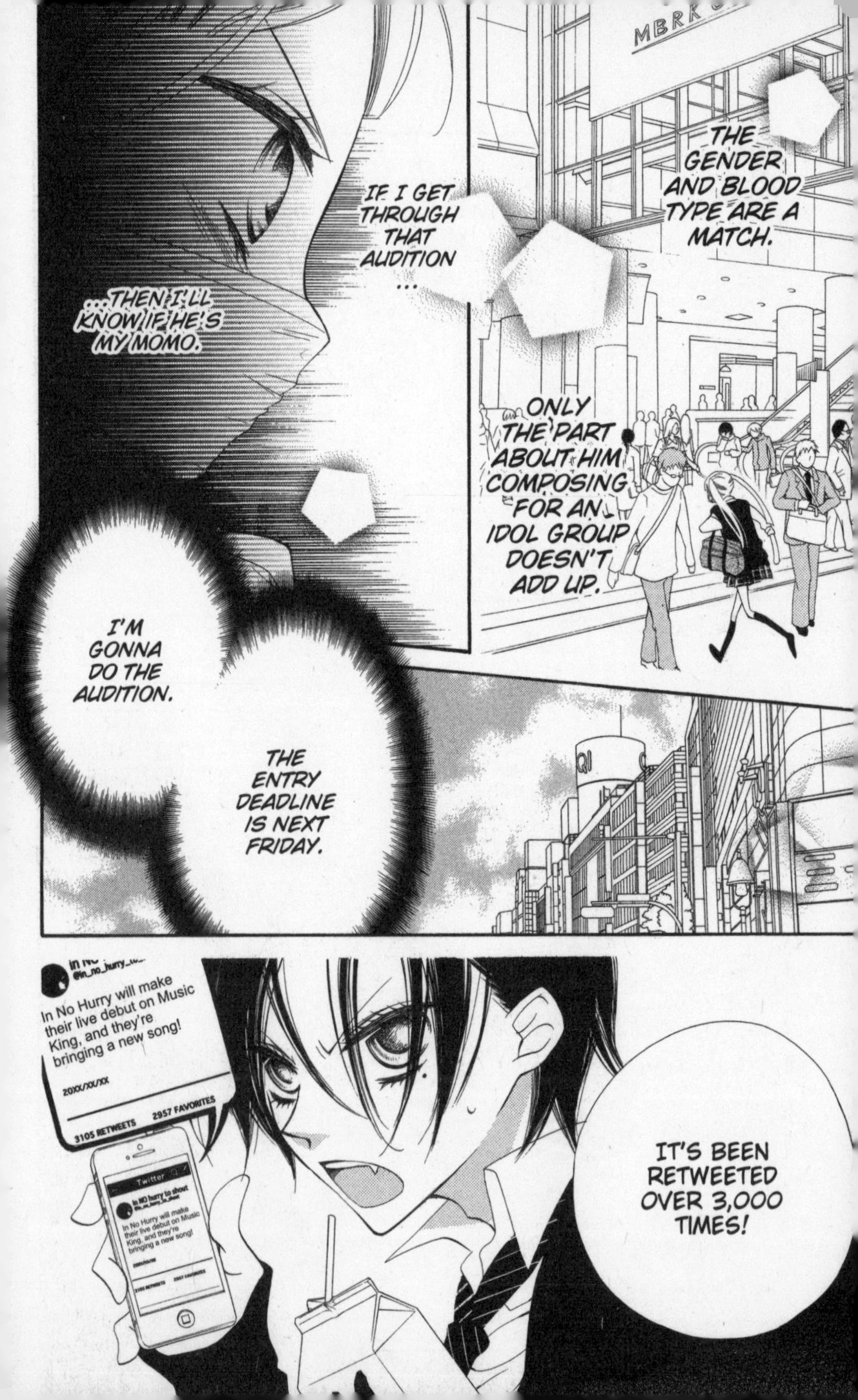
MBRK
THE GENDER AND BLOOD TYPE ARE A MATCH.
ONLY THE PART ABOUT HIM COMPOSING FOR AN IDOL GROUP DOESN'T ADD UP.
IF I GET THROUGH THAT AUDITION ...
...THEN I'LL KNOW IF HE'S MY MOMO.
I'M GONNA DO THE AUDITION.
THE ENTRY DEADLINE IS NEXT FRIDAY.
IT'S BEEN RETWEETED OVER 3,000 TIMES!
In No Hurry will make their live debut on Music King, and they're bringing a new song!
20XX/XX/XX
3105 RETWEETS
2957 FAVORITES

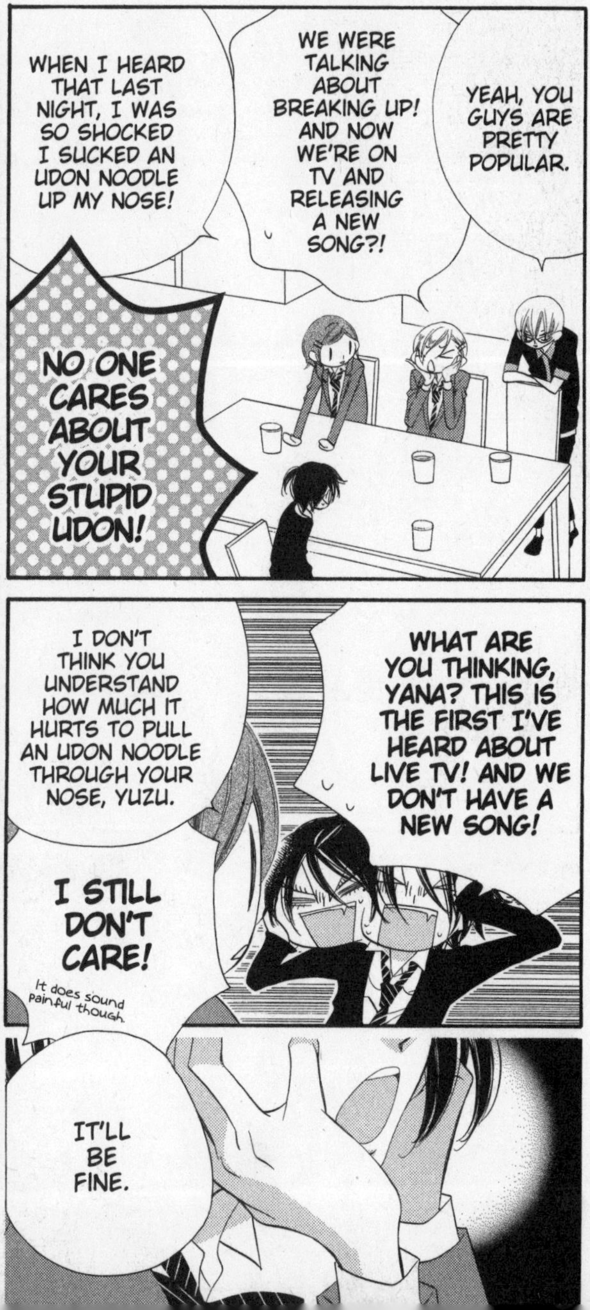
YEAH, YOU GUYS ARE PRETTY POPULAR.
WE WERE TALKING ABOUT BREAKING UP! AND NOW WE'RE ON TV AND RELEASING A NEW SONG?!
WHEN I HEARD THAT LAST NIGHT, I WAS SO SHOCKED I SUCKED AN UDON NOODLE UP MY NOSE!
NO ONE CARES ABOUT YOUR STUPID UDON!
WHAT ARE YOU THINKING, YANA? THIS IS THE FIRST I'VE HEARD ABOUT LIVE TV! AND WE DON'T HAVE A NEW SONG!
I DON'T THINK YOU UNDERSTAND HOW MUCH IT HURTS TO PULL AN UDON NOODLE THROUGH YOUR NOSE, YUZU.
I STILL DON'T CARE!
It does sound painful though.
IT'LL BE FINE.

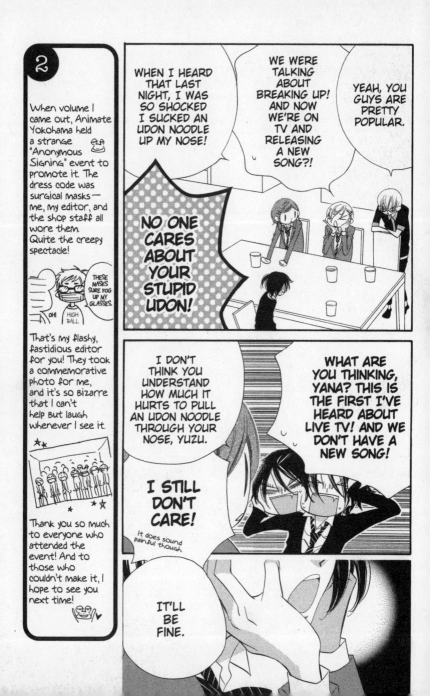

2

When volume 1 came out, Animate Yokohama held a strange "Anonymous Signing" event to promote it. The dress code was surgical masks—me, my editor, and the shop staff all wore them. Quite the creepy spectacle!

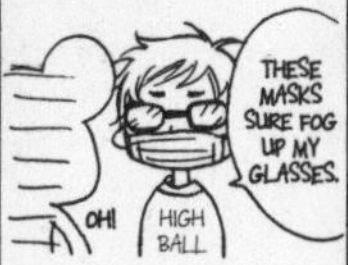
THESE MASKS SURE FOG UP MY GLASSES.
OH!
HIGH BALL

That's my flashy, fastidious editor for you! They took a commemorative photo for me, and it's so bizarre that I can't help but laugh whenever I see it.

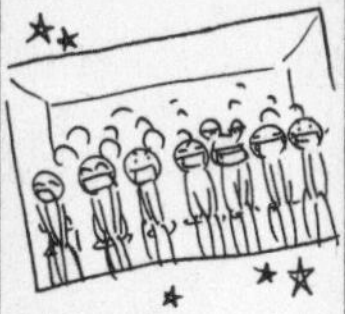

Thank you so much to everyone who attended the event! And to those who couldn't make it, I hope to see you next time!

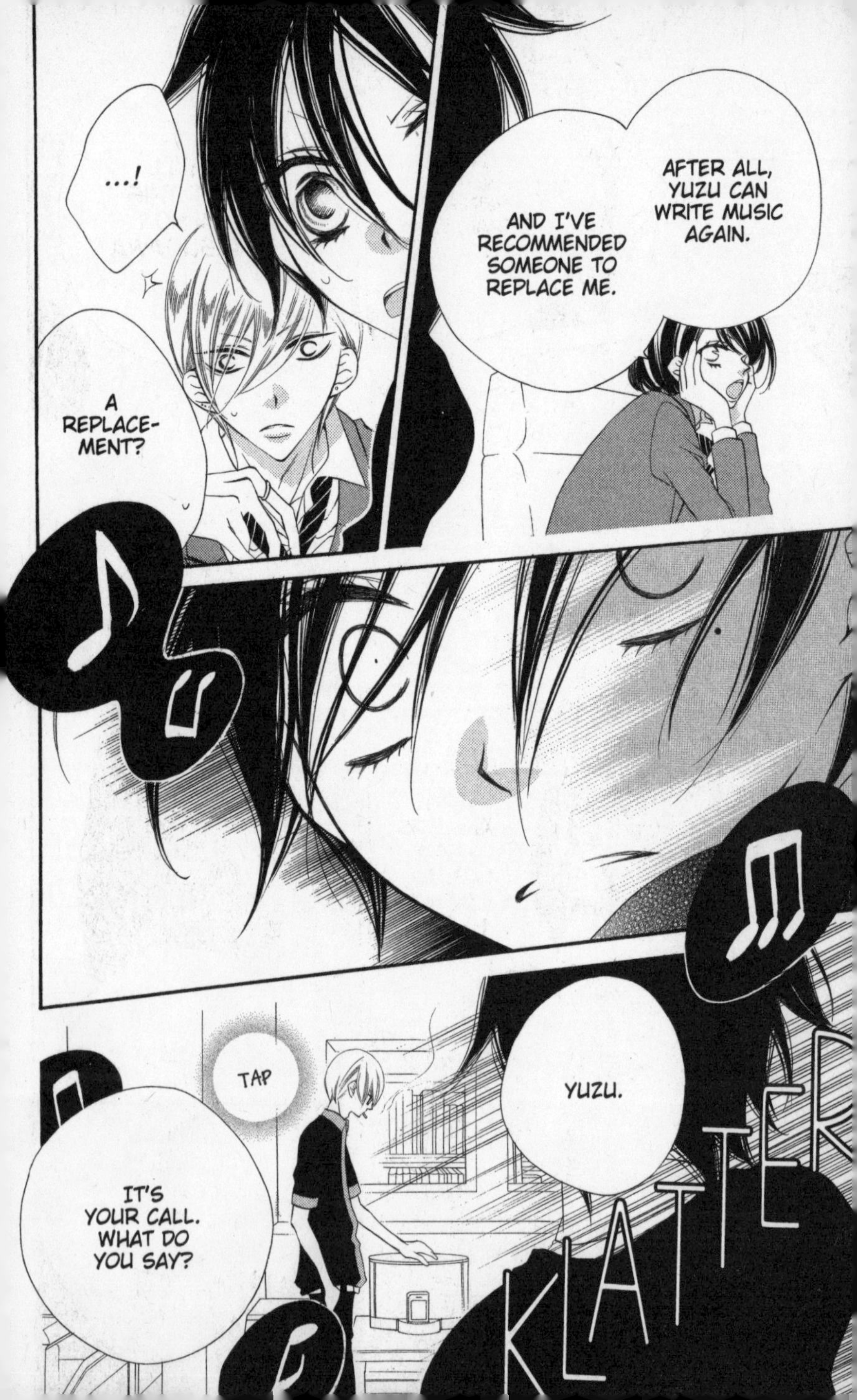
AFTER ALL, YUZU CAN WRITE MUSIC AGAIN.
AND I'VE RECOMMENDED SOMEONE TO REPLACE ME.
...!
A REPLACE-MENT?
YUZU.
KLATTER
TAP
IT'S YOUR CALL. WHAT DO YOU SAY?

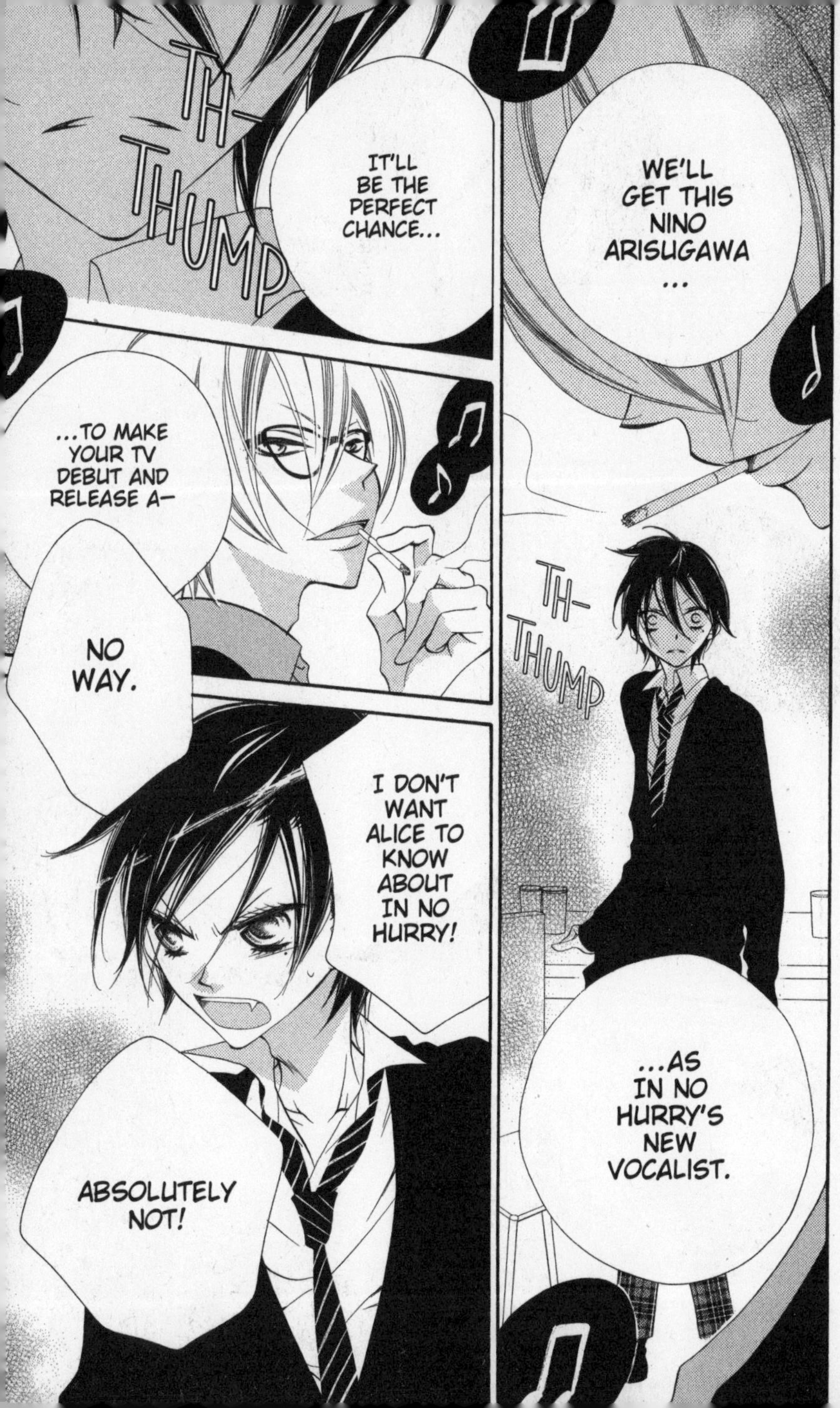
WE'LL GET THIS NINO ARISUGAWA ...
TH-THUMP
...AS IN NO HURRY'S NEW VOCALIST.
TH-THUMP
IT'LL BE THE PERFECT CHANCE...
...TO MAKE YOUR TV DEBUT AND RELEASE A—
NO WAY.
I DON'T WANT ALICE TO KNOW ABOUT IN NO HURRY!
ABSOLUTELY NOT!

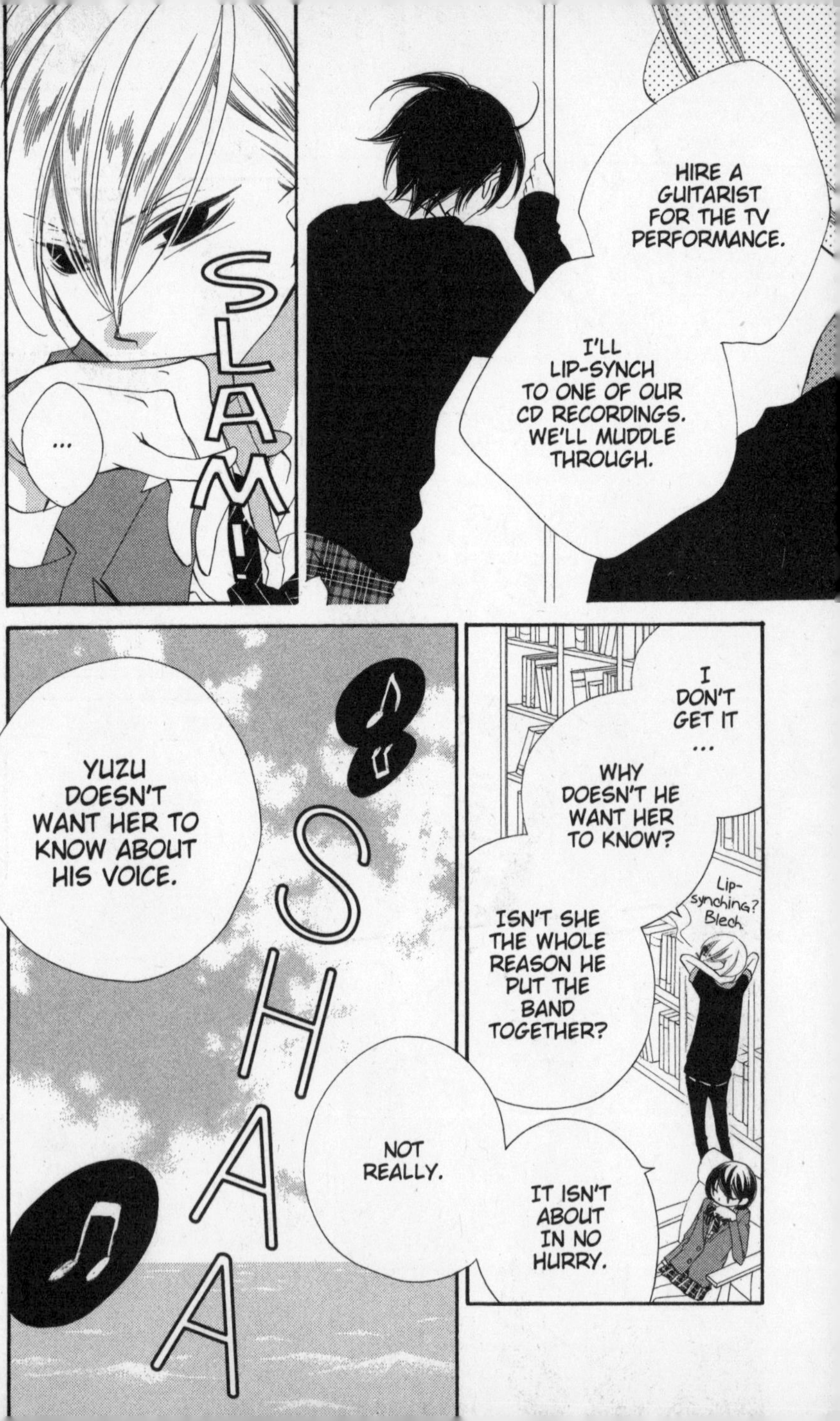
HIRE A GUITARIST FOR THE TV PERFORMANCE.
I'LL LIP-SYNCH TO ONE OF OUR CD RECORDINGS. WE'LL MUDDLE THROUGH.
SLAM!
...
I DON'T GET IT ...
WHY DOESN'T HE WANT HER TO KNOW?
Lip-synching? Blech.
ISN'T SHE THE WHOLE REASON HE PUT THE BAND TOGETHER?
NOT REALLY.
IT ISN'T ABOUT IN NO HURRY.
YUZU DOESN'T WANT HER TO KNOW ABOUT HIS VOICE.
SHAAA

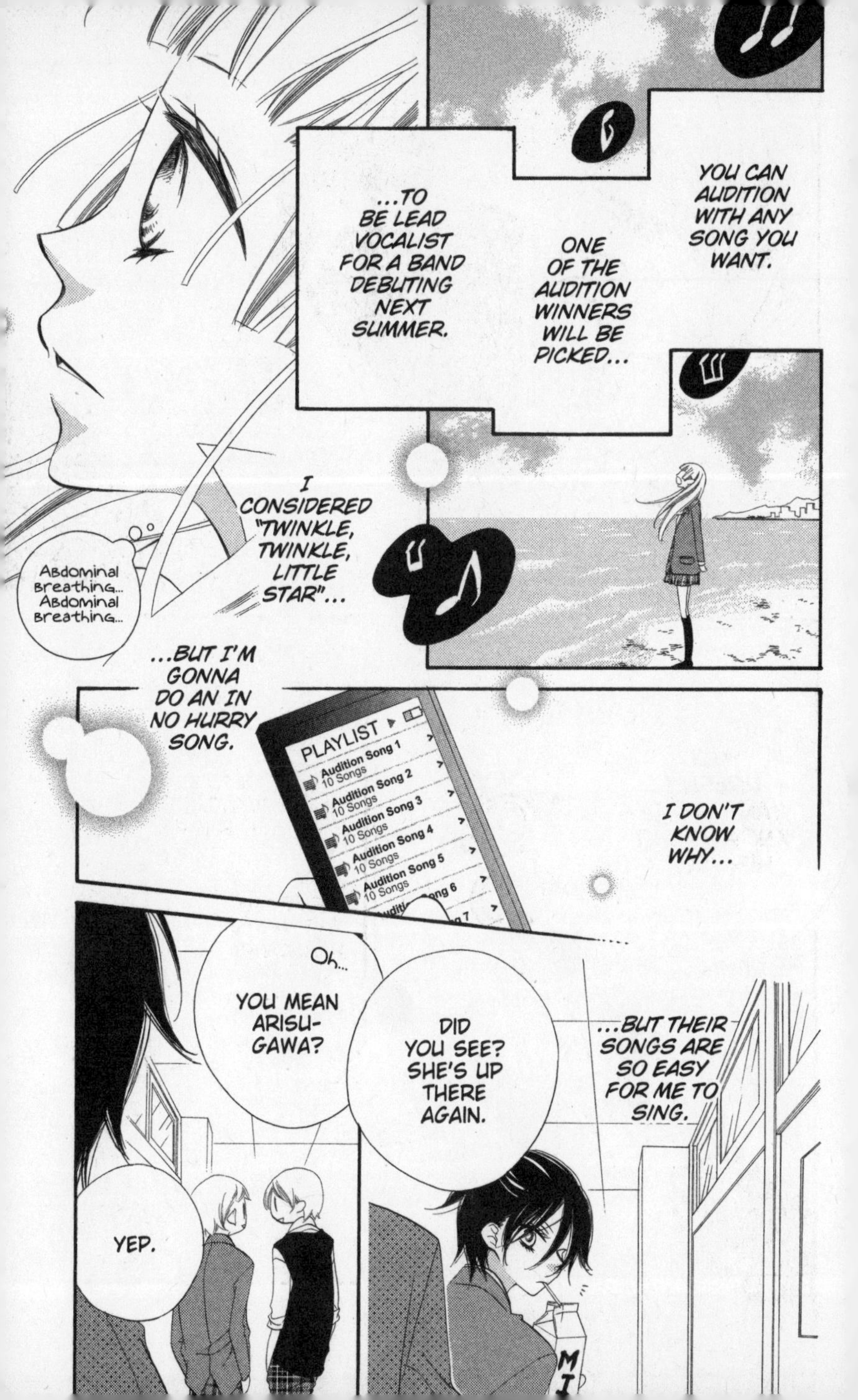
YOU CAN AUDITION WITH ANY SONG YOU WANT.
ONE OF THE AUDITION WINNERS WILL BE PICKED...
...TO BE LEAD VOCALIST FOR A BAND DEBUTING NEXT SUMMER.
I CONSIDERED "TWINKLE, TWINKLE, LITTLE STAR"...
Abdominal breathing... Abdominal breathing...
...BUT I'M GONNA DO AN IN NO HURRY SONG.
PLAYLIST
Audition Song 1
10 Songs
Audition Song 2
10 Songs
Audition Song 3
10 Songs
Audition Song 4
10 Songs
Audition Song 5
10 Songs
Audition Song 6
I DON'T KNOW WHY...
...BUT THEIR SONGS ARE SO EASY FOR ME TO SING.
DID YOU SEE? SHE'S UP THERE AGAIN.
Oh...
YOU MEAN ARISUGAWA?
YEP.

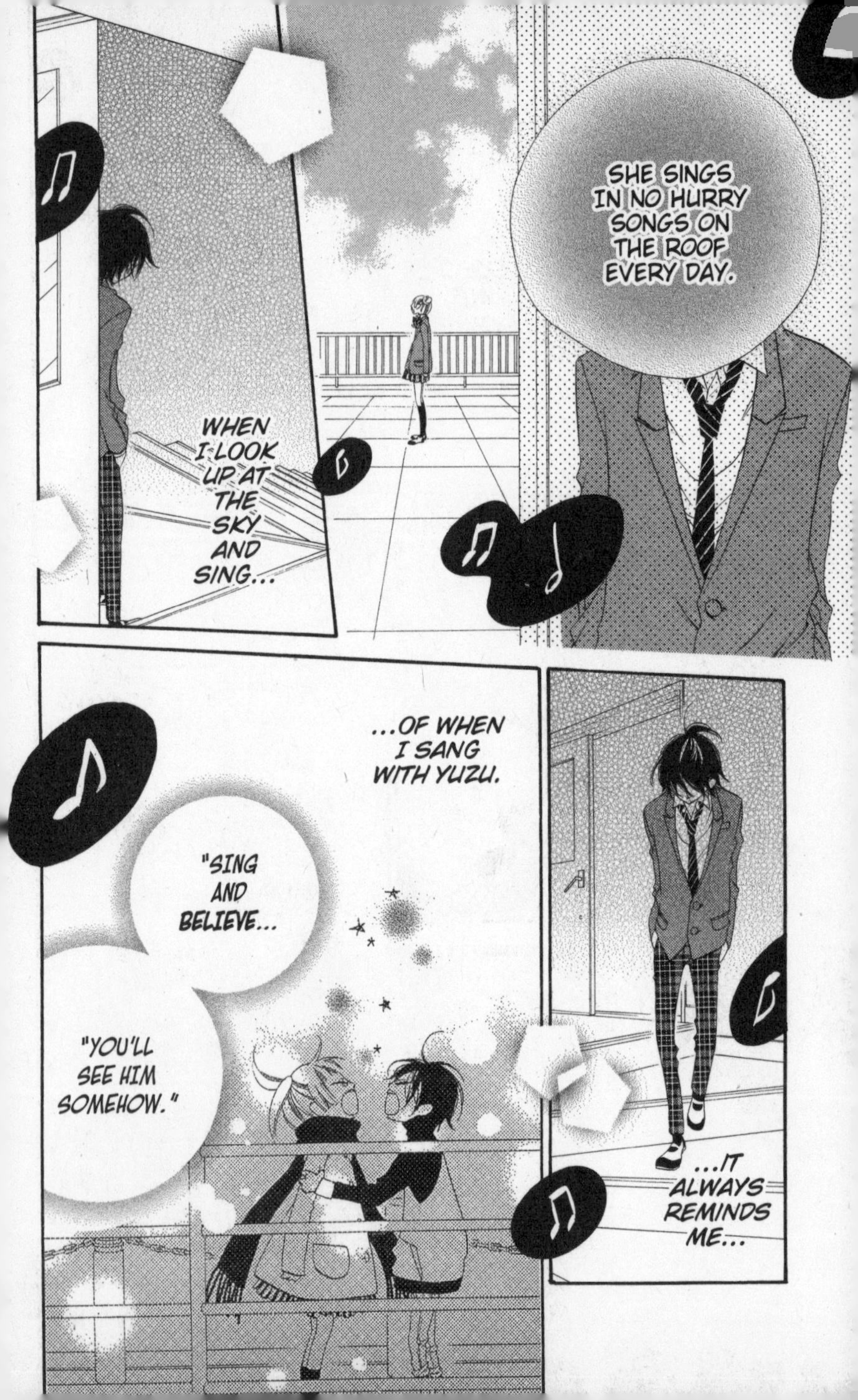
SHE SINGS IN NO HURRY SONGS ON THE ROOF EVERY DAY.
WHEN I LOOK UP AT THE SKY AND SING...
...IT ALWAYS REMINDS ME...
...OF WHEN I SANG WITH YUZU.
"SING AND BELIEVE...
"YOU'LL SEE HIM SOMEHOW."

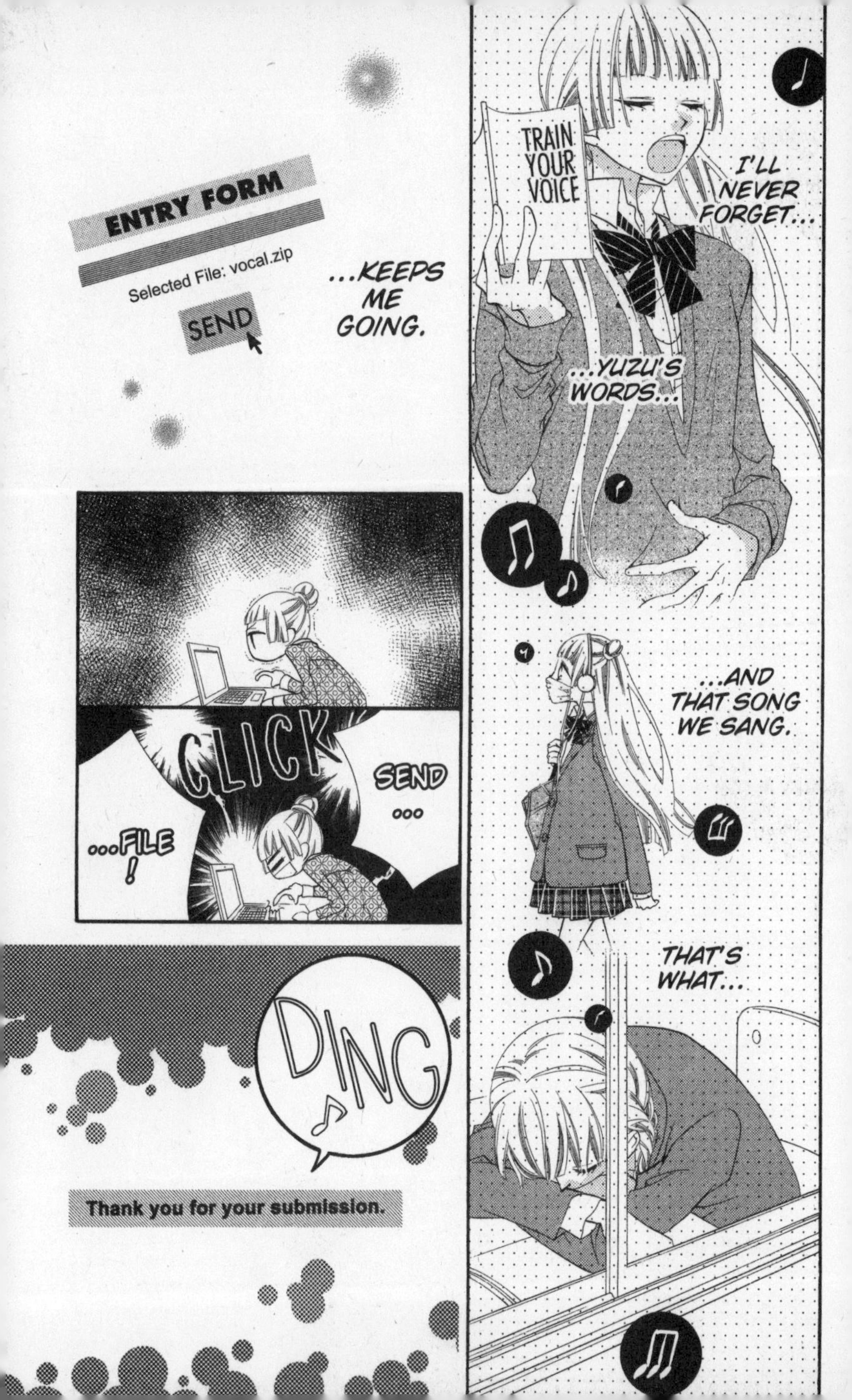
TRAIN YOUR VOICE
I'LL NEVER FORGET...
...YUZU'S WORDS...
...AND THAT SONG WE SANG.
THAT'S WHAT...
...KEEPS ME GOING.
ENTRY FORM
Selected File: vocal.zip
SEND
SEND...
CLICK
...FILE!
DING
Thank you for your submission.

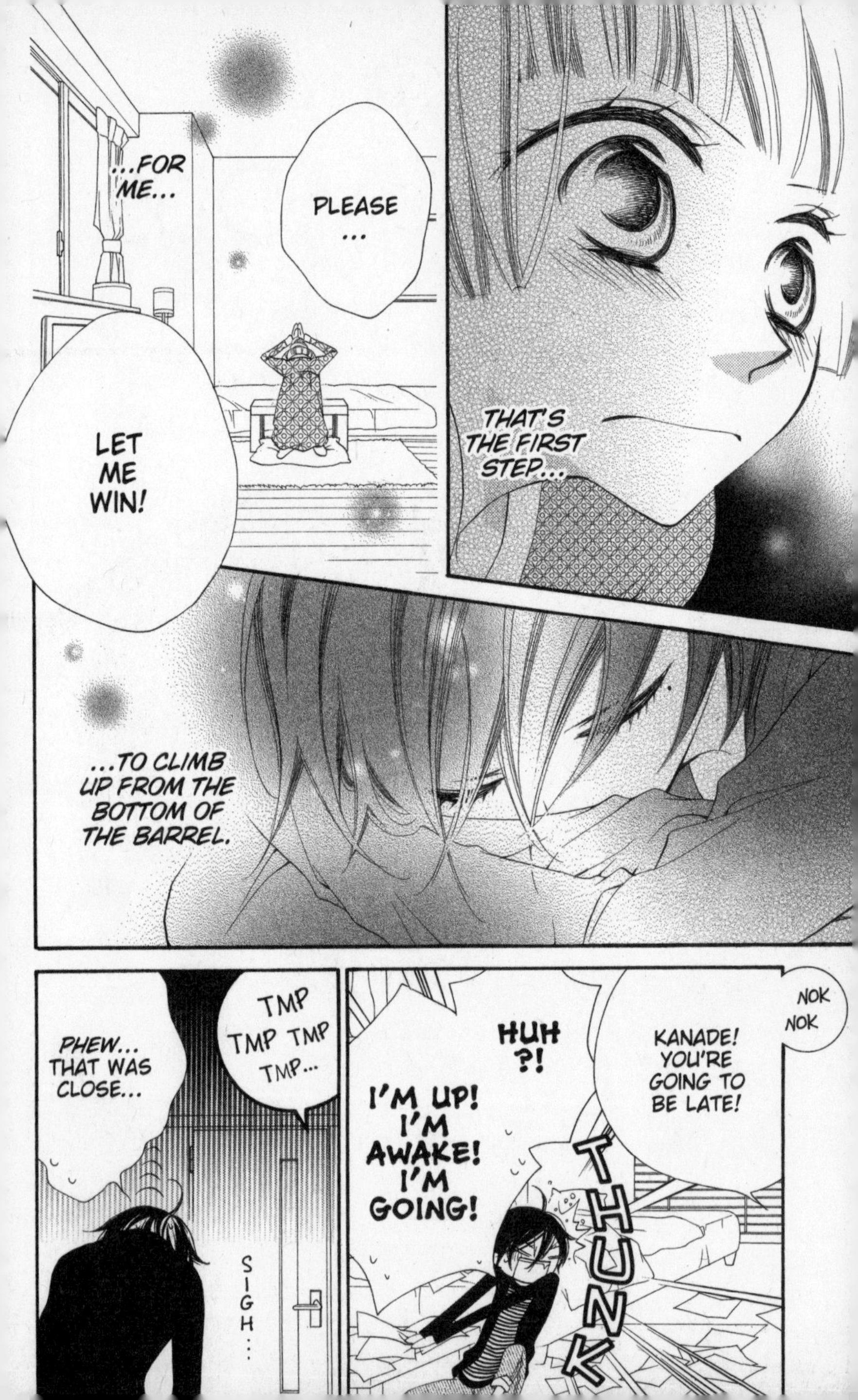
THAT'S THE FIRST STEP...
PLEASE ...
...FOR ME...
LET ME WIN!
...TO CLIMB UP FROM THE BOTTOM OF THE BARREL.
NOK NOK
KANADE! YOU'RE GOING TO BE LATE!
HUH ?!
THUNK
I'M UP! I'M AWAKE! I'M GOING!
TMP TMP TMP TMP...
PHEW... THAT WAS CLOSE...
SIGH...

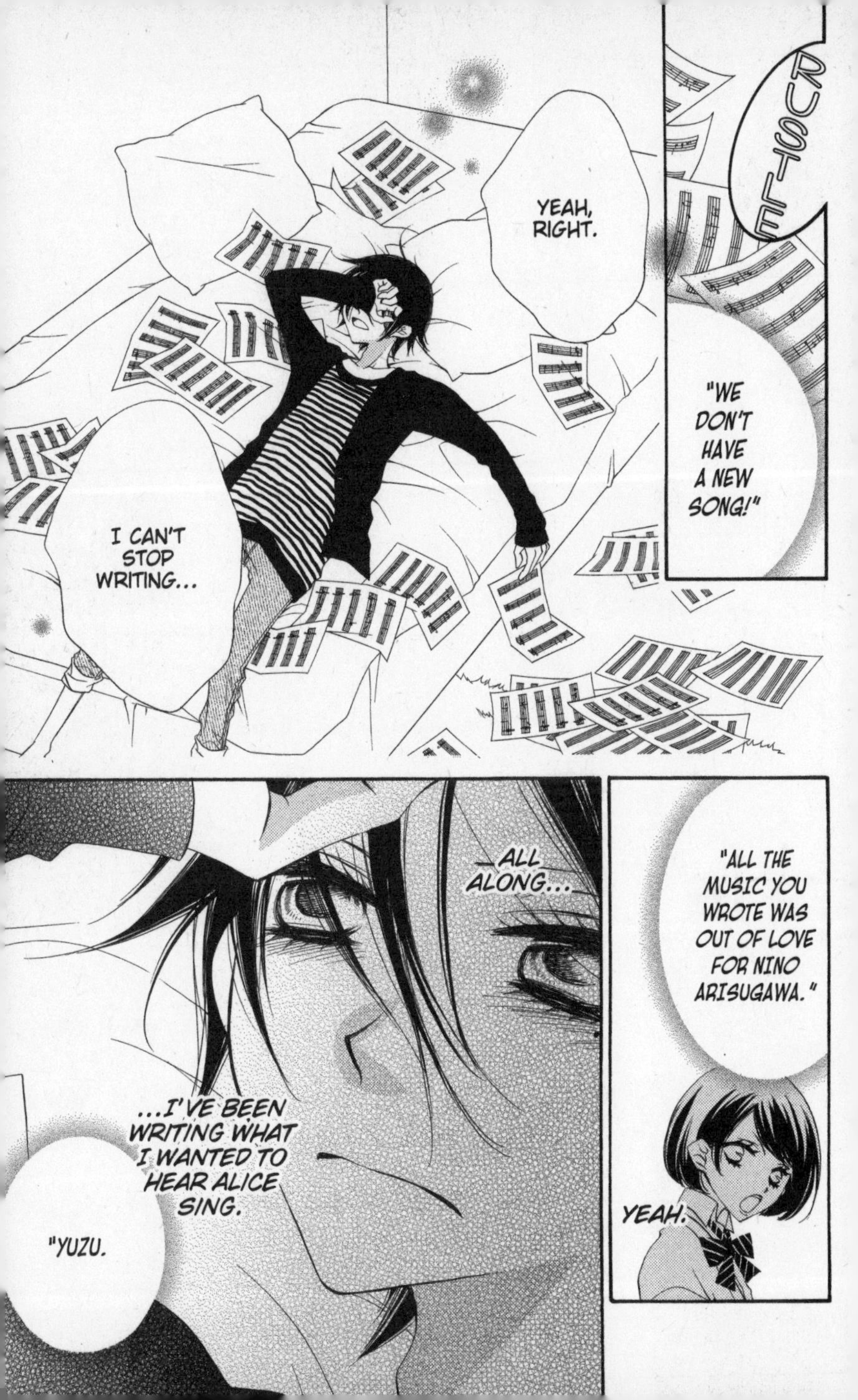
RUSTLE
"WE DON'T HAVE A NEW SONG!"
YEAH, RIGHT.
I CAN'T STOP WRITING...
"ALL THE MUSIC YOU WROTE WAS OUT OF LOVE FOR NINO ARISUGAWA."
YEAH.
—ALL ALONG...
...I'VE BEEN WRITING WHAT I WANTED TO HEAR ALICE SING.
"YUZU.

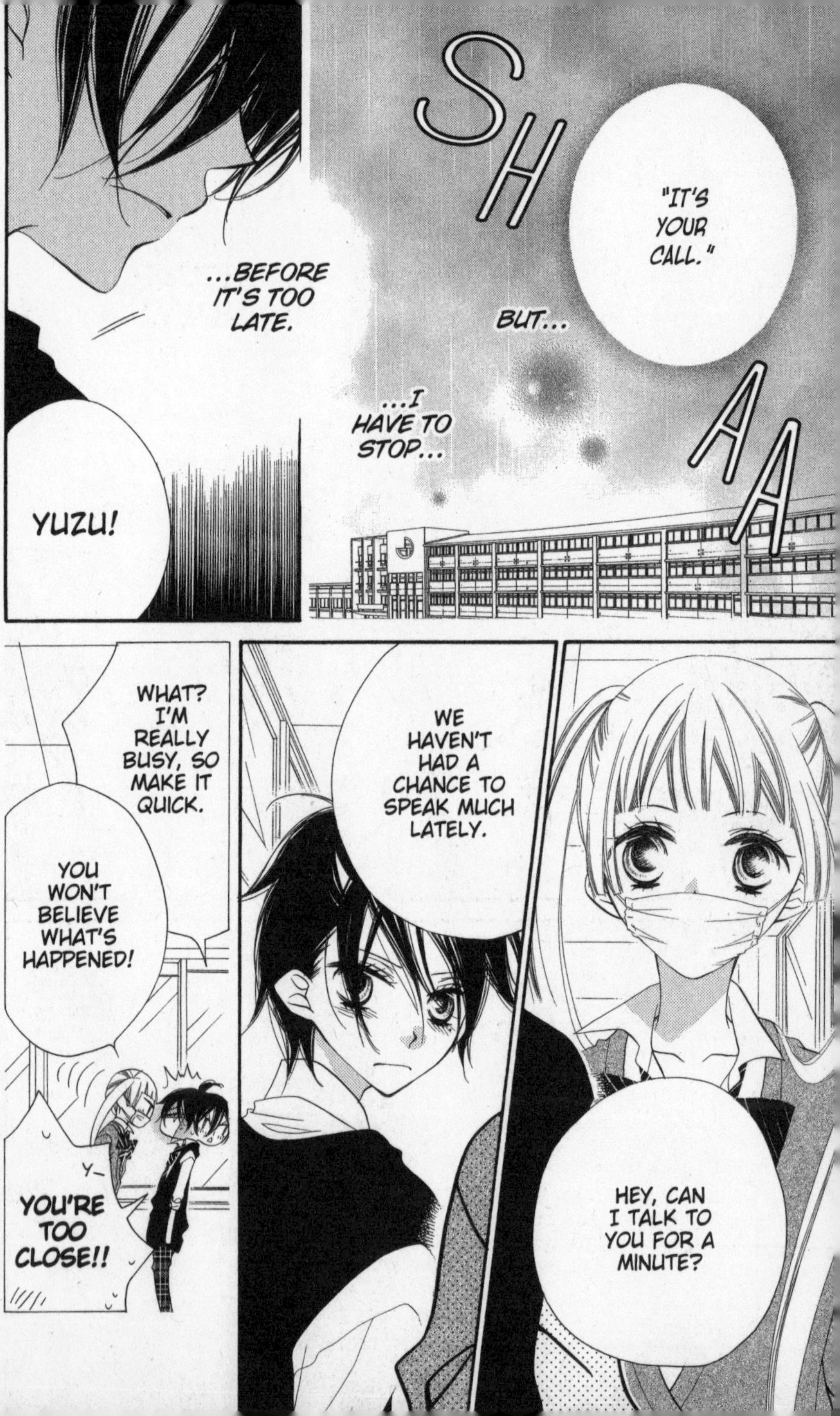
"IT'S YOUR CALL."
SHAA
BUT...
...I HAVE TO STOP...
...BEFORE IT'S TOO LATE.
YUZU!
HEY, CAN I TALK TO YOU FOR A MINUTE?
WE HAVEN'T HAD A CHANCE TO SPEAK MUCH LATELY.
WHAT? I'M REALLY BUSY, SO MAKE IT QUICK.
YOU WON'T BELIEVE WHAT'S HAPPENED!
Y—
YOU'RE TOO CLOSE!!

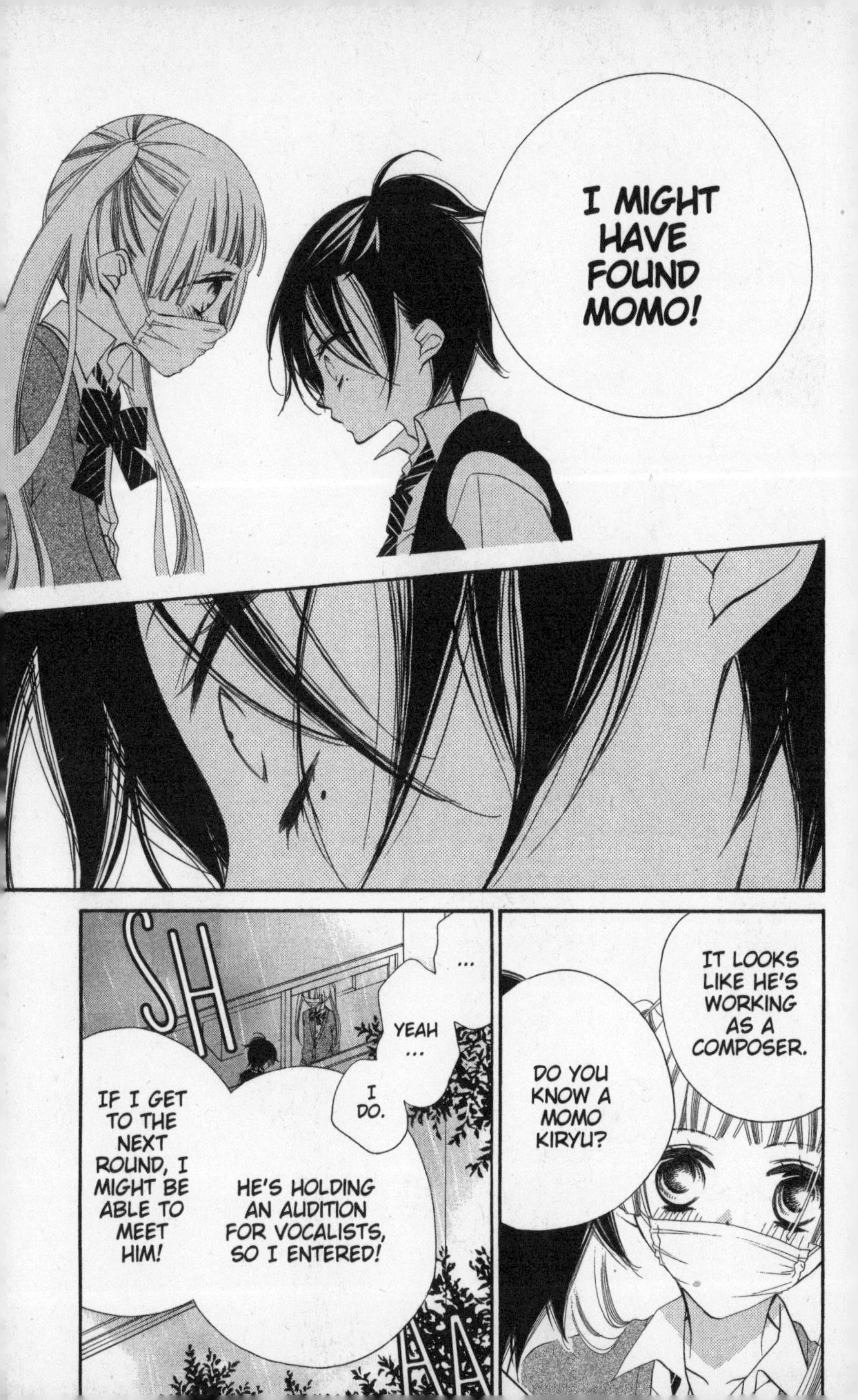
I MIGHT HAVE FOUND MOMO!
IT LOOKS LIKE HE'S WORKING AS A COMPOSER.
DO YOU KNOW A MOMO KIRYU?
...
YEAH ...
SH
I DO.
HE'S HOLDING AN AUDITION FOR VOCALISTS, SO I ENTERED!
IF I GET TO THE NEXT ROUND, I MIGHT BE ABLE TO MEET HIM!
AA

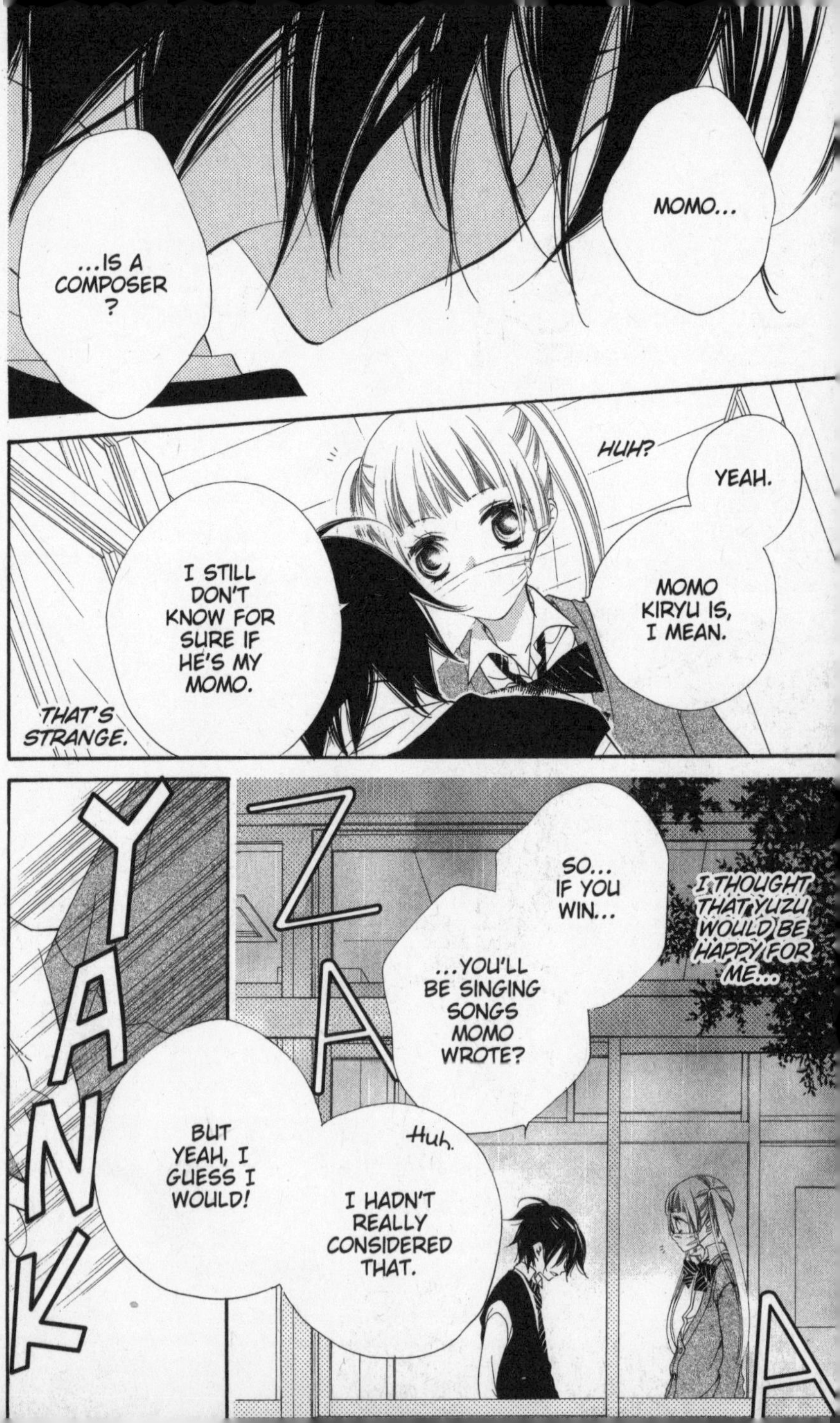
MOMO...
...IS A COMPOSER ?
HUH?
YEAH.
MOMO KIRYU IS, I MEAN.
I STILL DON'T KNOW FOR SURE IF HE'S MY MOMO.
THAT'S STRANGE.
I THOUGHT THAT YUZU WOULD BE HAPPY FOR ME...
SO... IF YOU WIN...
...YOU'LL BE SINGING SONGS MOMO WROTE?
Huh.
I HADN'T REALLY CONSIDERED THAT.
BUT YEAH, I GUESS I WOULD!
ZAA
YANK

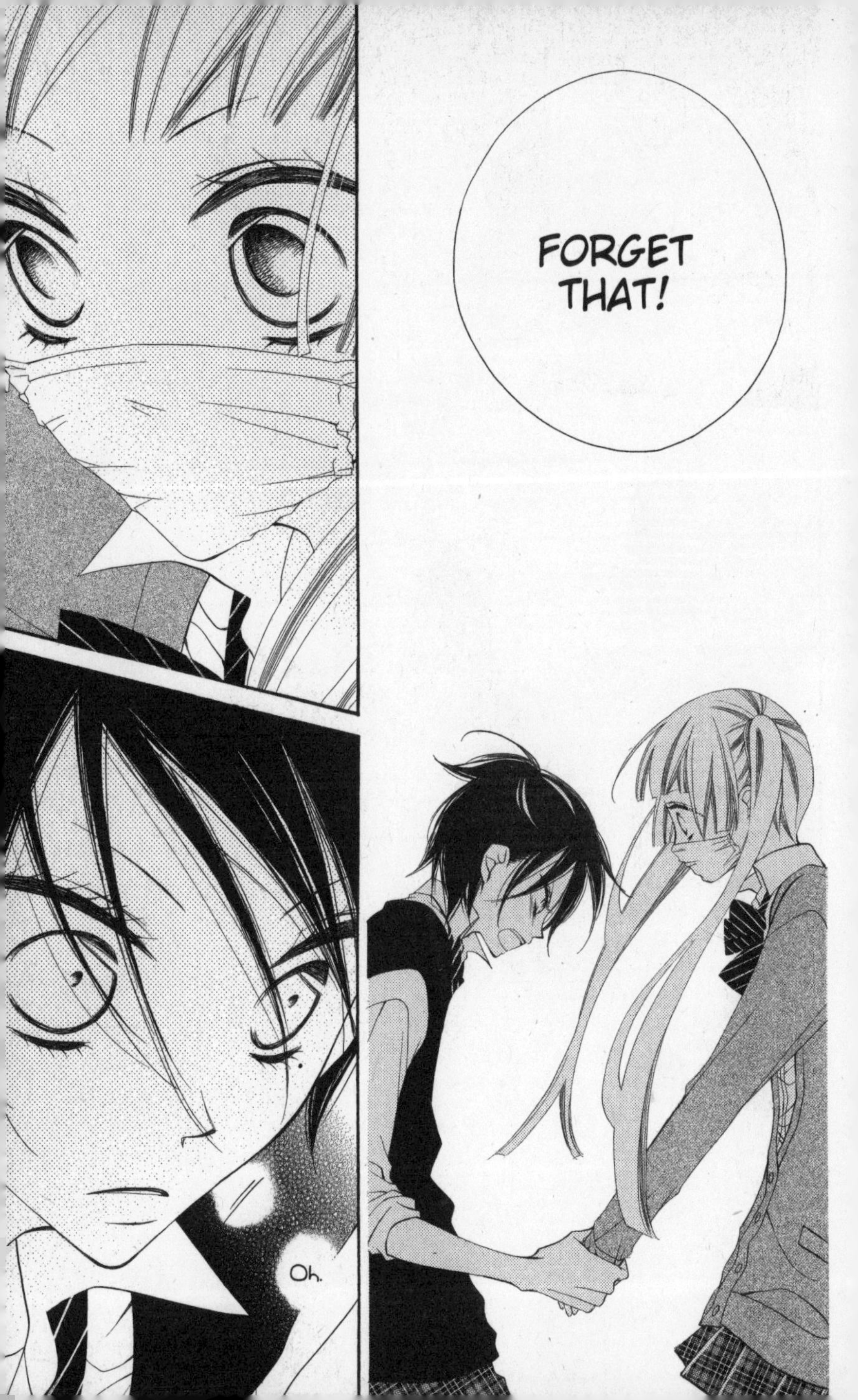
FORGET THAT!
Oh.

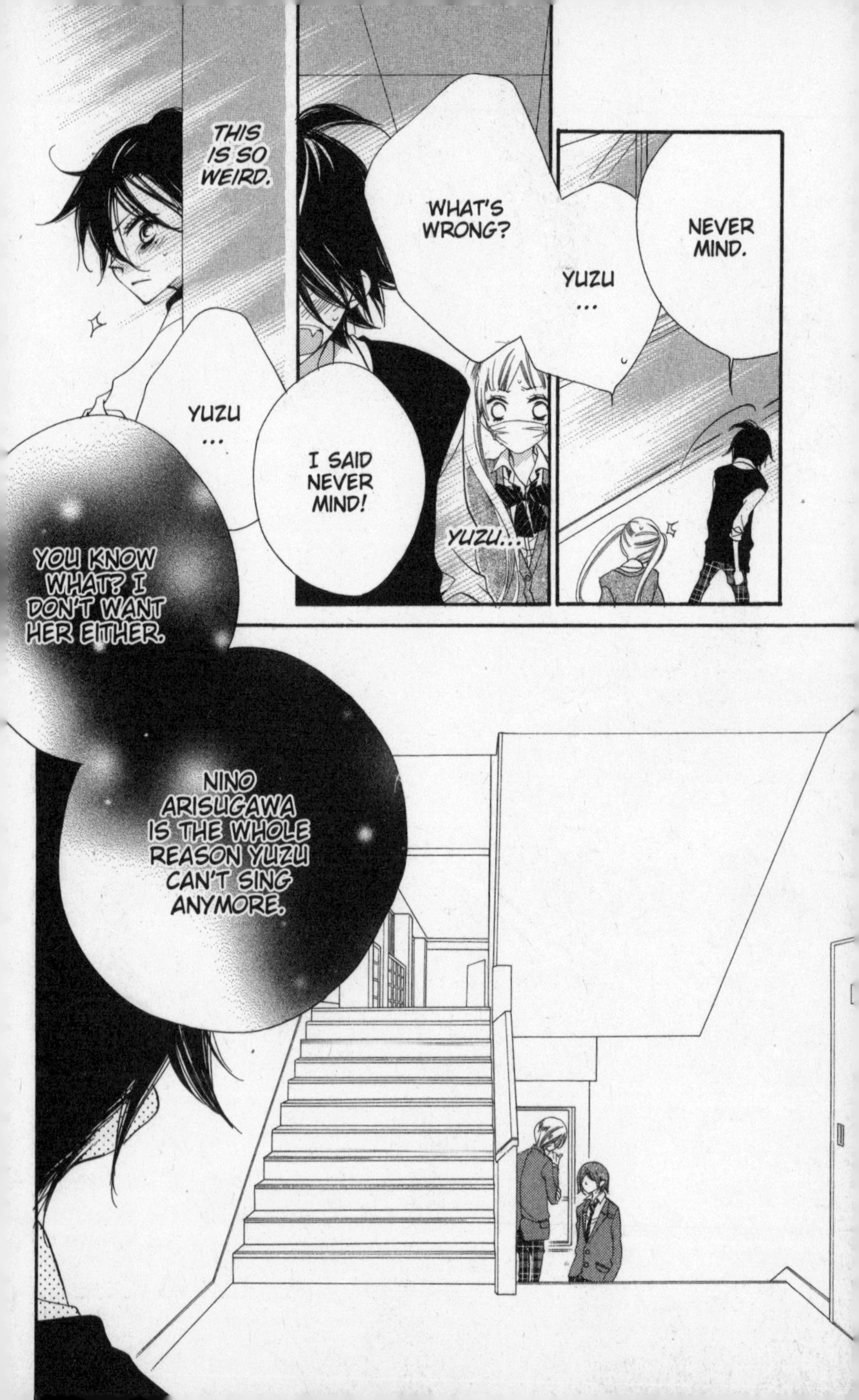

WHAT'S WRONG?
NEVER MIND.
YUZU ...
I SAID NEVER MIND!
YUZU...
THIS IS SO WEIRD.
YUZU ...
YOU KNOW WHAT? I DON'T WANT HER EITHER.
NINO ARISUGAWA IS THE WHOLE REASON YUZU CAN'T SING ANYMORE.

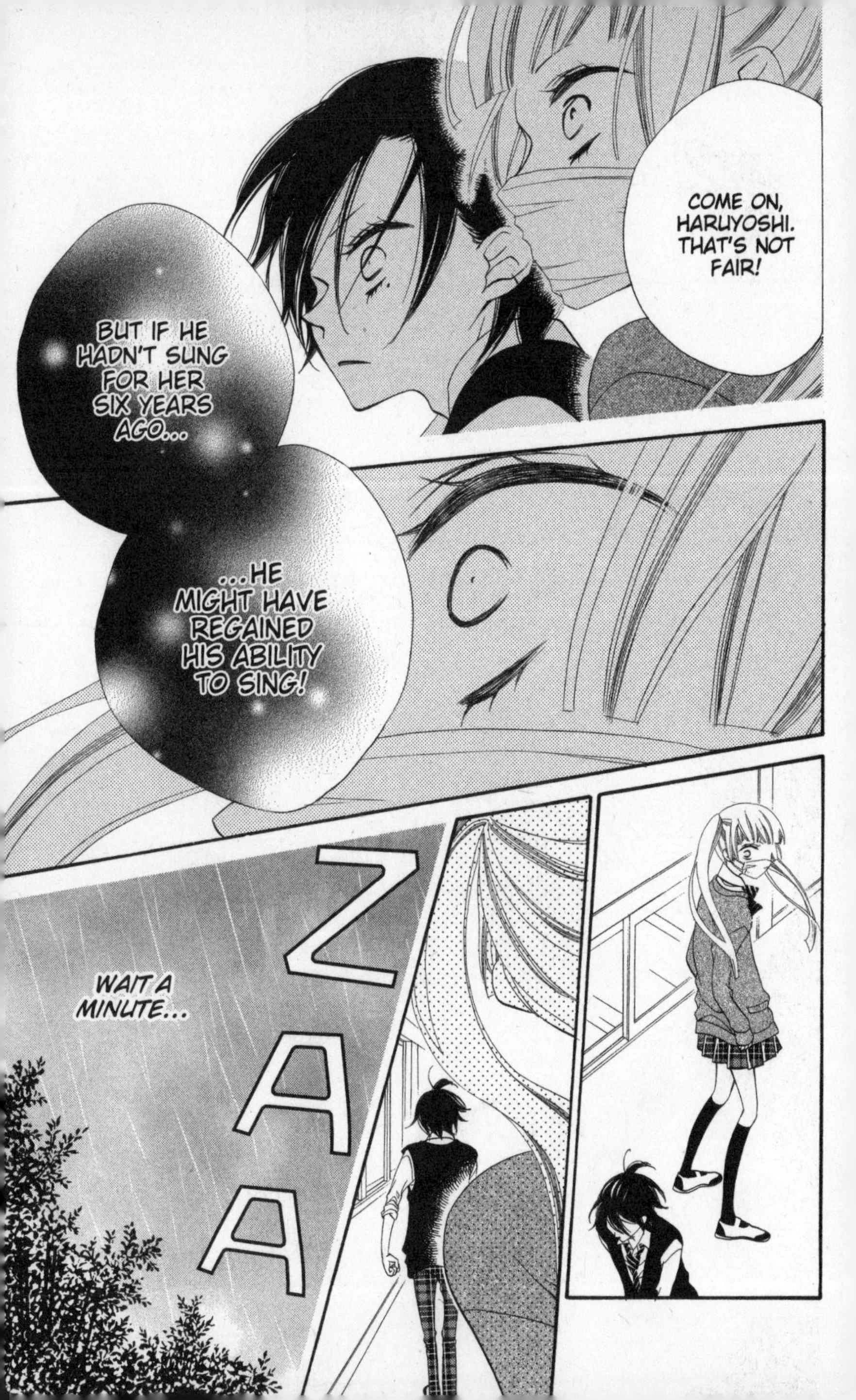

COME ON, HARUYOSHI. THAT'S NOT FAIR!
BUT IF HE HADN'T SUNG FOR HER SIX YEARS AGO...
...HE MIGHT HAVE REGAINED HIS ABILITY TO SING!
ZAAA
WAIT A MINUTE...

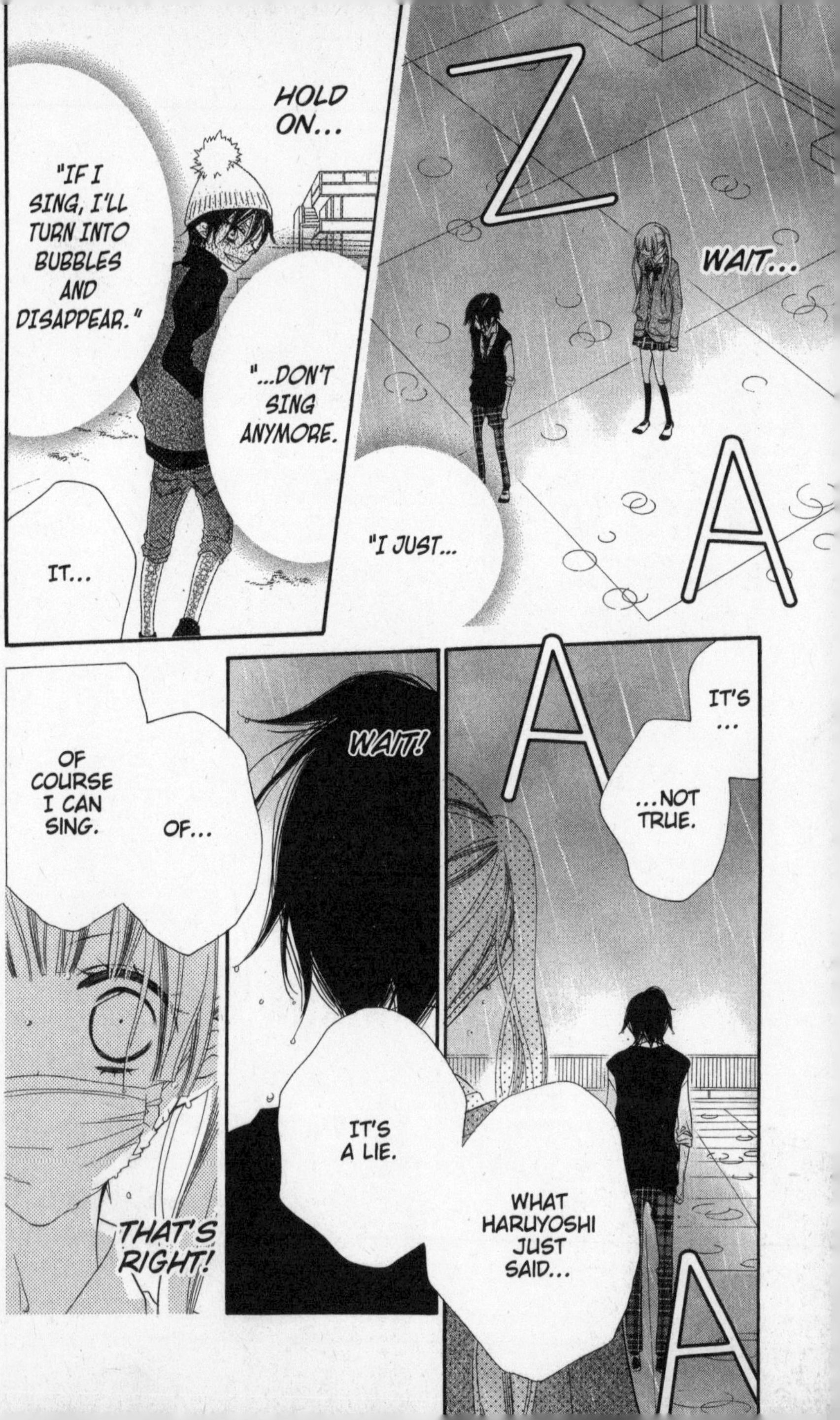
ZAAA
WAIT...
HOLD ON...
"IF I SING, I'LL TURN INTO BUBBLES AND DISAPPEAR."
"...DON'T SING ANYMORE.
"I JUST...
IT...
IT'S ...
...NOT TRUE.
WHAT HARUYOSHI JUST SAID...
IT'S A LIE.
WAIT!
OF...
OF COURSE I CAN SING.
THAT'S RIGHT!

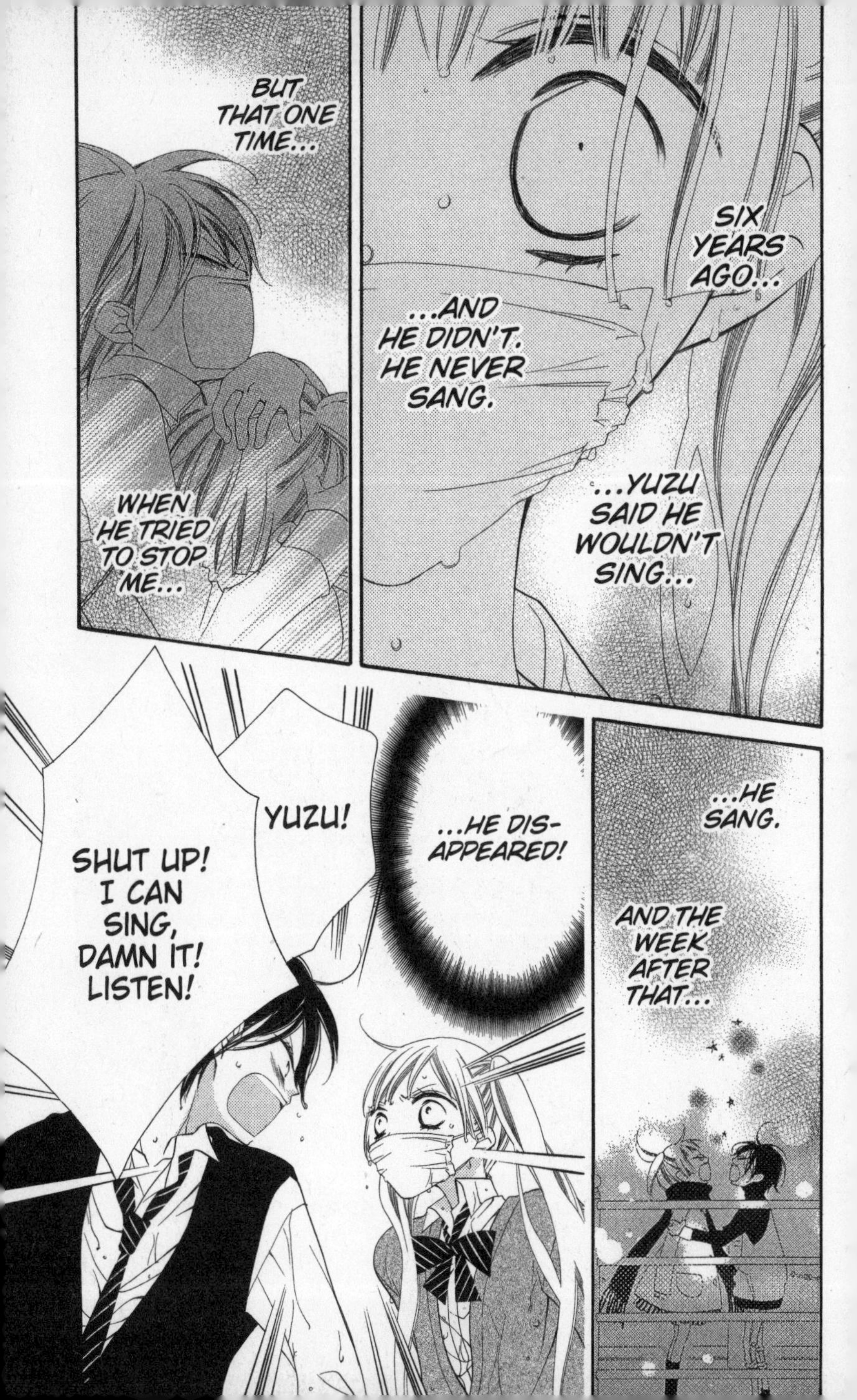
SIX YEARS AGO...
...YUZU SAID HE WOULDN'T SING...
...AND HE DIDN'T. HE NEVER SANG.
BUT THAT ONE TIME...
WHEN HE TRIED TO STOP ME...
...HE SANG.
AND THE WEEK AFTER THAT...
...HE DIS-APPEARED!
YUZU!
SHUT UP! I CAN SING, DAMN IT! LISTEN!

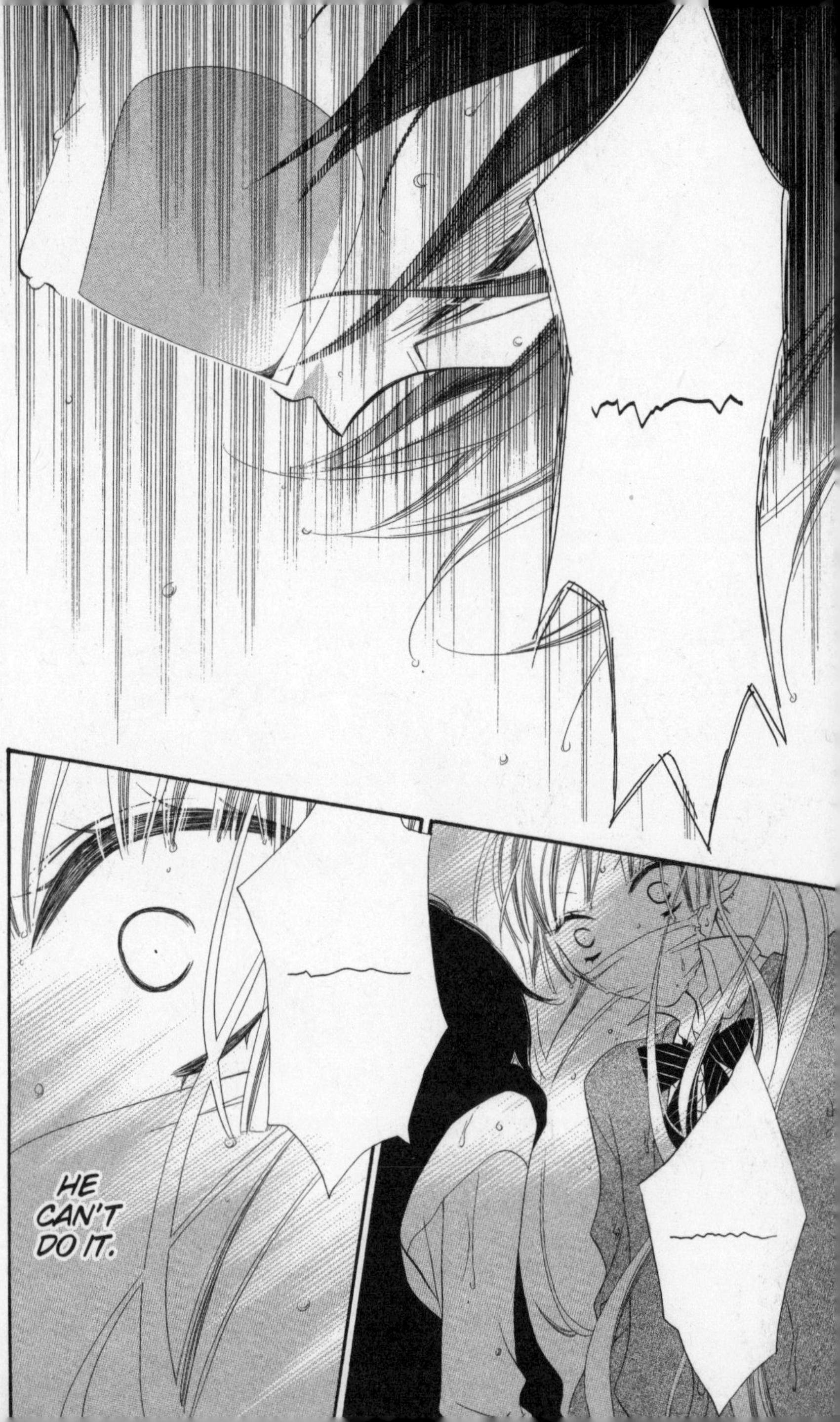
HE CAN'T DO IT.

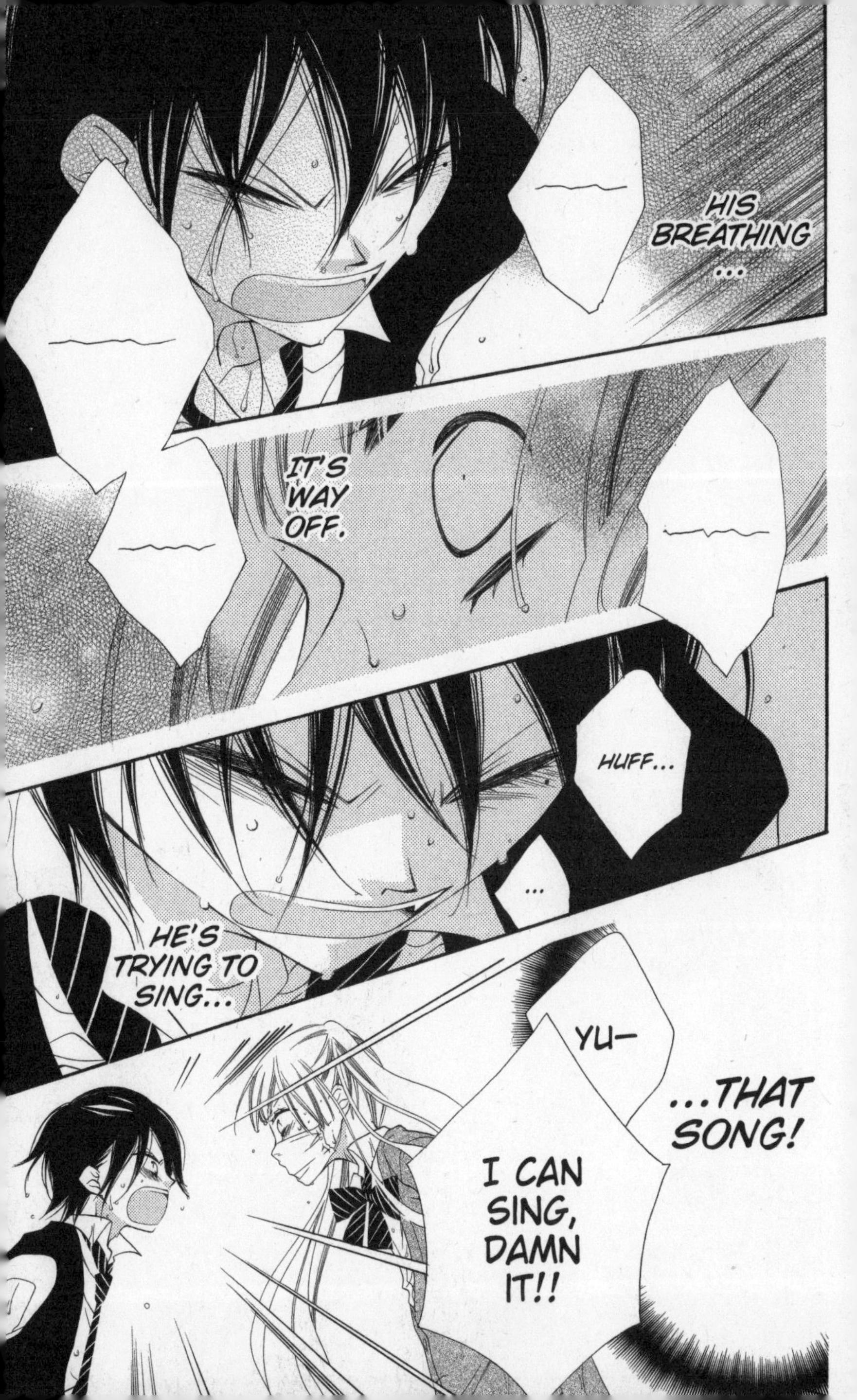

—
HIS BREATHING...
—
—
IT'S WAY OFF.
—
HUFF...
...
HE'S TRYING TO SING...
YU—
...THAT SONG!
I CAN SING, DAMN IT!!

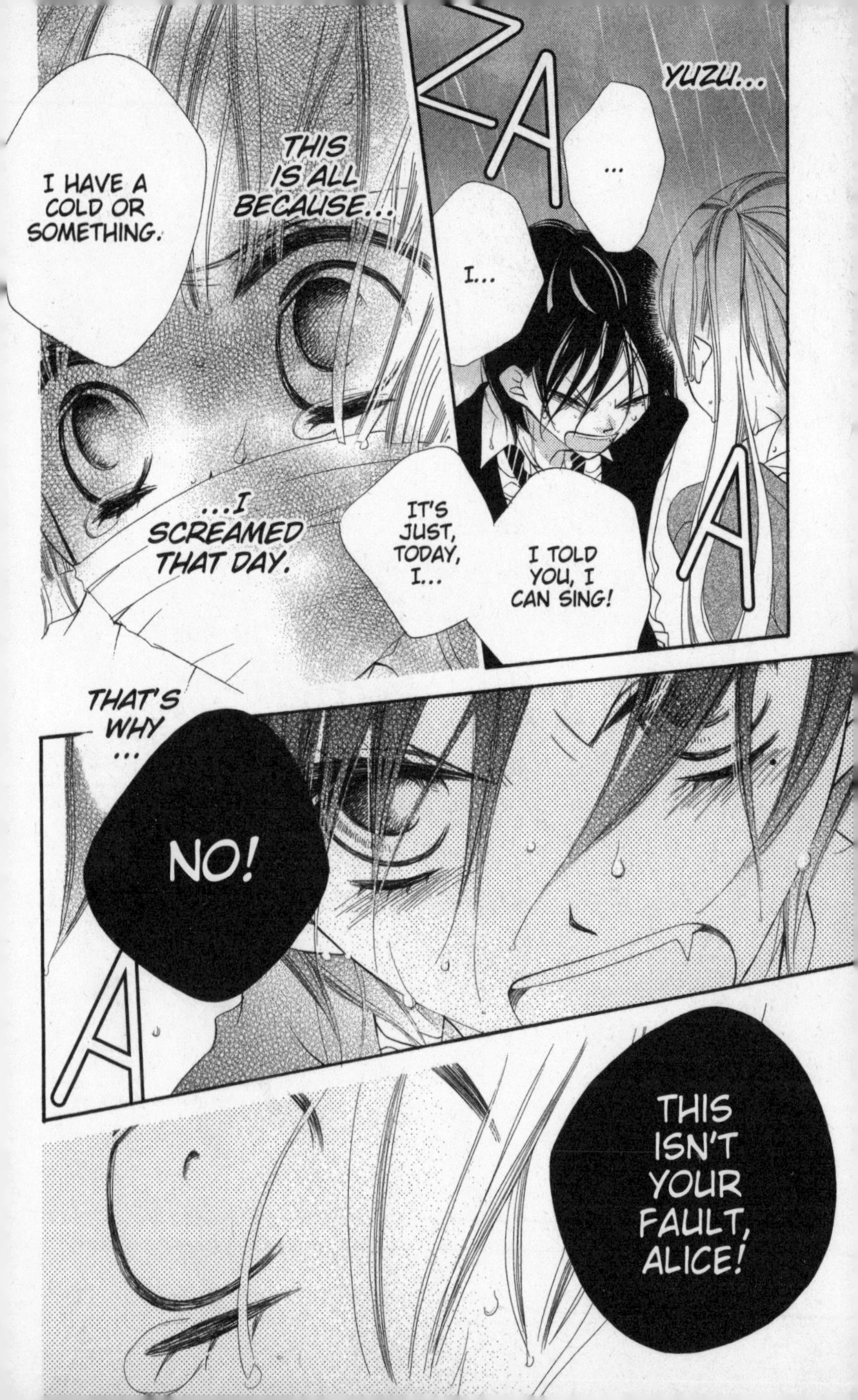
ZA
A
YUZU...
...
I...
I TOLD YOU, I CAN SING!
IT'S JUST, TODAY, I...
A
THIS IS ALL BECAUSE...
I HAVE A COLD OR SOMETHING.
...I SCREAMED THAT DAY.
THAT'S WHY...
NO!
A
THIS ISN'T YOUR FAULT, ALICE!

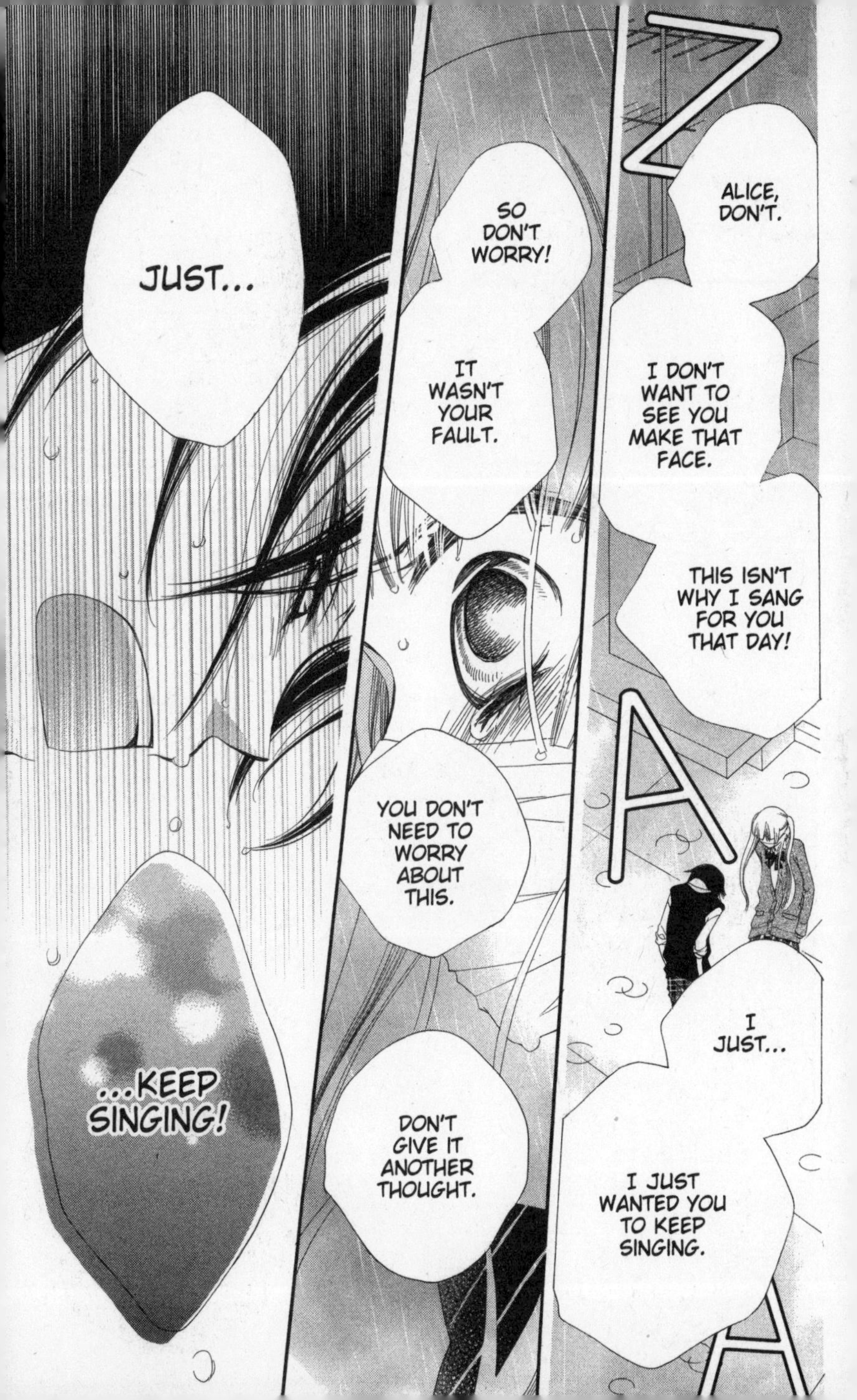
ALICE, DON'T.
I DON'T WANT TO SEE YOU MAKE THAT FACE.
THIS ISN'T WHY I SANG FOR YOU THAT DAY!
I JUST...
I JUST WANTED YOU TO KEEP SINGING.
SO DON'T WORRY!
IT WASN'T YOUR FAULT.
YOU DON'T NEED TO WORRY ABOUT THIS.
DON'T GIVE IT ANOTHER THOUGHT.
JUST...
...KEEP SINGING!

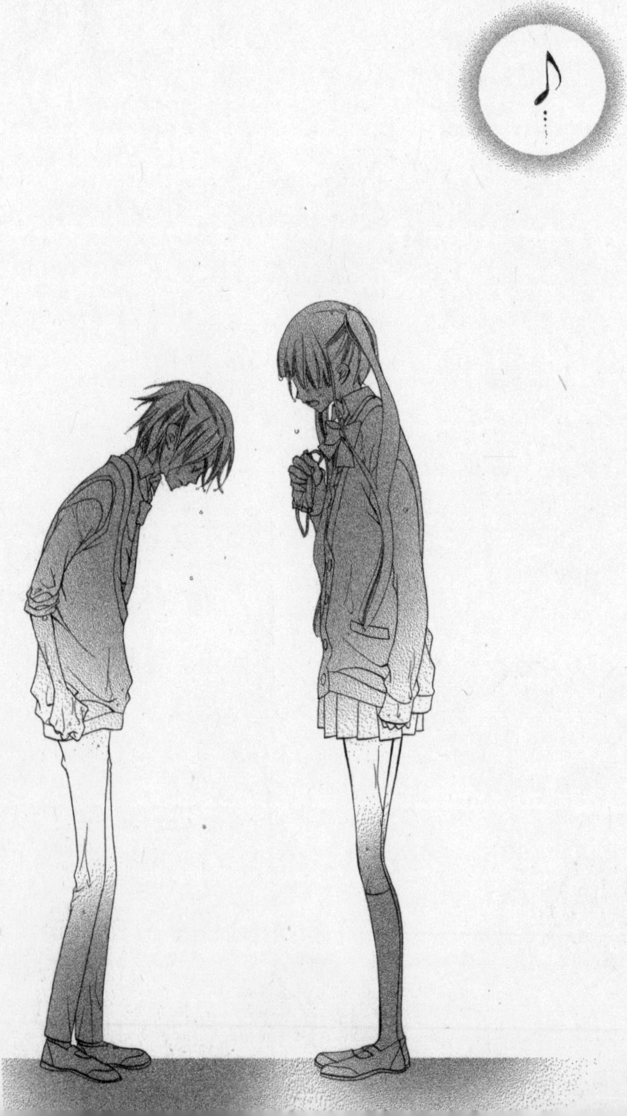

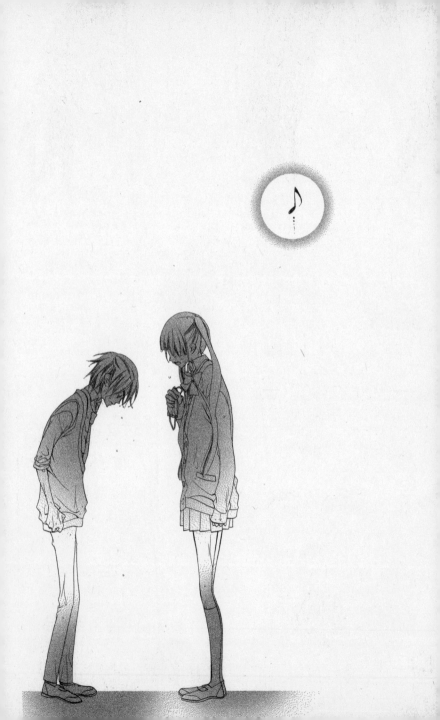

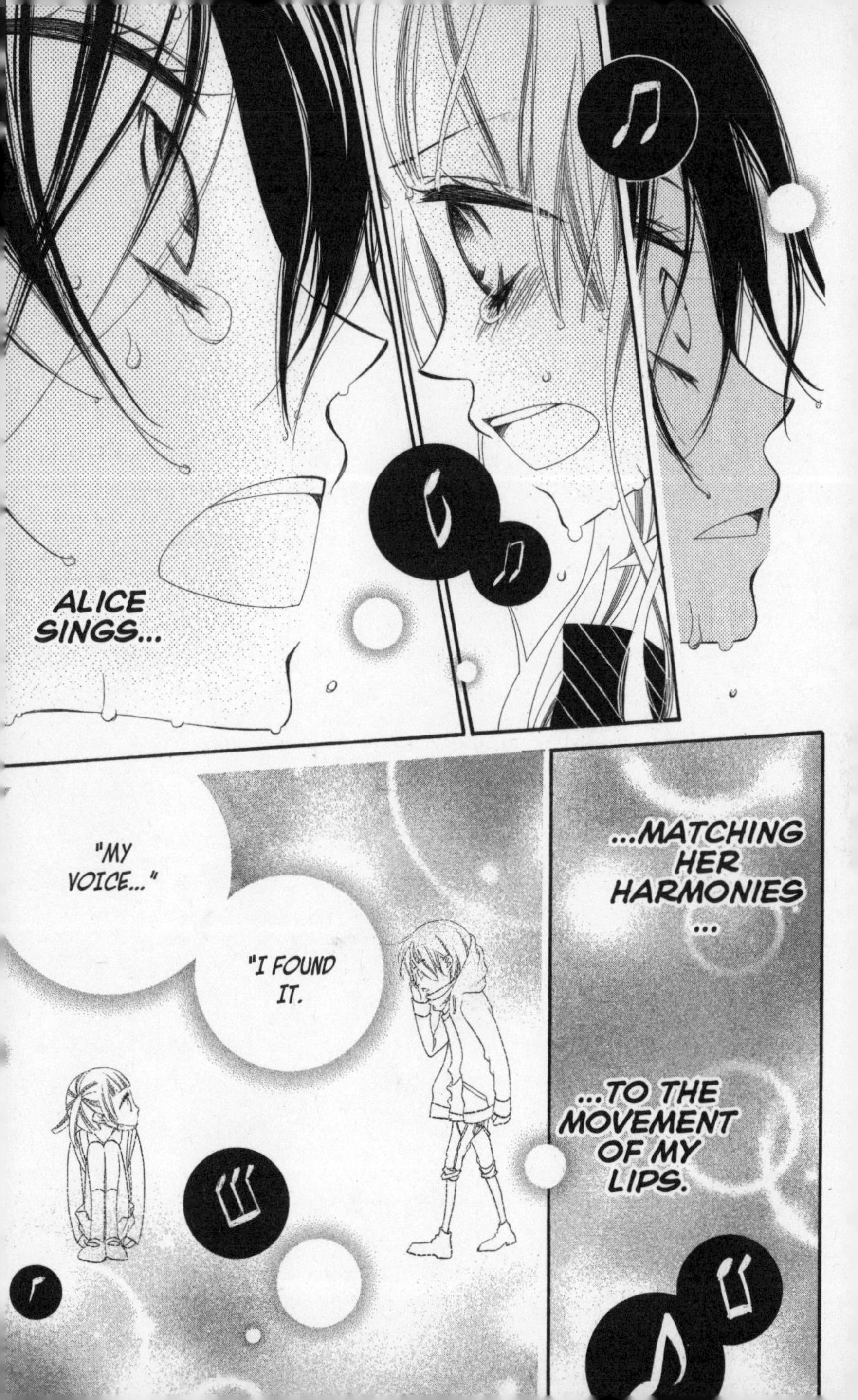
ALICE SINGS...
...MATCHING HER HARMONIES ...
...TO THE MOVEMENT OF MY LIPS.
"MY VOICE..."
"I FOUND IT.

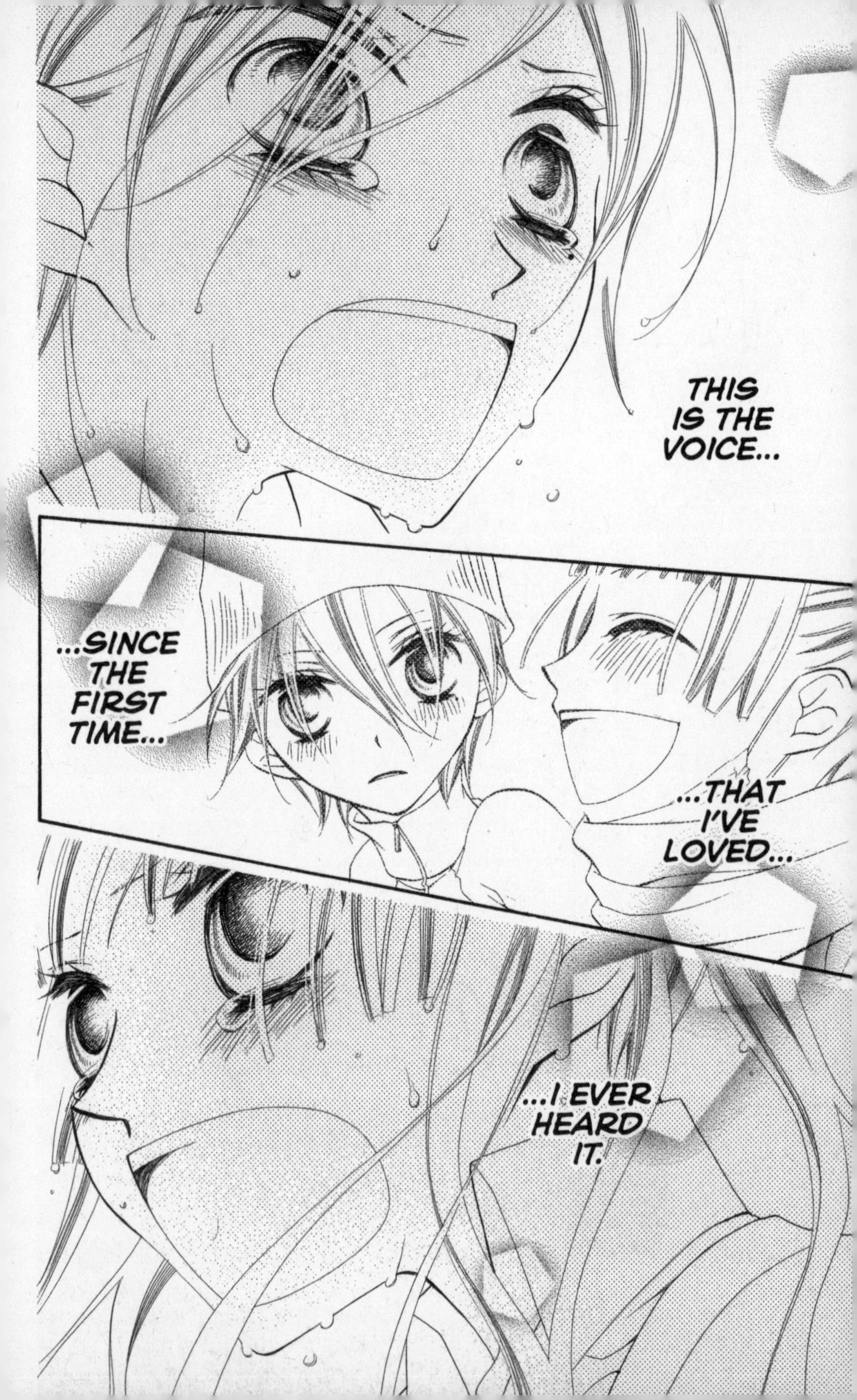
THIS IS THE VOICE...
...THAT I'VE LOVED...
...SINCE THE FIRST TIME...
...I EVER HEARD IT.

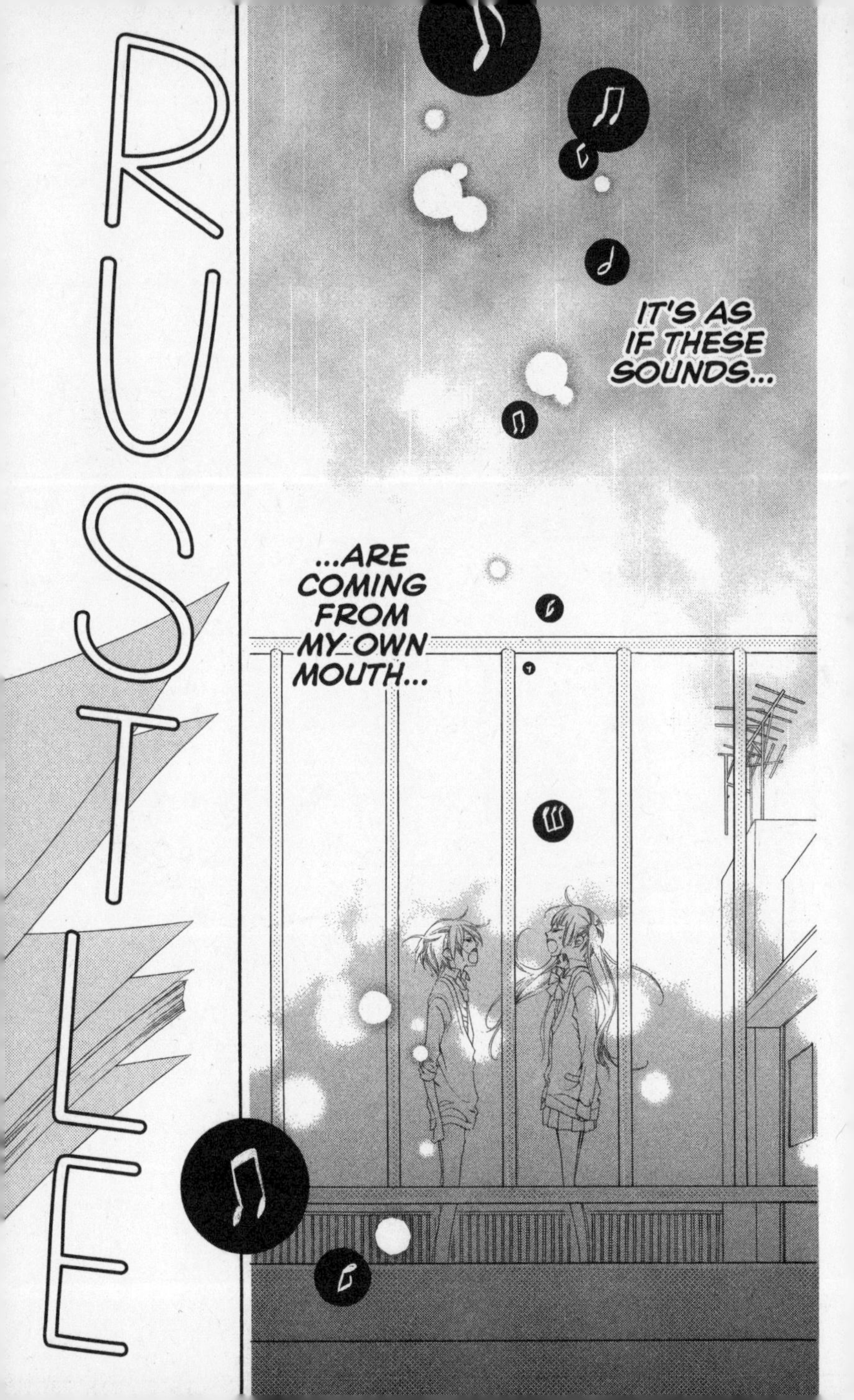
IT'S AS IF THESE SOUNDS...
...ARE COMING FROM MY OWN MOUTH...
RUSTLE

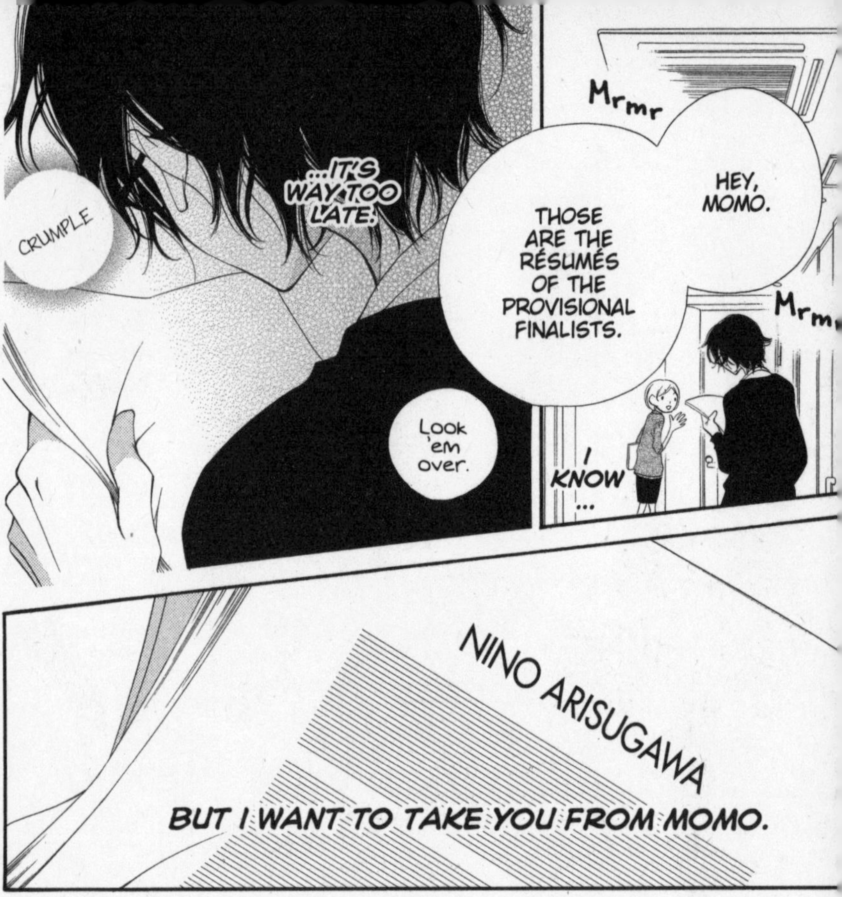
Mrmr
HEY, MOMO.
THOSE ARE THE RÉSUMÉS OF THE PROVISIONAL FINALISTS.
Mrmr
I KNOW ...
Look 'em over.
...IT'S WAY TOO LATE!
CRUMPLE
NINO ARISUGAWA
BUT I WANT TO TAKE YOU FROM MOMO.

SOMEHOW.

AND SOON.

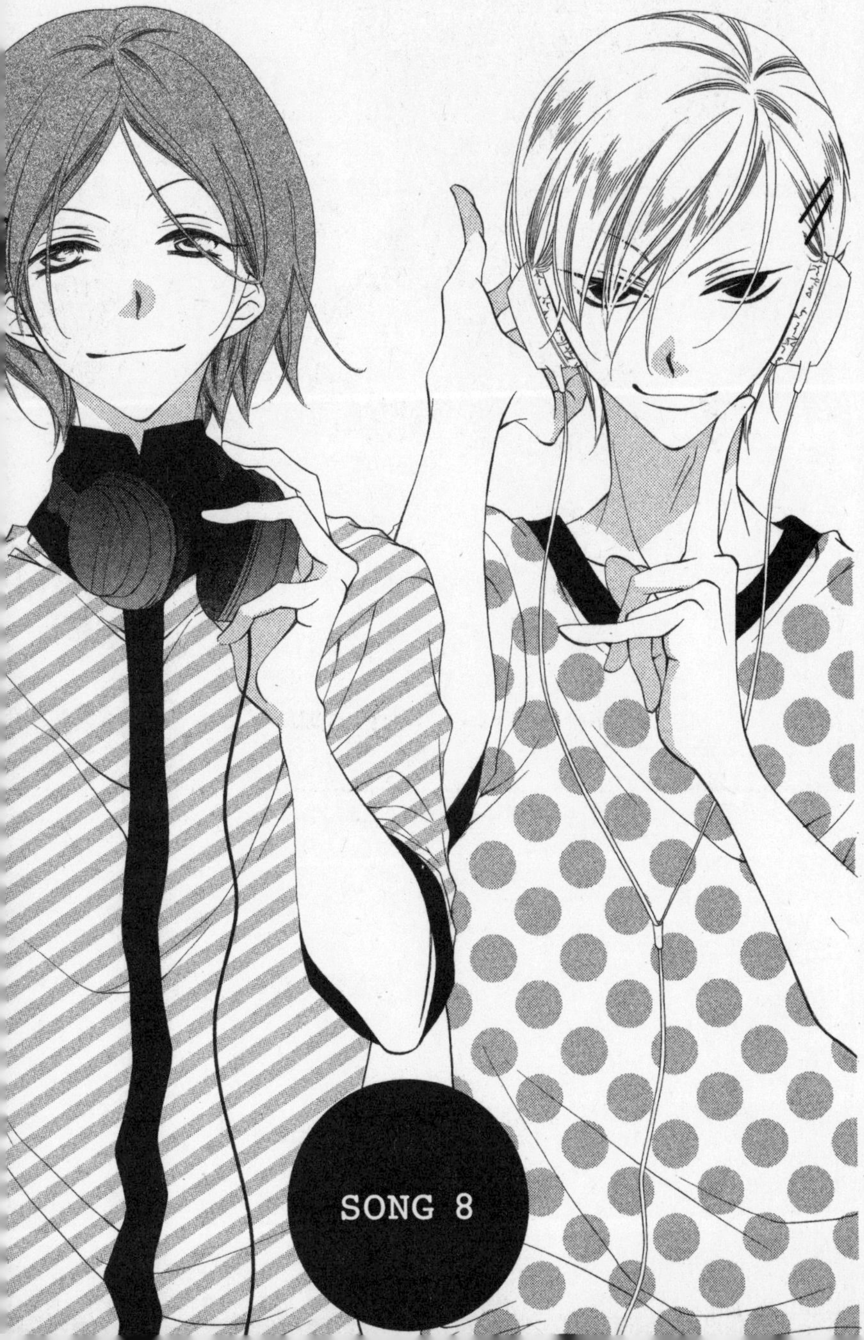
SONG 8

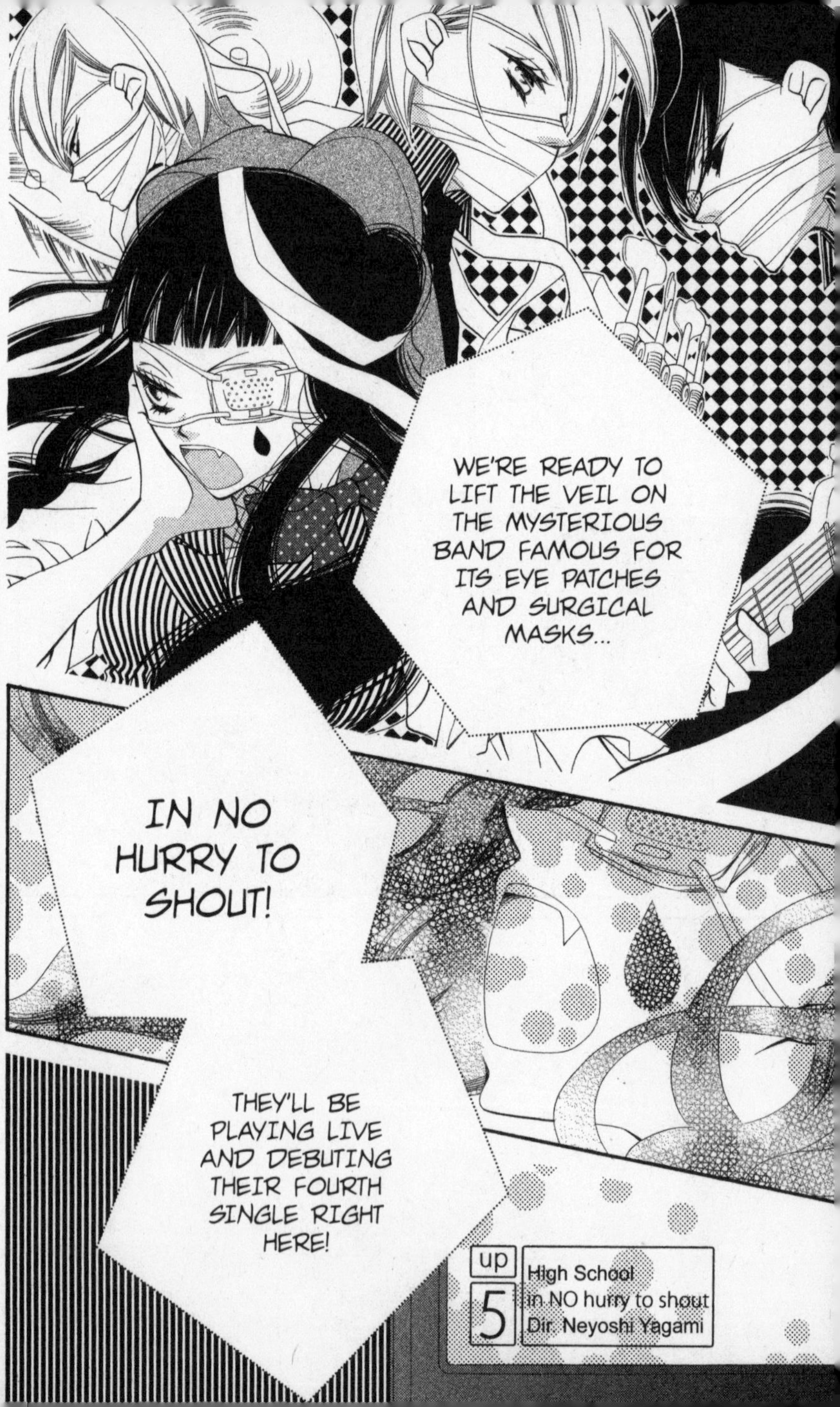
WE'RE READY TO LIFT THE VEIL ON THE MYSTERIOUS BAND FAMOUS FOR ITS EYE PATCHES AND SURGICAL MASKS...
IN NO HURRY TO SHOUT!
THEY'LL BE PLAYING LIVE AND DEBUTING THEIR FOURTH SINGLE RIGHT HERE!
up
5
High School
in NO hurry to shout
Dir. Neyoshi Yagami

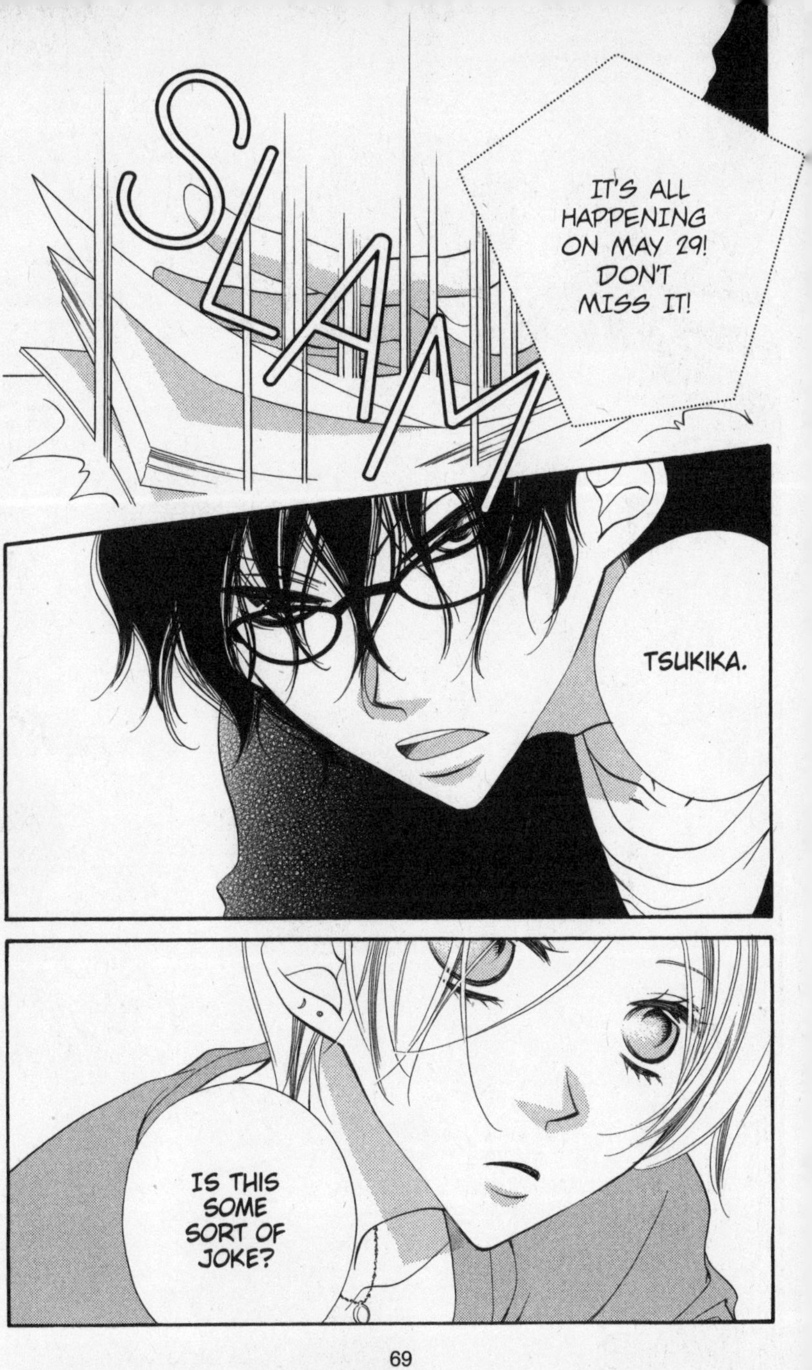
IT'S ALL HAPPENING ON MAY 29! DON'T MISS IT!
SLAM
TSUKIKA.
IS THIS SOME SORT OF JOKE?

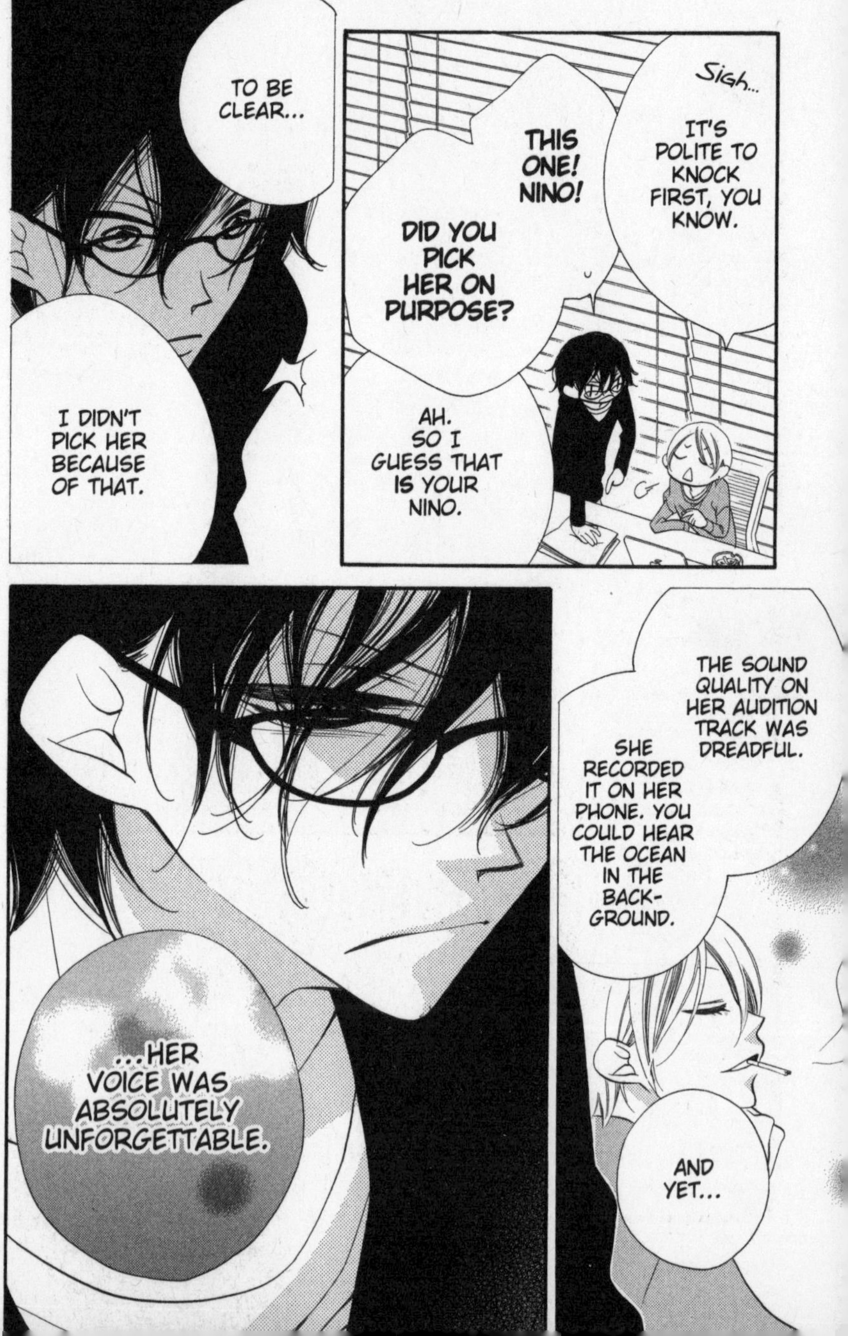
Sigh...
IT'S POLITE TO KNOCK FIRST, YOU KNOW.
THIS ONE! NINO!
DID YOU PICK HER ON PURPOSE?
AH. SO I GUESS THAT IS YOUR NINO.
TO BE CLEAR...
I DIDN'T PICK HER BECAUSE OF THAT.
THE SOUND QUALITY ON HER AUDITION TRACK WAS DREADFUL.
SHE RECORDED IT ON HER PHONE. YOU COULD HEAR THE OCEAN IN THE BACK-GROUND.
AND YET...
...HER VOICE WAS ABSOLUTELY UNFORGETTABLE.

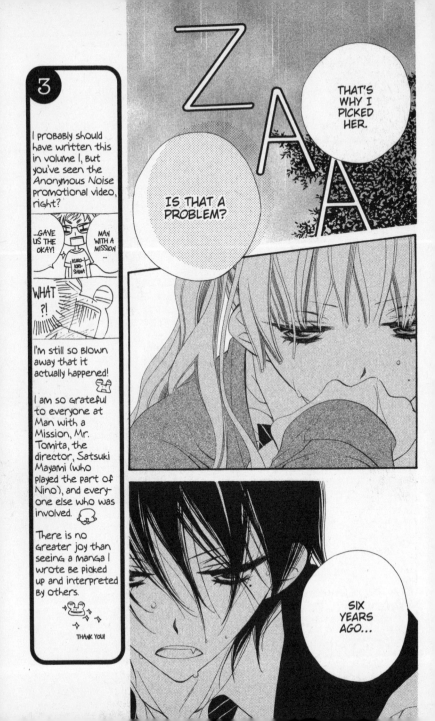

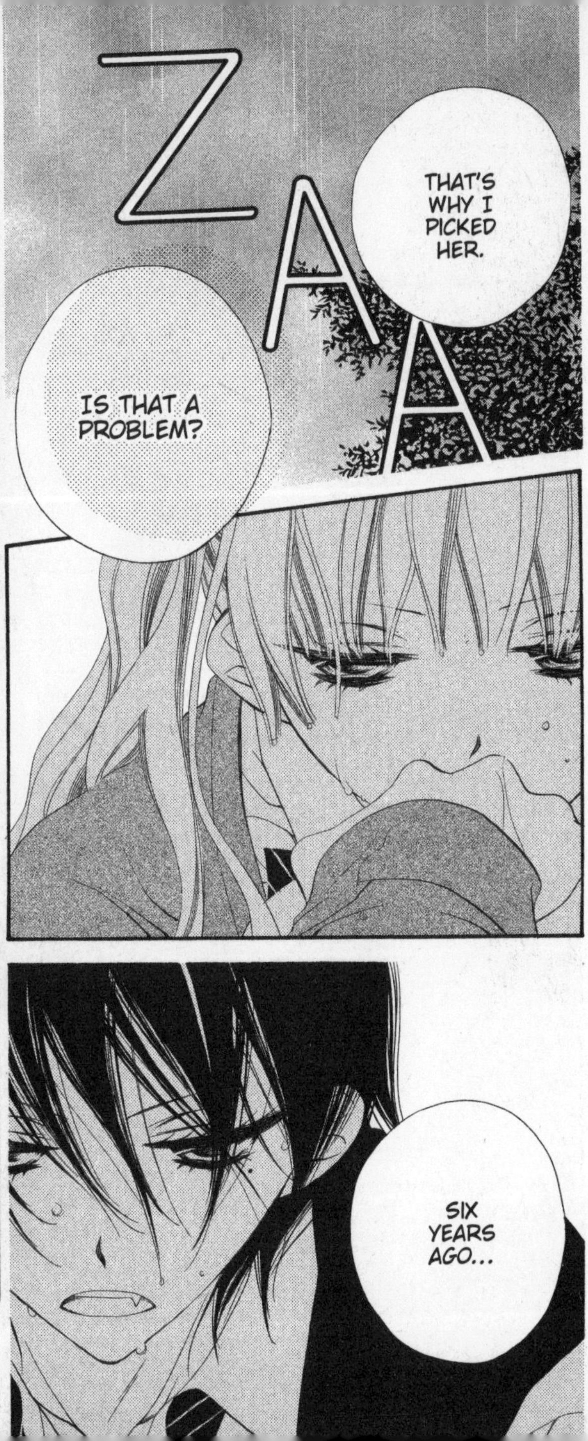
ZAAA
THAT'S WHY I PICKED HER.
IS THAT A PROBLEM?
SIX YEARS AGO...

3

I probably should have written this in volume 1, but you've seen the Anonymous Noise promotional video, right?

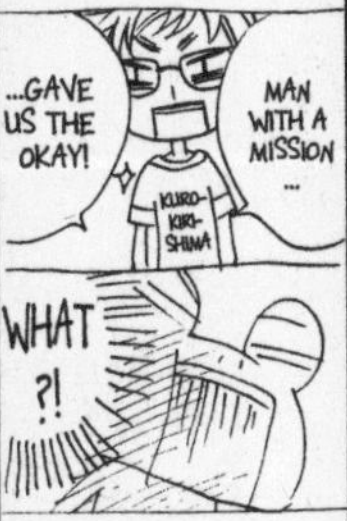
MAN WITH A MISSION...
...GAVE US THE OKAY!
KURO-KIRI-SHIMA
WHAT?!

I'm still so blown away that it actually happened!

I am so grateful to everyone at Man with a Mission, Mr. Tomita, the director, Satsuki Mayami (who played the part of Nino), and every-one else who was involved.

There is no greater joy than seeing a manga I wrote be picked up and interpreted by others.

THANK YOU!

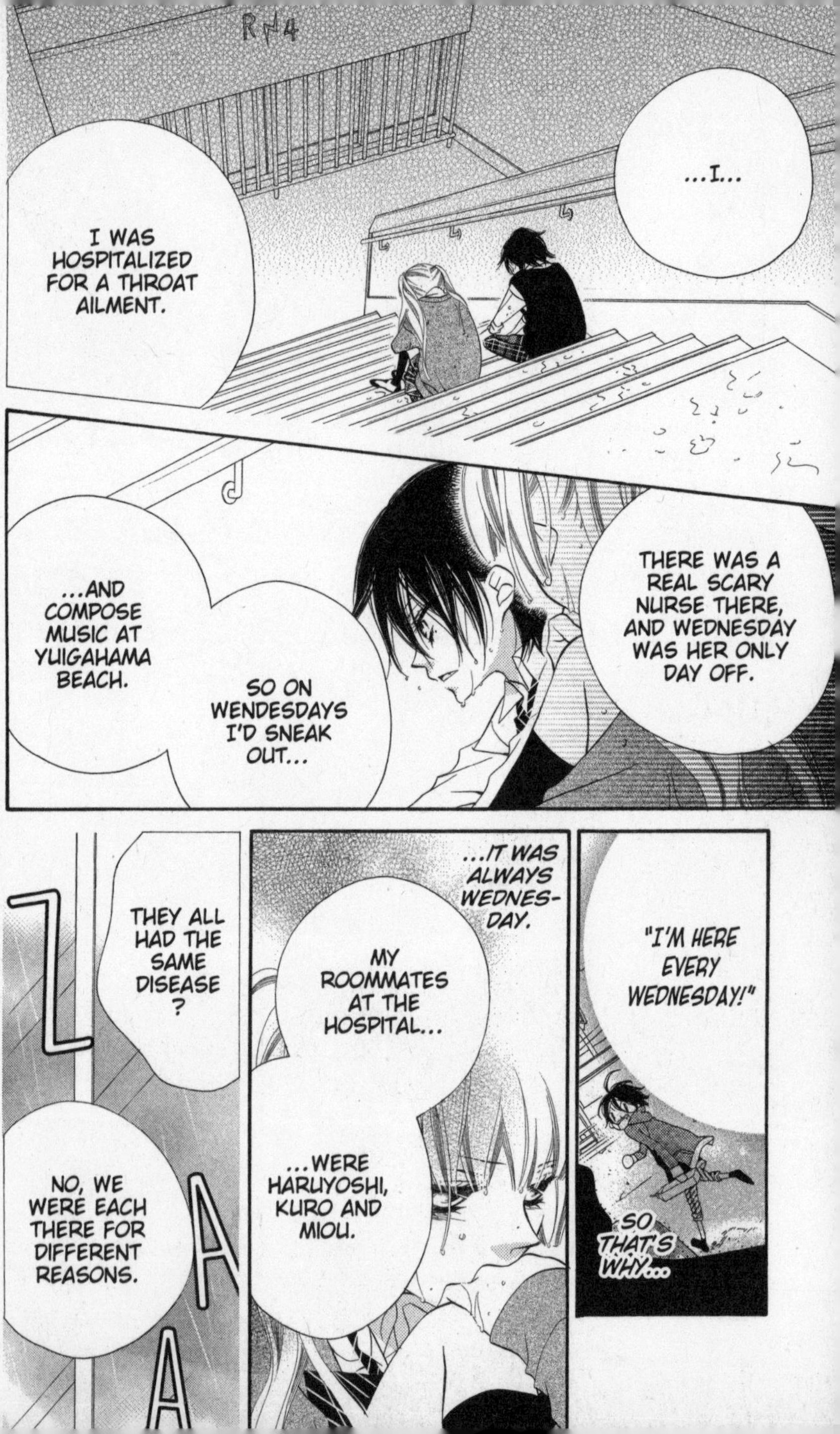
...I...
I WAS HOSPITALIZED FOR A THROAT AILMENT.
THERE WAS A REAL SCARY NURSE THERE, AND WEDNESDAY WAS HER ONLY DAY OFF.
SO ON WENDESDAYS I'D SNEAK OUT...
...AND COMPOSE MUSIC AT YUIGAHAMA BEACH.
"I'M HERE EVERY WEDNESDAY!"
SO THAT'S WHY...
...IT WAS ALWAYS WEDNES-DAY.
MY ROOMMATES AT THE HOSPITAL...
...WERE HARUYOSHI, KURO AND MIOU.
THEY ALL HAD THE SAME DISEASE?
NO, WE WERE EACH THERE FOR DIFFERENT REASONS.
ZAA

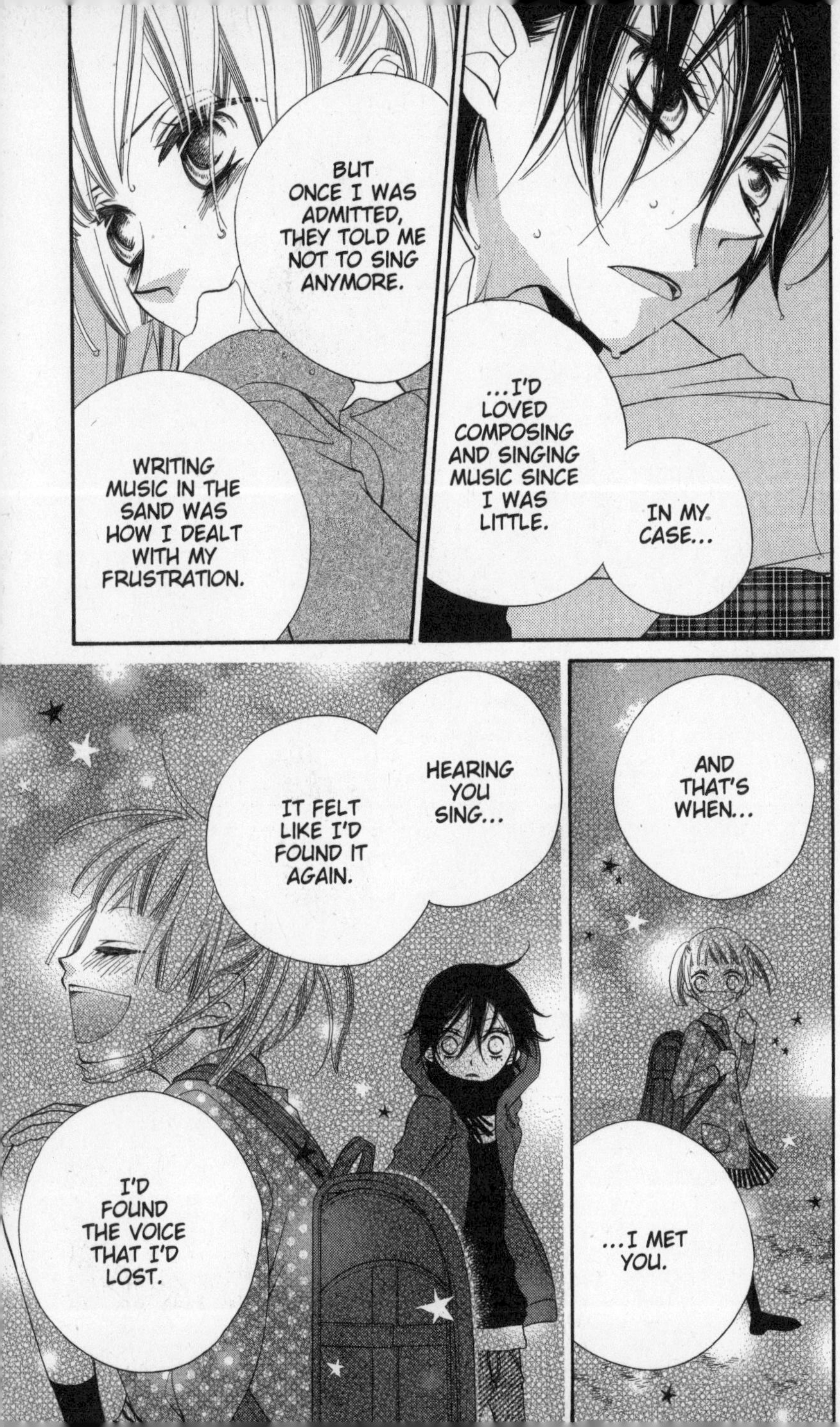
IN MY CASE...
...I'D LOVED COMPOSING AND SINGING MUSIC SINCE I WAS LITTLE.
BUT ONCE I WAS ADMITTED, THEY TOLD ME NOT TO SING ANYMORE.
WRITING MUSIC IN THE SAND WAS HOW I DEALT WITH MY FRUSTRATION.
AND THAT'S WHEN...
...I MET YOU.
HEARING YOU SING...
IT FELT LIKE I'D FOUND IT AGAIN.
I'D FOUND THE VOICE THAT I'D LOST.

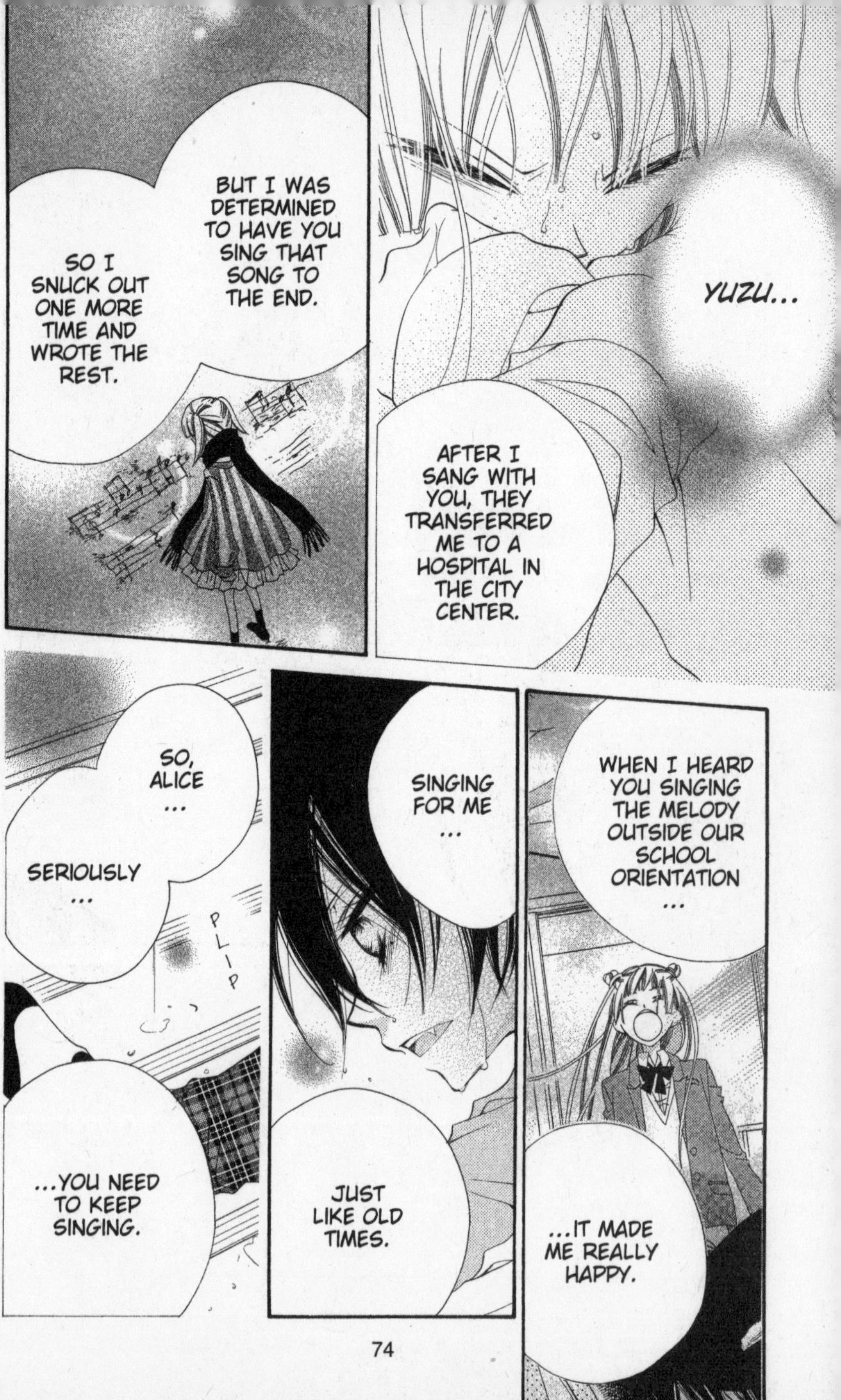
YUZU...
AFTER I SANG WITH YOU, THEY TRANSFERRED ME TO A HOSPITAL IN THE CITY CENTER.
BUT I WAS DETERMINED TO HAVE YOU SING THAT SONG TO THE END.
SO I SNUCK OUT ONE MORE TIME AND WROTE THE REST.
WHEN I HEARD YOU SINGING THE MELODY OUTSIDE OUR SCHOOL ORIENTATION...
...IT MADE ME REALLY HAPPY.
SINGING FOR ME...
JUST LIKE OLD TIMES.
SO, ALICE...
SERIOUSLY...
PLIP
...YOU NEED TO KEEP SINGING.

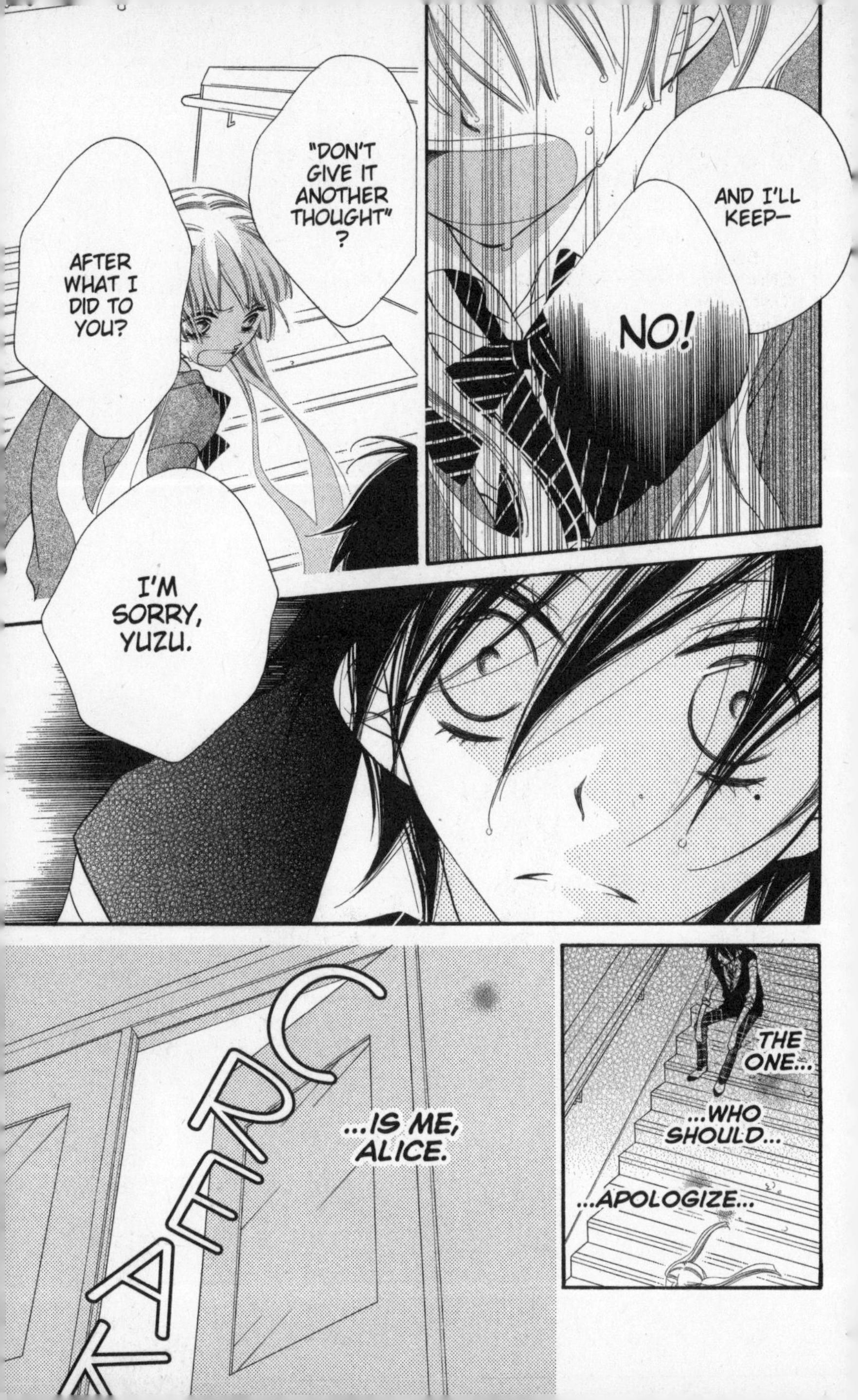
AND I'LL KEEP—
NO!
"DON'T GIVE IT ANOTHER THOUGHT"?
AFTER WHAT I DID TO YOU?
I'M SORRY, YUZU.
THE ONE...
...WHO SHOULD...
...APOLOGIZE...
...IS ME, ALICE.

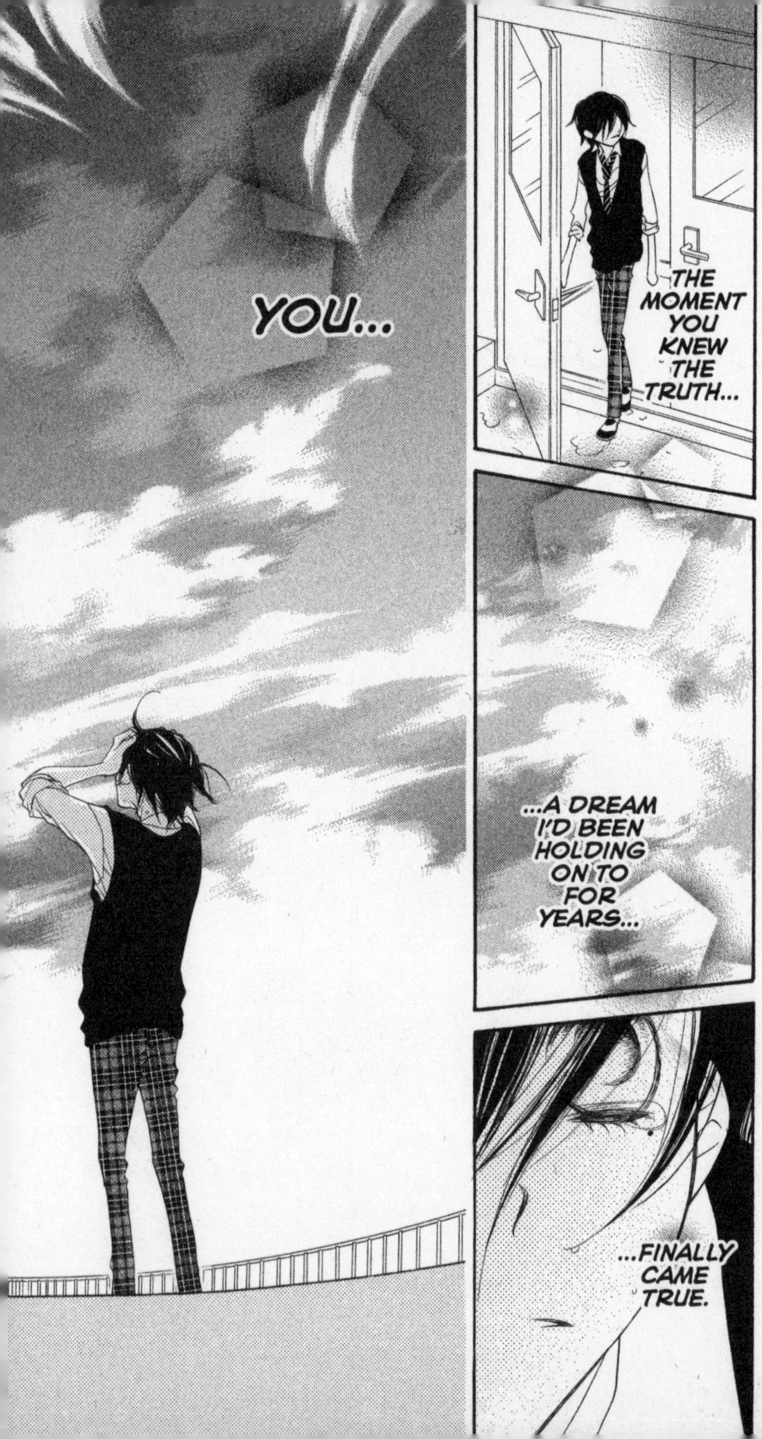
THE MOMENT YOU KNEW THE TRUTH...
...A DREAM I'D BEEN HOLDING ON TO FOR YEARS...
...FINALLY CAME TRUE.
YOU...

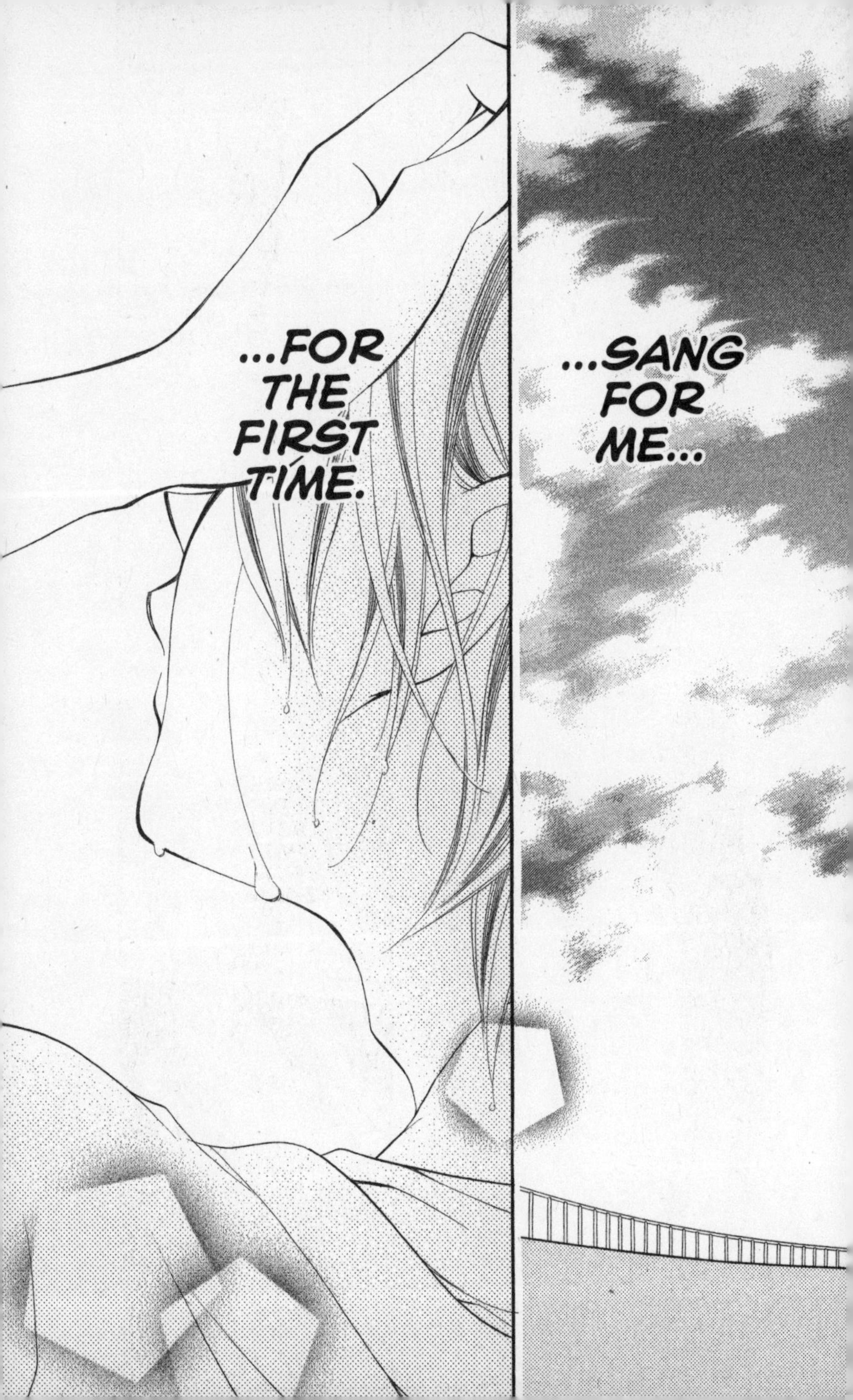
...SANG FOR ME...
...FOR THE FIRST TIME.

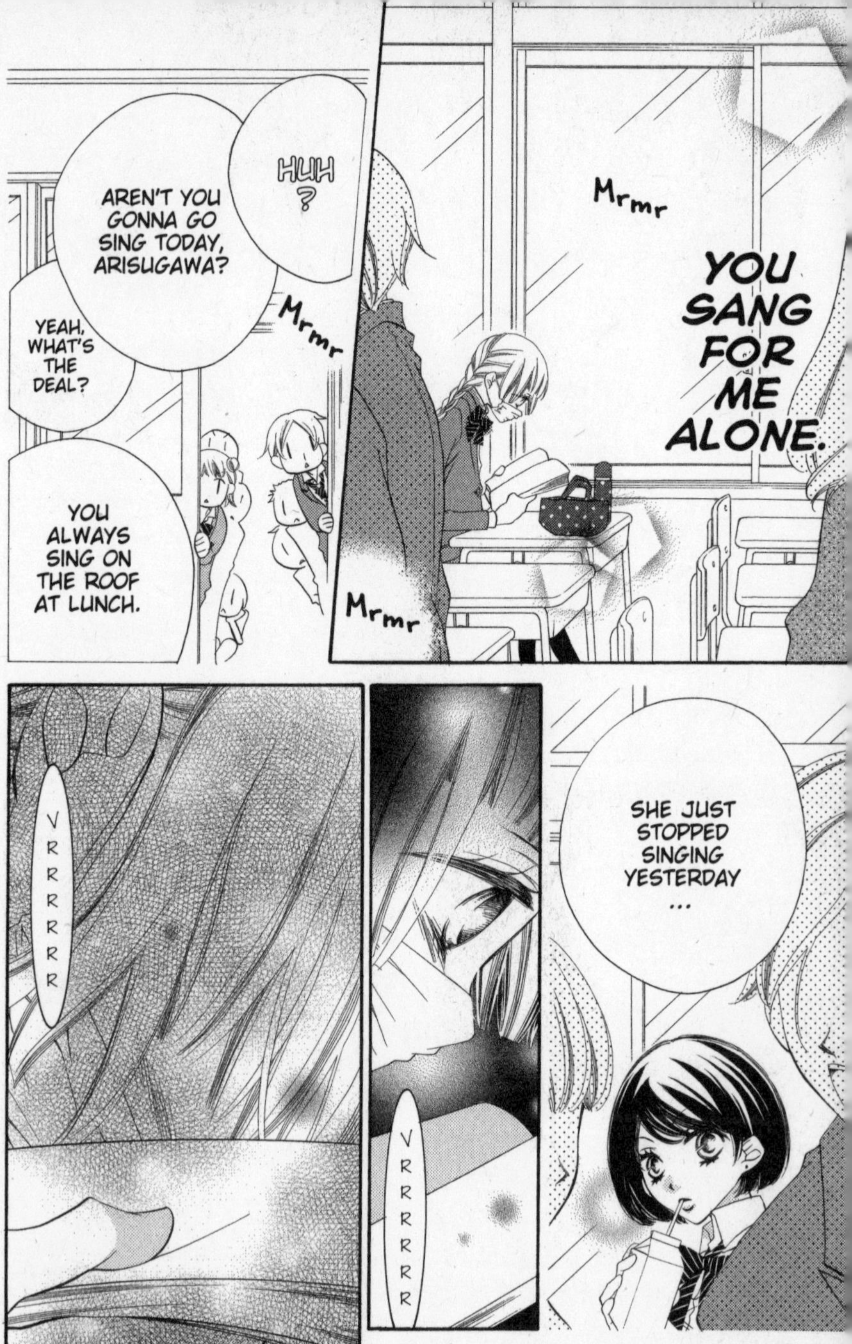
Mrmr
YOU SANG FOR ME ALONE.
Mrmr
HUH?
AREN'T YOU GONNA GO SING TODAY, ARISUGAWA?
Mrmr
YEAH, WHAT'S THE DEAL?
YOU ALWAYS SING ON THE ROOF AT LUNCH.
SHE JUST STOPPED SINGING YESTERDAY...
VRRRRRR
VRRRRRR

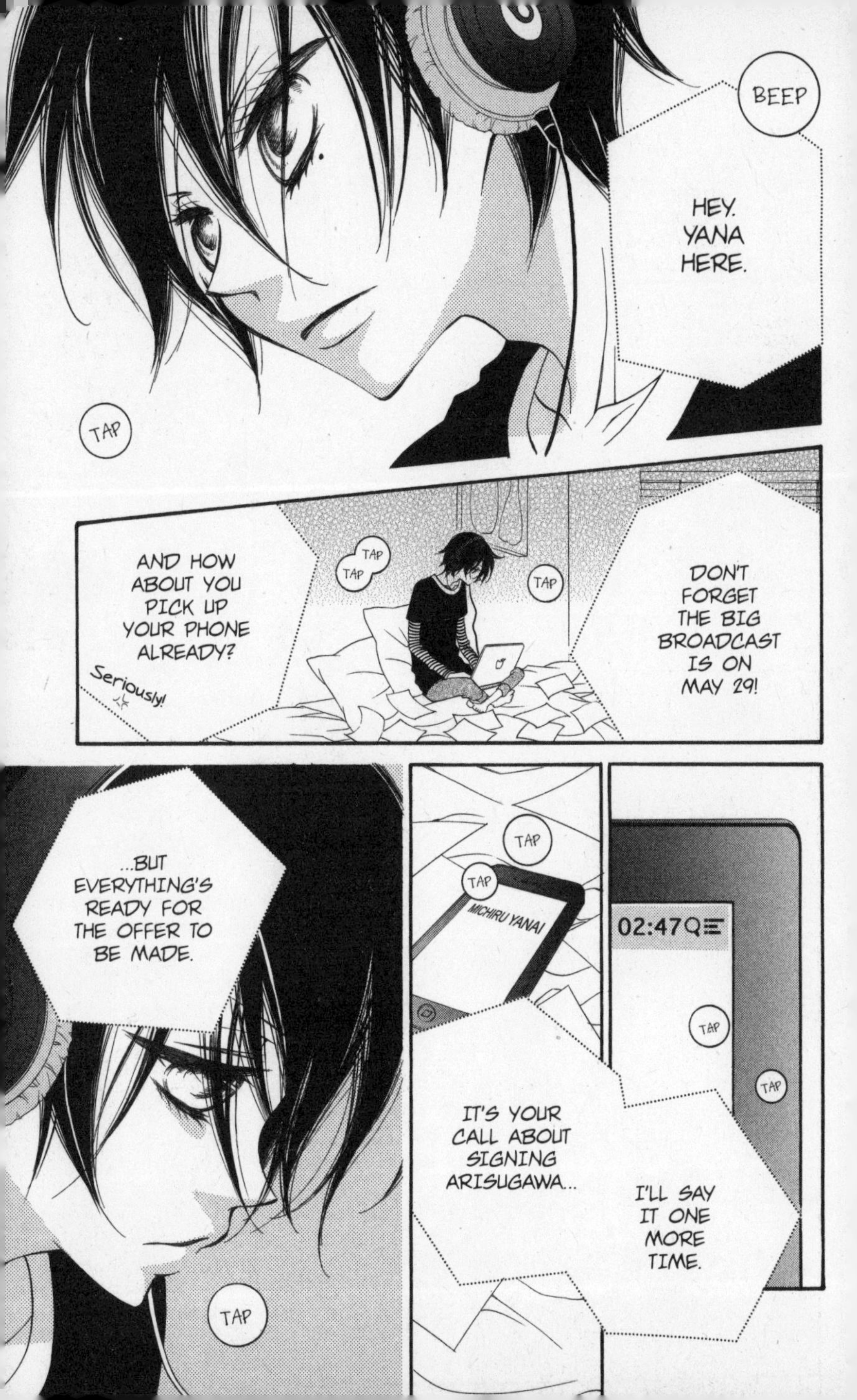
BEEP
HEY. YANA HERE.
TAP
DON'T FORGET THE BIG BROADCAST IS ON MAY 29!
TAP
TAP
TAP
AND HOW ABOUT YOU PICK UP YOUR PHONE ALREADY?
Seriously!
02:47
TAP
TAP
I'LL SAY IT ONE MORE TIME.
TAP
TAP
MICHIRU YANAI
IT'S YOUR CALL ABOUT SIGNING ARISUGAWA...
...BUT EVERYTHING'S READY FOR THE OFFER TO BE MADE.
TAP

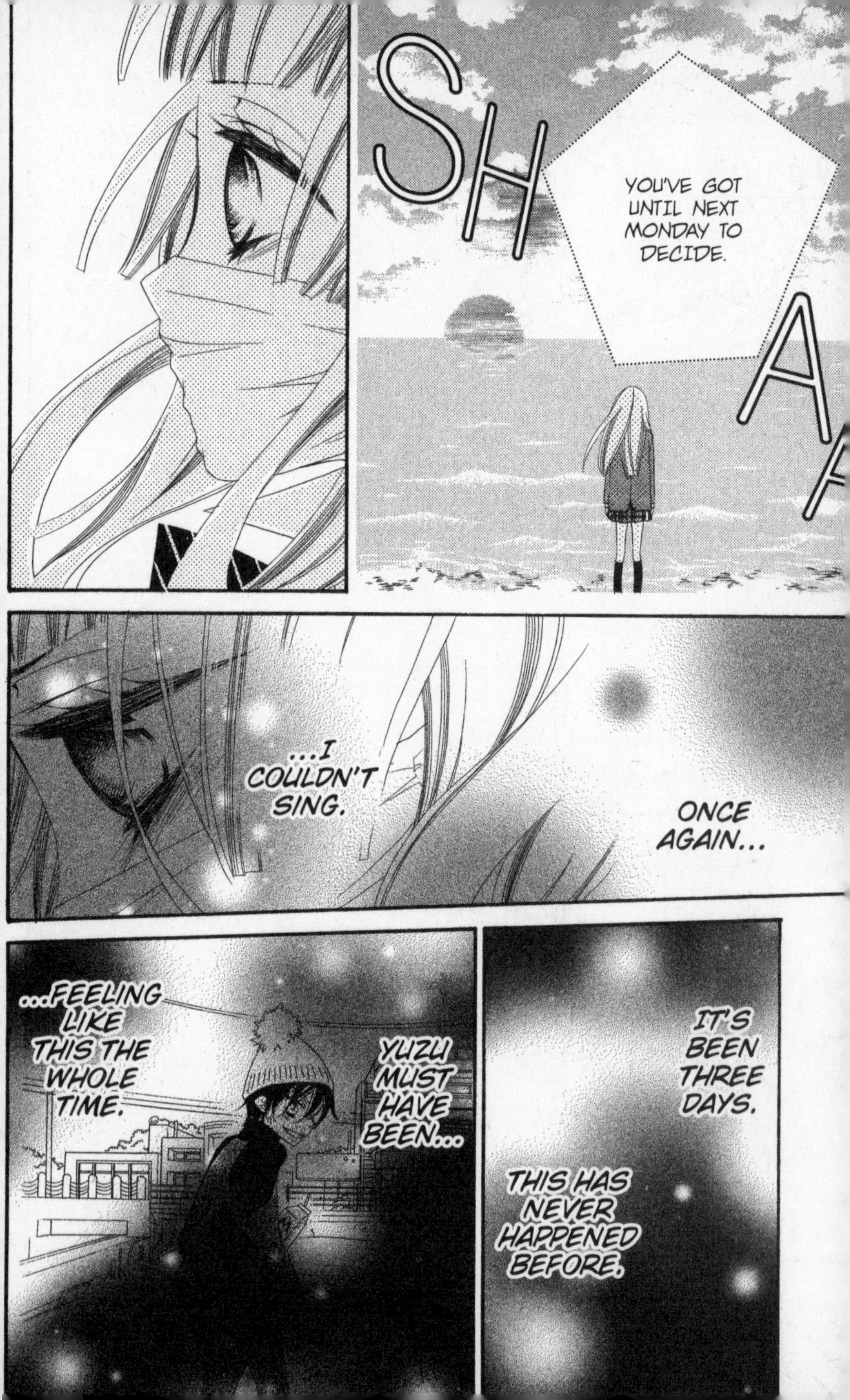

SHA
YOU'VE GOT UNTIL NEXT MONDAY TO DECIDE.
ONCE AGAIN...
...I COULDN'T SING.
IT'S BEEN THREE DAYS.
THIS HAS NEVER HAPPENED BEFORE.
YUZU MUST HAVE BEEN...
...FEELING LIKE THIS THE WHOLE TIME.

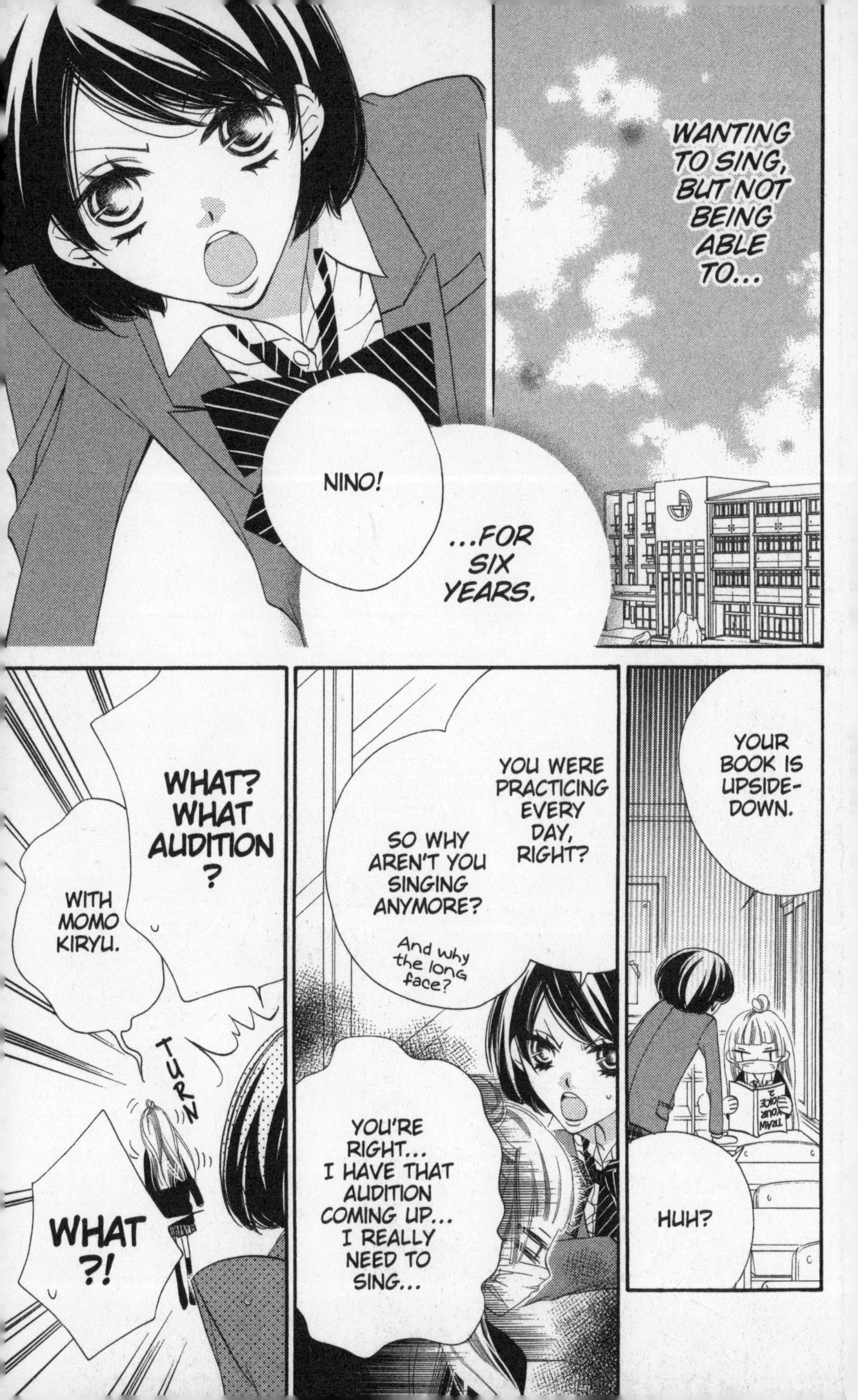
WANTING TO SING, BUT NOT BEING ABLE TO...
...FOR SIX YEARS.
NINO!
YOUR BOOK IS UPSIDE-DOWN.
HUH?
YOU WERE PRACTICING EVERY DAY, RIGHT?
SO WHY AREN'T YOU SINGING ANYMORE?
And why the long face?
YOU'RE RIGHT... I HAVE THAT AUDITION COMING UP... I REALLY NEED TO SING...
WHAT? WHAT AUDITION ?
WITH MOMO KIRYU.
TURN
WHAT ?!

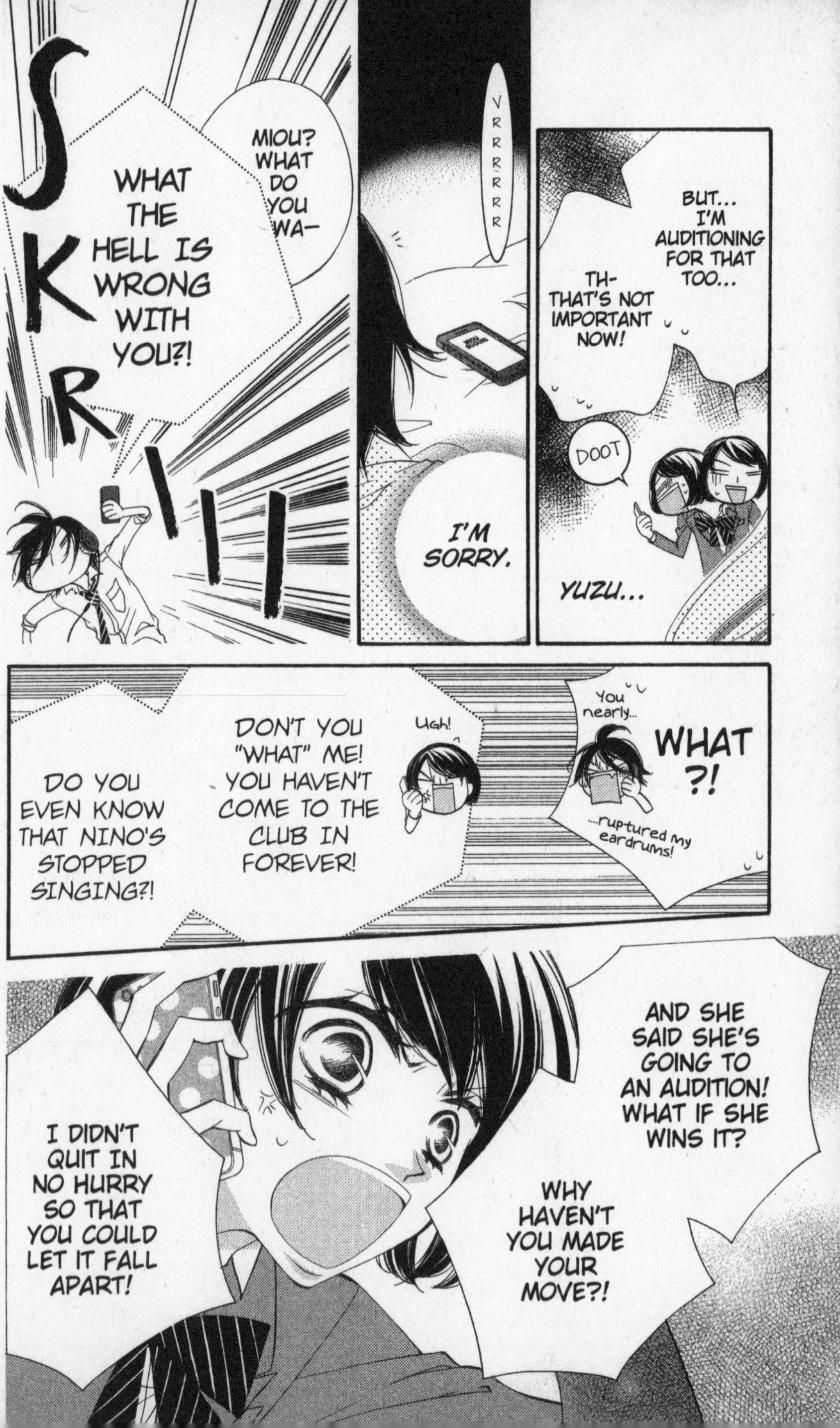
BUT... I'M AUDITIONING FOR THAT TOO...
TH-THAT'S NOT IMPORTANT NOW!
DOOT
YUZU...
VRRRRRR
I'M SORRY.
MIOU? WHAT DO YOU WA-
SKRIII
WHAT THE HELL IS WRONG WITH YOU?!
You nearly...
WHAT?!
...ruptured my eardrums!
Ugh!
DON'T YOU "WHAT" ME! YOU HAVEN'T COME TO THE CLUB IN FOREVER!
DO YOU EVEN KNOW THAT NINO'S STOPPED SINGING?!
AND SHE SAID SHE'S GOING TO AN AUDITION! WHAT IF SHE WINS IT?
WHY HAVEN'T YOU MADE YOUR MOVE?!
I DIDN'T QUIT IN NO HURRY SO THAT YOU COULD LET IT FALL APART!

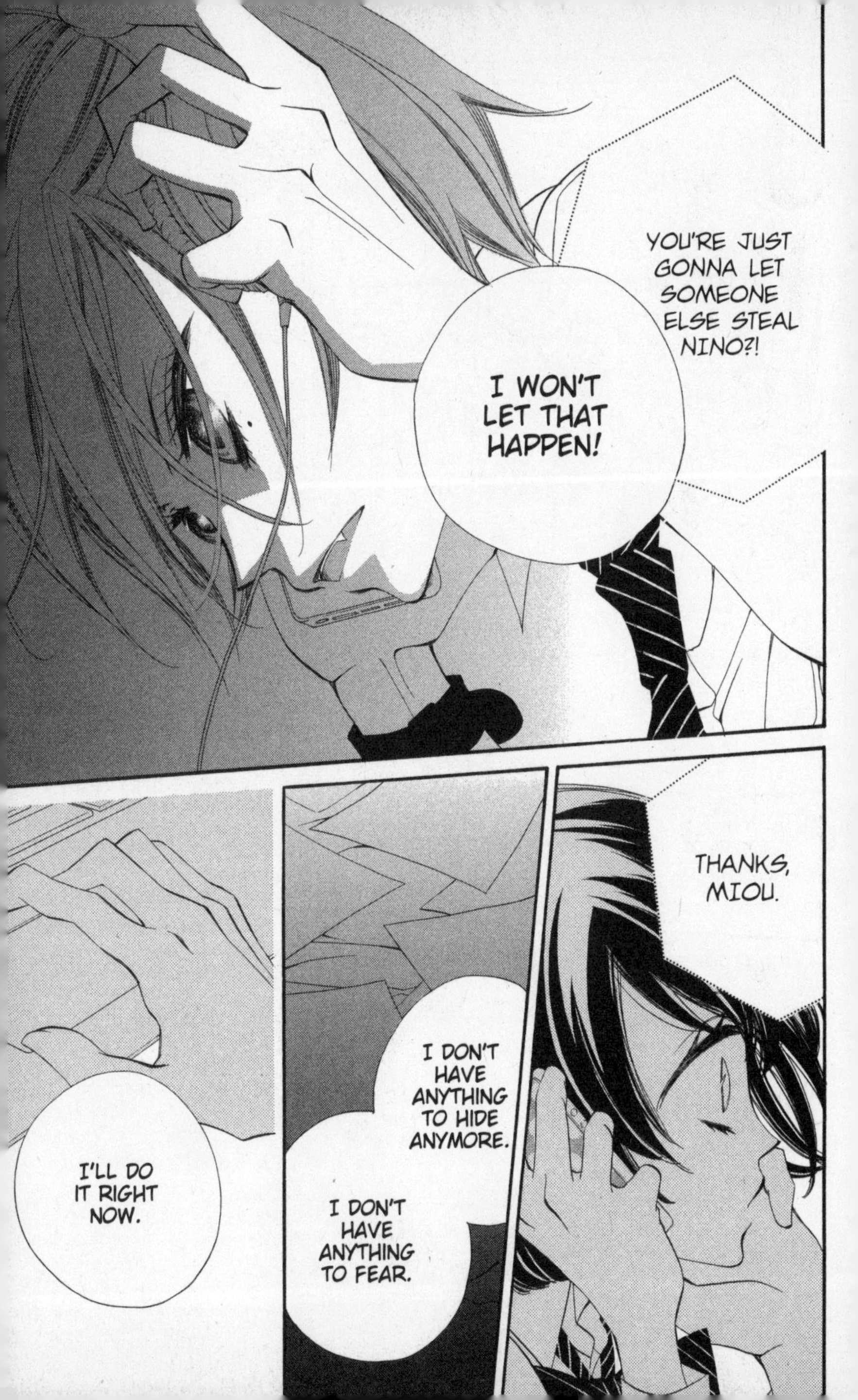
YOU'RE JUST GONNA LET SOMEONE ELSE STEAL NINO?!
I WON'T LET THAT HAPPEN!
THANKS, MIOU.
I DON'T HAVE ANYTHING TO HIDE ANYMORE.
I DON'T HAVE ANYTHING TO FEAR.
I'LL DO IT RIGHT NOW.

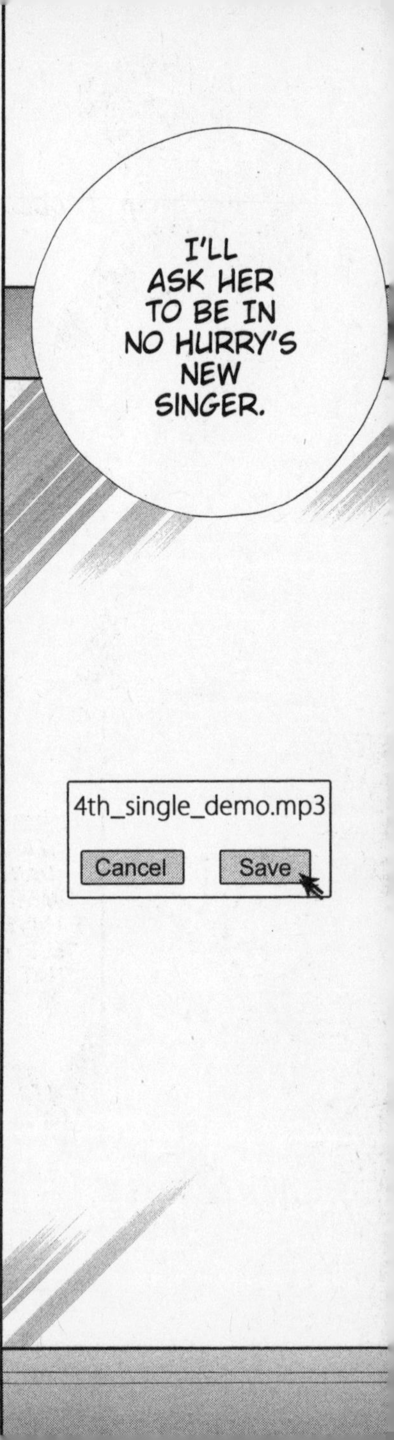
I'LL ASK HER TO BE IN NO HURRY'S NEW SINGER.
4th_single_demo.mp3
Cancel
Save

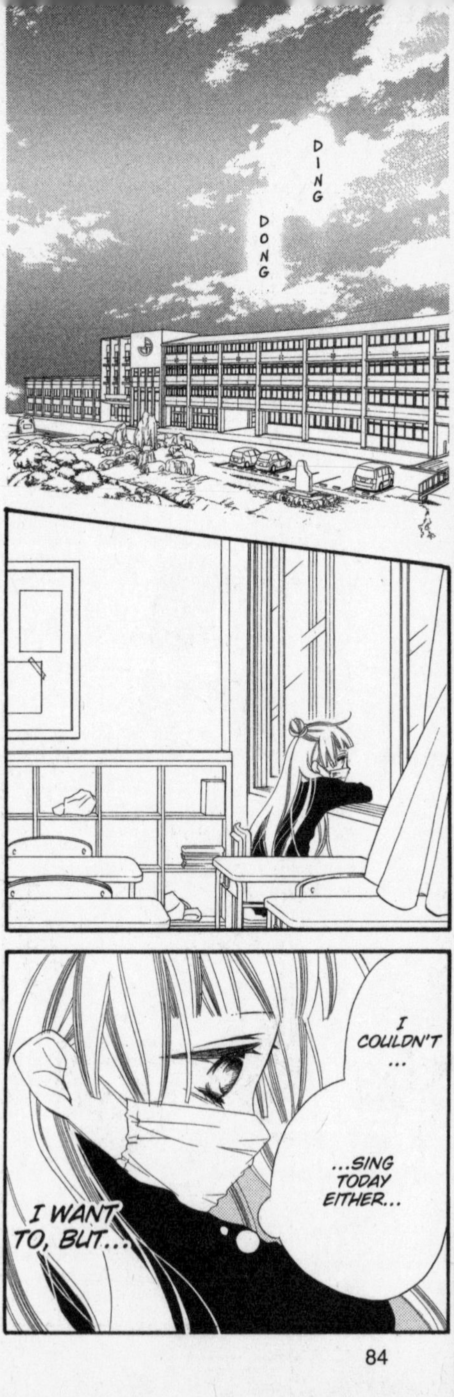
DING
DONG
I COULDN'T ...
...SING TODAY EITHER...
I WANT TO, BUT...

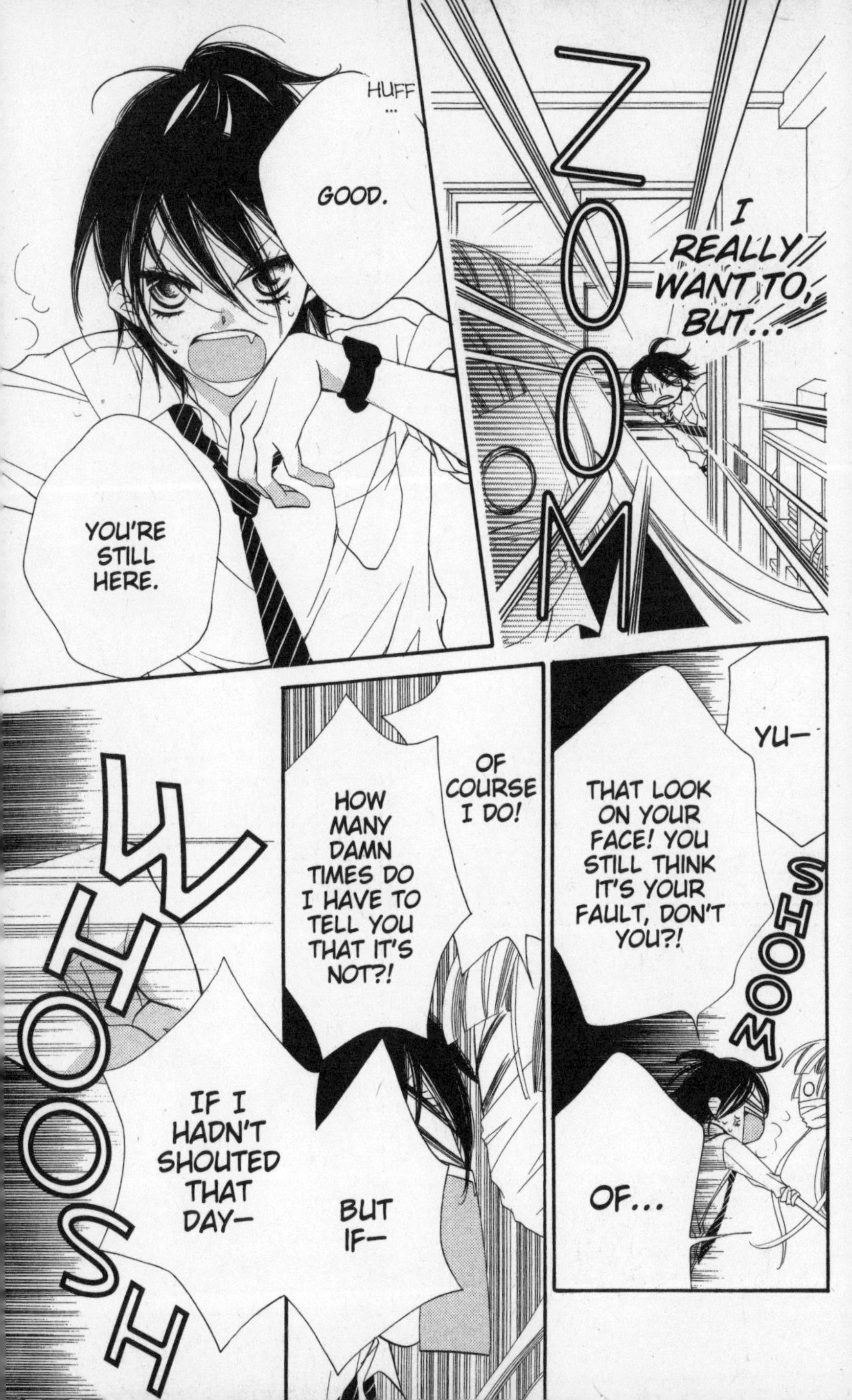
ZOOOM
I REALLY WANT TO, BUT...
HUFF ...
GOOD.
YOU'RE STILL HERE.
YU—
THAT LOOK ON YOUR FACE! YOU STILL THINK IT'S YOUR FAULT, DON'T YOU?!
SHOOM
OF...
OF COURSE I DO!
HOW MANY DAMN TIMES DO I HAVE TO TELL YOU THAT IT'S NOT?!
BUT IF—
WHOOSH
IF I HADN'T SHOUTED THAT DAY—

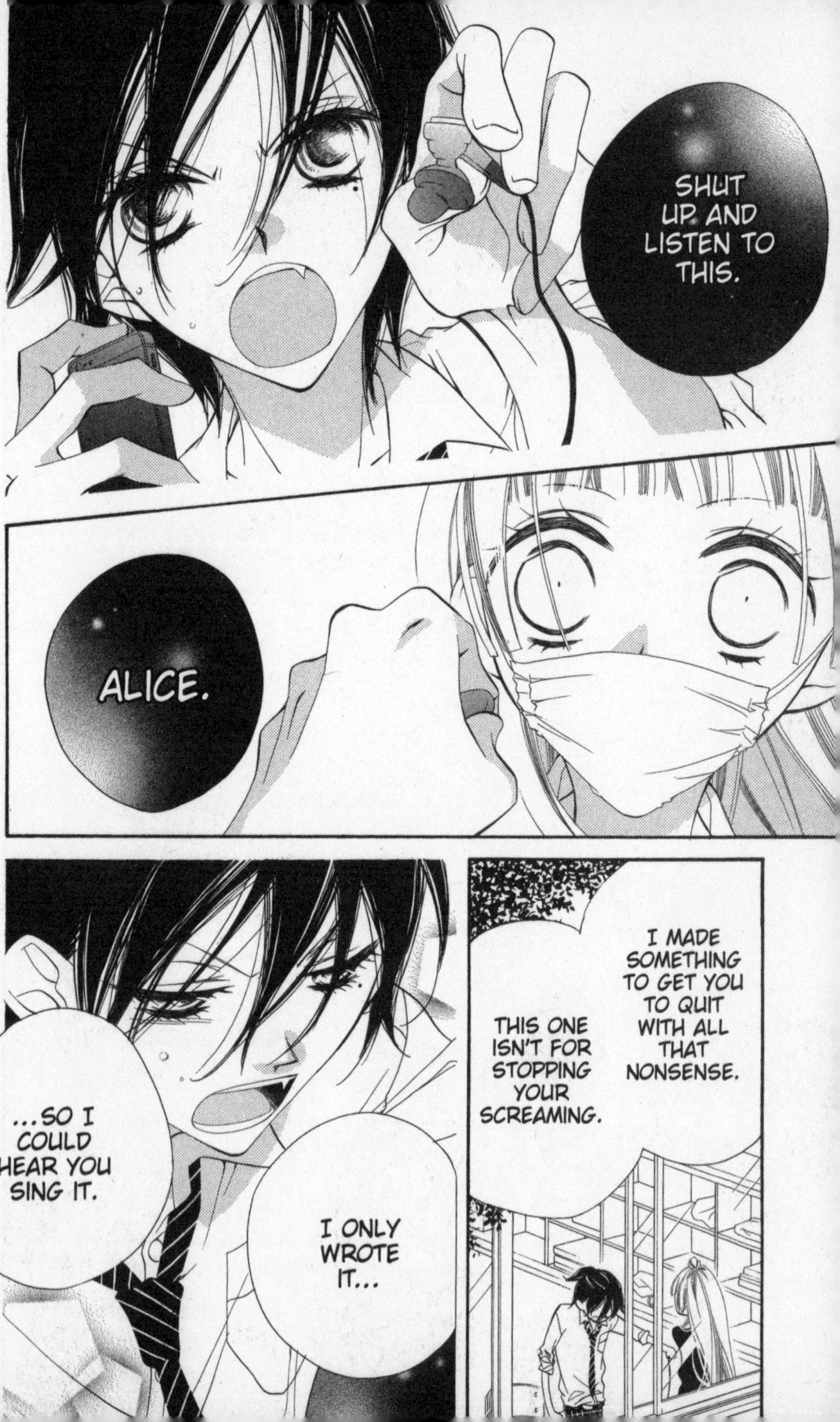
SHUT UP AND LISTEN TO THIS.
ALICE.
I MADE SOMETHING TO GET YOU TO QUIT WITH ALL THAT NONSENSE.
THIS ONE ISN'T FOR STOPPING YOUR SCREAMING.
I ONLY WROTE IT...
...SO I COULD HEAR YOU SING IT.

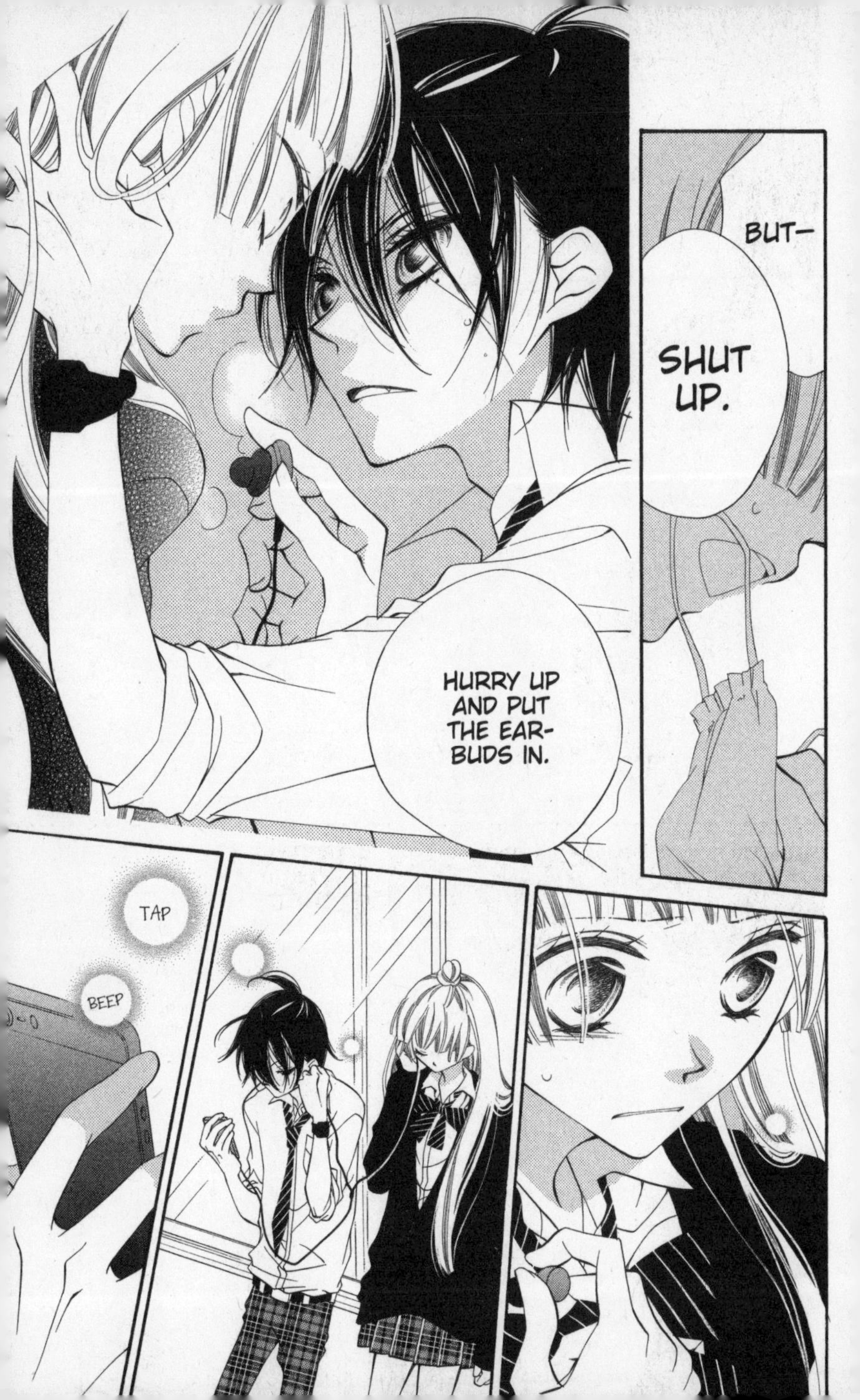
BUT—
SHUT UP.
HURRY UP AND PUT THE EAR-BUDS IN.
TAP
BEEP

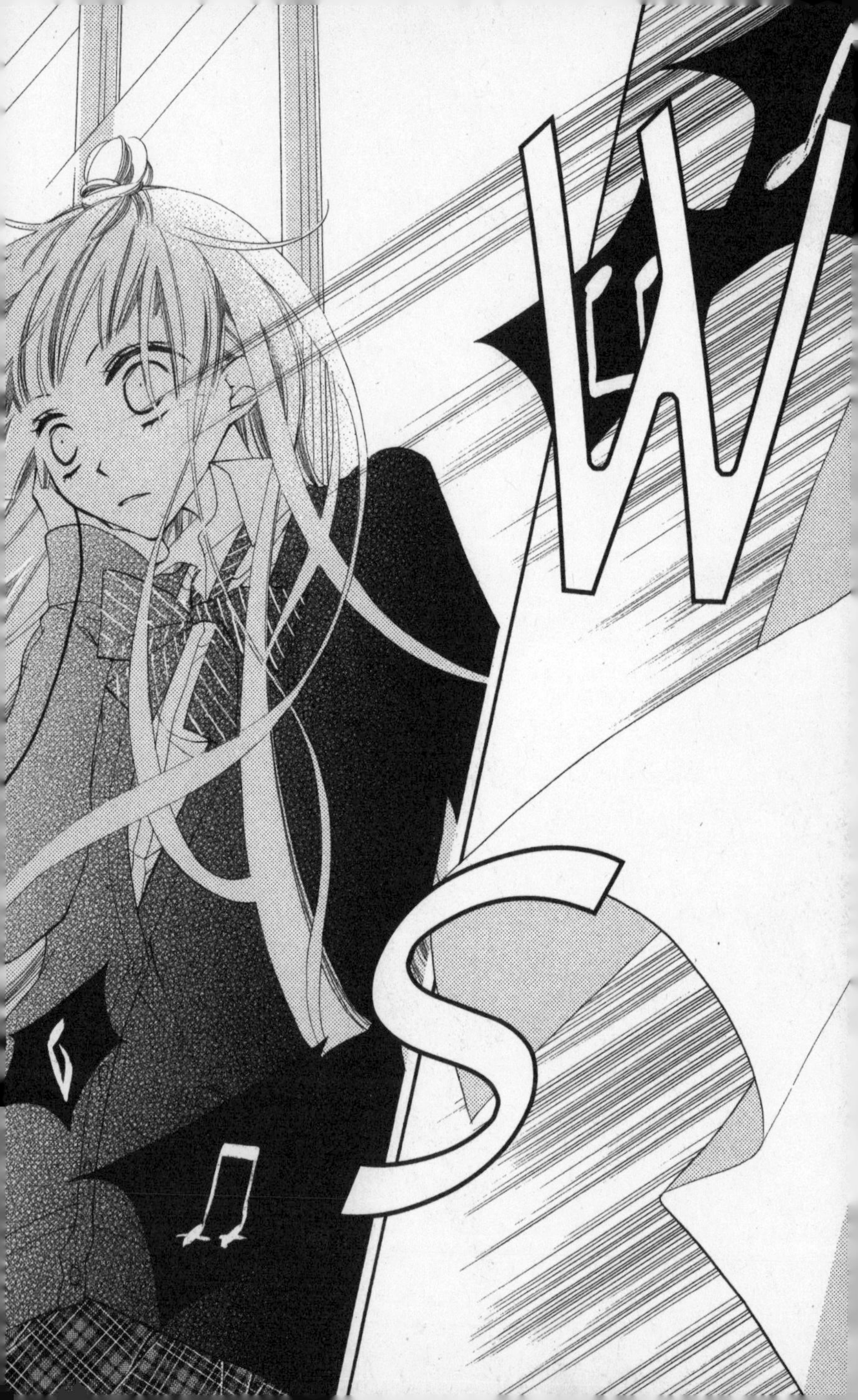
SW

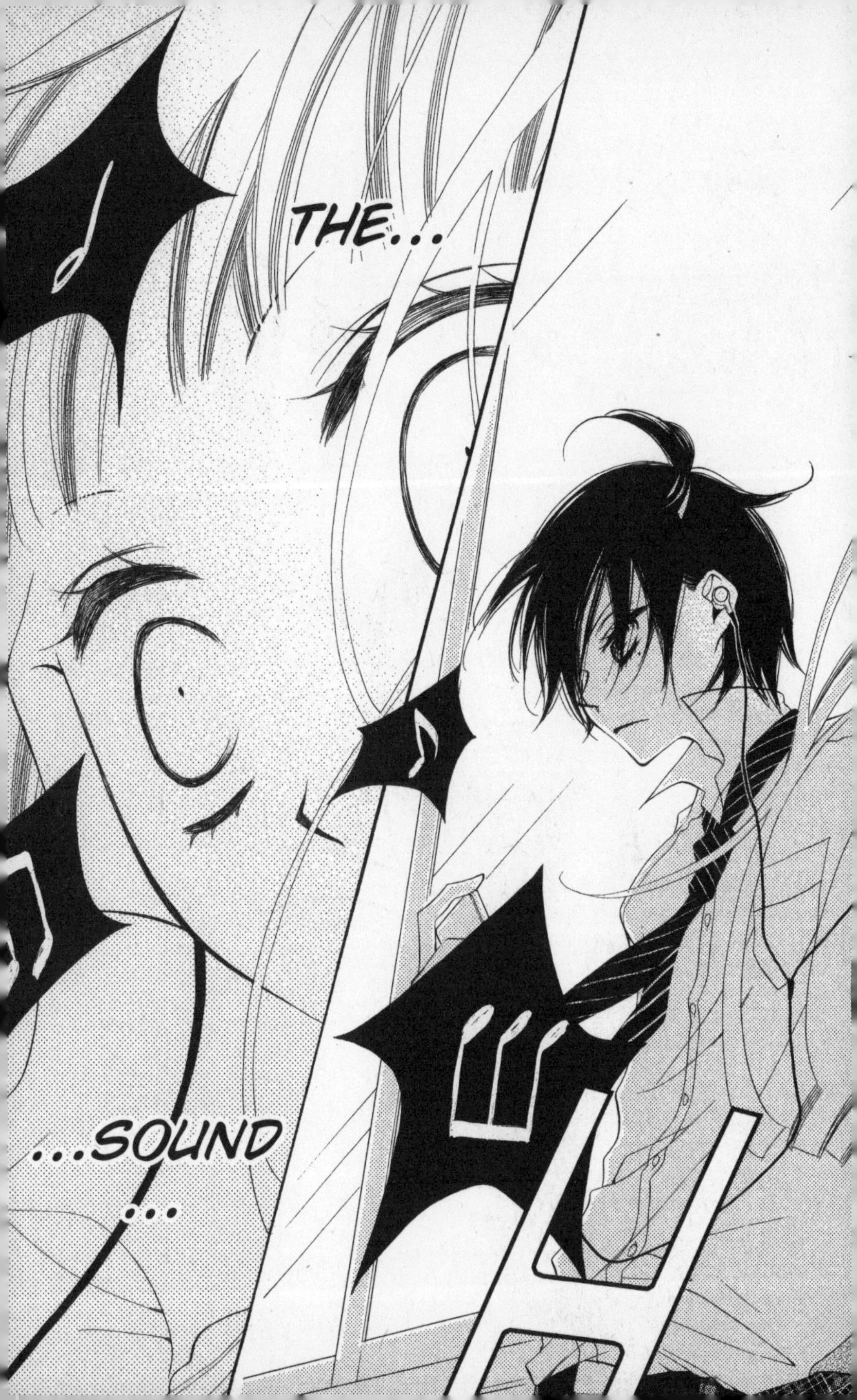
THE...
...SOUND
...

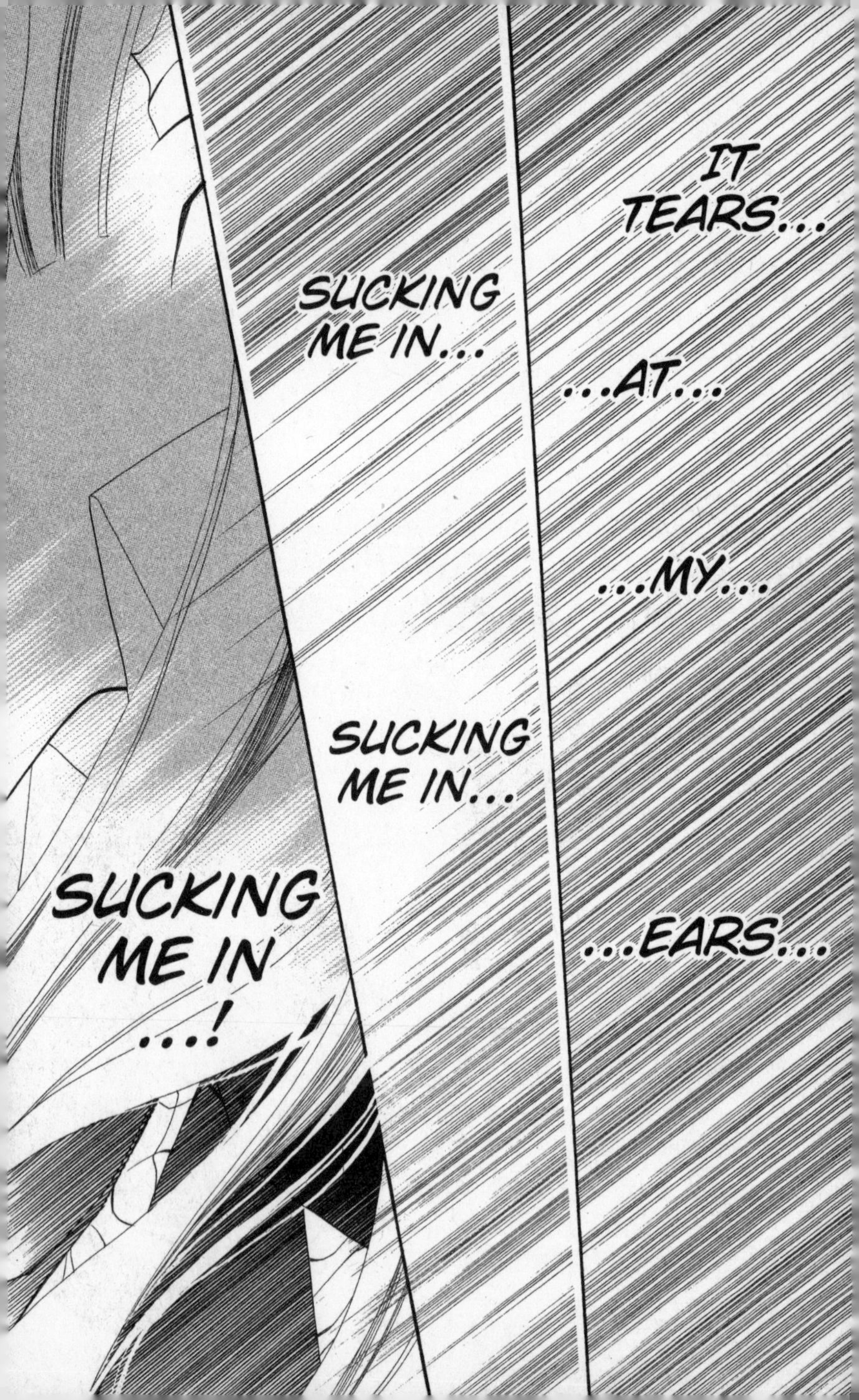
IT TEARS...
...AT...
...MY...
...EARS...
SUCKING ME IN...
SUCKING ME IN...
SUCKING ME IN ...!

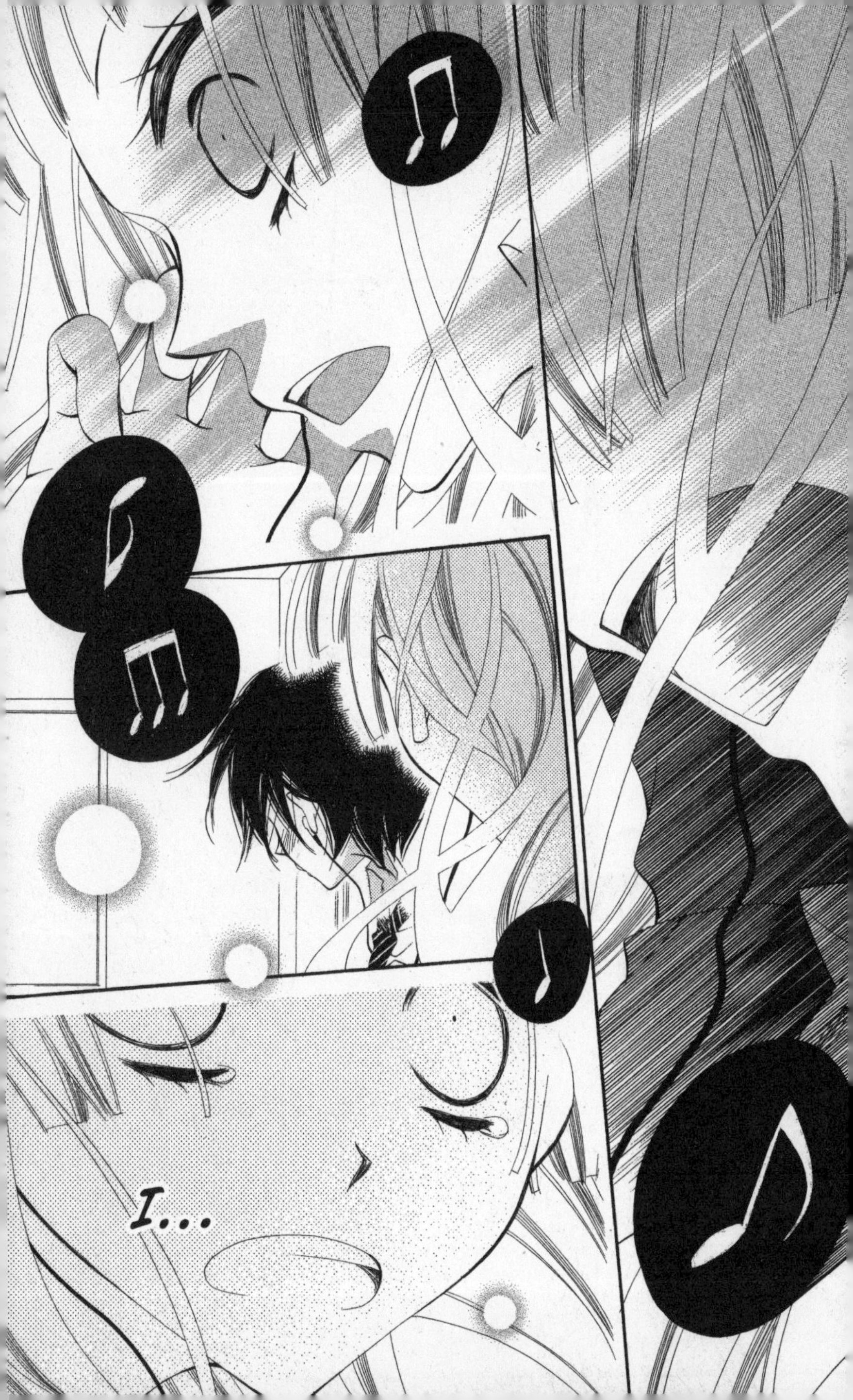
I...

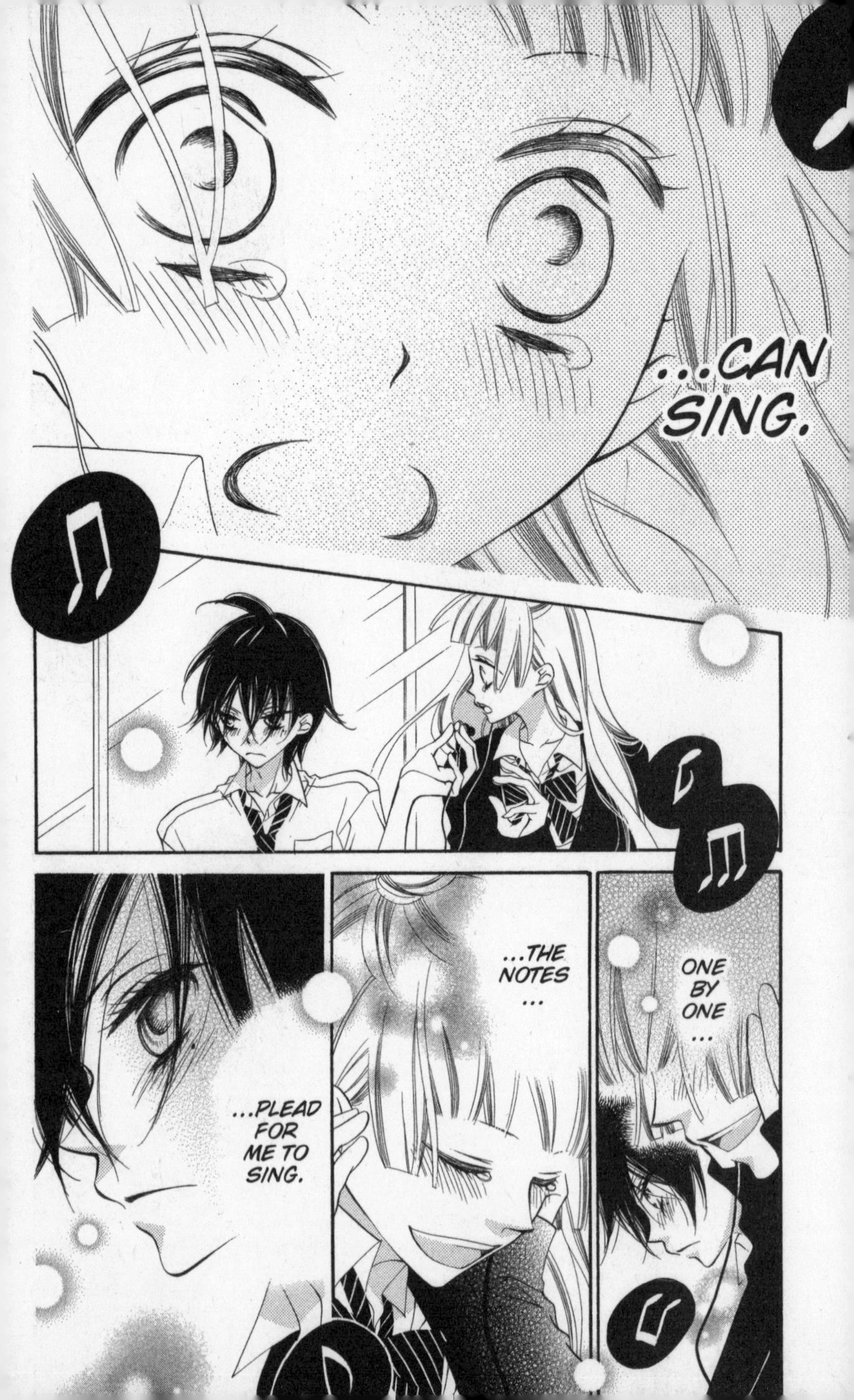
...CAN SING.
ONE BY ONE ...
...THE NOTES ...
...PLEAD FOR ME TO SING.

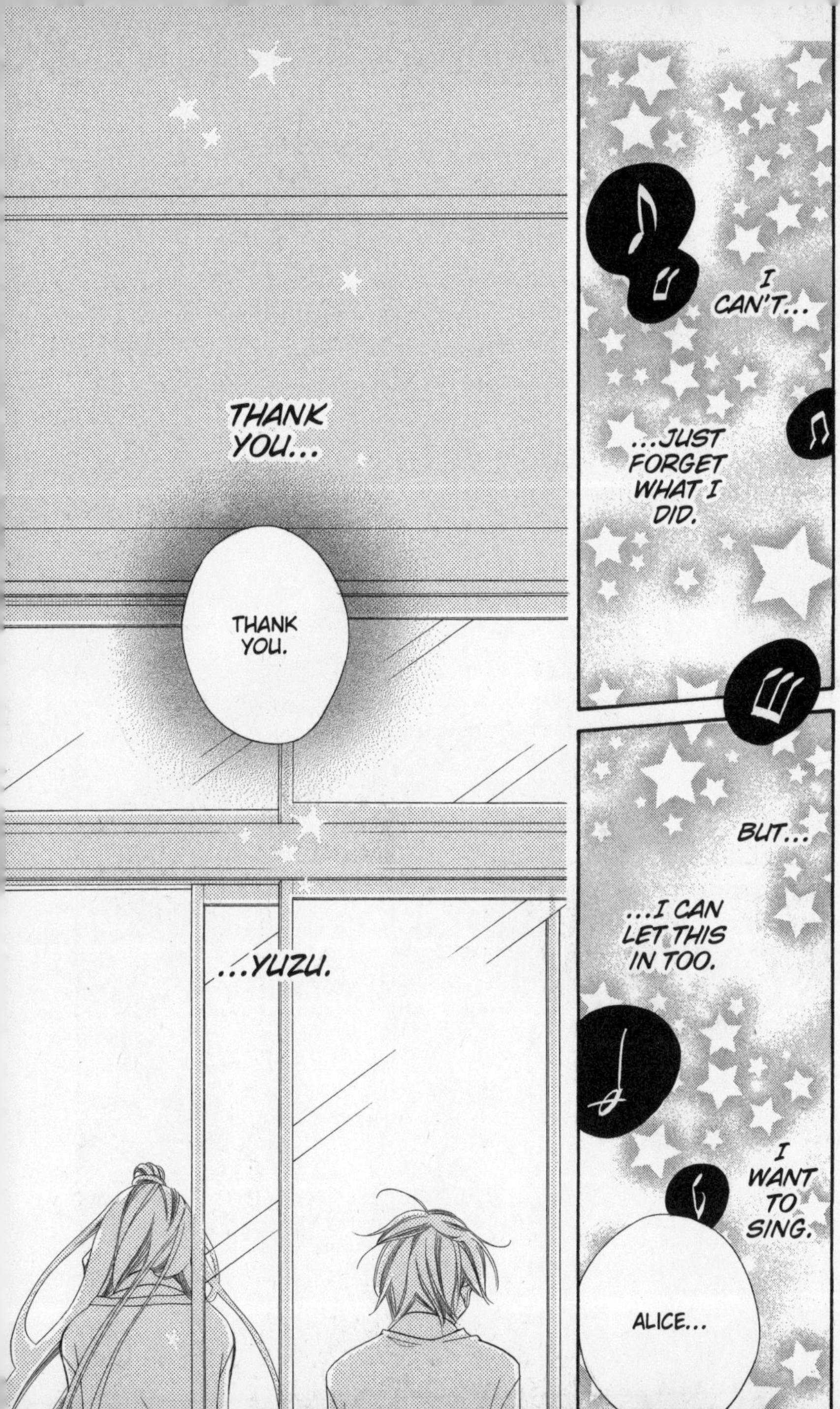

I CAN'T...
...JUST FORGET WHAT I DID.
BUT...
...I CAN LET THIS IN TOO.
I WANT TO SING.
ALICE...
THANK YOU...
THANK YOU.
...YUZU.

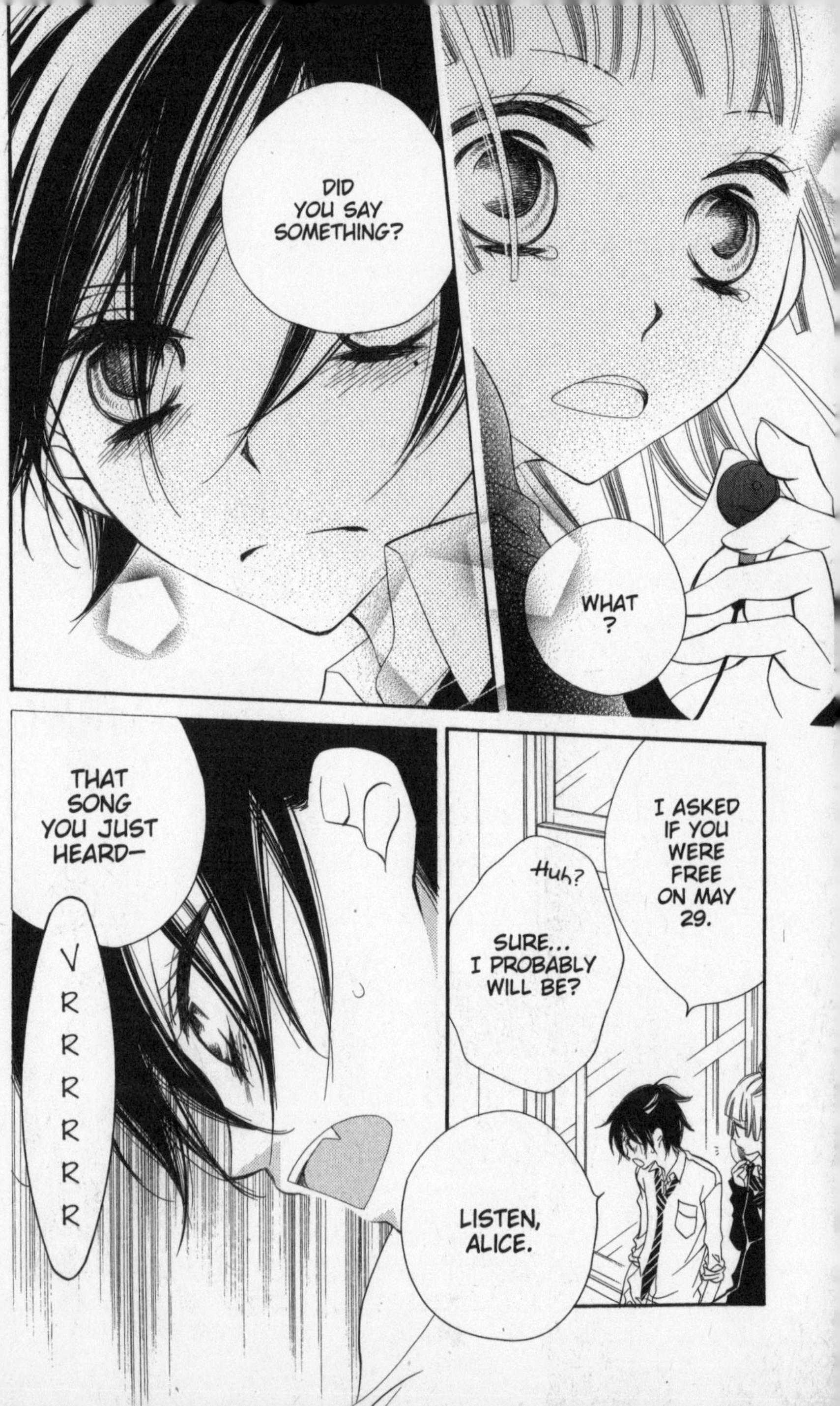
WHAT?
DID YOU SAY SOMETHING?
I ASKED IF YOU WERE FREE ON MAY 29.
Huh?
SURE... I PROBABLY WILL BE?
LISTEN, ALICE.
THAT SONG YOU JUST HEARD—
VRRRRRR

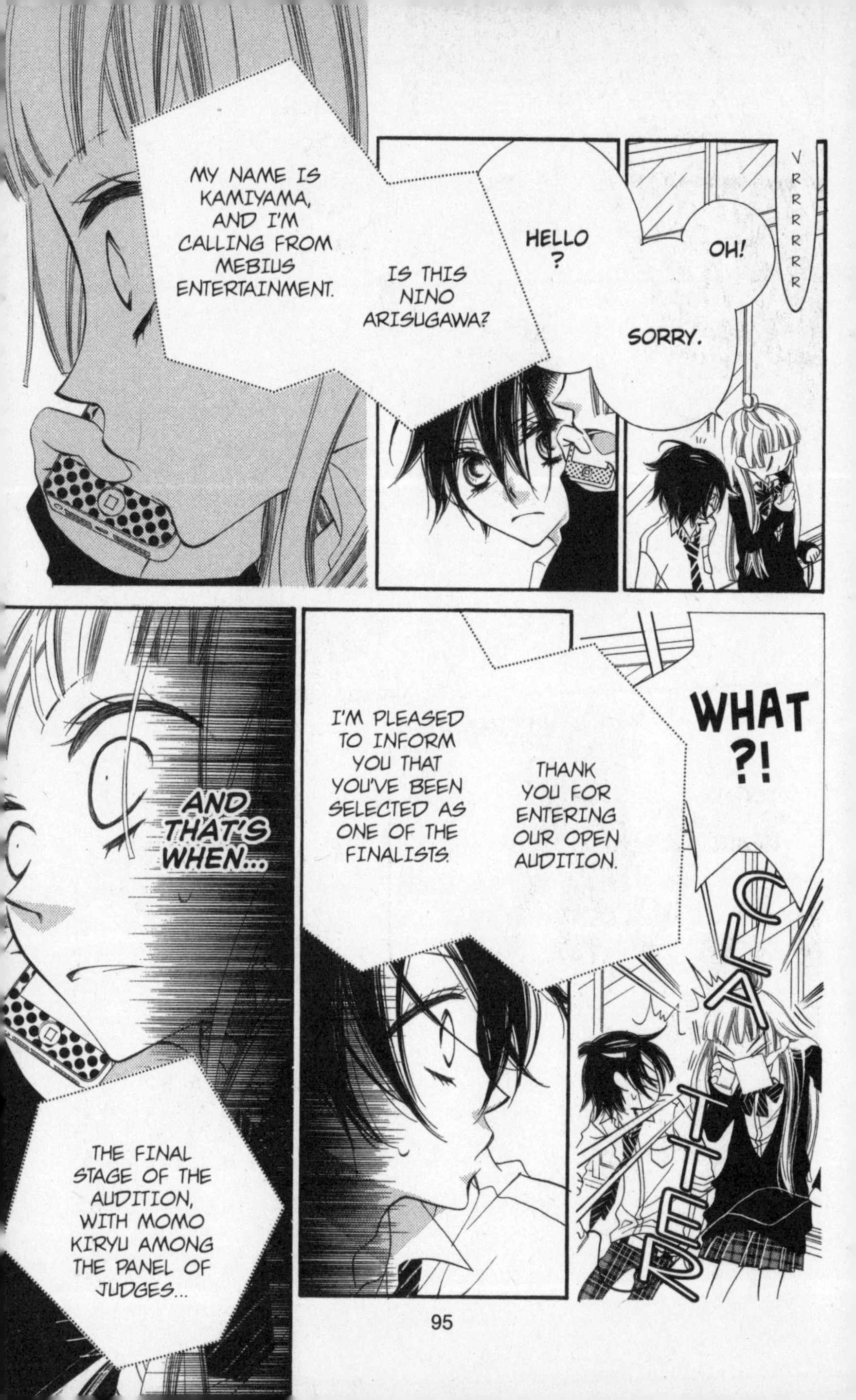
VRRRRRR
OH!
SORRY.
HELLO?
MY NAME IS KAMIYAMA, AND I'M CALLING FROM MEBIUS ENTERTAINMENT.
IS THIS NINO ARISUGAWA?
WHAT?!
CLATTER
THANK YOU FOR ENTERING OUR OPEN AUDITION.
I'M PLEASED TO INFORM YOU THAT YOU'VE BEEN SELECTED AS ONE OF THE FINALISTS.
AND THAT'S WHEN...
THE FINAL STAGE OF THE AUDITION, WITH MOMO KIRYU AMONG THE PANEL OF JUDGES...

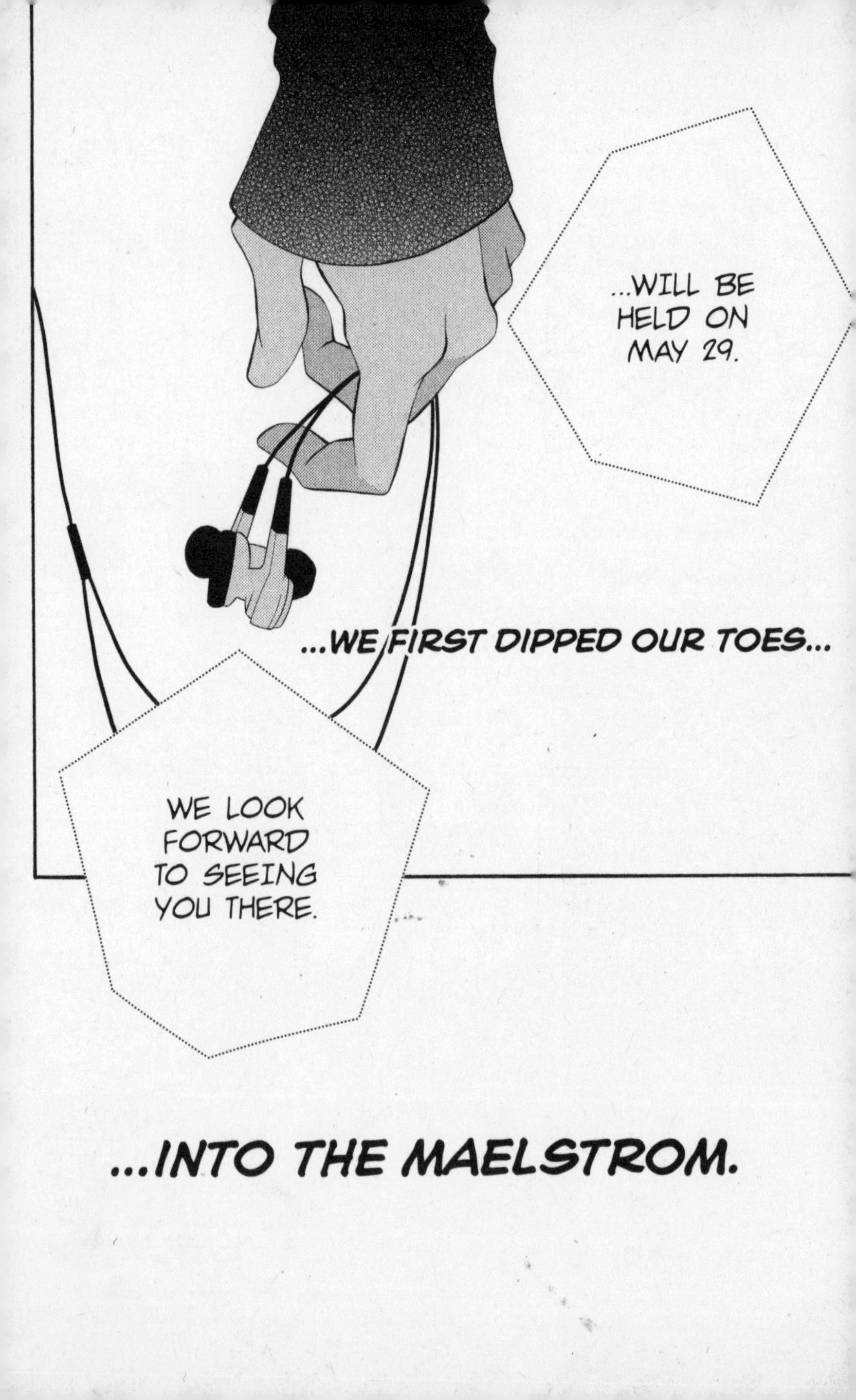
...WILL BE HELD ON MAY 29.
...WE FIRST DIPPED OUR TOES...
WE LOOK FORWARD TO SEEING YOU THERE.
...INTO THE MAELSTROM.

THE HEART-POUNDING EPIC SAGA OF **YUZU AND HIS MILK** EPISODE 3

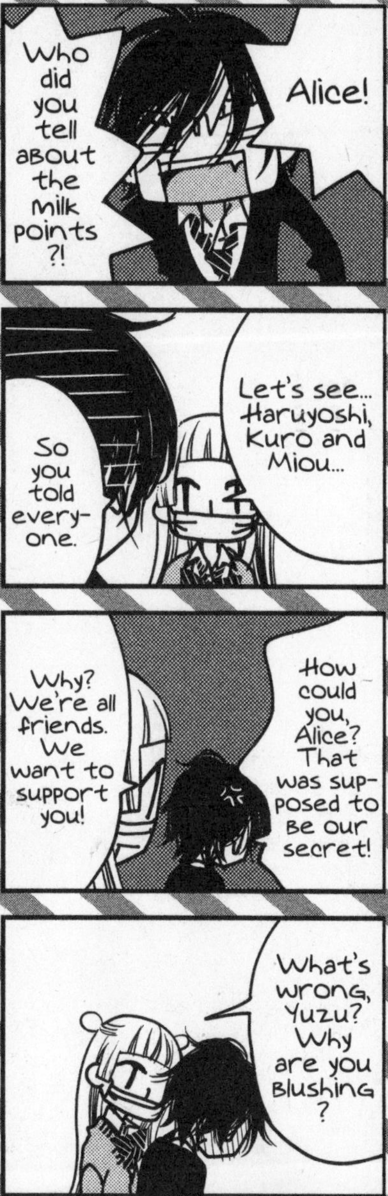
Alice!
Who did you tell about the milk points?!
Let's see... Haruyoshi, Kuro and Miou...
So you told every-one.
How could you, Alice? That was sup-posed to be our secret!
Why? We're all friends. We want to support you!
What's wrong, Yuzu? Why are you blushing?

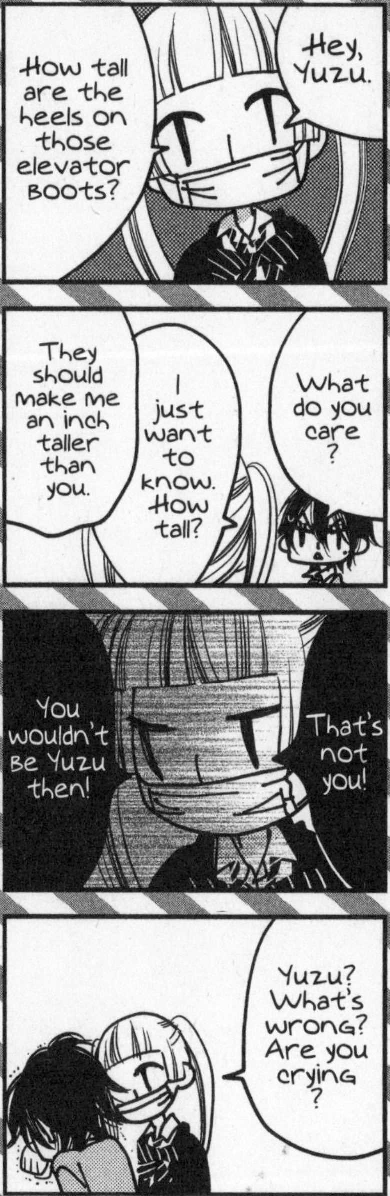
Hey, Yuzu.
How tall are the heels on those elevator boots?
What do you care?
I just want to know. How tall?
They should make me an inch taller than you.
That's not you!
You wouldn't be Yuzu then!
Yuzu? What's wrong? Are you crying?

TO BE CONTINUED

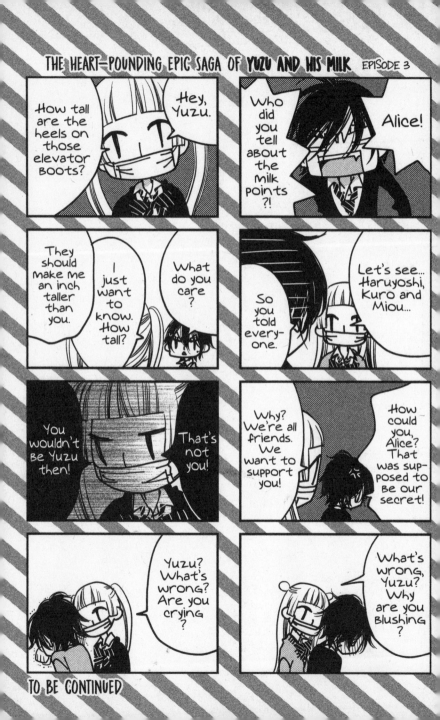

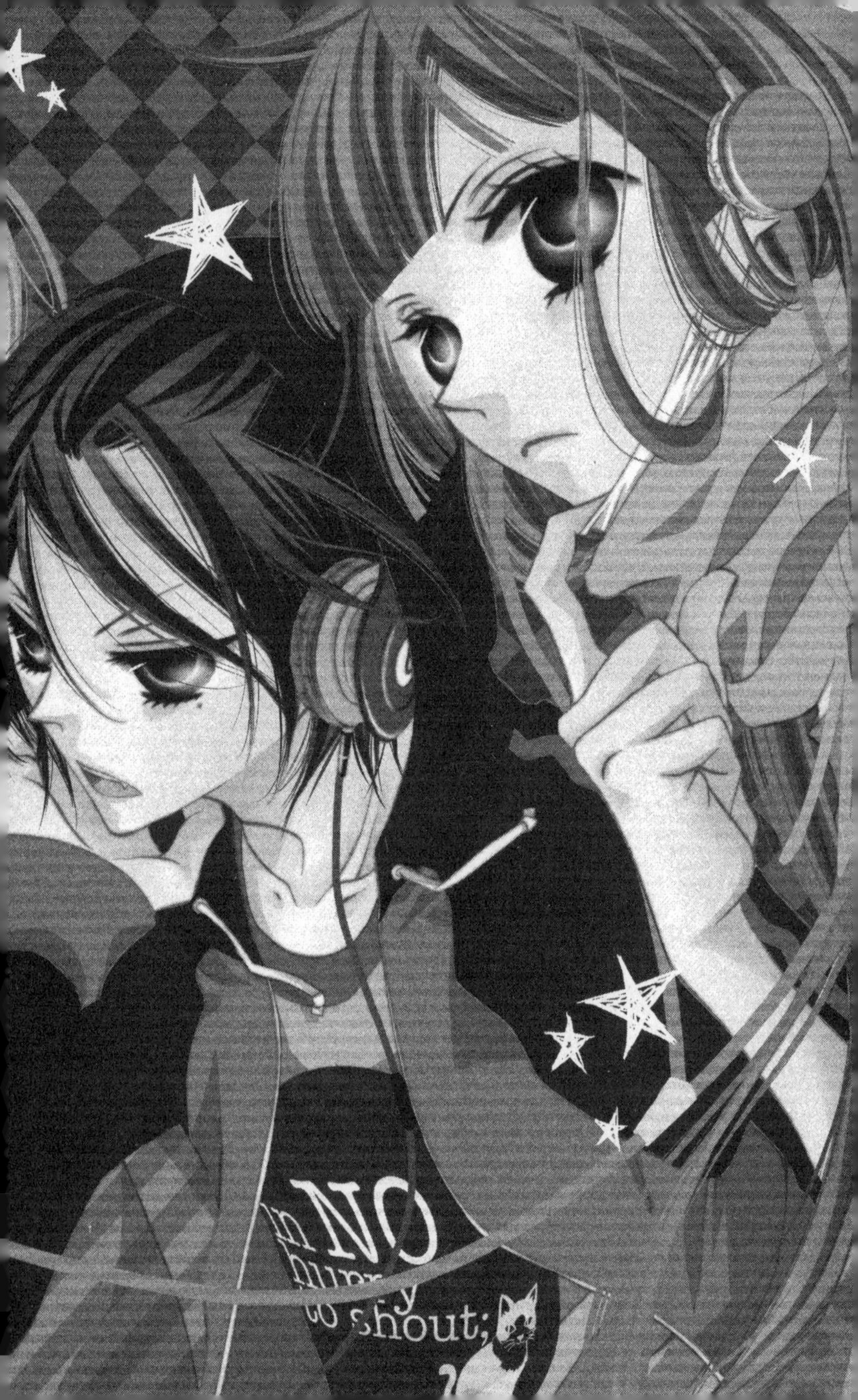
in NO
hurry
to shout;

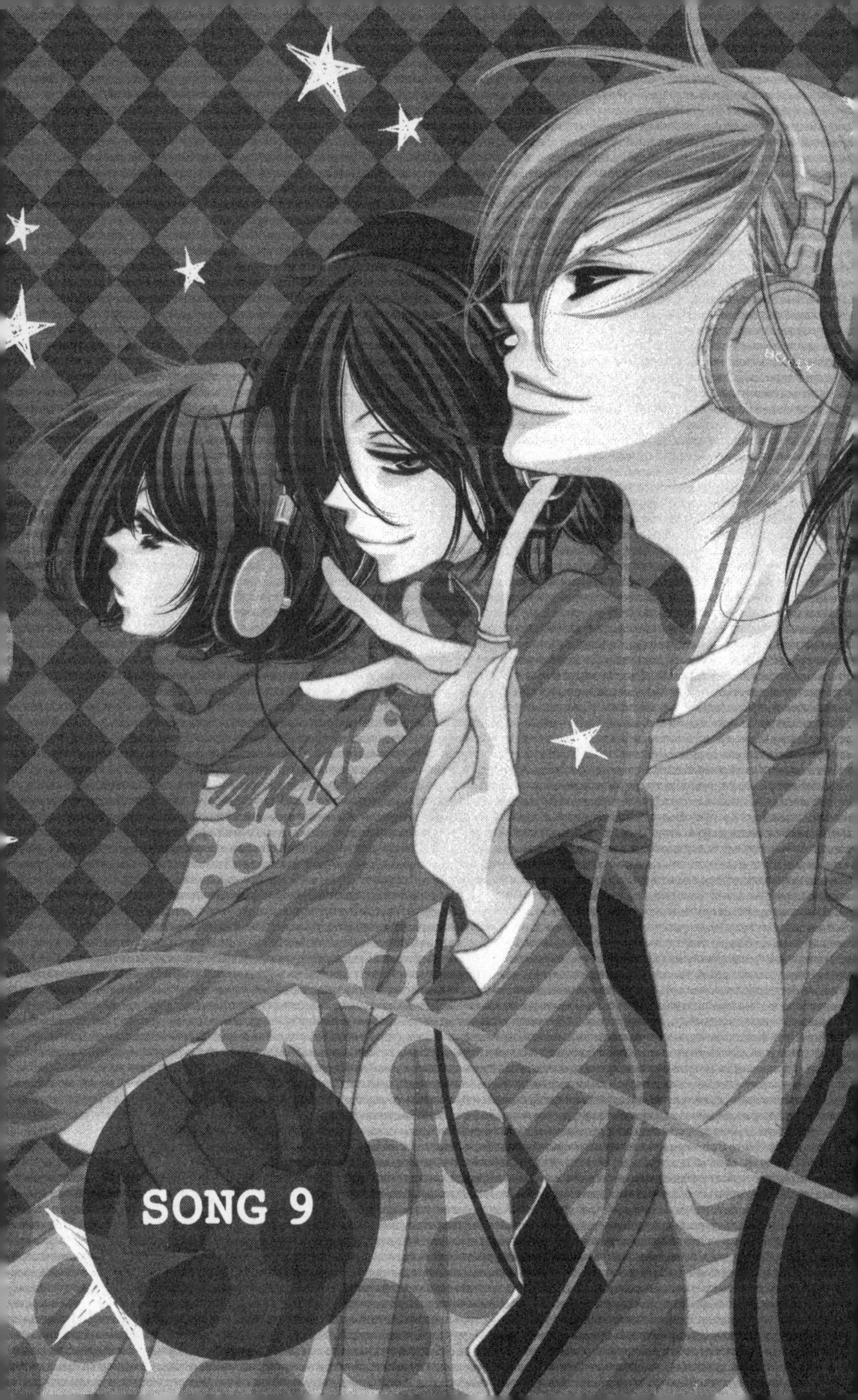
SONG 9

ANONYMOUS DRAMA CD POSTPRODUCTION REPORT!

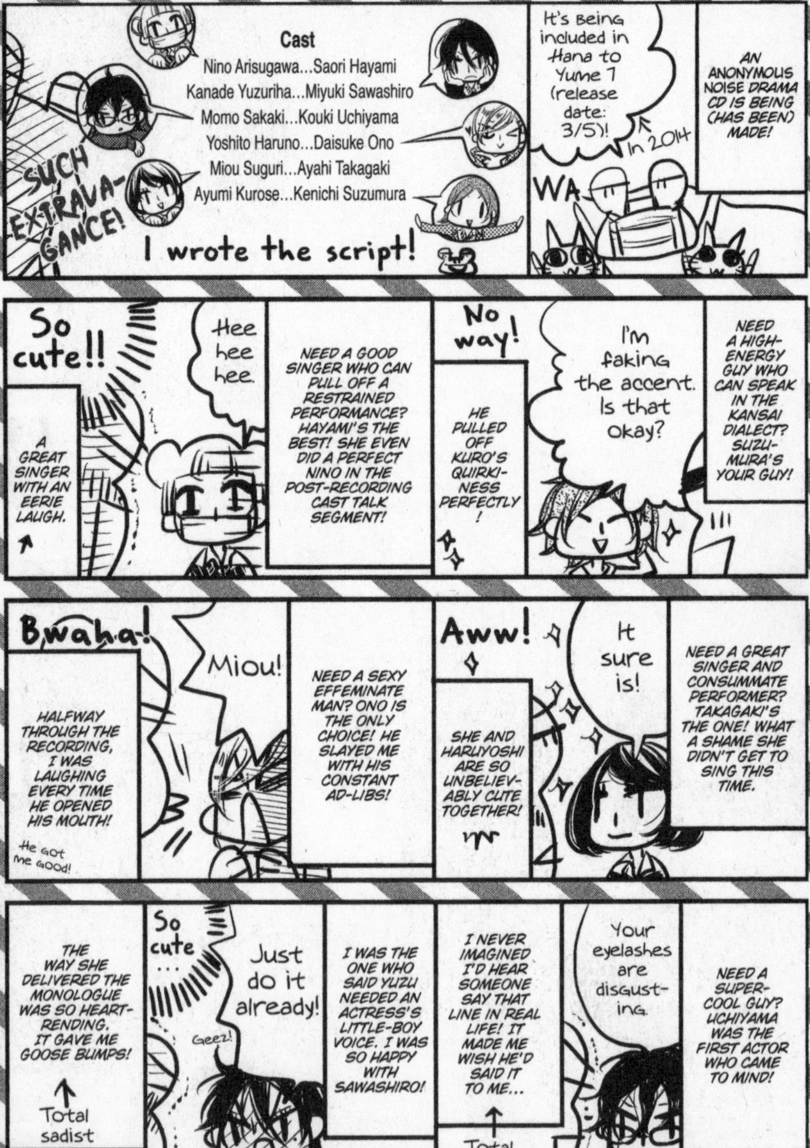
AN ANONYMOUS NOISE DRAMA CD IS BEING (HAS BEEN) MADE!
It's being included in Hana to Yume 7 (release date: 3/5)!
In 2014
WA
Cast
Nino Arisugawa...Saori Hayami
Kanade Yuzuriha...Miyuki Sawashiro
Momo Sakaki...Kouki Uchiyama
Yoshito Haruno...Daisuke Ono
Miou Suguri...Ayahi Takagaki
Ayumi Kurose...Kenichi Suzumura
SUCH EXTRAVA-GANCE!
I wrote the script!
NEED A HIGH-ENERGY GUY WHO CAN SPEAK IN THE KANSAI DIALECT? SUZU-MURA'S YOUR GUY!
I'm faking the accent. Is that okay?
No way!
HE PULLED OFF KURO'S QUIRKI-NESS PERFECTLY!
NEED A GOOD SINGER WHO CAN PULL OFF A RESTRAINED PERFORMANCE? HAYAMI'S THE BEST! SHE EVEN DID A PERFECT NINO IN THE POST-RECORDING CAST TALK SEGMENT!
Hee hee hee.
So cute!!
A GREAT SINGER WITH AN EERIE LAUGH.
NEED A GREAT SINGER AND CONSUMMATE PERFORMER? TAKAGAKI'S THE ONE! WHAT A SHAME SHE DIDN'T GET TO SING THIS TIME.
It sure is!
Aww!
SHE AND HARUYOSHI ARE SO UNBELIEV-ABLY CUTE TOGETHER!
NEED A SEXY EFFEMINATE MAN? ONO IS THE ONLY CHOICE! HE SLAYED ME WITH HIS CONSTANT AD-LIBS!
Miou!
Bwaha!
HALFWAY THROUGH THE RECORDING, I WAS LAUGHING EVERY TIME HE OPENED HIS MOUTH!
He got me good!
NEED A SUPER-COOL GUY? UCHIYAMA WAS THE FIRST ACTOR WHO CAME TO MIND!
Your eyelashes are disgust-ing.
I NEVER IMAGINED I'D HEAR SOMEONE SAY THAT LINE IN REAL LIFE! IT MADE ME WISH HE'D SAID IT TO ME...
Total masochist
I WAS THE ONE WHO SAID YUZU NEEDED AN ACTRESS'S LITTLE-BOY VOICE. I WAS SO HAPPY WITH SAWASHIRO!
Just do it already!
Geez!
So cute...
THE WAY SHE DELIVERED THE MONOLOGUE WAS SO HEART-RENDING. IT GAVE ME GOOSE BUMPS!
Total sadist

CONTINUED IN AUTHOR'S NOTE 4!

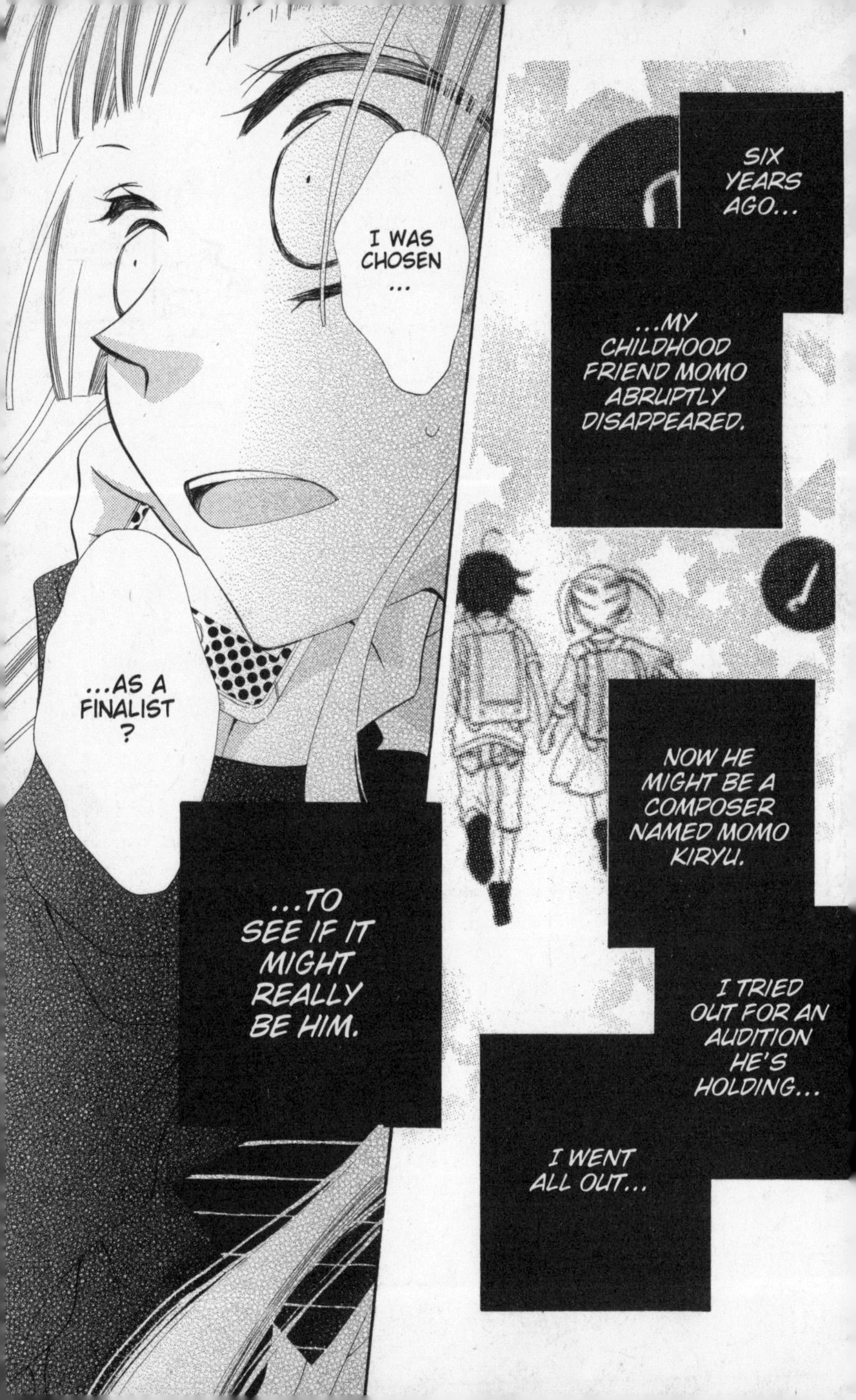
SIX YEARS AGO...
...MY CHILDHOOD FRIEND MOMO ABRUPTLY DISAPPEARED.
NOW HE MIGHT BE A COMPOSER NAMED MOMO KIRYU.
I TRIED OUT FOR AN AUDITION HE'S HOLDING...
I WENT ALL OUT...
I WAS CHOSEN ...
...AS A FINALIST ?
...TO SEE IF IT MIGHT REALLY BE HIM.

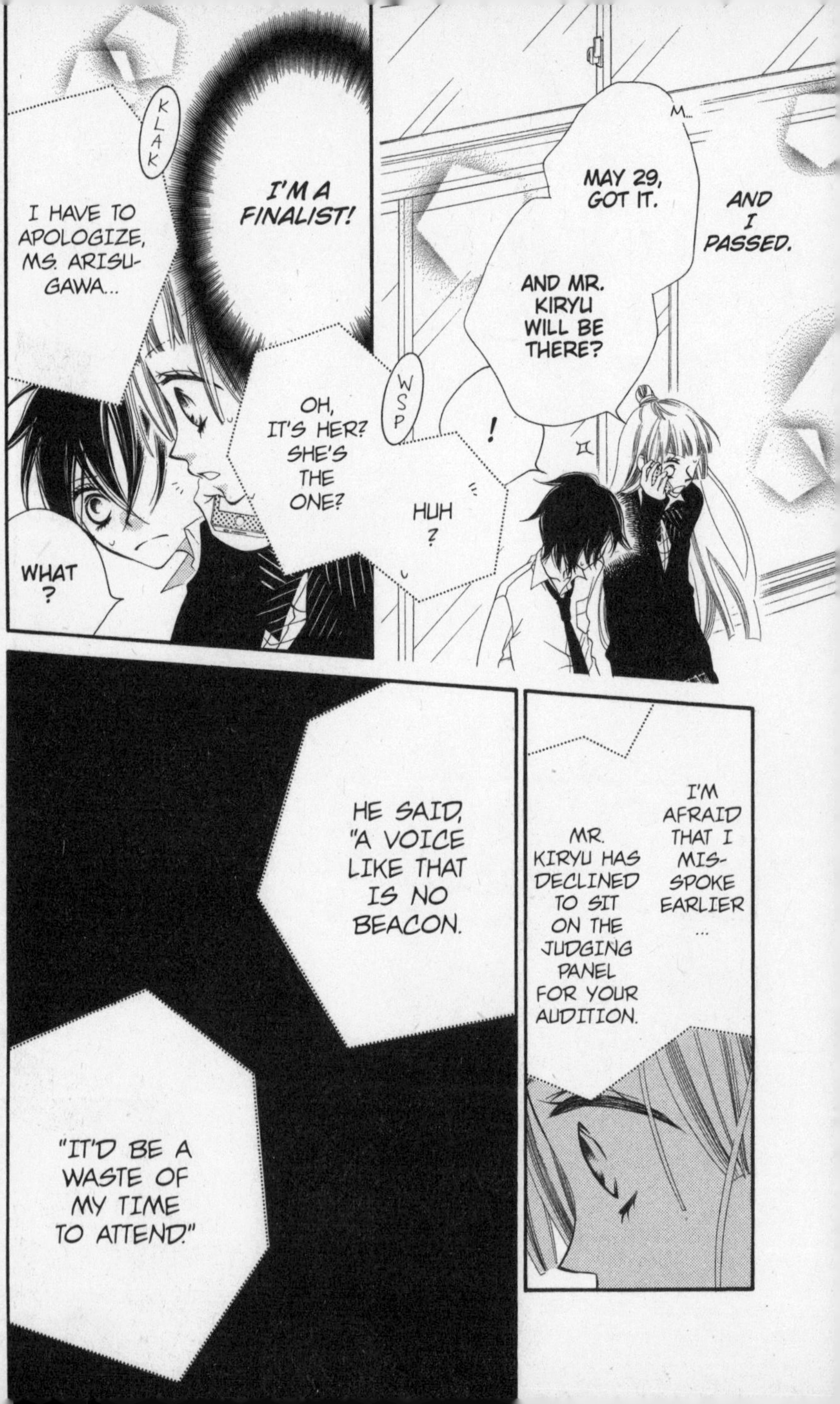
M...
AND I PASSED.
MAY 29, GOT IT.
AND MR. KIRYU WILL BE THERE?
!
HUH?
I'M A FINALIST!
KLAK
I HAVE TO APOLOGIZE, MS. ARISUGAWA...
WSP
OH, IT'S HER? SHE'S THE ONE?
WHAT?
I'M AFRAID THAT I MIS-SPOKE EARLIER...
MR. KIRYU HAS DECLINED TO SIT ON THE JUDGING PANEL FOR YOUR AUDITION.
HE SAID, "A VOICE LIKE THAT IS NO BEACON.
"IT'D BE A WASTE OF MY TIME TO ATTEND."

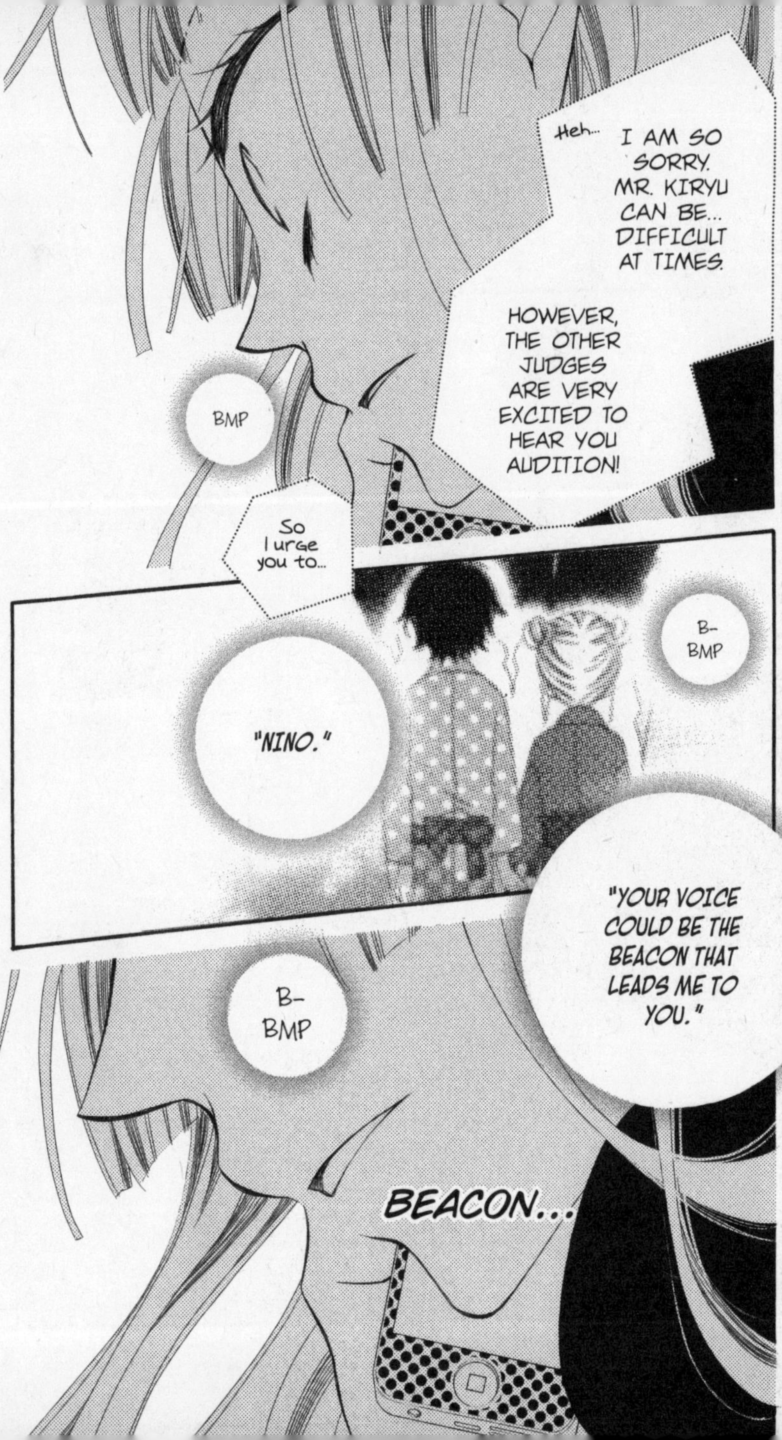
Heh...
I AM SO SORRY. MR. KIRYU CAN BE... DIFFICULT AT TIMES.
HOWEVER, THE OTHER JUDGES ARE VERY EXCITED TO HEAR YOU AUDITION!
BMP
So I urge you to...
B-BMP
"NINO."
"YOUR VOICE COULD BE THE BEACON THAT LEADS ME TO YOU."
B-BMP
BEACON...

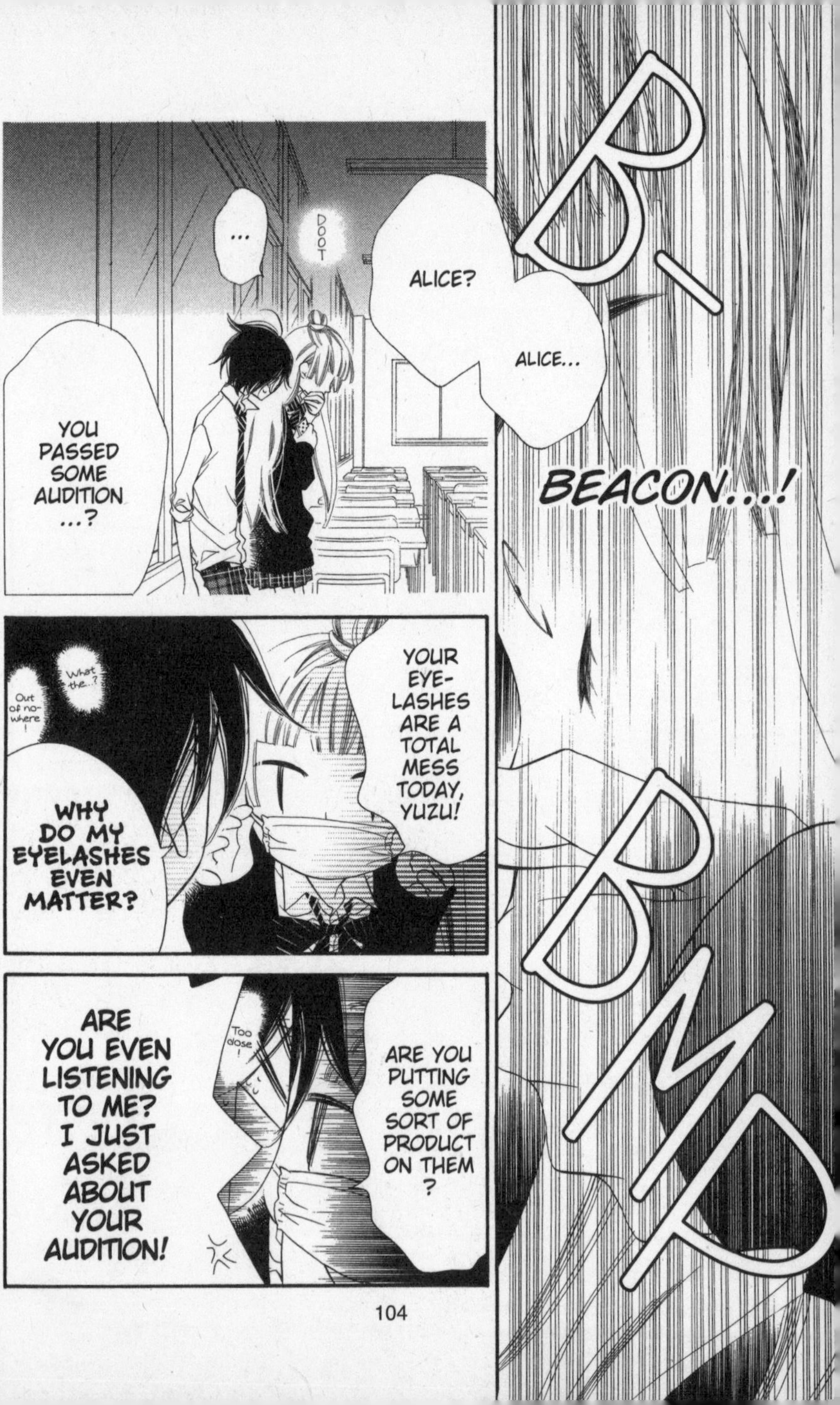
BA-
BUMP
BEACON...!
ALICE?
ALICE...
DOOT
...
YOU PASSED SOME AUDITION ...?
YOUR EYE-LASHES ARE A TOTAL MESS TODAY, YUZU!
What the...?
Out of no-where!
WHY DO MY EYELASHES EVEN MATTER?
ARE YOU PUTTING SOME SORT OF PRODUCT ON THEM?
Too close!
ARE YOU EVEN LISTENING TO ME? I JUST ASKED ABOUT YOUR AUDITION!

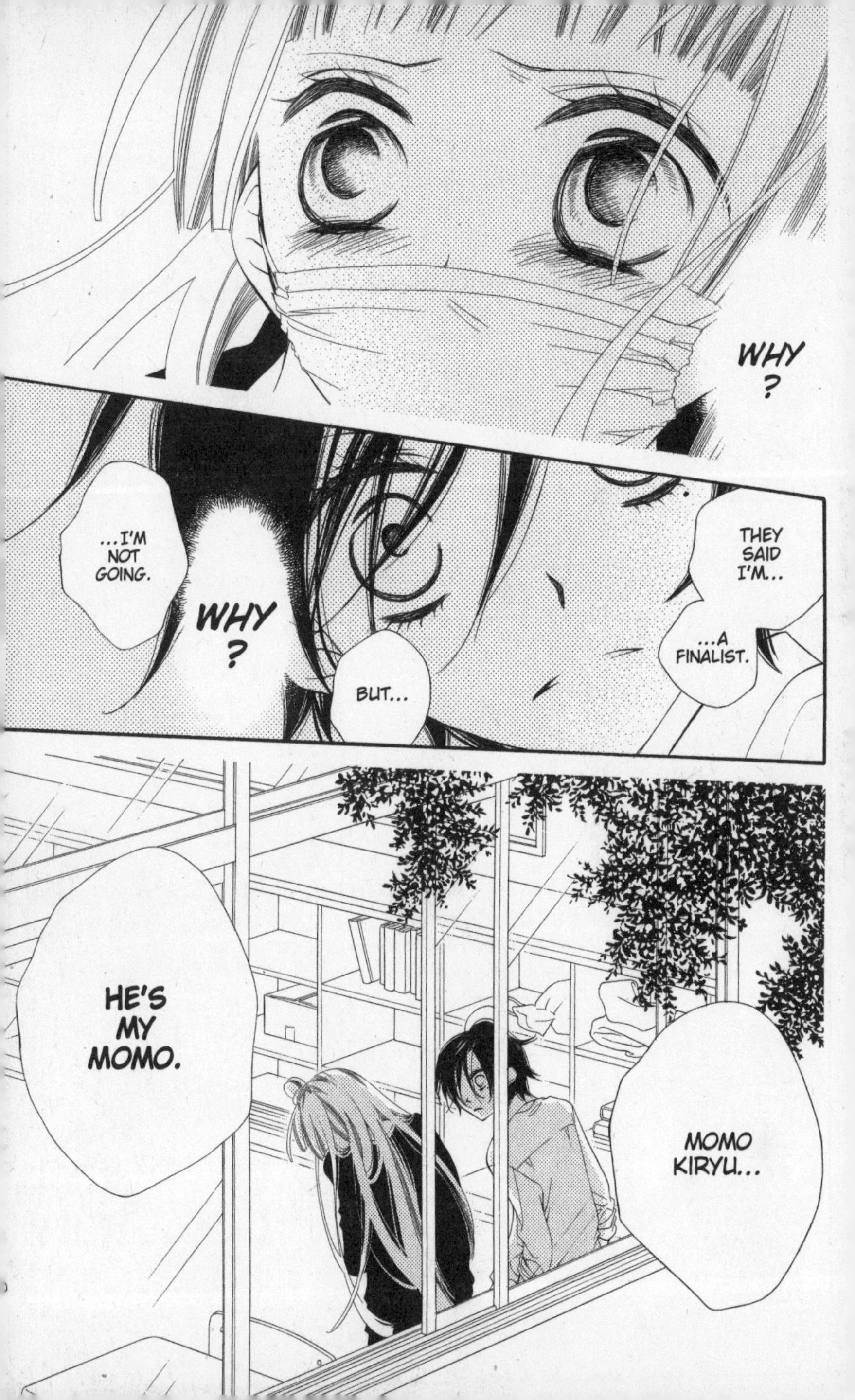
WHY ?
THEY SAID I'M...
...A FINALIST.
BUT...
WHY ?
...I'M NOT GOING.
MOMO KIRYU...
HE'S MY MOMO.

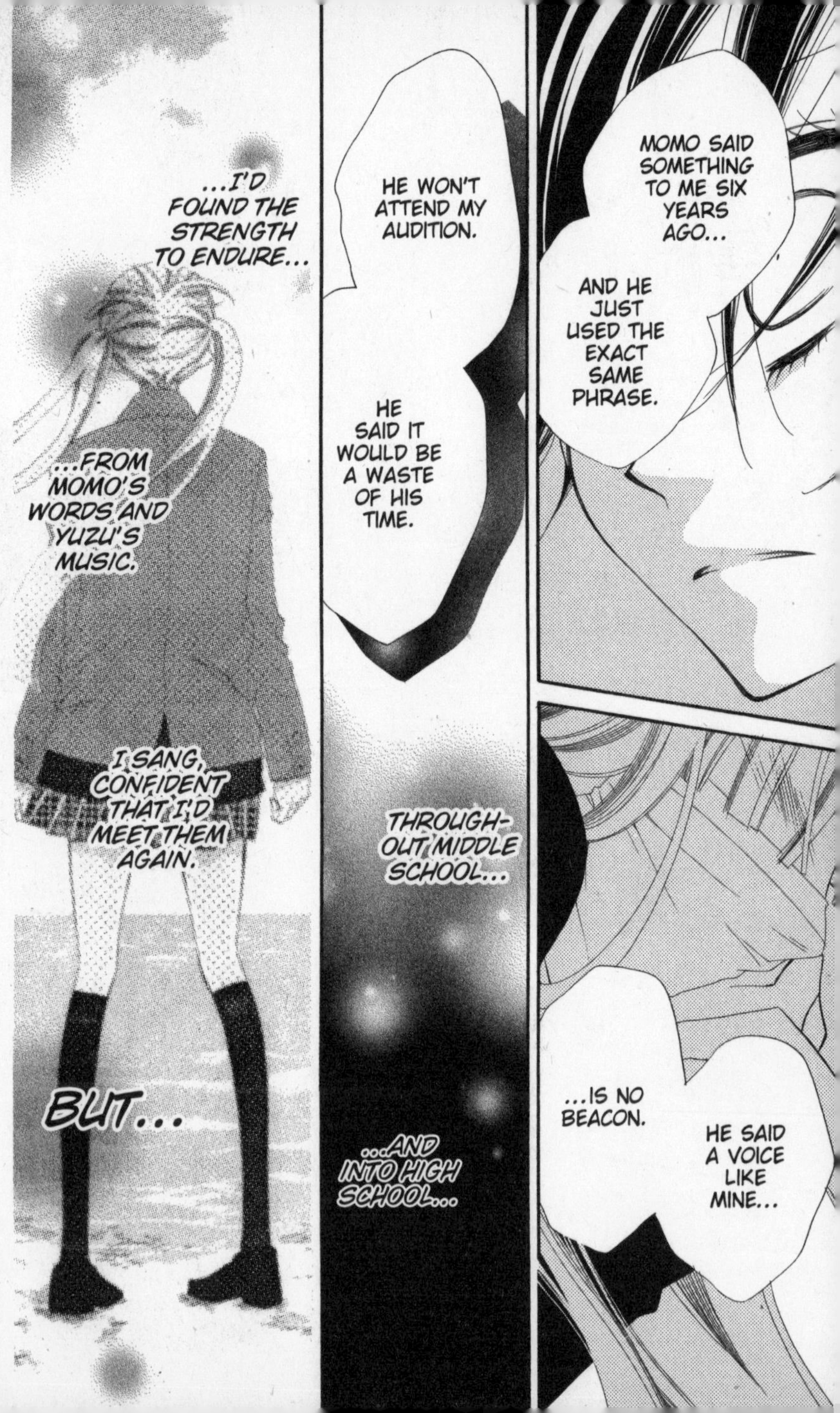
MOMO SAID SOMETHING TO ME SIX YEARS AGO...
AND HE JUST USED THE EXACT SAME PHRASE.
HE SAID A VOICE LIKE MINE...
...IS NO BEACON.
HE WON'T ATTEND MY AUDITION.
HE SAID IT WOULD BE A WASTE OF HIS TIME.
THROUGH-OUT MIDDLE SCHOOL...
...AND INTO HIGH SCHOOL...
...I'D FOUND THE STRENGTH TO ENDURE...
...FROM MOMO'S WORDS AND YUZU'S MUSIC.
I SANG, CONFIDENT THAT I'D MEET THEM AGAIN.
BUT...

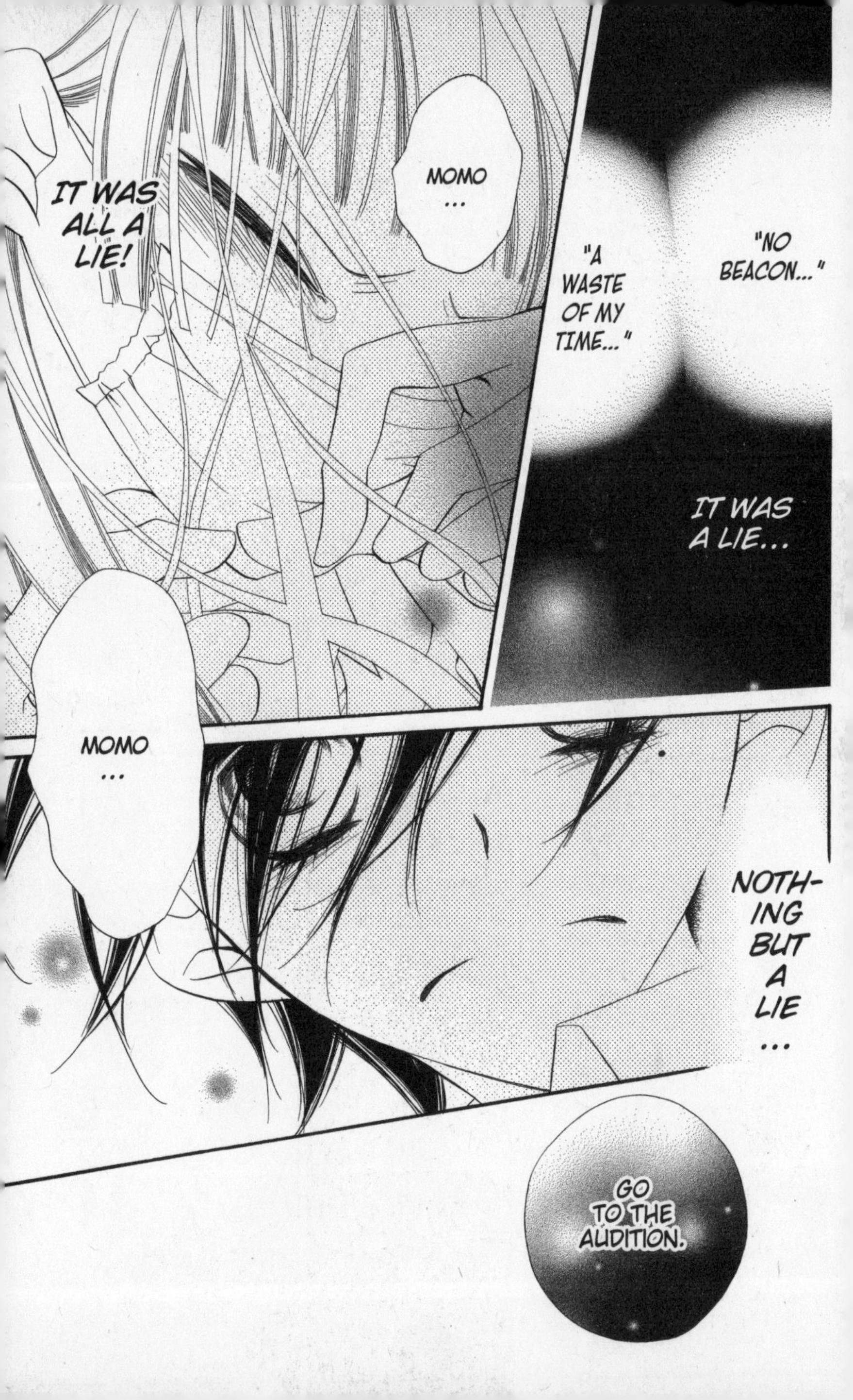
"NO BEACON..."
"A WASTE OF MY TIME..."
IT WAS A LIE...
MOMO...
IT WAS ALL A LIE!
NOTH-ING BUT A LIE...
MOMO...
GO TO THE AUDITION.

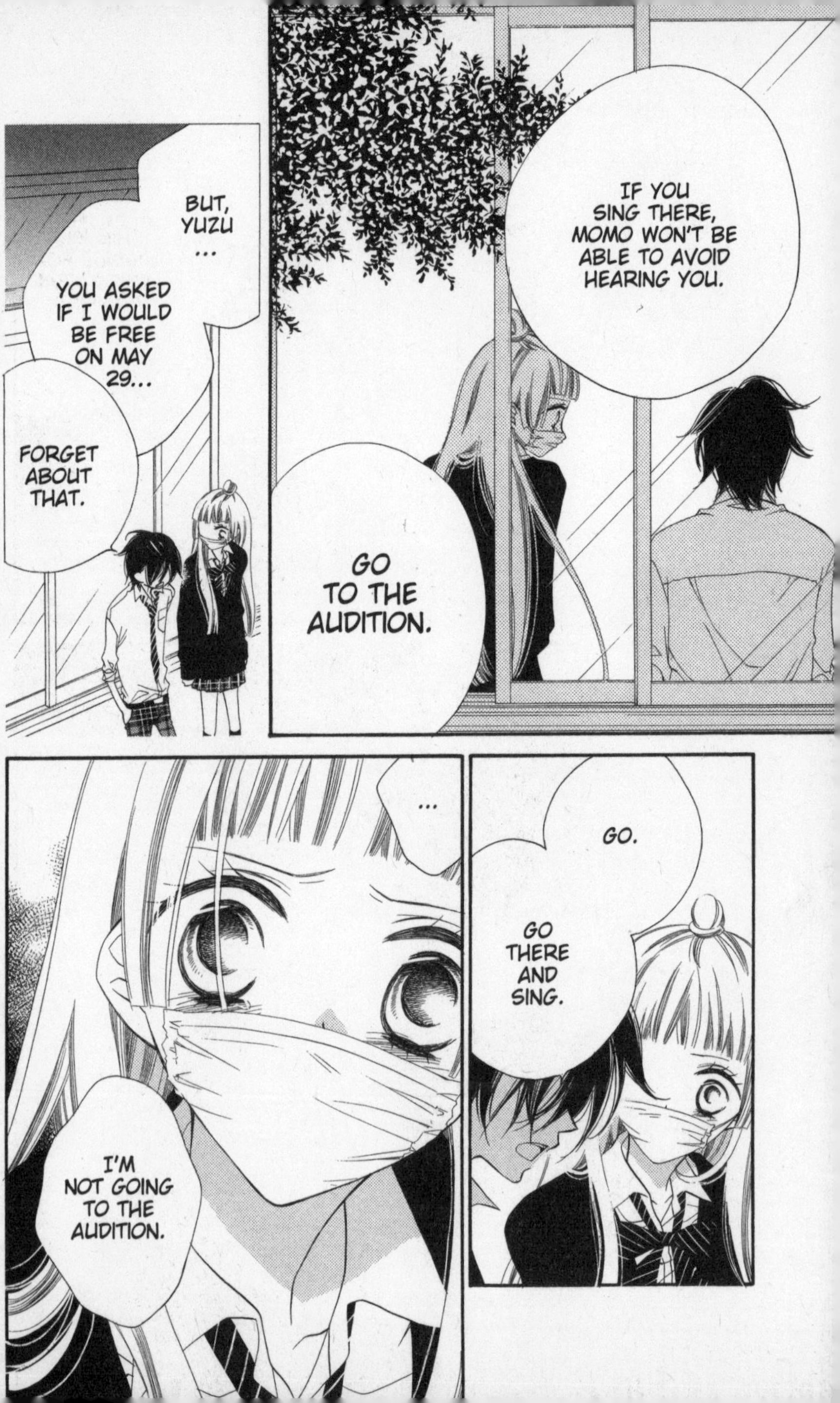
IF YOU SING THERE, MOMO WON'T BE ABLE TO AVOID HEARING YOU.
GO TO THE AUDITION.
BUT, YUZU ...
YOU ASKED IF I WOULD BE FREE ON MAY 29...
FORGET ABOUT THAT.
GO.
GO THERE AND SING.
...
I'M NOT GOING TO THE AUDITION.

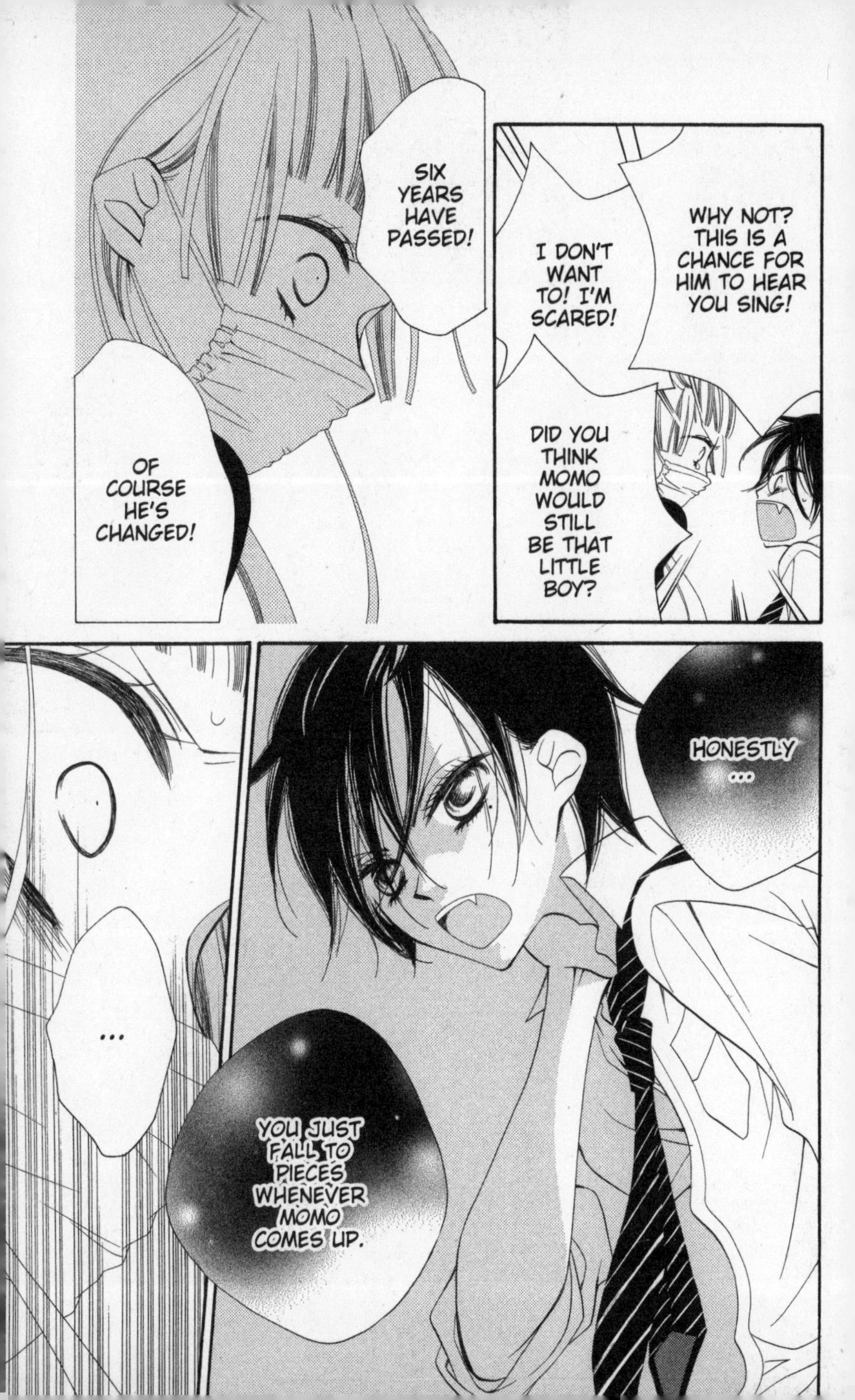

WHY NOT? THIS IS A CHANCE FOR HIM TO HEAR YOU SING!
I DON'T WANT TO! I'M SCARED!
DID YOU THINK MOMO WOULD STILL BE THAT LITTLE BOY?
SIX YEARS HAVE PASSED!
OF COURSE HE'S CHANGED!
HONESTLY...
YOU JUST FALL TO PIECES WHENEVER MOMO COMES UP.
...

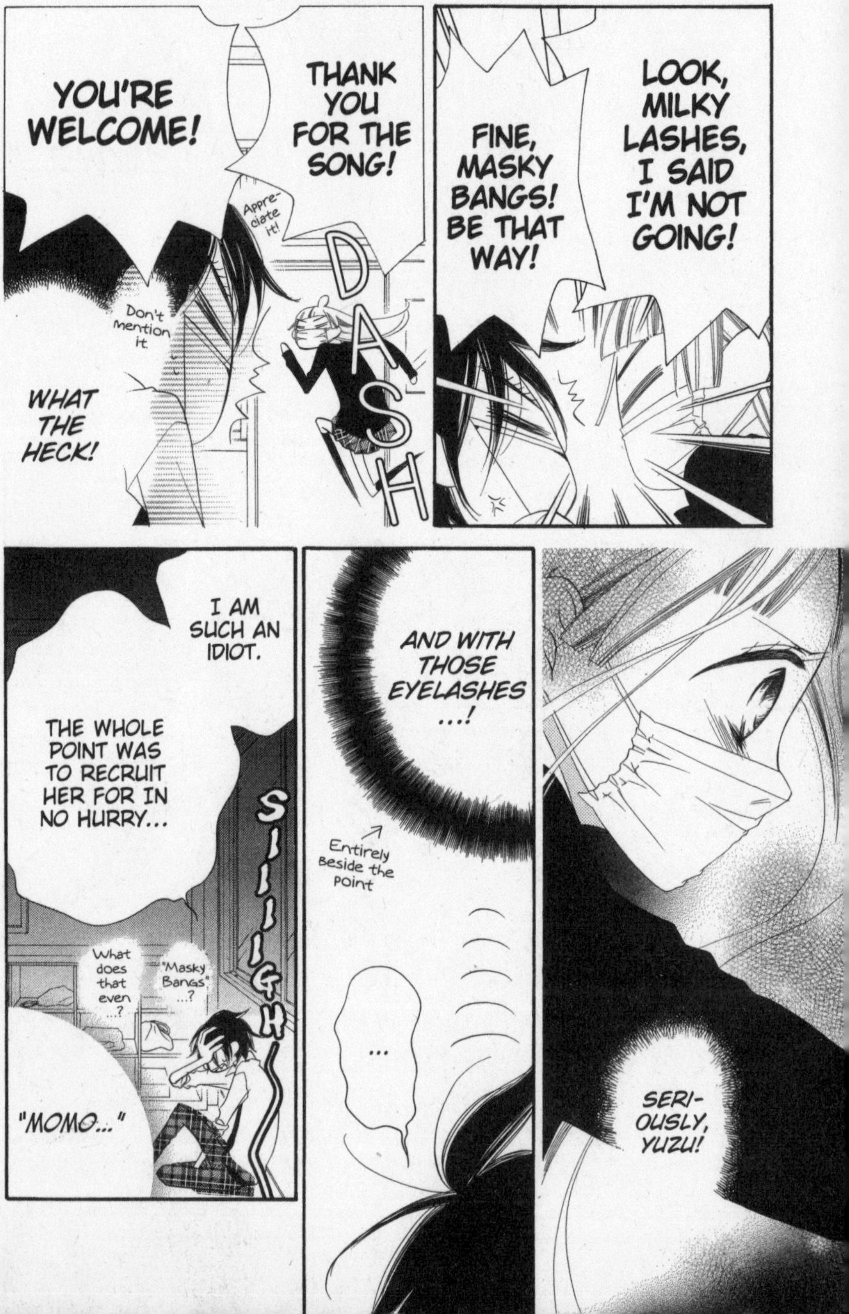
LOOK, MILKY LASHES, I SAID I'M NOT GOING!
FINE, MASKY BANGS! BE THAT WAY!
THANK YOU FOR THE SONG!
Appre-ciate it!
DASH
YOU'RE WELCOME!
Don't mention it.
WHAT THE HECK!
SERI-OUSLY, YUZU!
AND WITH THOSE EYELASHES ...!
Entirely Beside the point
...
I AM SUCH AN IDIOT.
THE WHOLE POINT WAS TO RECRUIT HER FOR IN NO HURRY...
SIIIIIGH
"Masky Bangs" ...?
What does that even ...?
"MOMO..."

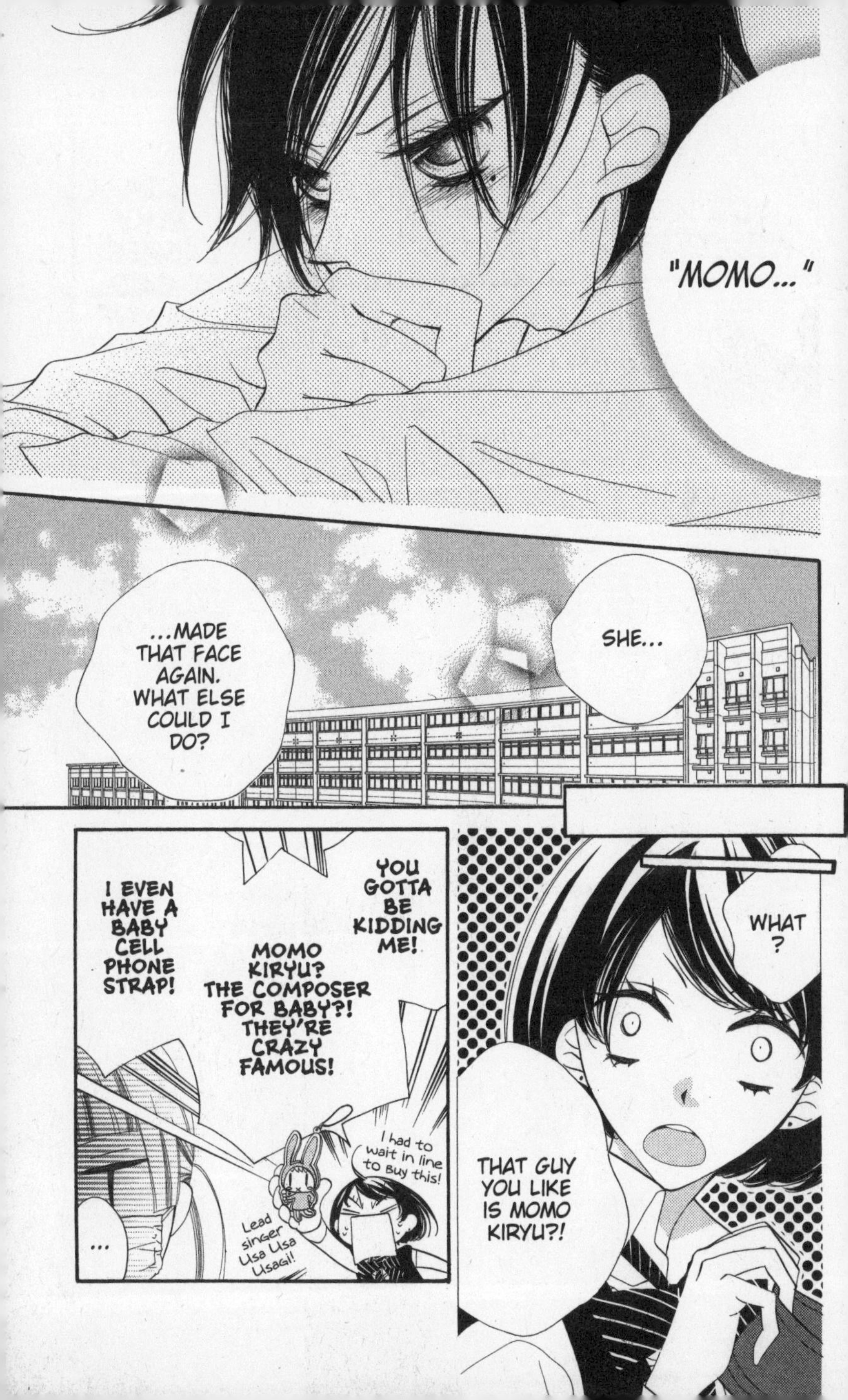
"MOMO..."
SHE...
...MADE THAT FACE AGAIN. WHAT ELSE COULD I DO?
WHAT?
THAT GUY YOU LIKE IS MOMO KIRYU?!
YOU GOTTA BE KIDDING ME!
MOMO KIRYU? THE COMPOSER FOR BABY?! THEY'RE CRAZY FAMOUS!
I EVEN HAVE A BABY CELL PHONE STRAP!
I had to wait in line to buy this!
Lead singer Usa Usa Usagi!
...

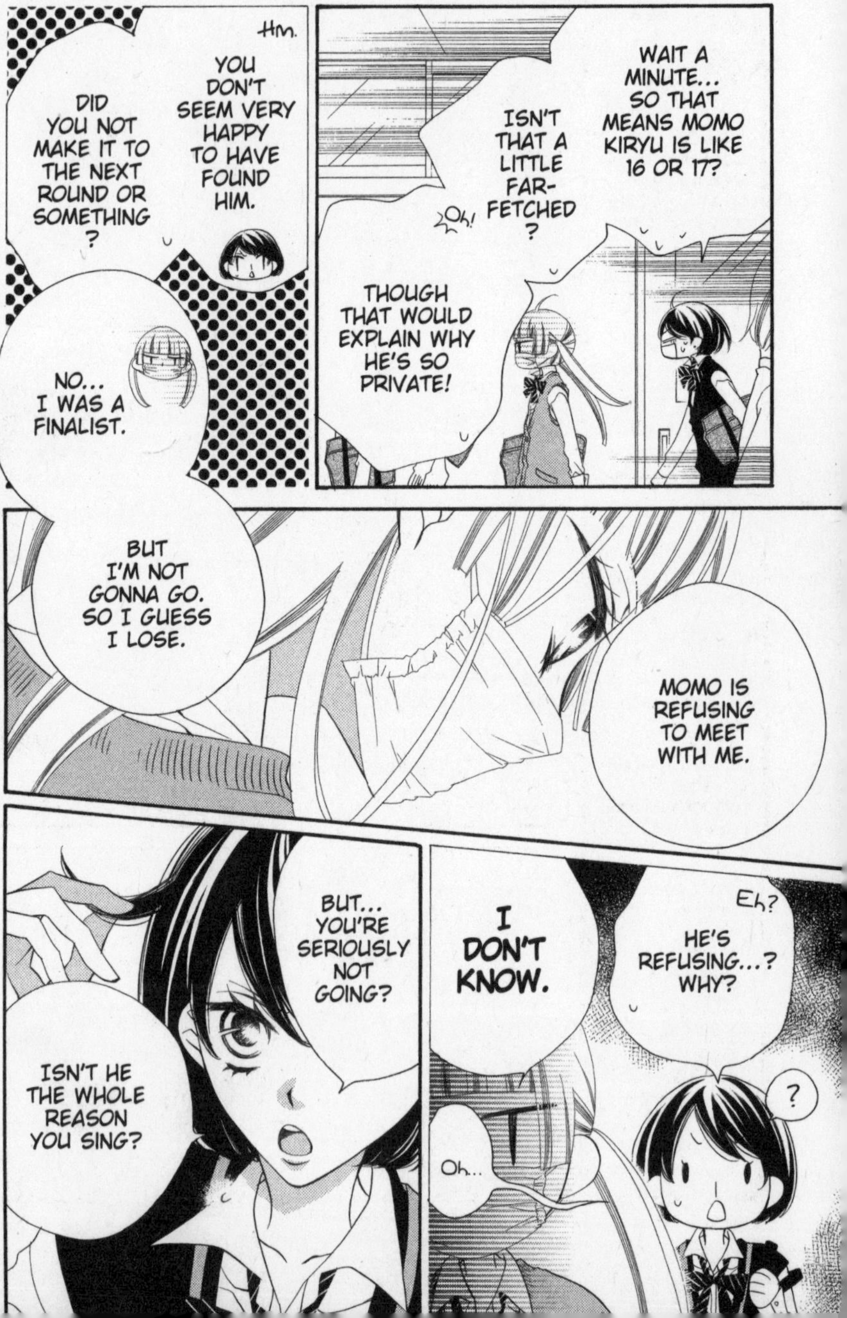
WAIT A MINUTE... SO THAT MEANS MOMO KIRYU IS LIKE 16 OR 17?
ISN'T THAT A LITTLE FAR-FETCHED?
Oh!
THOUGH THAT WOULD EXPLAIN WHY HE'S SO PRIVATE!
Hm.
YOU DON'T SEEM VERY HAPPY TO HAVE FOUND HIM.
DID YOU NOT MAKE IT TO THE NEXT ROUND OR SOMETHING?
NO... I WAS A FINALIST.
BUT I'M NOT GONNA GO. SO I GUESS I LOSE.
MOMO IS REFUSING TO MEET WITH ME.
Eh?
HE'S REFUSING...? WHY?
I DON'T KNOW.
Oh...
BUT... YOU'RE SERIOUSLY NOT GOING?
ISN'T HE THE WHOLE REASON YOU SING?

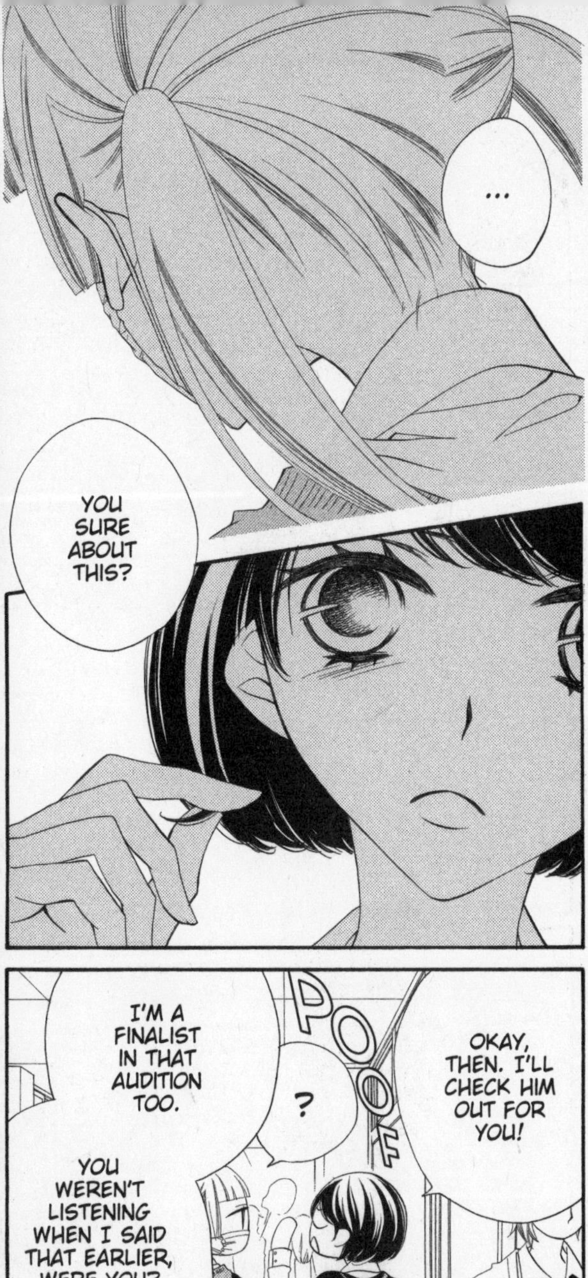
...
YOU SURE ABOUT THIS?
OKAY, THEN. I'LL CHECK HIM OUT FOR YOU!
POOF
I'M A FINALIST IN THAT AUDITION TOO.
?
YOU WEREN'T LISTENING WHEN I SAID THAT EARLIER, WERE YOU?

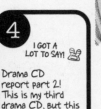

4

I GOT A LOT TO SAY!

Drama CD report part 2! This is my third drama CD, but this was the first time that the director had me speak with the cast to help them develop their characters before the recording. It was a fascinating experience!

They asked questions like "How much do Yuzu and Momo like each other?" (Sawashiro) and "Is Haruyoshi a man at heart?" (Ono). We talked more after the recording too. It goes without saying, but I have so much respect for the great work they did. During the Cast Talk segment, you can hear how enthustiastic everyone was and how they got along so well—the whole recording was like that! There were so many times when I couldn't stop laughing! I hope everyone who's heard it enjoyed it and that everyone else gets a chance to enjoy it too!

REPORT OVER! THANKS!

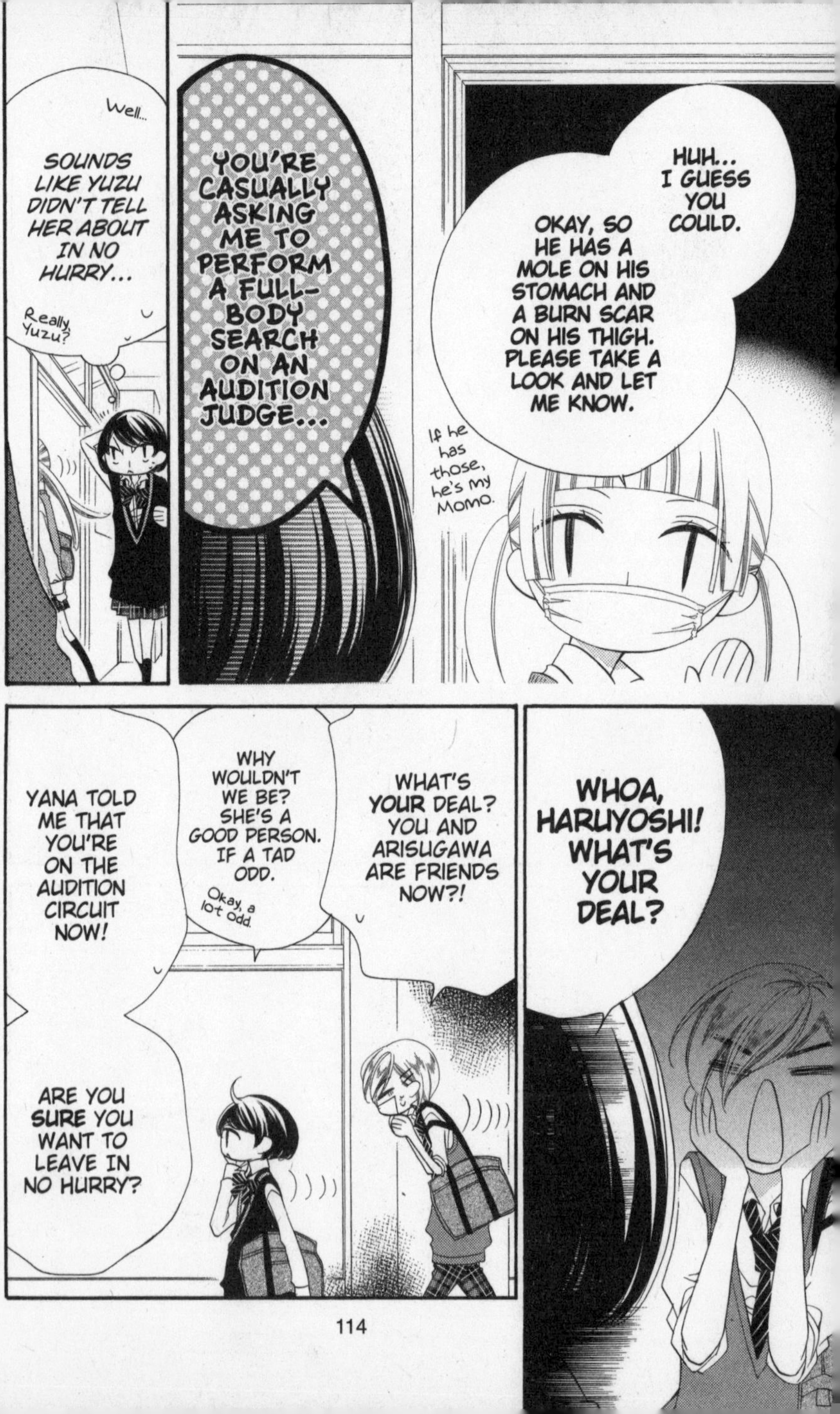
HUH... I GUESS YOU COULD.
OKAY, SO HE HAS A MOLE ON HIS STOMACH AND A BURN SCAR ON HIS THIGH. PLEASE TAKE A LOOK AND LET ME KNOW.
If he has those, he's my Momo.
YOU'RE CASUALLY ASKING ME TO PERFORM A FULL-BODY SEARCH ON AN AUDITION JUDGE...
Well...
SOUNDS LIKE YUZU DIDN'T TELL HER ABOUT IN NO HURRY...
Really, Yuzu?
WHOA, HARUYOSHI! WHAT'S YOUR DEAL?
WHAT'S YOUR DEAL? YOU AND ARISUGAWA ARE FRIENDS NOW?!
WHY WOULDN'T WE BE? SHE'S A GOOD PERSON. IF A TAD ODD.
Okay, a lot odd.
YANA TOLD ME THAT YOU'RE ON THE AUDITION CIRCUIT NOW!
ARE YOU SURE YOU WANT TO LEAVE IN NO HURRY?

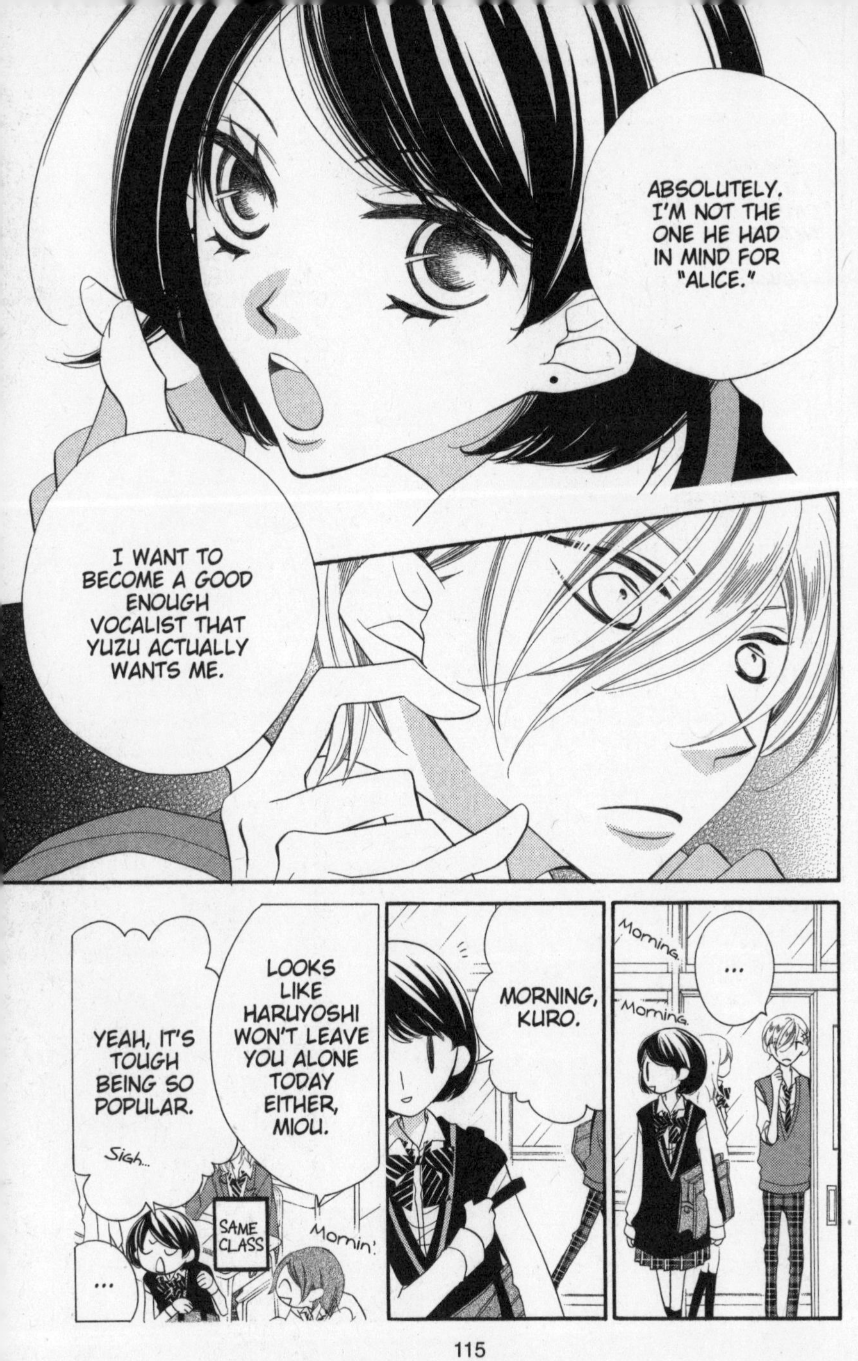
ABSOLUTELY. I'M NOT THE ONE HE HAD IN MIND FOR "ALICE."
I WANT TO BECOME A GOOD ENOUGH VOCALIST THAT YUZU ACTUALLY WANTS ME.
Morning.
Morning.
...
MORNING, KURO.
LOOKS LIKE HARUYOSHI WON'T LEAVE YOU ALONE TODAY EITHER, MIOU.
YEAH, IT'S TOUGH BEING SO POPULAR.
Sigh...
SAME CLASS
Mornin'
...

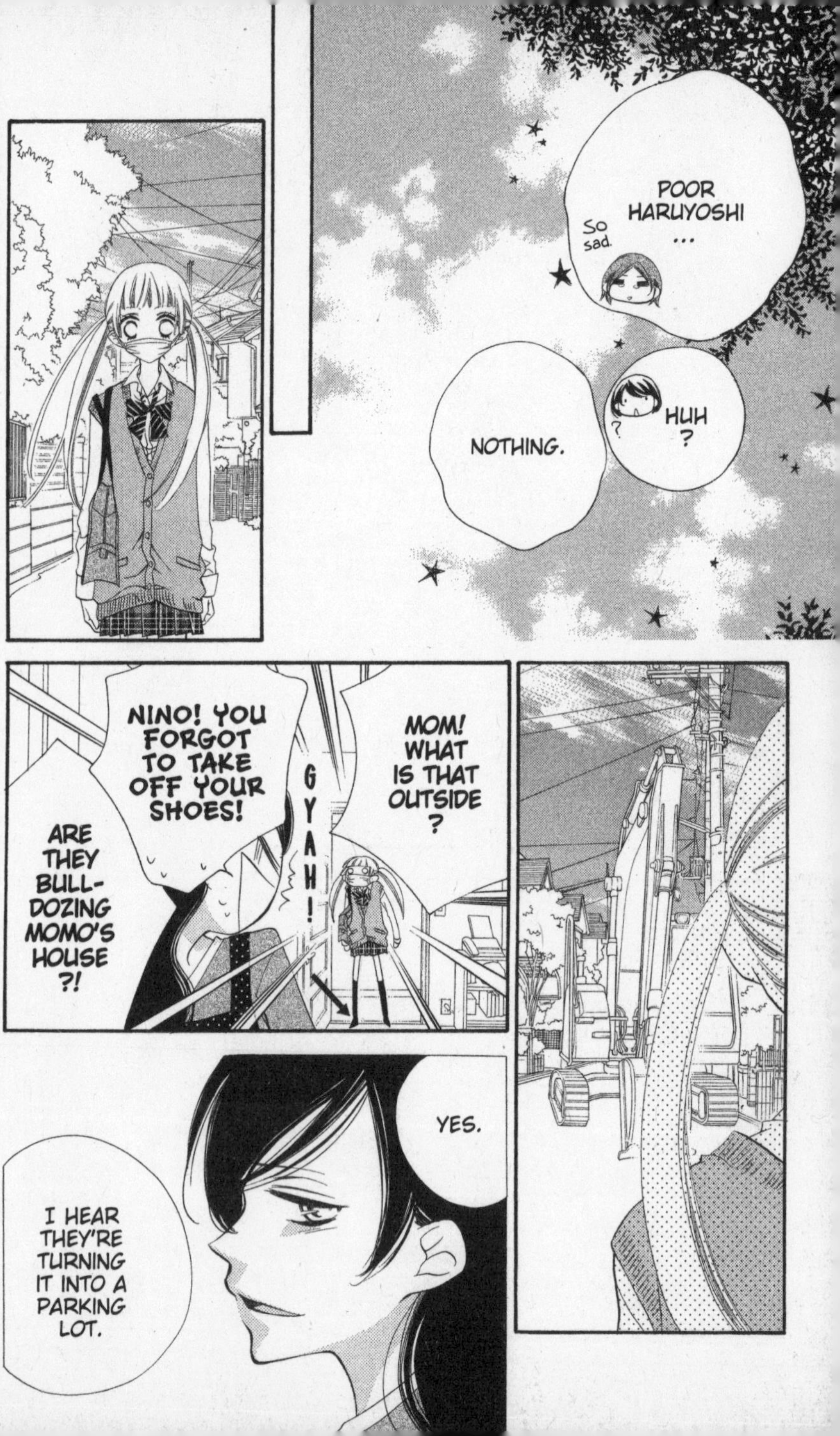
POOR HARUYOSHI ...
So sad.
HUH ?
NOTHING.
MOM! WHAT IS THAT OUTSIDE ?
GYAH!
NINO! YOU FORGOT TO TAKE OFF YOUR SHOES!
ARE THEY BULL-DOZING MOMO'S HOUSE ?!
YES.
I HEAR THEY'RE TURNING IT INTO A PARKING LOT.

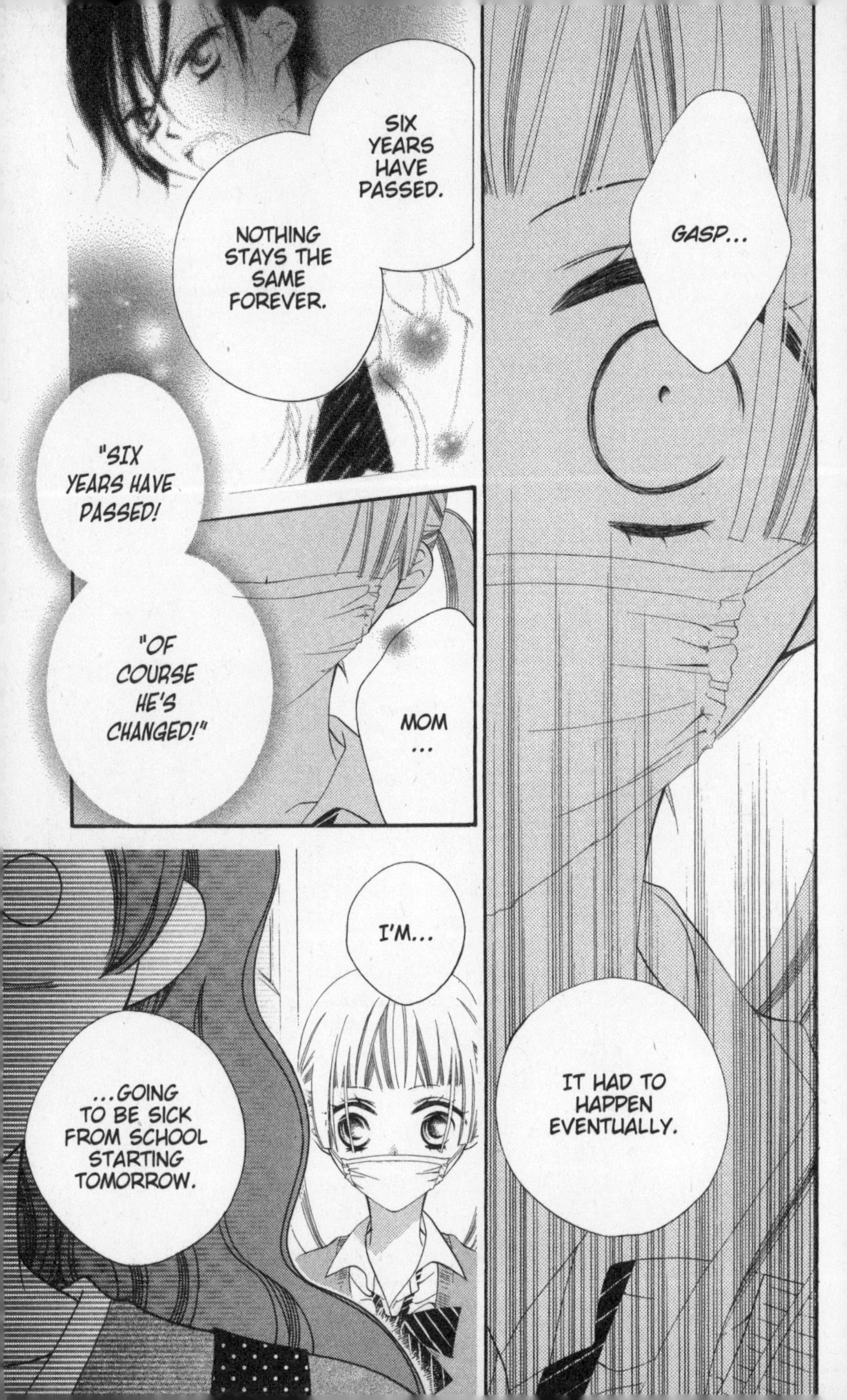
GASP...
IT HAD TO HAPPEN EVENTUALLY.
SIX YEARS HAVE PASSED.
NOTHING STAYS THE SAME FOREVER.
"SIX YEARS HAVE PASSED!
"OF COURSE HE'S CHANGED!"
MOM ...
I'M...
...GOING TO BE SICK FROM SCHOOL STARTING TOMORROW.

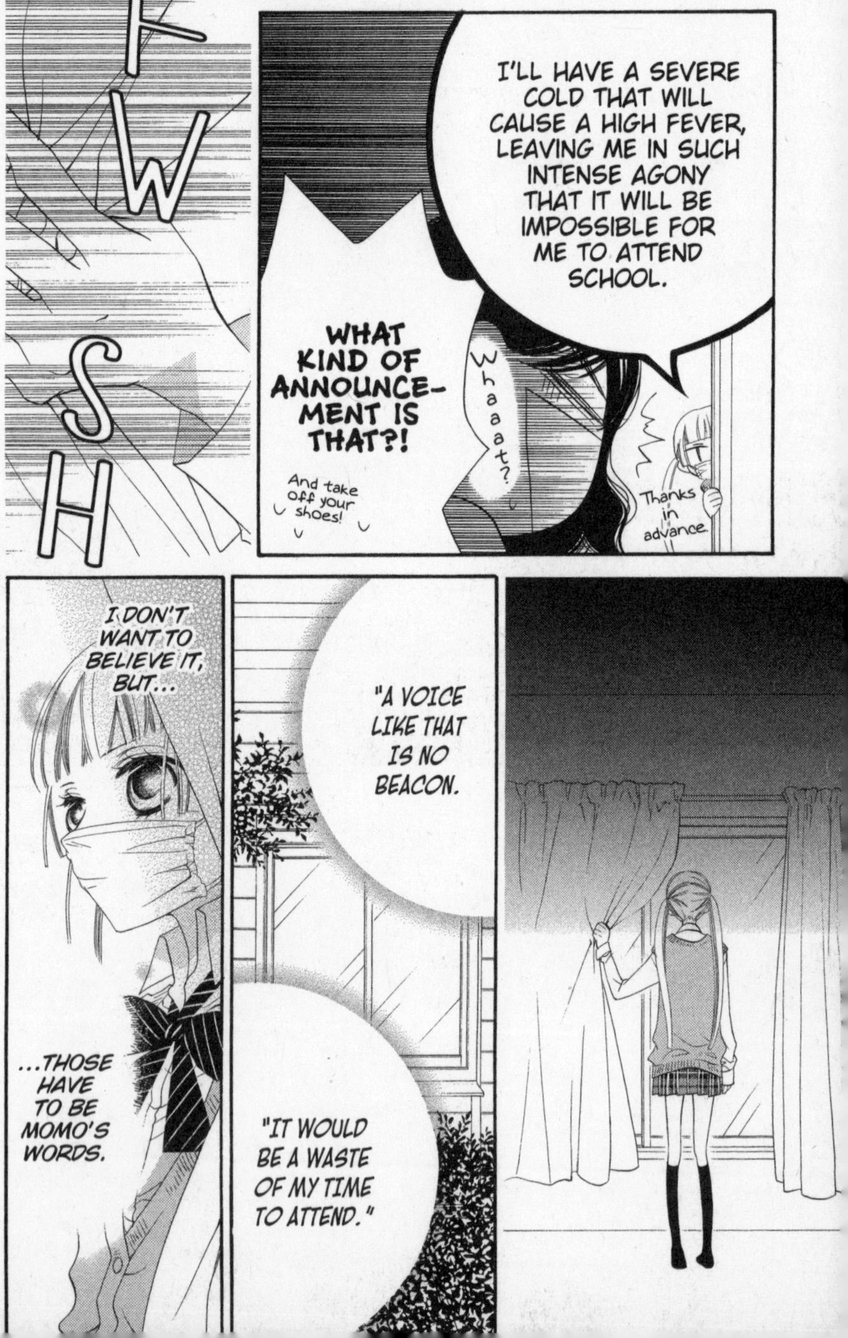
I'LL HAVE A SEVERE COLD THAT WILL CAUSE A HIGH FEVER, LEAVING ME IN SUCH INTENSE AGONY THAT IT WILL BE IMPOSSIBLE FOR ME TO ATTEND SCHOOL.
Thanks in advance
Whaaat?
WHAT KIND OF ANNOUNCE-MENT IS THAT?!
And take off your shoes!
FWSH
"A VOICE LIKE THAT IS NO BEACON.
"IT WOULD BE A WASTE OF MY TIME TO ATTEND."
I DON'T WANT TO BELIEVE IT, BUT...
...THOSE HAVE TO BE MOMO'S WORDS.

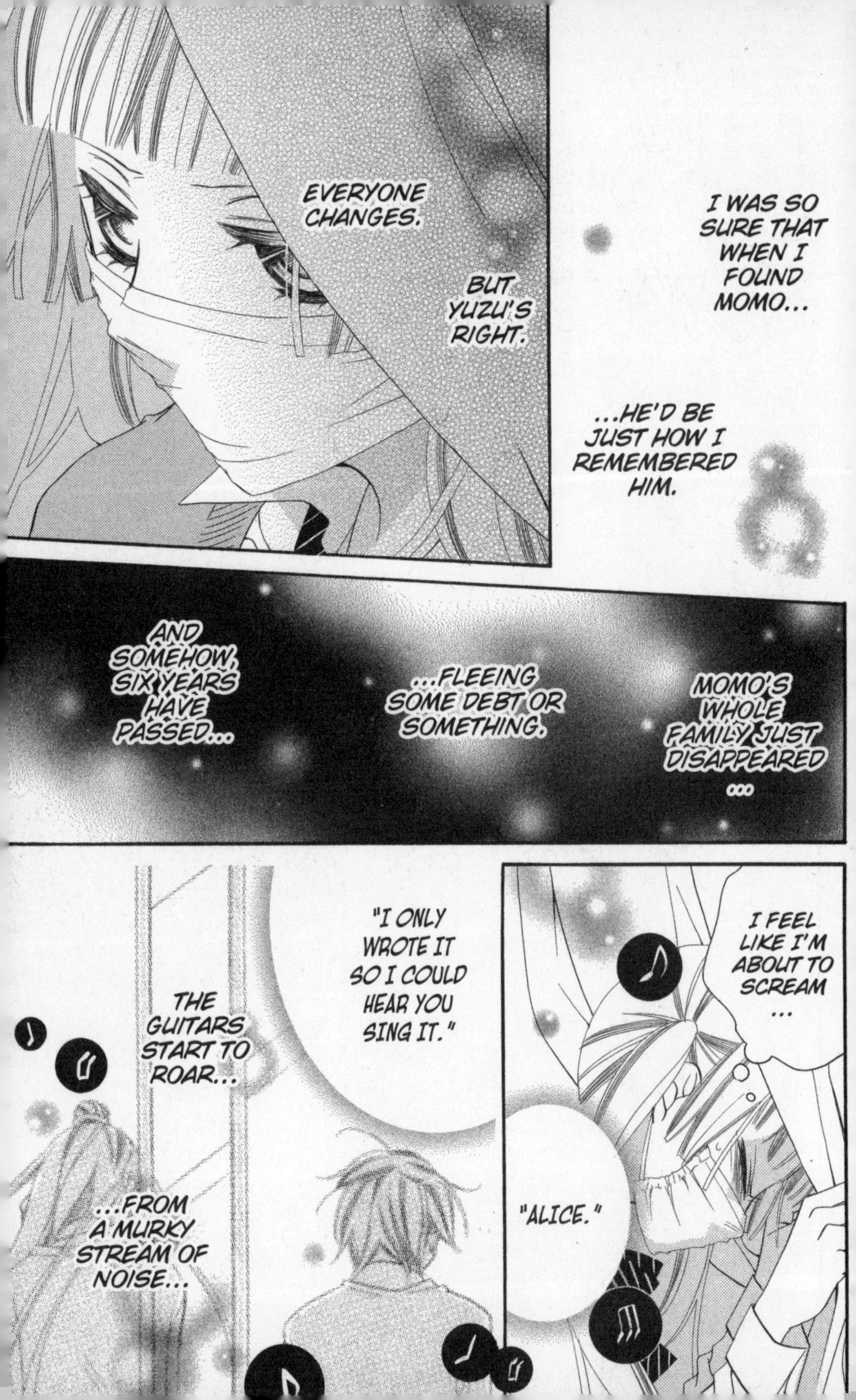
I WAS SO SURE THAT WHEN I FOUND MOMO...
...HE'D BE JUST HOW I REMEMBERED HIM.
BUT YUZU'S RIGHT.
EVERYONE CHANGES.
MOMO'S WHOLE FAMILY JUST DISAPPEARED...
...FLEEING SOME DEBT OR SOMETHING.
AND SOMEHOW, SIX YEARS HAVE PASSED...
I FEEL LIKE I'M ABOUT TO SCREAM...
"ALICE."
"I ONLY WROTE IT SO I COULD HEAR YOU SING IT."
THE GUITARS START TO ROAR...
...FROM A MURKY STREAM OF NOISE...

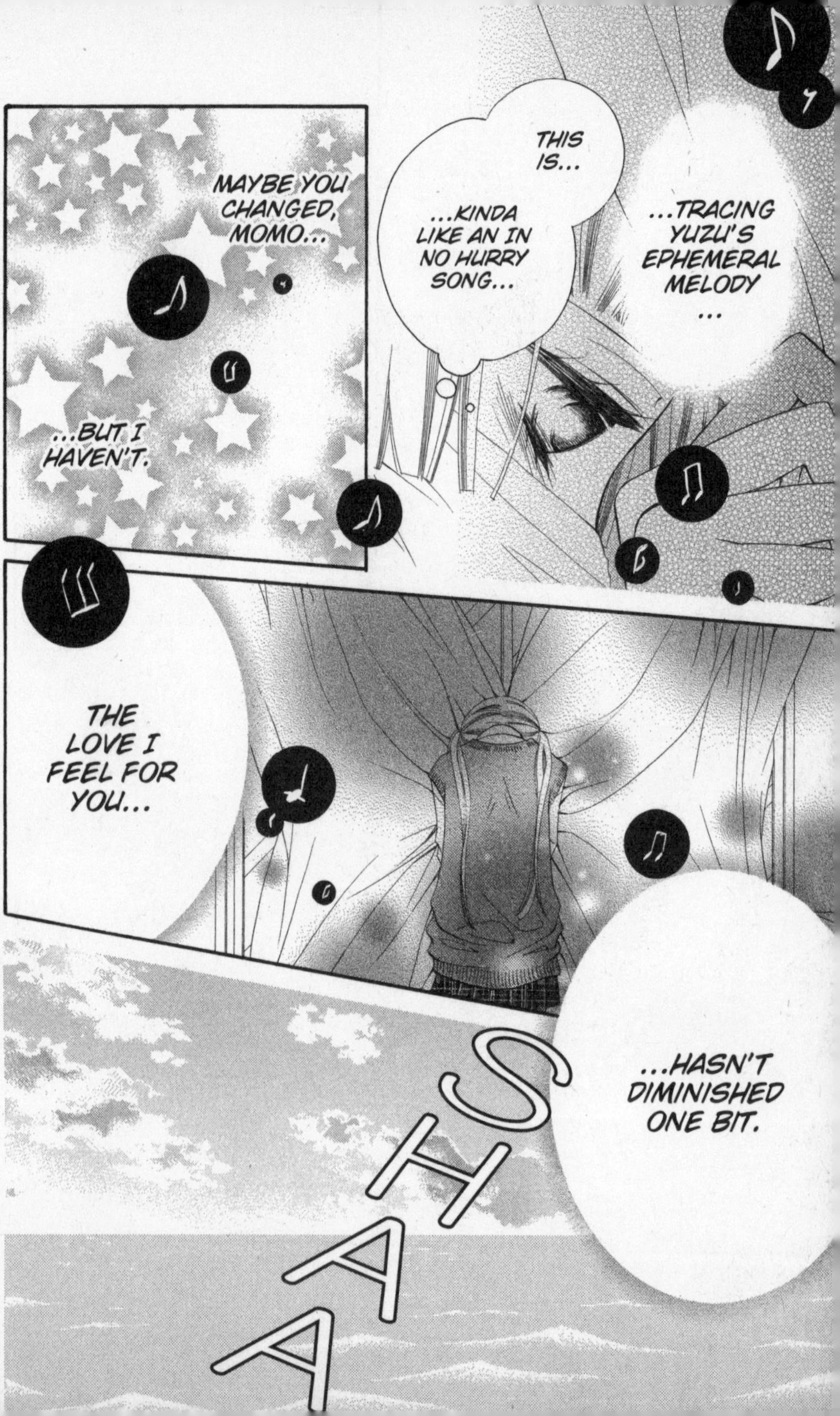
...TRACING YUZU'S EPHEMERAL MELODY...
THIS IS...
...KINDA LIKE AN IN NO HURRY SONG...
MAYBE YOU CHANGED, MOMO...
...BUT I HAVEN'T.
THE LOVE I FEEL FOR YOU...
...HASN'T DIMINISHED ONE BIT.
SHAA

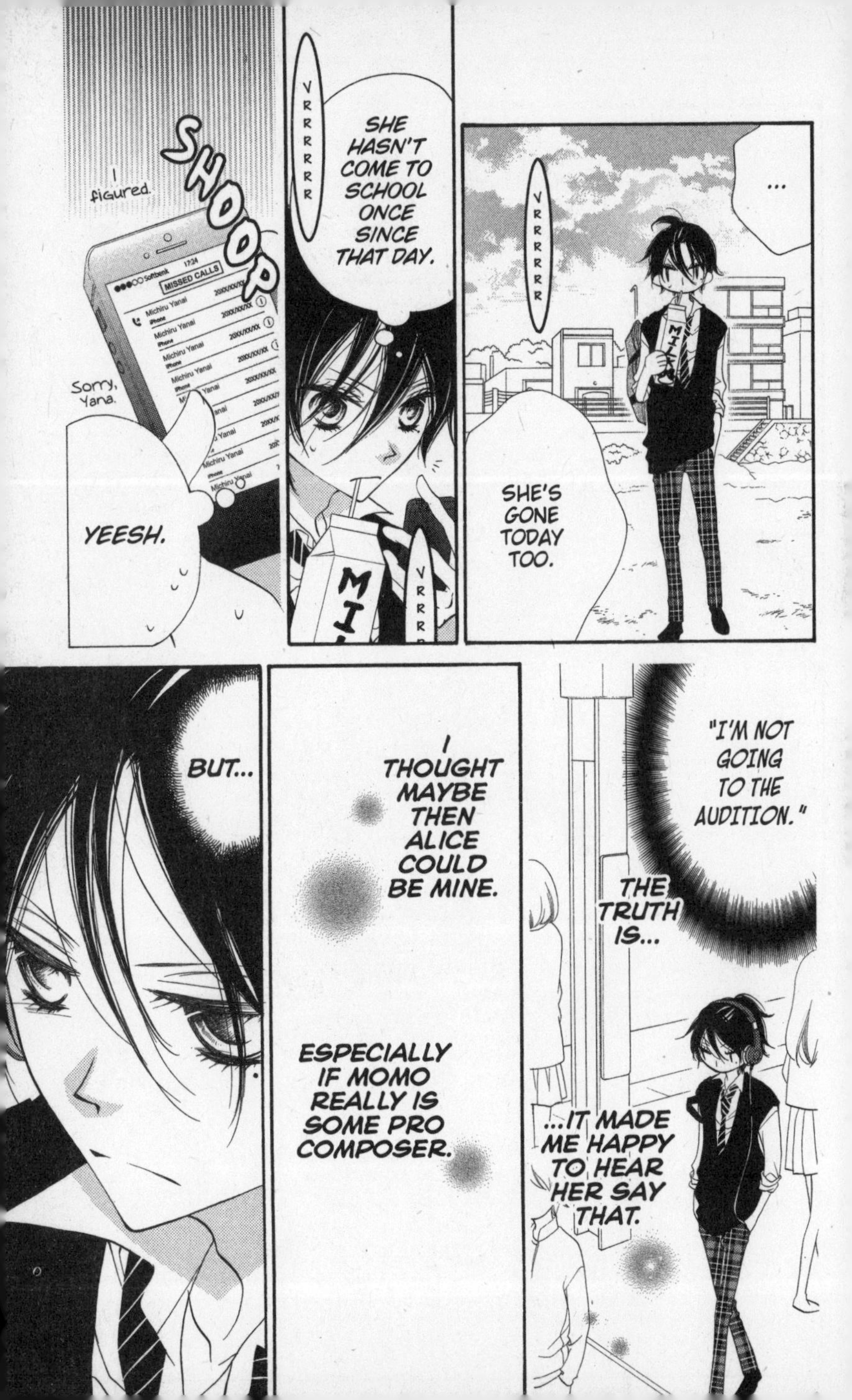
...
VRRRRR
SHE'S GONE TODAY TOO.
VRRRRR
SHE HASN'T COME TO SCHOOL ONCE SINCE THAT DAY.
VRRR
SHOOP
I figured.
Softbank 17:24
MISSED CALLS
Michiru Yanai
Michiru Yanai
Michiru Yanai
Michiru Yanai
Michiru Yanai
Michiru Yanai
Sorry, Yana.
YEESH.
"I'M NOT GOING TO THE AUDITION."
THE TRUTH IS...
...IT MADE ME HAPPY TO HEAR HER SAY THAT.
I THOUGHT MAYBE THEN ALICE COULD BE MINE.
ESPECIALLY IF MOMO REALLY IS SOME PRO COMPOSER.
BUT...

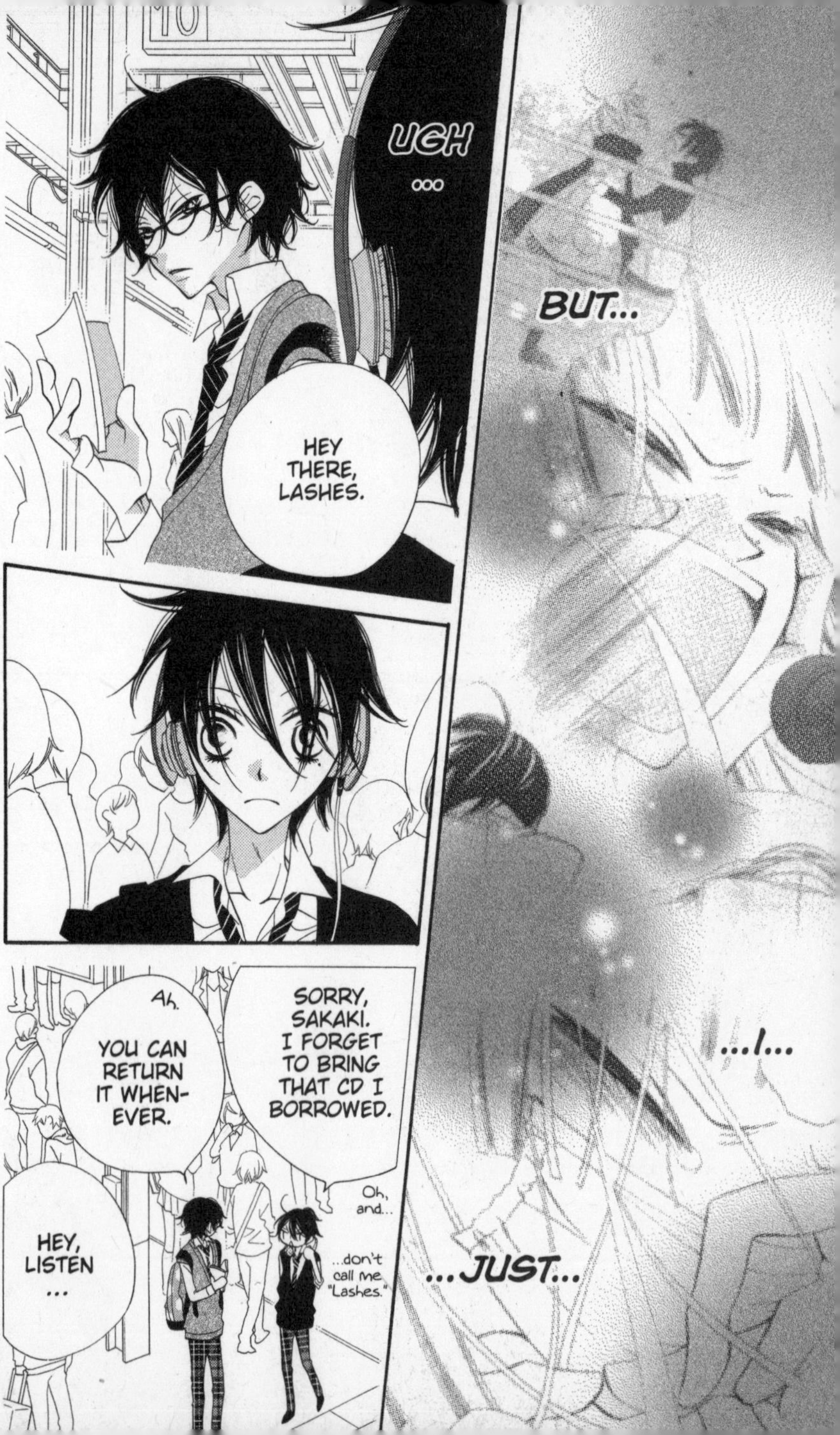
BUT...
...I...
...JUST...
UGH ...
HEY THERE, LASHES.
SORRY, SAKAKI. I FORGET TO BRING THAT CD I BORROWED.
Ah.
YOU CAN RETURN IT WHEN-EVER.
Oh, and...
...don't call me "Lashes."
HEY, LISTEN ...

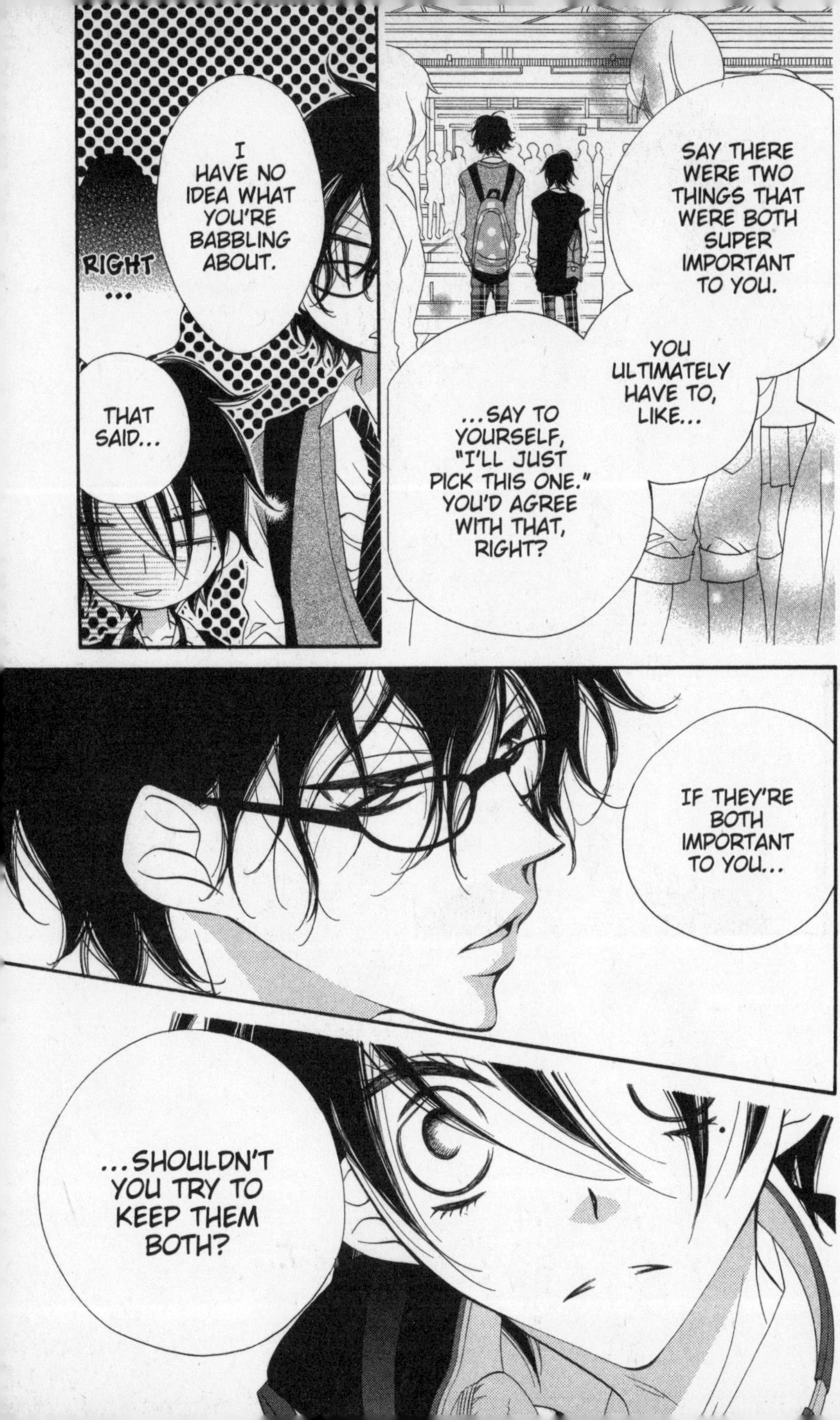
SAY THERE WERE TWO THINGS THAT WERE BOTH SUPER IMPORTANT TO YOU.
YOU ULTIMATELY HAVE TO, LIKE...
...SAY TO YOURSELF, "I'LL JUST PICK THIS ONE." YOU'D AGREE WITH THAT, RIGHT?
I HAVE NO IDEA WHAT YOU'RE BABBLING ABOUT.
RIGHT...
THAT SAID...
IF THEY'RE BOTH IMPORTANT TO YOU...
...SHOULDN'T YOU TRY TO KEEP THEM BOTH?

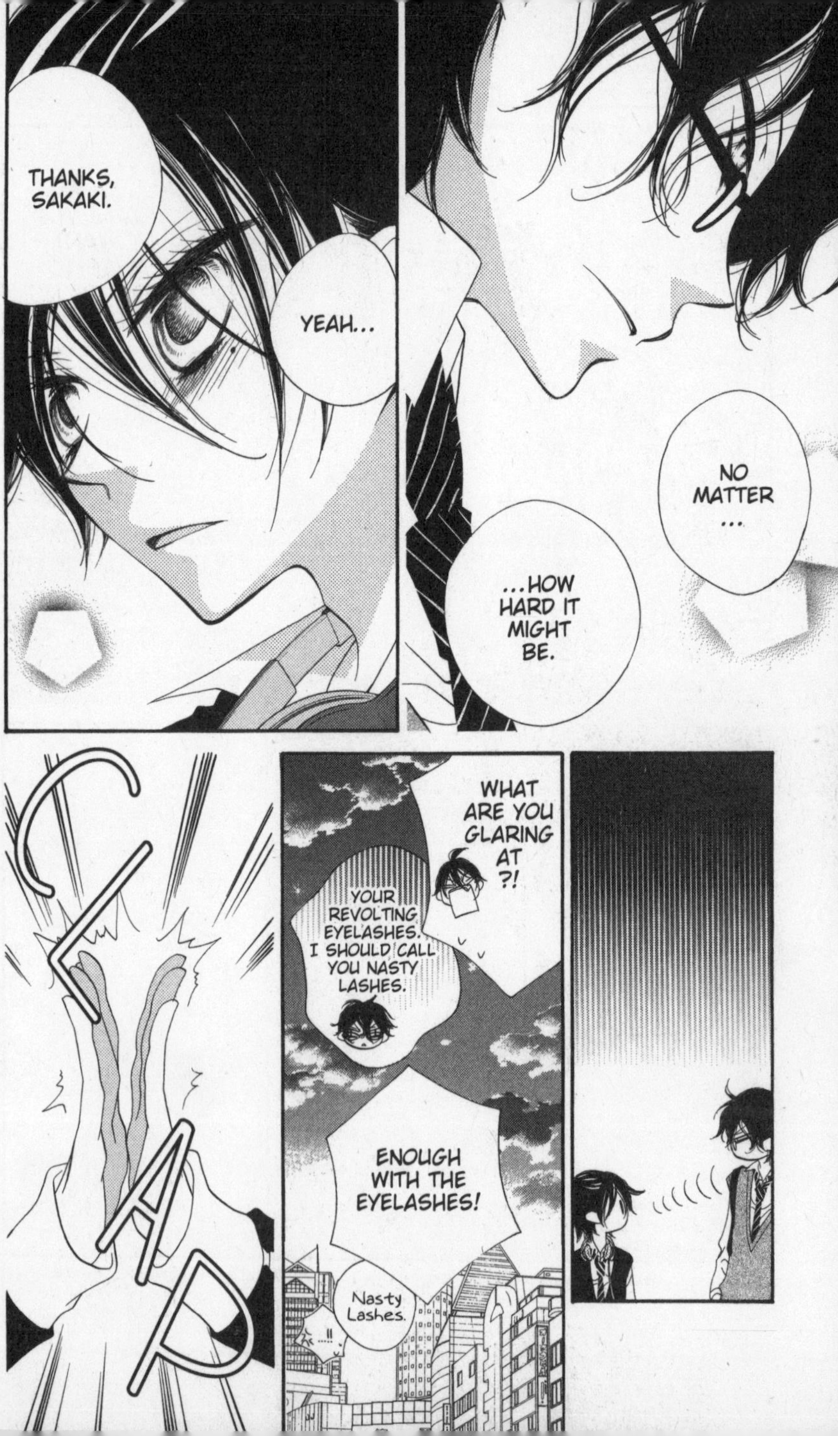
NO MATTER ...
...HOW HARD IT MIGHT BE.
THANKS, SAKAKI.
YEAH...
WHAT ARE YOU GLARING AT ?!
YOUR REVOLTING EYELASHES. I SHOULD CALL YOU NASTY LASHES.
ENOUGH WITH THE EYELASHES!
Nasty Lashes.
CLAP

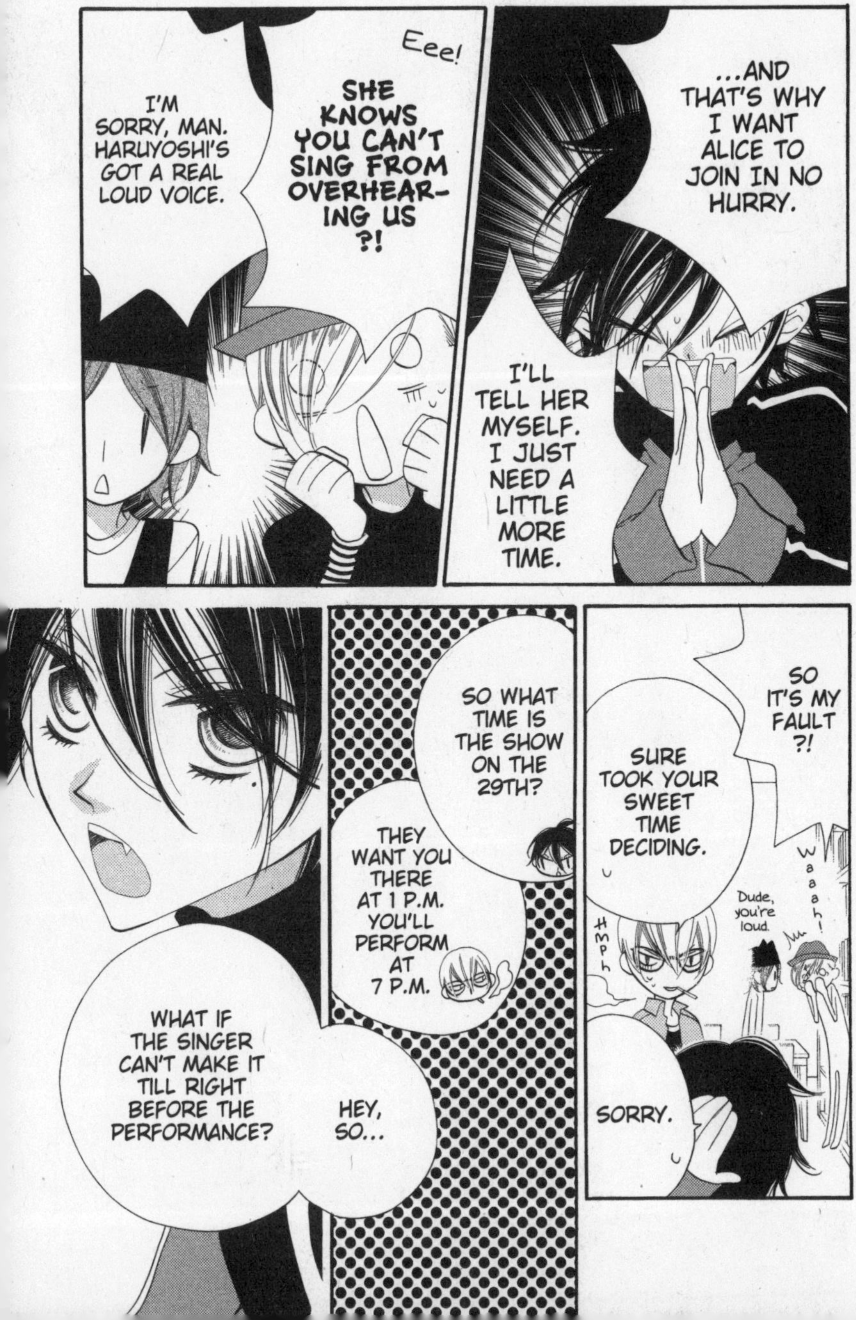
...AND THAT'S WHY I WANT ALICE TO JOIN IN NO HURRY.
I'LL TELL HER MYSELF. I JUST NEED A LITTLE MORE TIME.
Eee!
SHE KNOWS YOU CAN'T SING FROM OVERHEARING US ?!
I'M SORRY, MAN. HARUYOSHI'S GOT A REAL LOUD VOICE.
SO IT'S MY FAULT ?!
SURE TOOK YOUR SWEET TIME DECIDING.
Waaah!
Dude, you're loud.
Hmph
SORRY.
SO WHAT TIME IS THE SHOW ON THE 29TH?
THEY WANT YOU THERE AT 1 P.M. YOU'LL PERFORM AT 7 P.M.
HEY, SO...
WHAT IF THE SINGER CAN'T MAKE IT TILL RIGHT BEFORE THE PERFORMANCE?

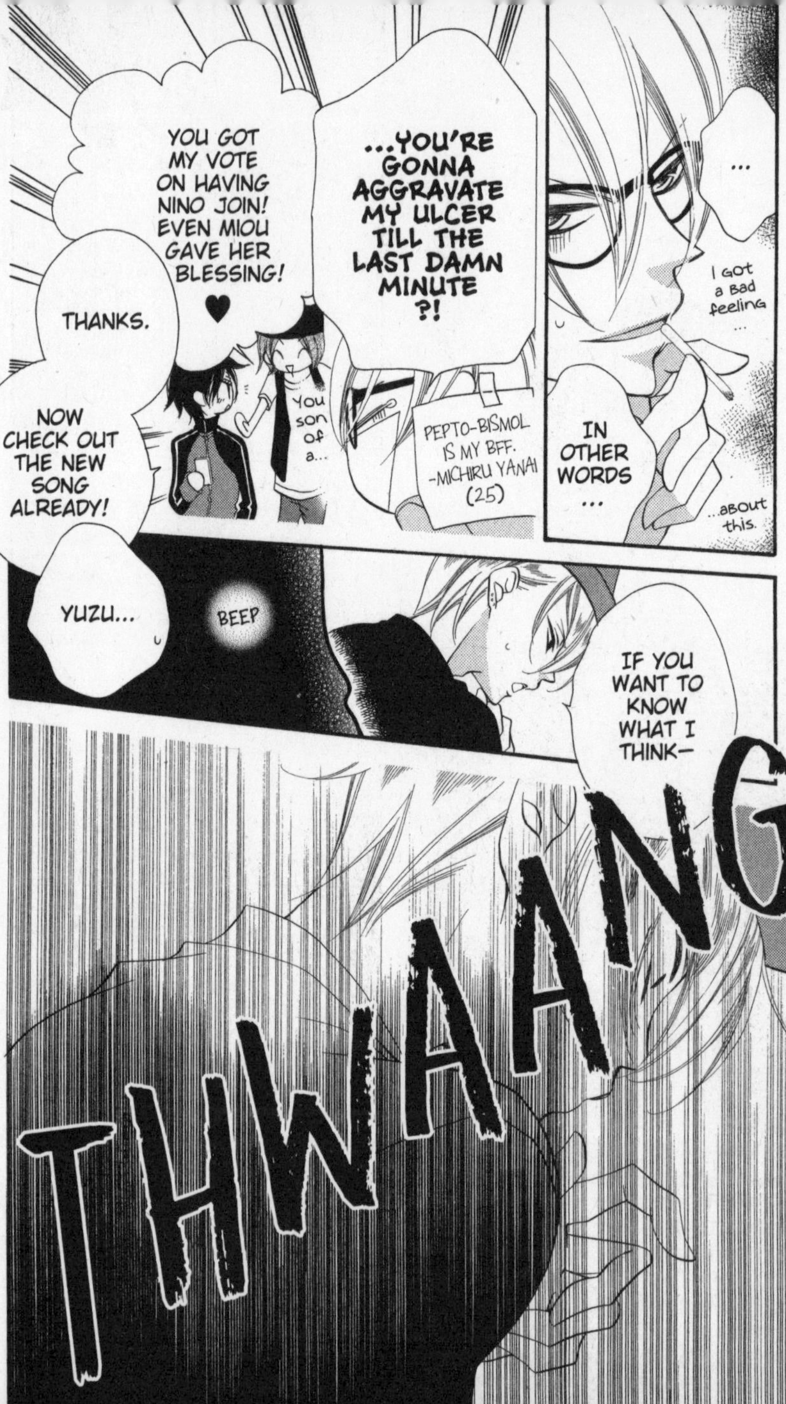
...
I got a bad feeling...
IN OTHER WORDS...
...about this.
...YOU'RE GONNA AGGRAVATE MY ULCER TILL THE LAST DAMN MINUTE?!
YOU GOT MY VOTE ON HAVING NINO JOIN! EVEN MIOU GAVE HER BLESSING! ♥
You son of a...
PEPTO-BISMOL IS MY BFF. -MICHIRU YANAI (25)
THANKS.
NOW CHECK OUT THE NEW SONG ALREADY!
IF YOU WANT TO KNOW WHAT I THINK—
BEEP
YUZU...
THWAANG

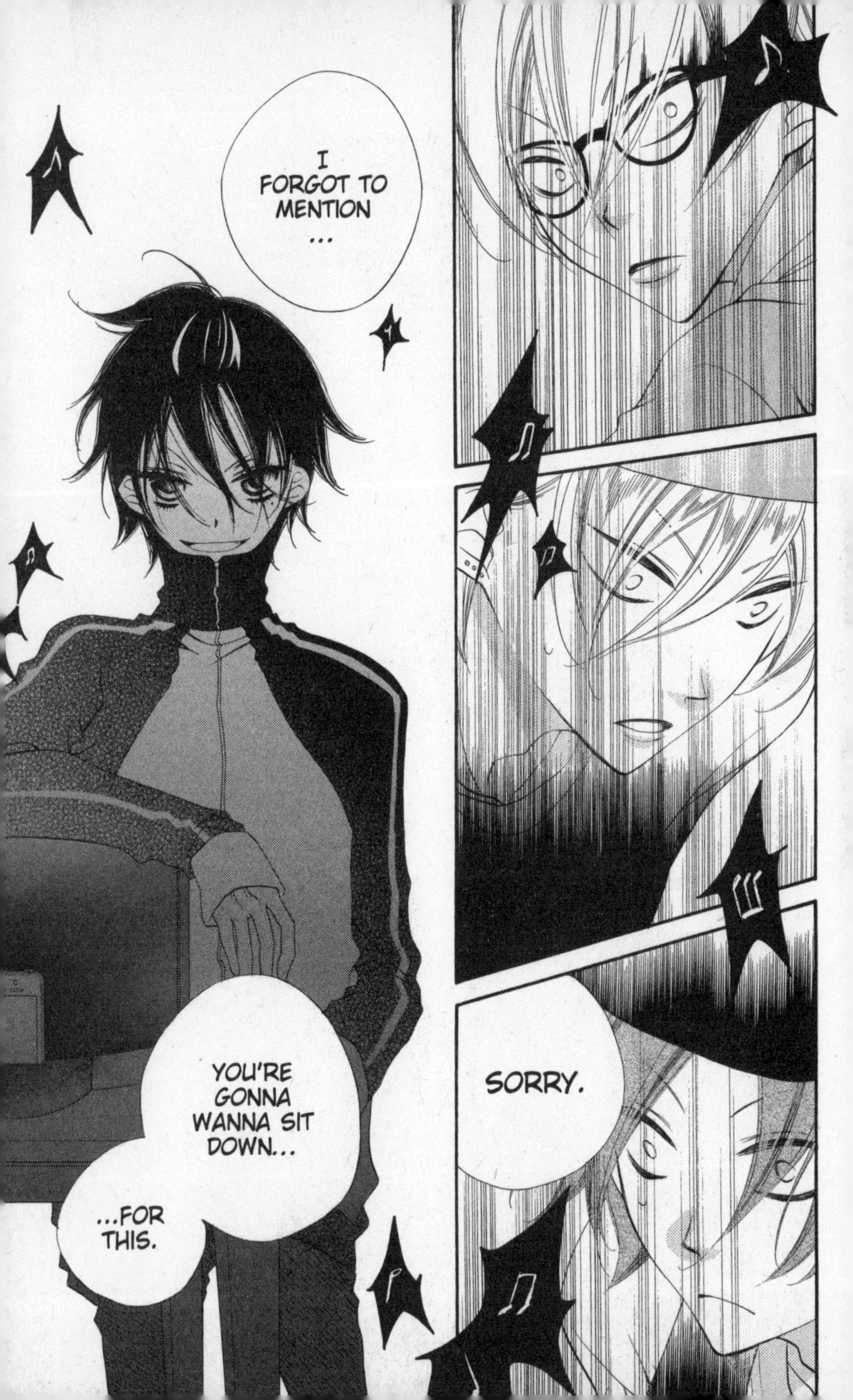
SORRY.
I FORGOT TO MENTION...
YOU'RE GONNA WANNA SIT DOWN...
...FOR THIS.

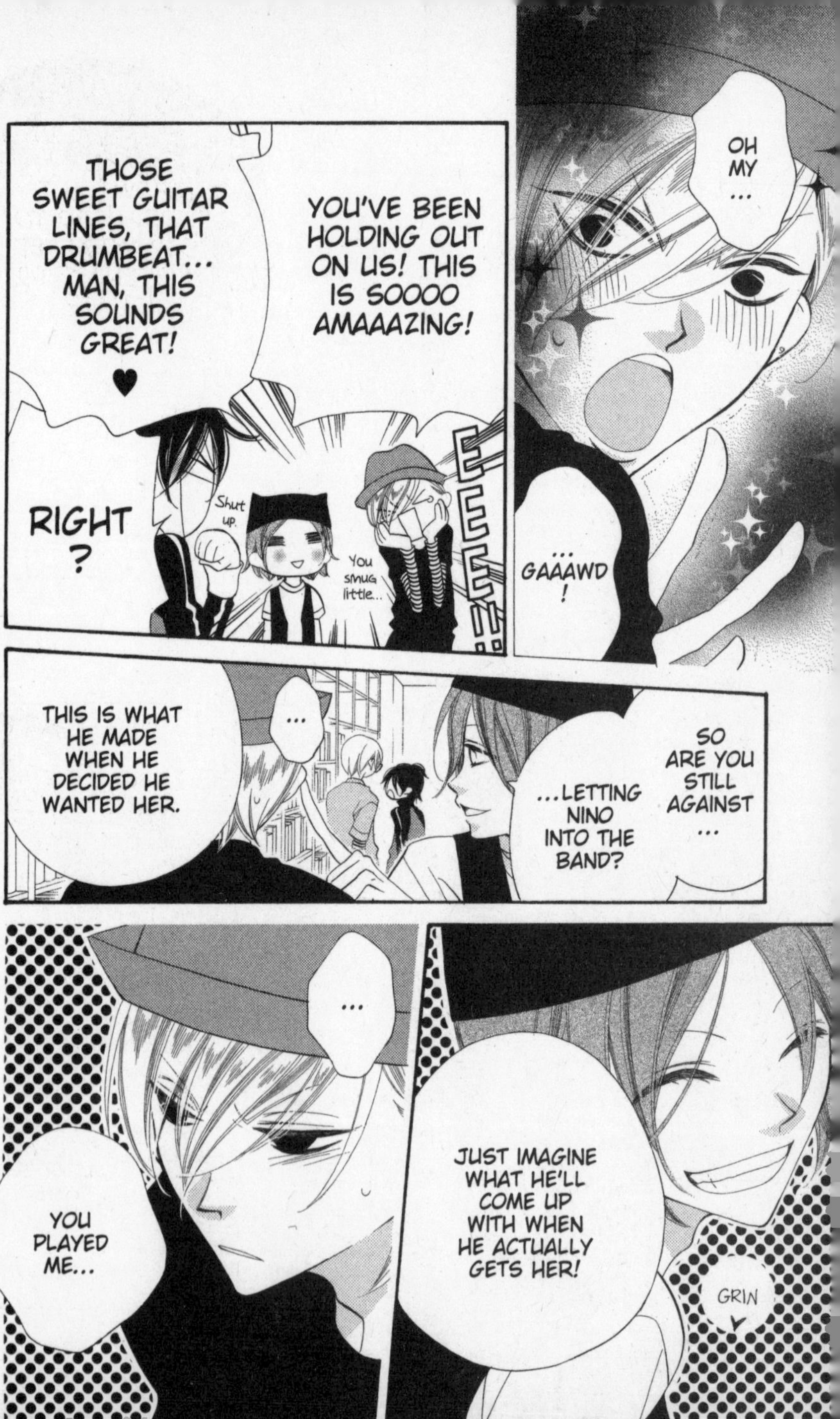
OH MY...
...GAAAWD!
YOU'VE BEEN HOLDING OUT ON US! THIS IS SOOOO AMAAAZING!
THOSE SWEET GUITAR LINES, THAT DRUMBEAT... MAN, THIS SOUNDS GREAT! ♥
EEEE!!
You smug little...
Shut up.
RIGHT?
SO ARE YOU STILL AGAINST...
...LETTING NINO INTO THE BAND?
...
THIS IS WHAT HE MADE WHEN HE DECIDED HE WANTED HER.
JUST IMAGINE WHAT HE'LL COME UP WITH WHEN HE ACTUALLY GETS HER!
GRIN
...
YOU PLAYED ME...

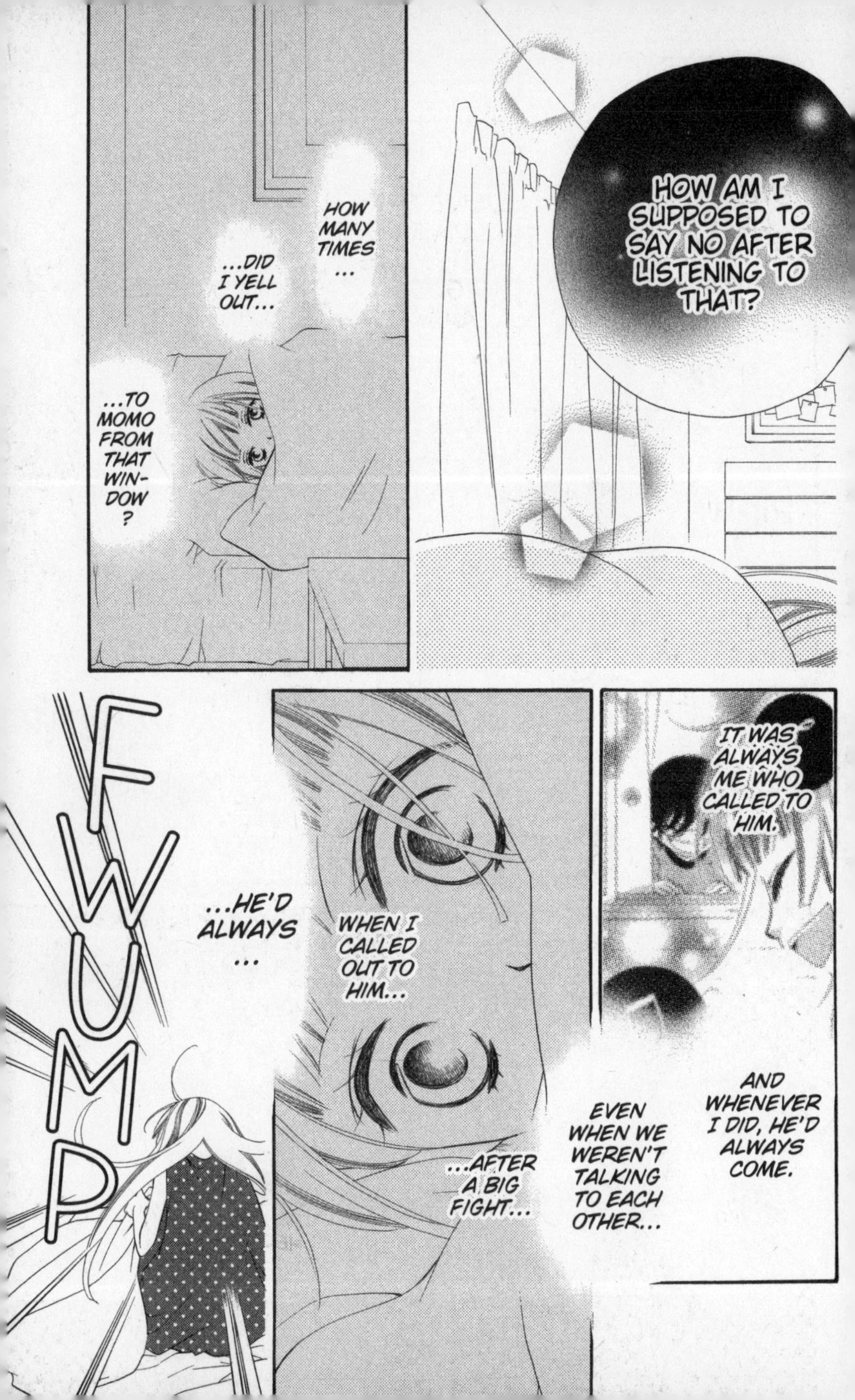
HOW AM I SUPPOSED TO SAY NO AFTER LISTENING TO THAT?
HOW MANY TIMES...
...DID I YELL OUT...
...TO MOMO FROM THAT WIN-DOW?
IT WAS ALWAYS ME WHO CALLED TO HIM.
AND WHENEVER I DID, HE'D ALWAYS COME.
EVEN WHEN WE WEREN'T TALKING TO EACH OTHER...
...AFTER A BIG FIGHT...
WHEN I CALLED OUT TO HIM...
...HE'D ALWAYS...
FWUMP

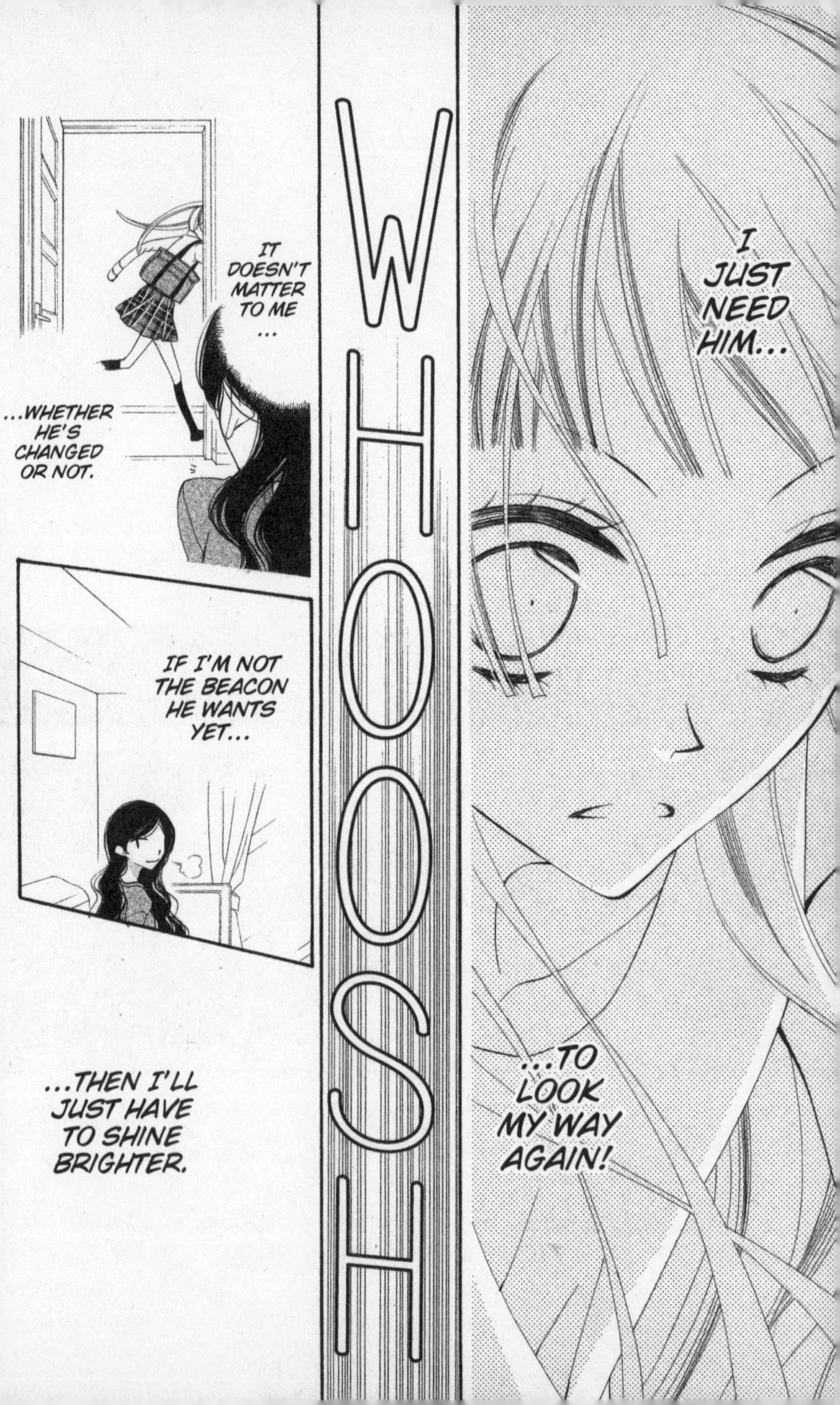
I JUST NEED HIM...
...TO LOOK MY WAY AGAIN!
WHOOSH
IT DOESN'T MATTER TO ME ...
...WHETHER HE'S CHANGED OR NOT.
IF I'M NOT THE BEACON HE WANTS YET...
...THEN I'LL JUST HAVE TO SHINE BRIGHTER.

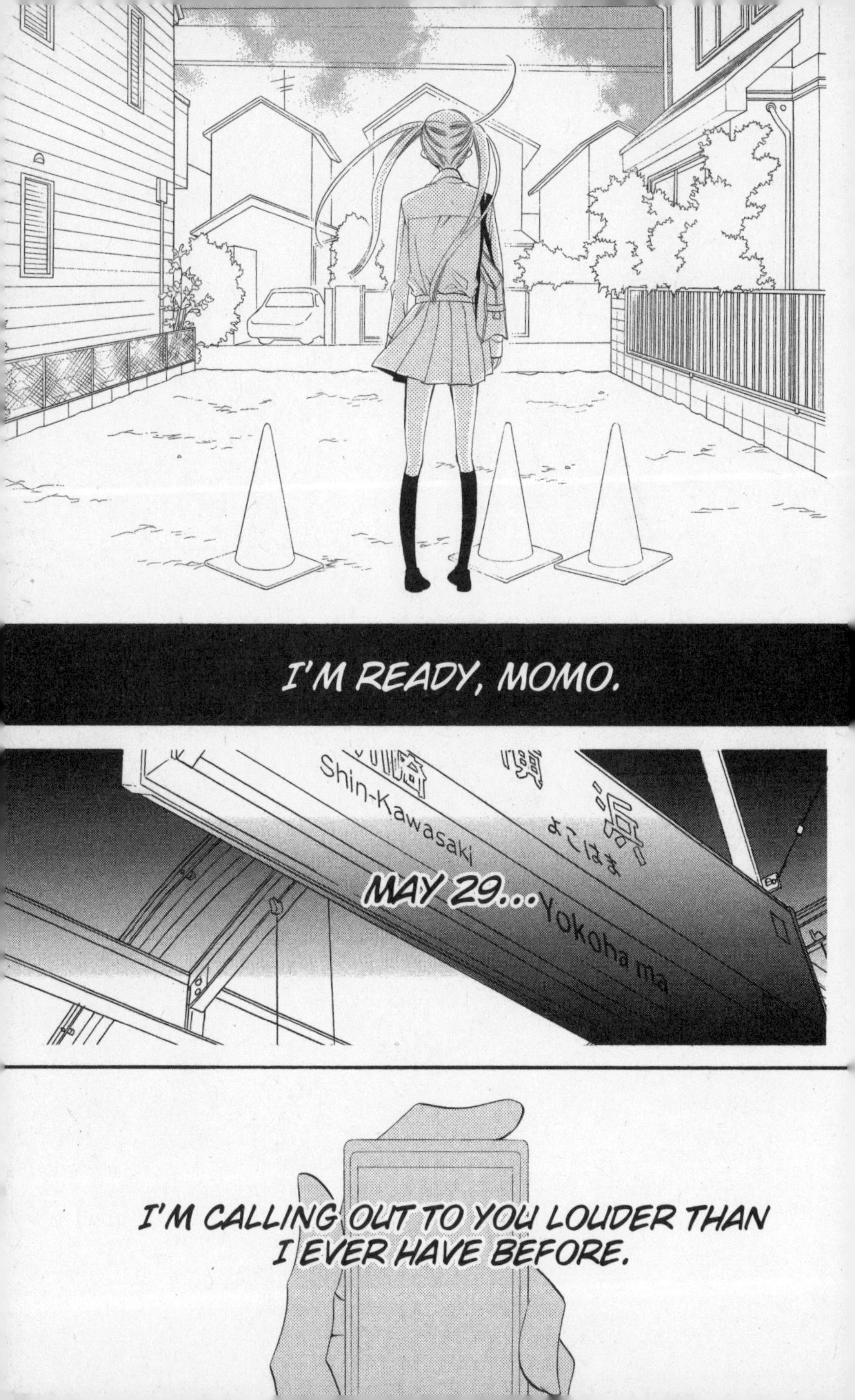
I'M READY, MOMO.
Shin-Kawasaki
よこはま
MAY 29...
Yokoha ma
I'M CALLING OUT TO YOU LOUDER THAN
I EVER HAVE BEFORE.

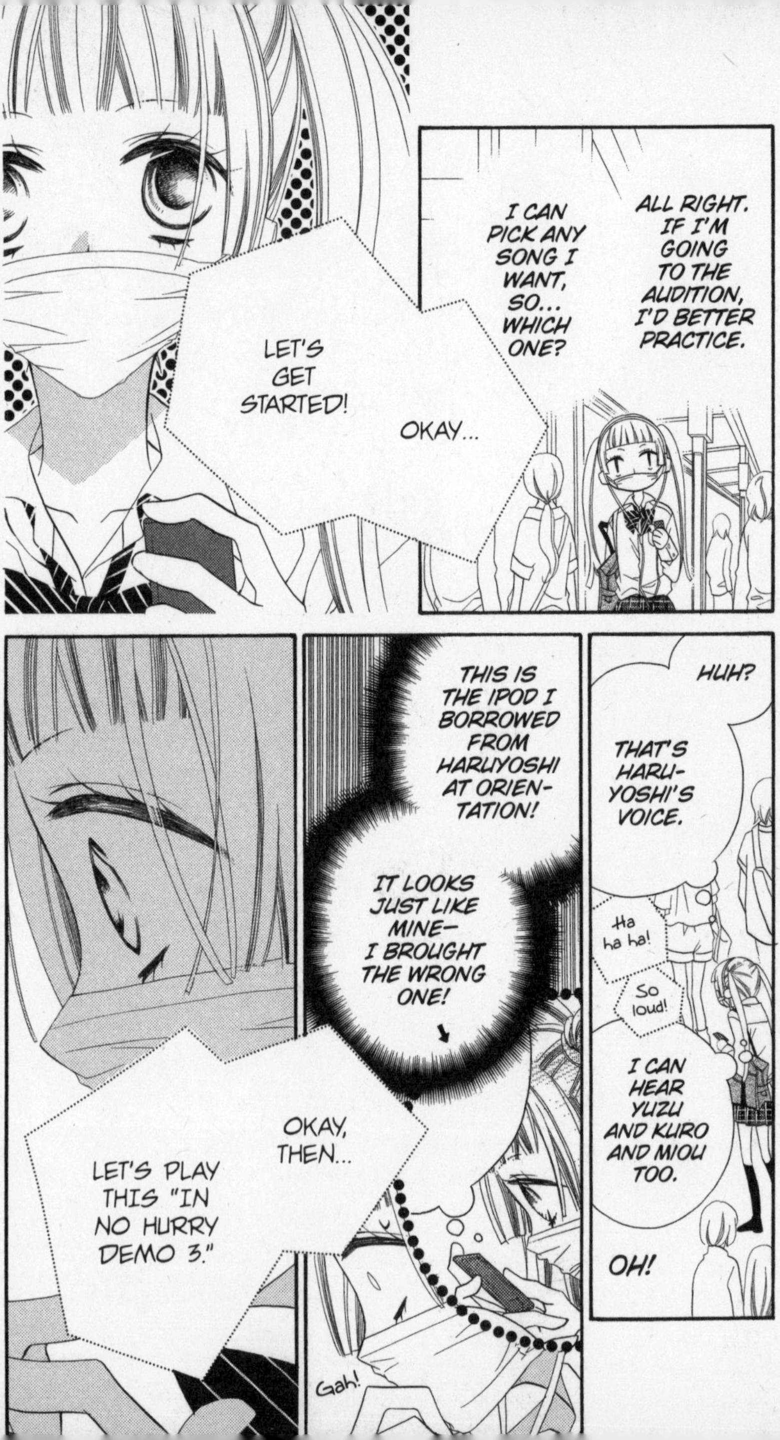
ALL RIGHT. IF I'M GOING TO THE AUDITION, I'D BETTER PRACTICE.
I CAN PICK ANY SONG I WANT, SO... WHICH ONE?
LET'S GET STARTED!
OKAY...
HUH?
THAT'S HARUYOSHI'S VOICE.
Ha ha ha!
So loud!
I CAN HEAR YUZU AND KURO AND MIOU TOO.
OH!
THIS IS THE IPOD I BORROWED FROM HARUYOSHI AT ORIENTATION!
IT LOOKS JUST LIKE MINE— I BROUGHT THE WRONG ONE!
Gah!
OKAY, THEN...
LET'S PLAY THIS "IN NO HURRY DEMO 3."

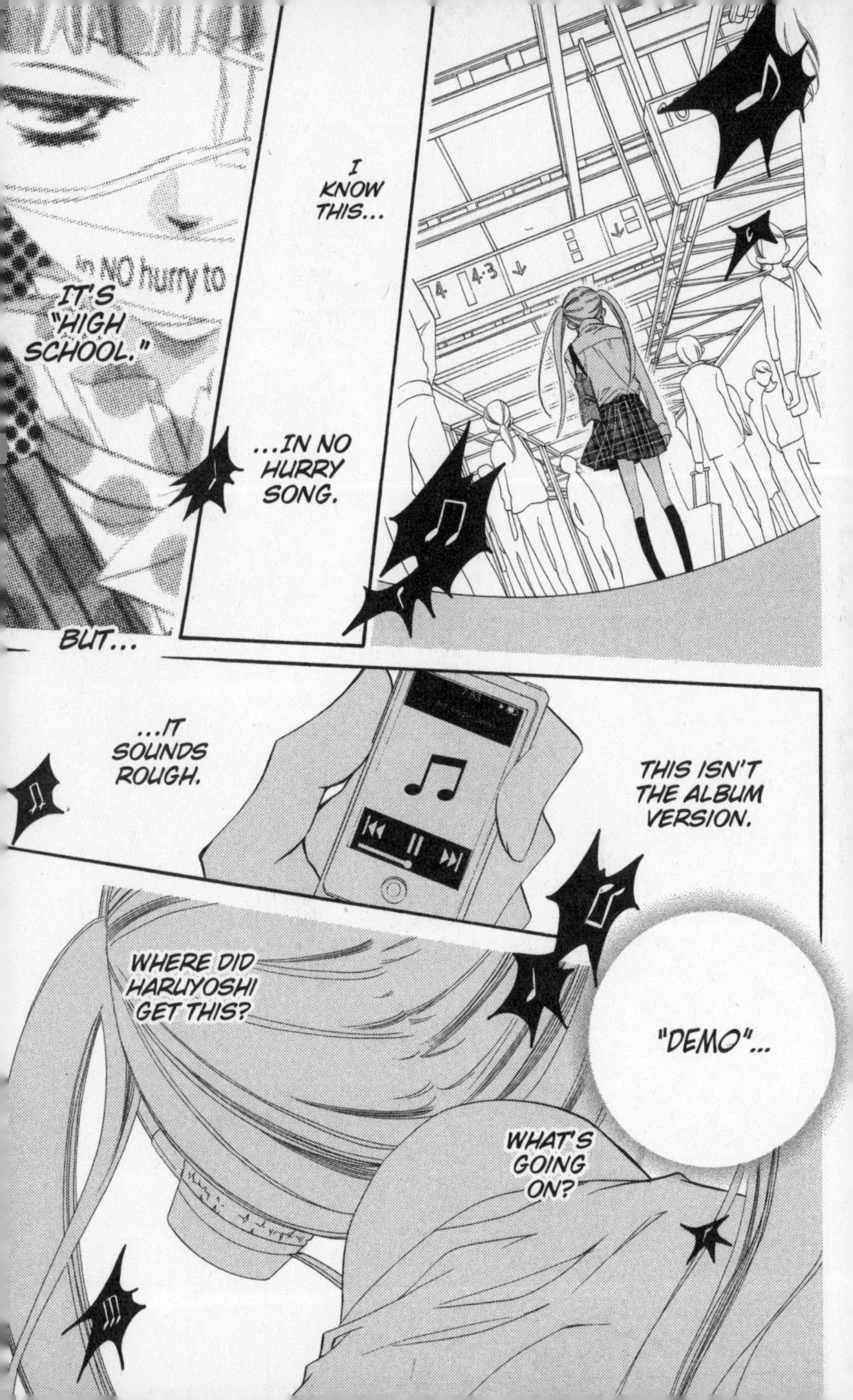
I KNOW THIS...
in NO hurry to
IT'S "HIGH SCHOOL."
...IN NO HURRY SONG.
BUT...
THIS ISN'T THE ALBUM VERSION.
...IT SOUNDS ROUGH.
"DEMO"...
WHERE DID HARUYOSHI GET THIS?
WHAT'S GOING ON?

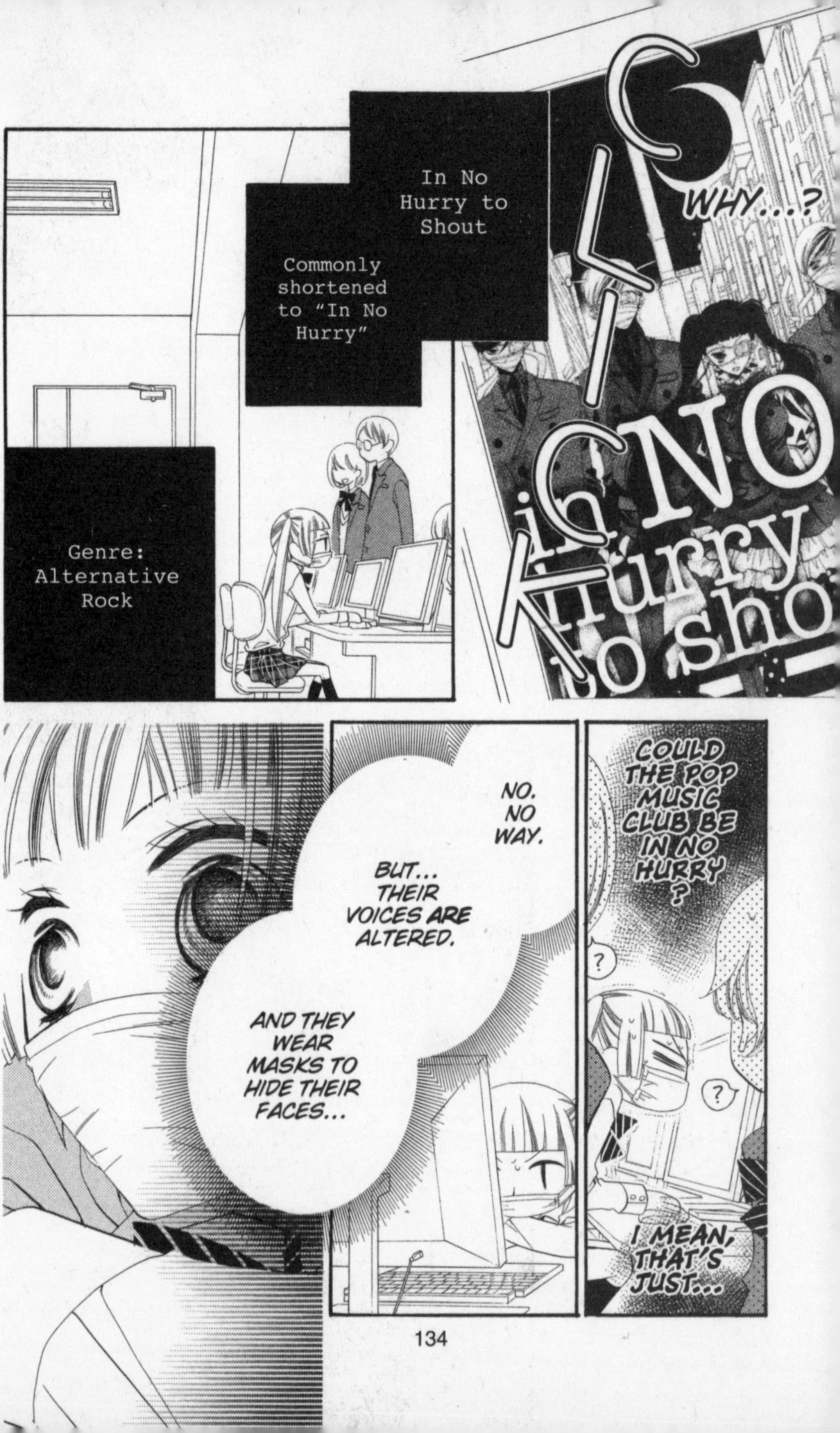
CLICK
WHY...?
in NO hurry to sho
In No Hurry to Shout
Commonly shortened to "In No Hurry"
Genre: Alternative Rock
COULD THE POP MUSIC CLUB BE IN NO HURRY?
?
?
I MEAN, THAT'S JUST...
NO. NO WAY.
BUT... THEIR VOICES ARE ALTERED.
AND THEY WEAR MASKS TO HIDE THEIR FACES...

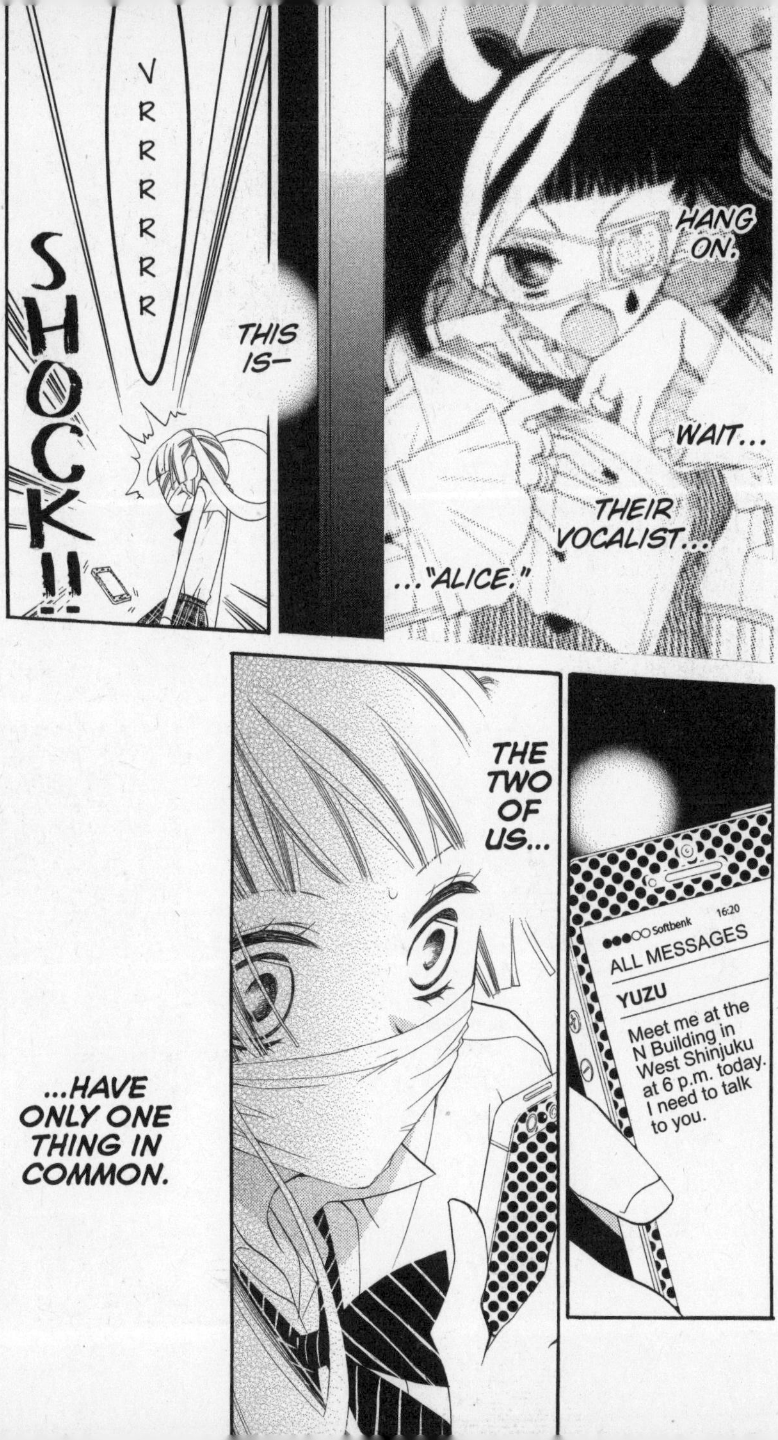
HANG ON.
WAIT...
THEIR VOCALIST...
..."ALICE."
THIS IS—
VRRRRRR
SHOCK!!
●●●○○ Softbenk 16:20
ALL MESSAGES
YUZU
Meet me at the N Building in West Shinjuku at 6 p.m. today. I need to talk to you.
THE TWO OF US...
...HAVE ONLY ONE THING IN COMMON.

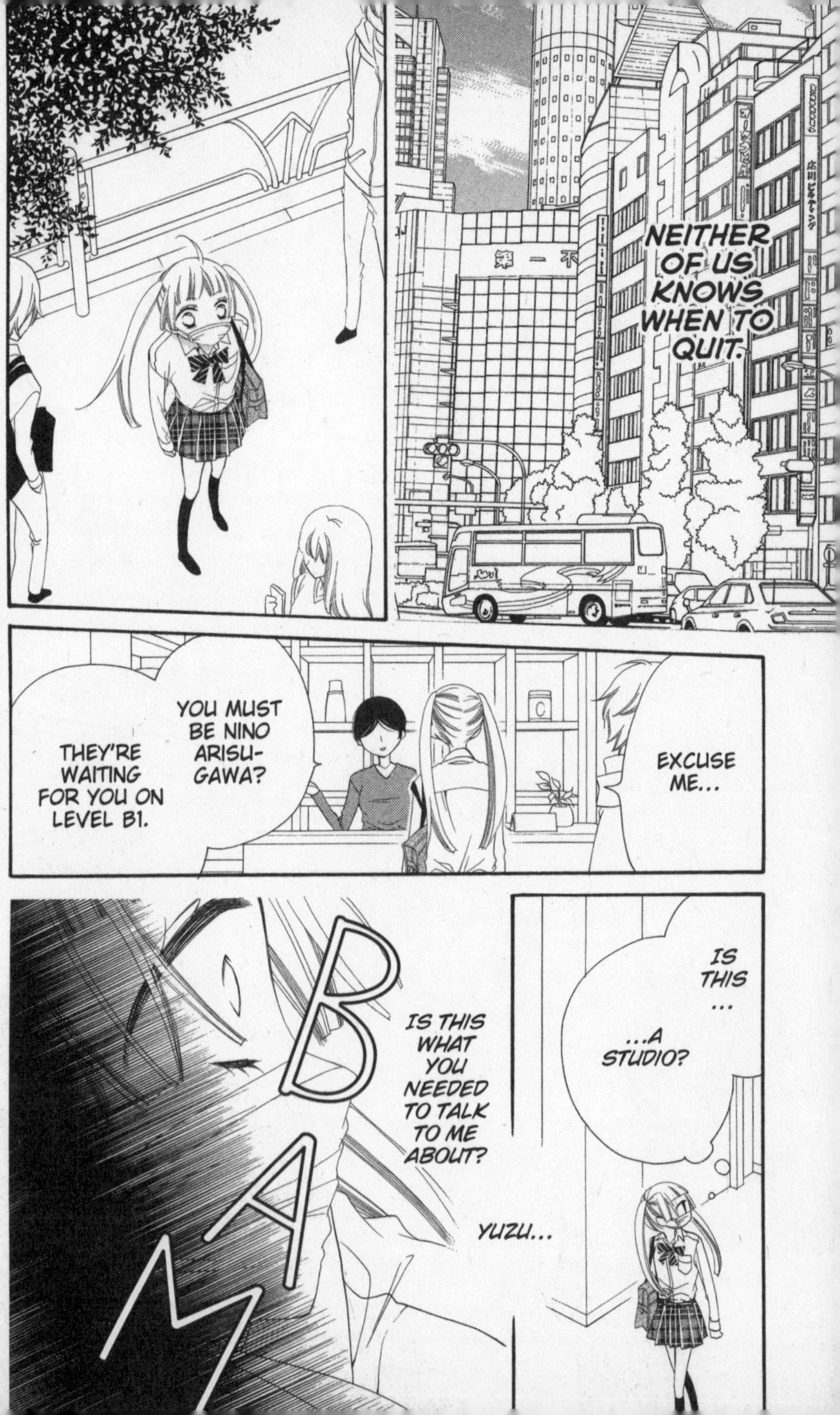
NEITHER OF US KNOWS WHEN TO QUIT.
EXCUSE ME...
YOU MUST BE NINO ARISUGAWA?
THEY'RE WAITING FOR YOU ON LEVEL B1.
IS THIS...
...A STUDIO?
IS THIS WHAT YOU NEEDED TO TALK TO ME ABOUT?
YUZU...
BAM

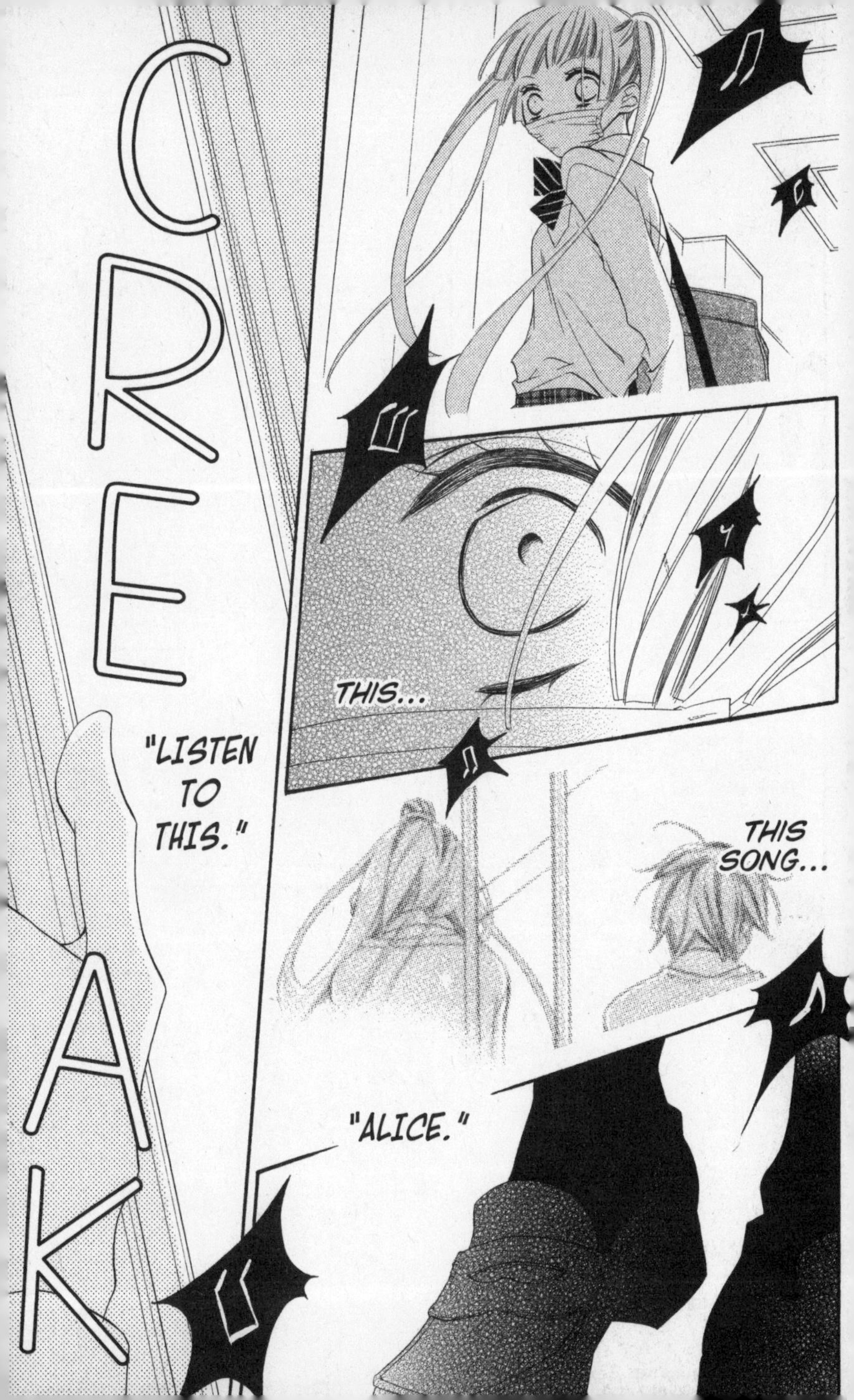
THIS...
THIS SONG...
"ALICE."
CREAK
"LISTEN TO THIS."

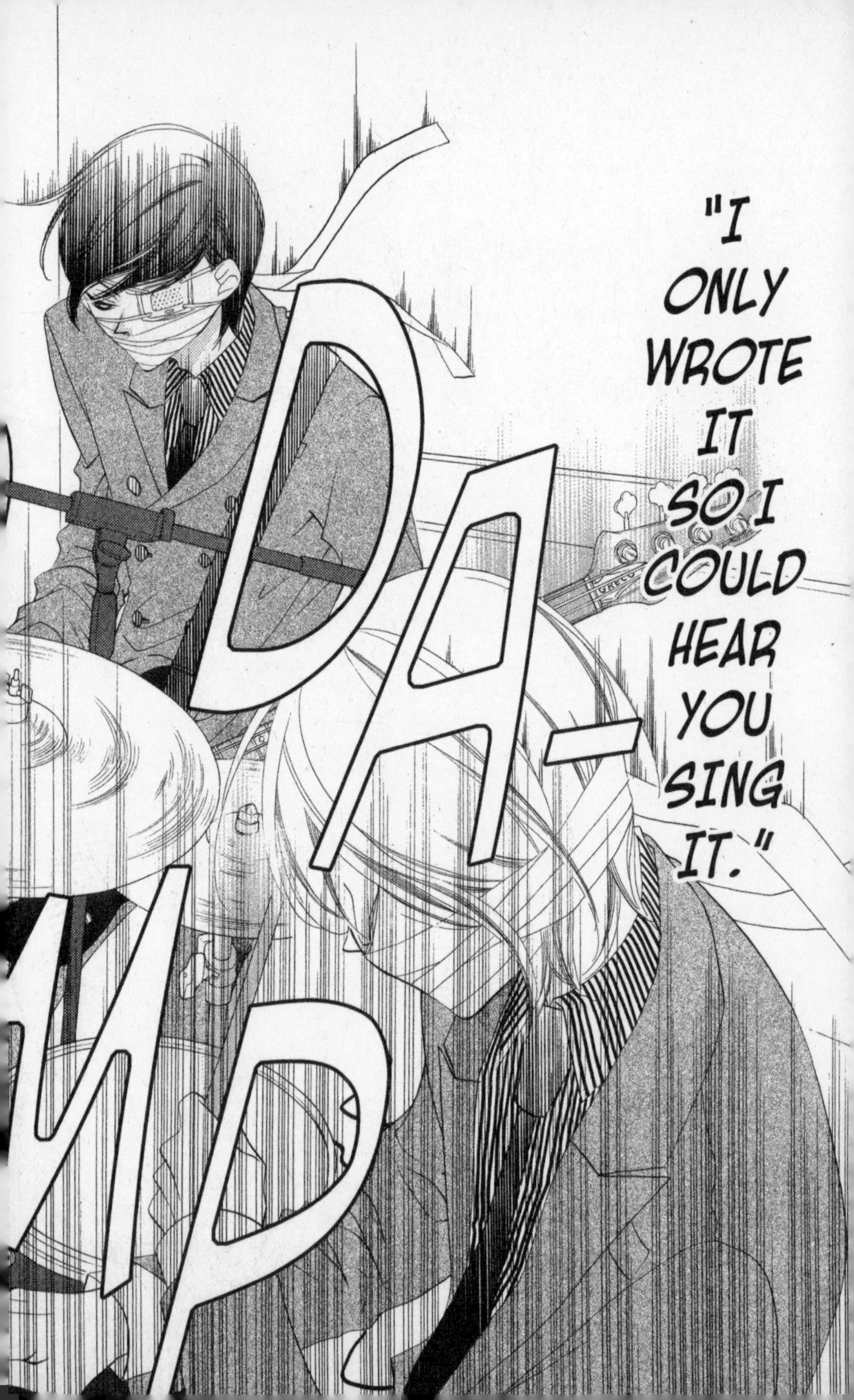
"I ONLY WROTE IT SO I COULD HEAR YOU SING IT."
DA-

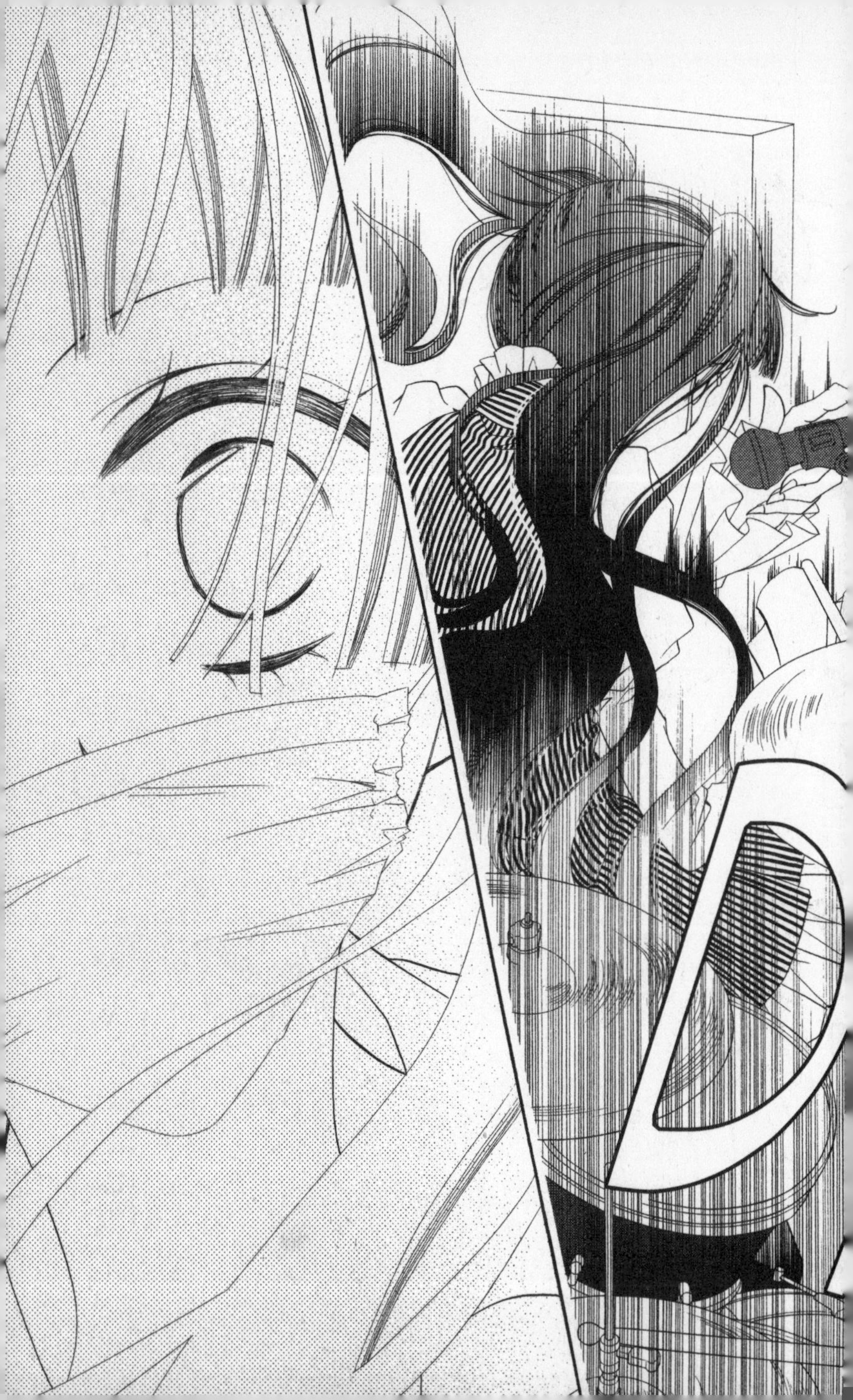

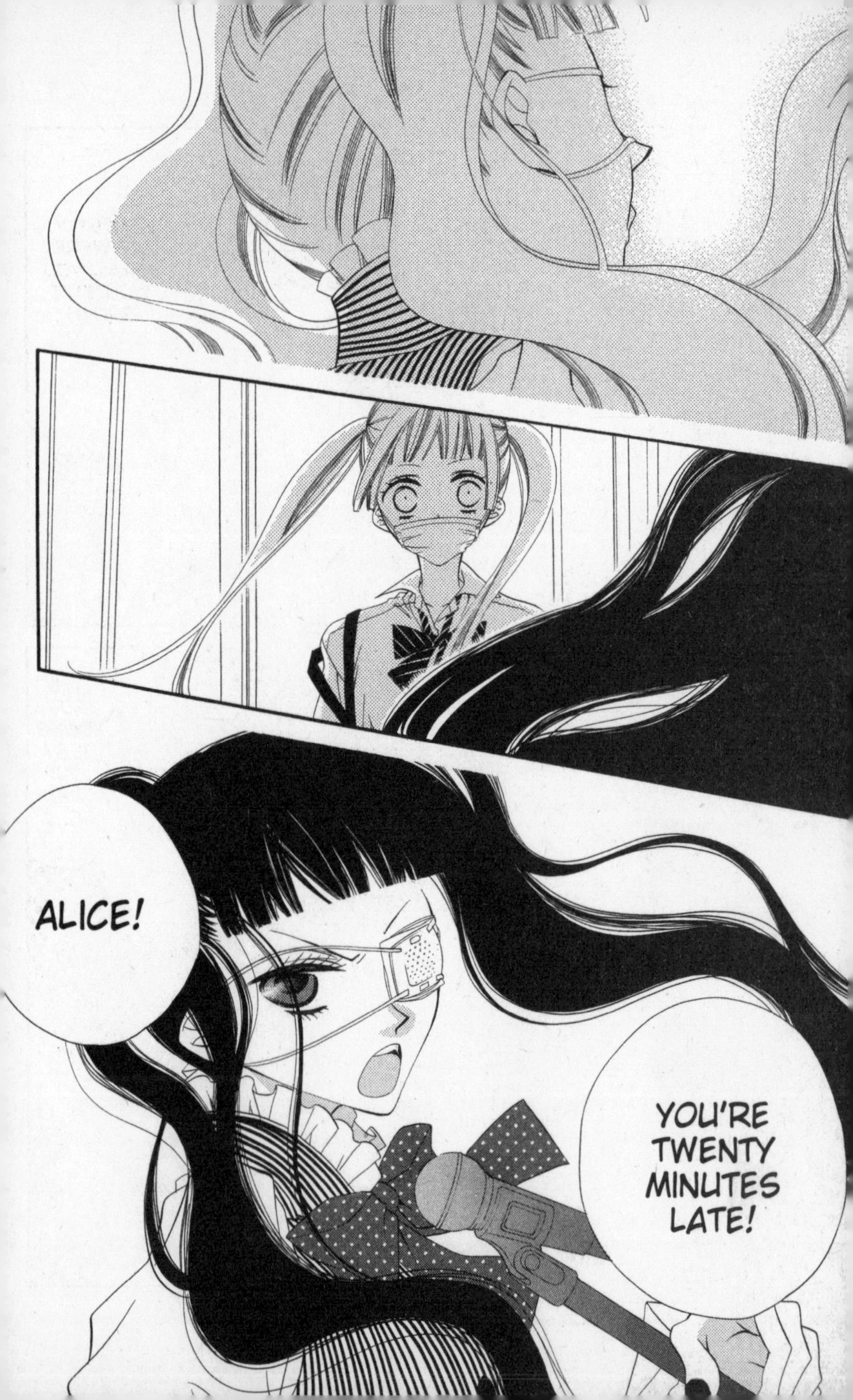
ALICE!
YOU'RE TWENTY MINUTES LATE!

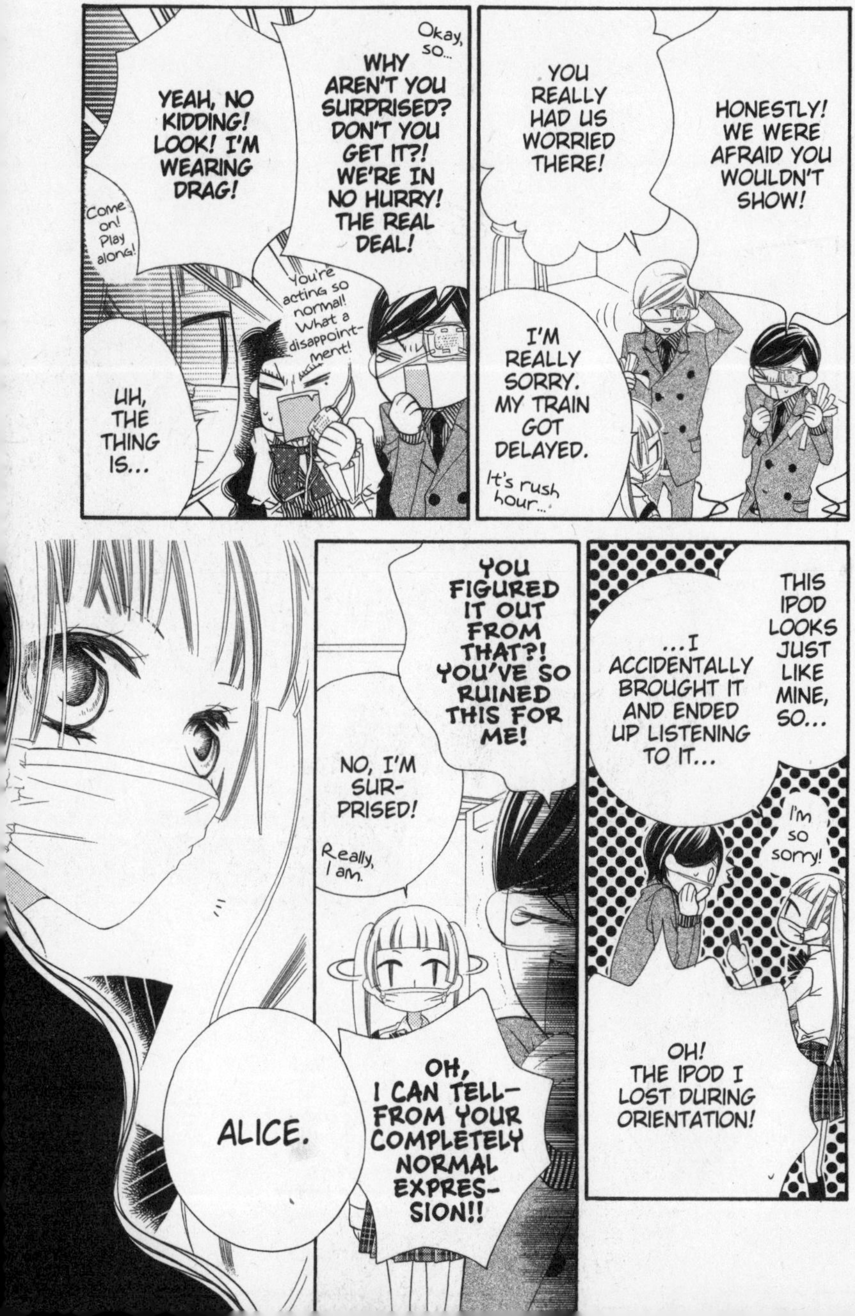
HONESTLY! WE WERE AFRAID YOU WOULDN'T SHOW!
YOU REALLY HAD US WORRIED THERE!
I'M REALLY SORRY. MY TRAIN GOT DELAYED.
It's rush hour...
Okay, so...
WHY AREN'T YOU SURPRISED? DON'T YOU GET IT?! WE'RE IN NO HURRY! THE REAL DEAL!
YEAH, NO KIDDING! LOOK! I'M WEARING DRAG!
Come on! Play along!
You're acting so normal! What a disappointment!
UH, THE THING IS...
THIS IPOD LOOKS JUST LIKE MINE, SO...
...I ACCIDENTALLY BROUGHT IT AND ENDED UP LISTENING TO IT...
I'm so sorry!
OH! THE IPOD I LOST DURING ORIENTATION!
YOU FIGURED IT OUT FROM THAT?! YOU'VE SO RUINED THIS FOR ME!
NO, I'M SUR-PRISED!
Really, I am.
OH, I CAN TELL— FROM YOUR COMPLETELY NORMAL EXPRES-SION!!
ALICE.

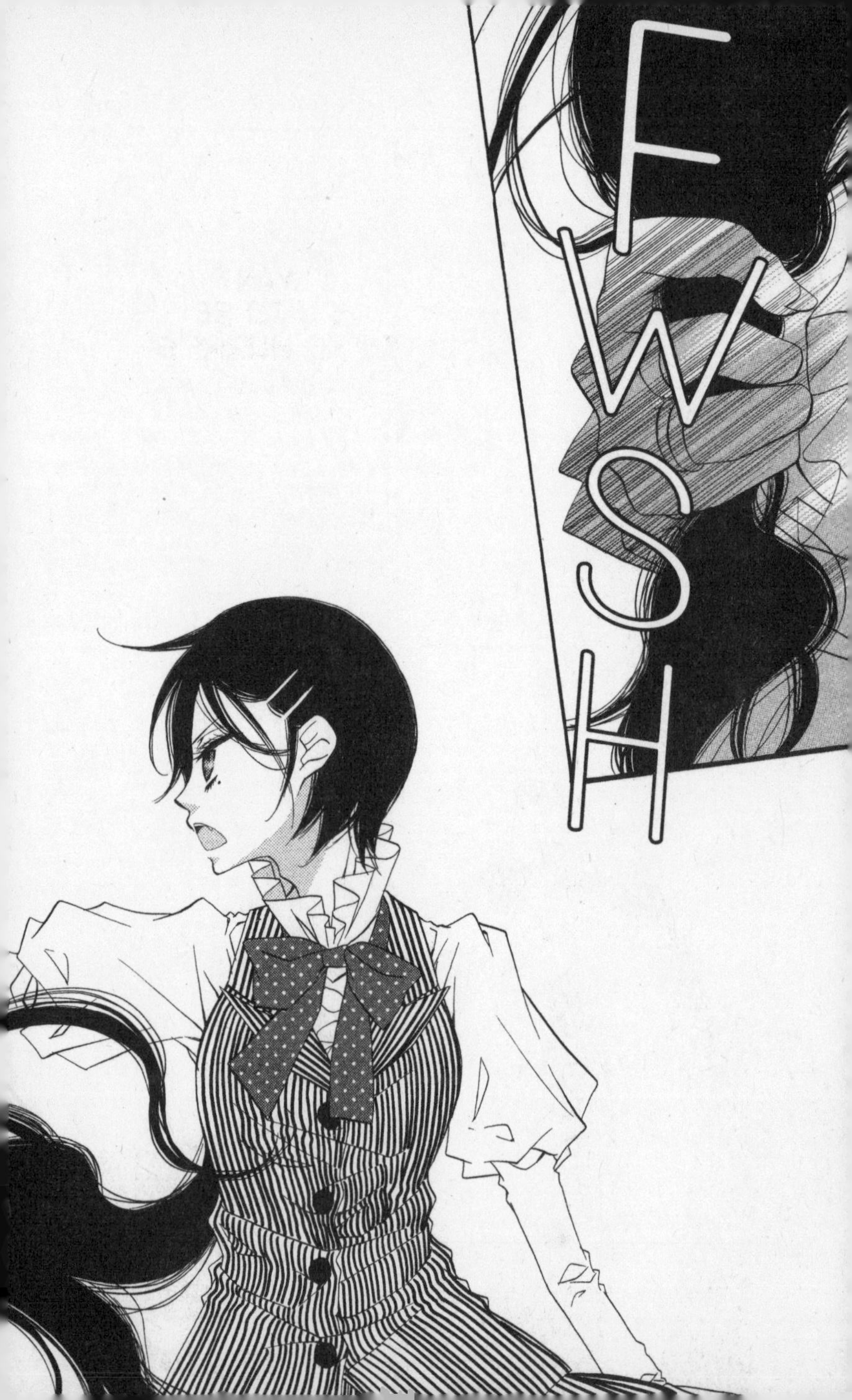
FWSH

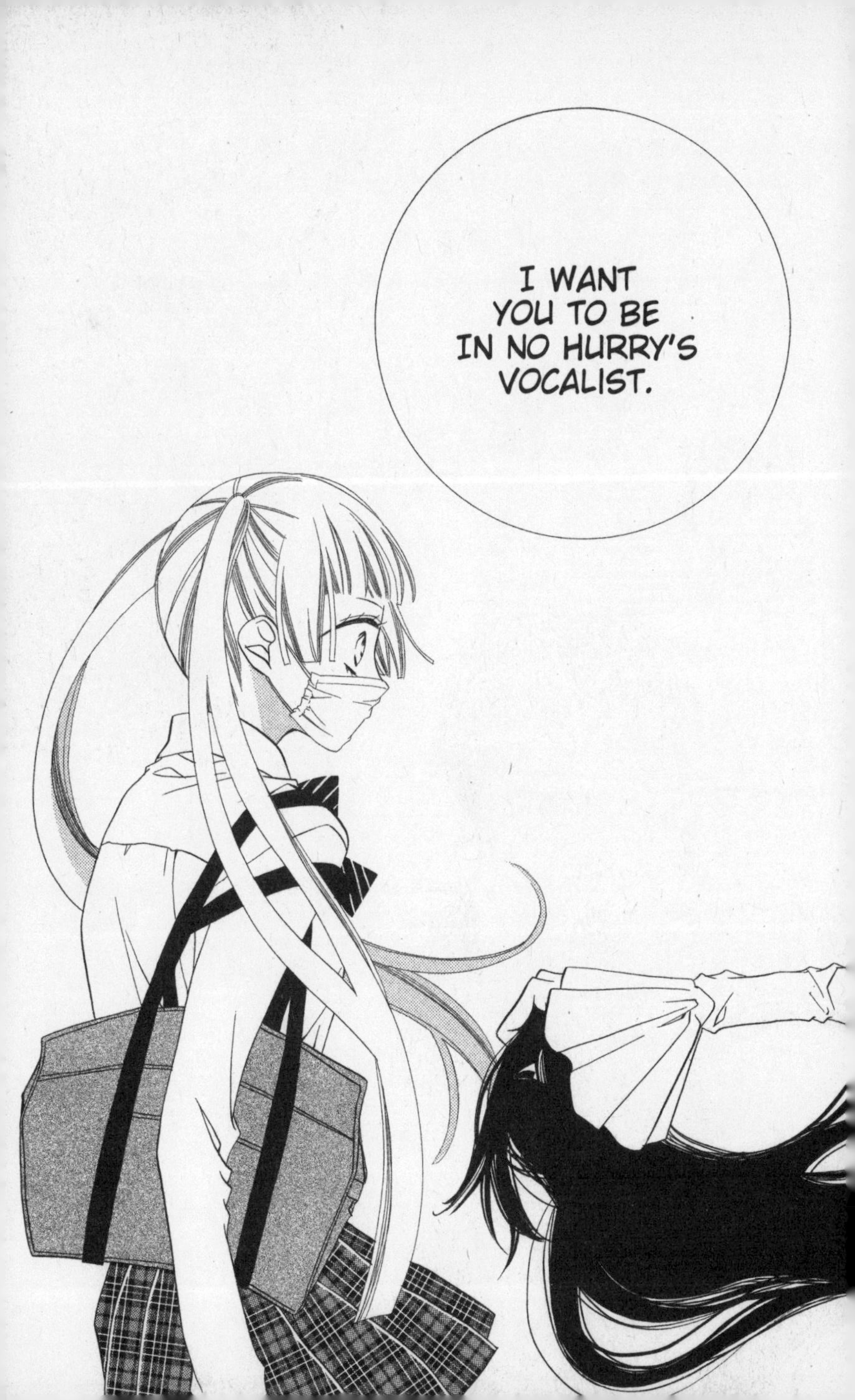
I WANT YOU TO BE IN NO HURRY'S VOCALIST.

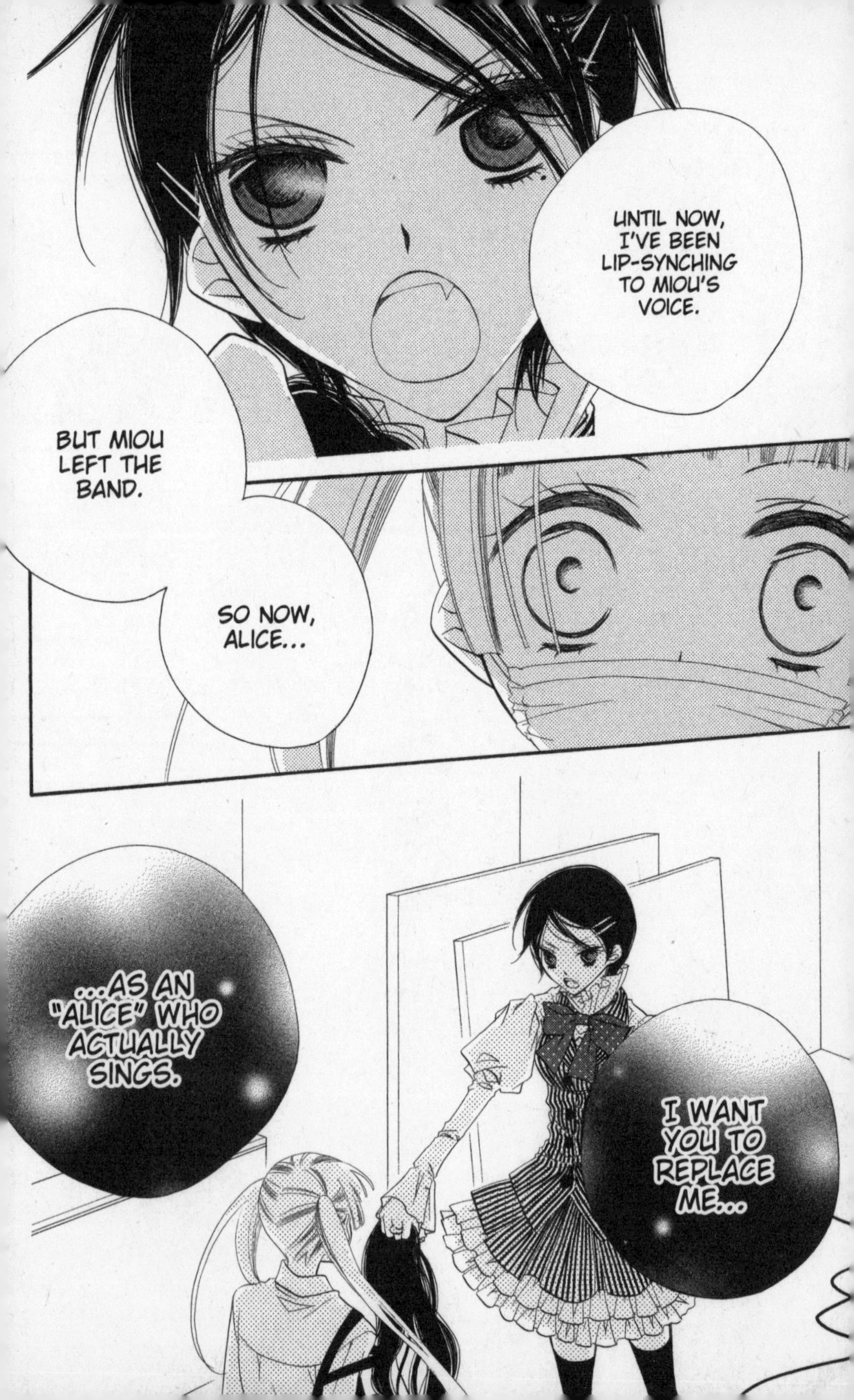
UNTIL NOW, I'VE BEEN LIP-SYNCHING TO MIOU'S VOICE.
BUT MIOU LEFT THE BAND.
SO NOW, ALICE...
I WANT YOU TO REPLACE ME...
...AS AN "ALICE" WHO ACTUALLY SINGS.

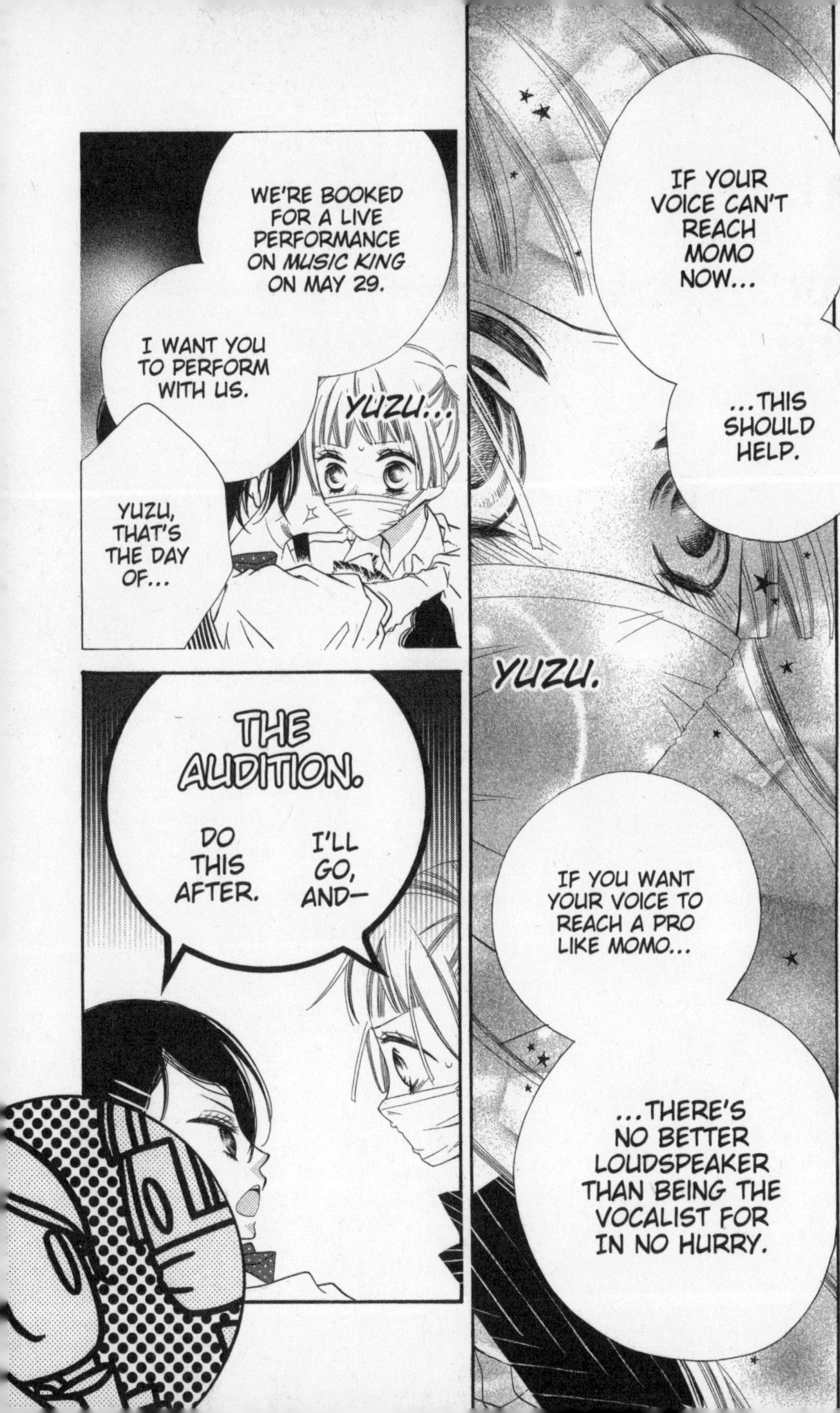
IF YOUR VOICE CAN'T REACH MOMO NOW...
...THIS SHOULD HELP.
YUZU.
IF YOU WANT YOUR VOICE TO REACH A PRO LIKE MOMO...
...THERE'S NO BETTER LOUDSPEAKER THAN BEING THE VOCALIST FOR IN NO HURRY.
WE'RE BOOKED FOR A LIVE PERFORMANCE ON MUSIC KING ON MAY 29.
I WANT YOU TO PERFORM WITH US.
YUZU...
YUZU, THAT'S THE DAY OF...
THE AUDITION.
I'LL GO, AND—
DO THIS AFTER.

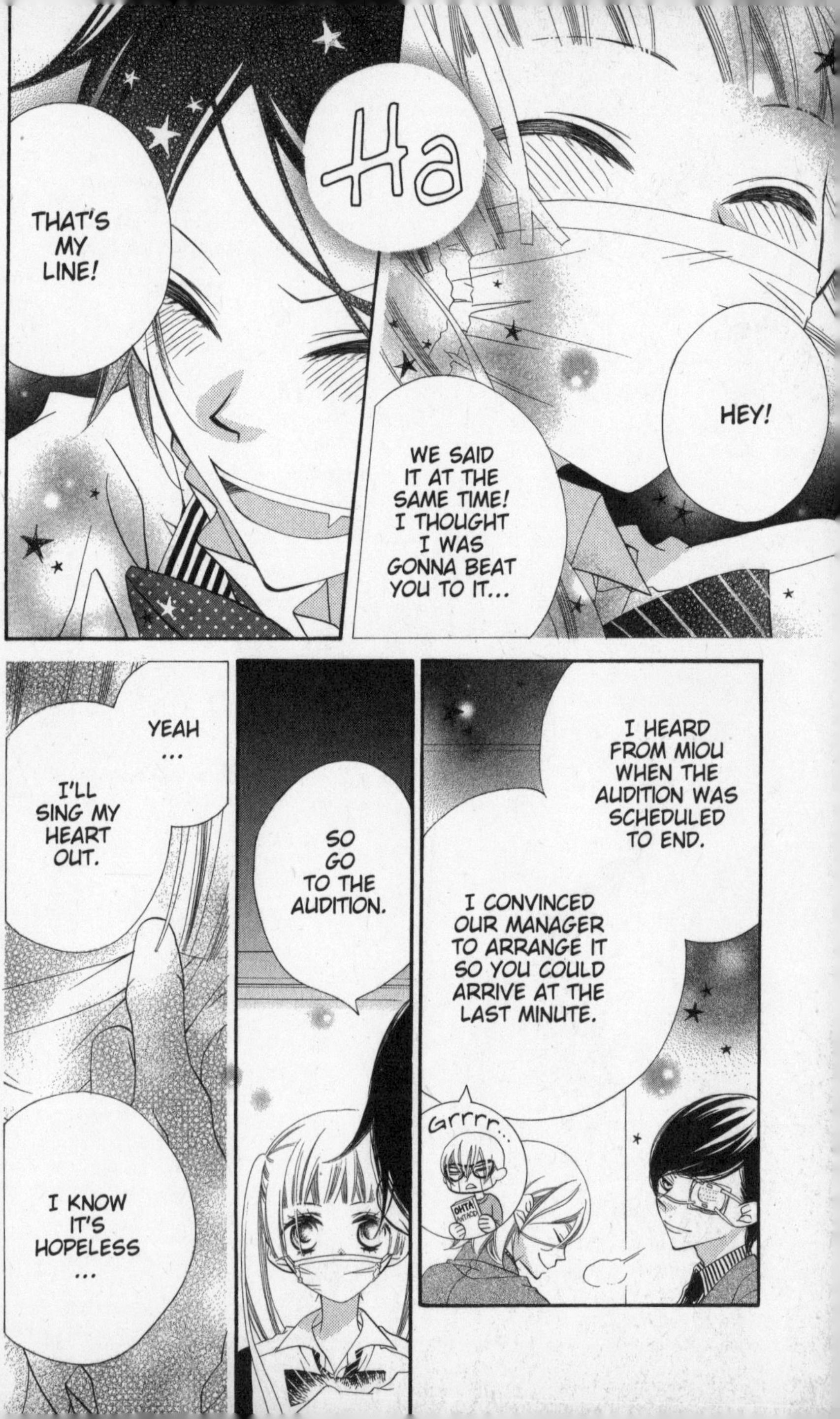
HEY!
WE SAID IT AT THE SAME TIME! I THOUGHT I WAS GONNA BEAT YOU TO IT...
Ha
THAT'S MY LINE!
I HEARD FROM MIOU WHEN THE AUDITION WAS SCHEDULED TO END.
I CONVINCED OUR MANAGER TO ARRANGE IT SO YOU COULD ARRIVE AT THE LAST MINUTE.
Grrrr...
SO GO TO THE AUDITION.
YEAH ...
I'LL SING MY HEART OUT.
I KNOW IT'S HOPELESS ...

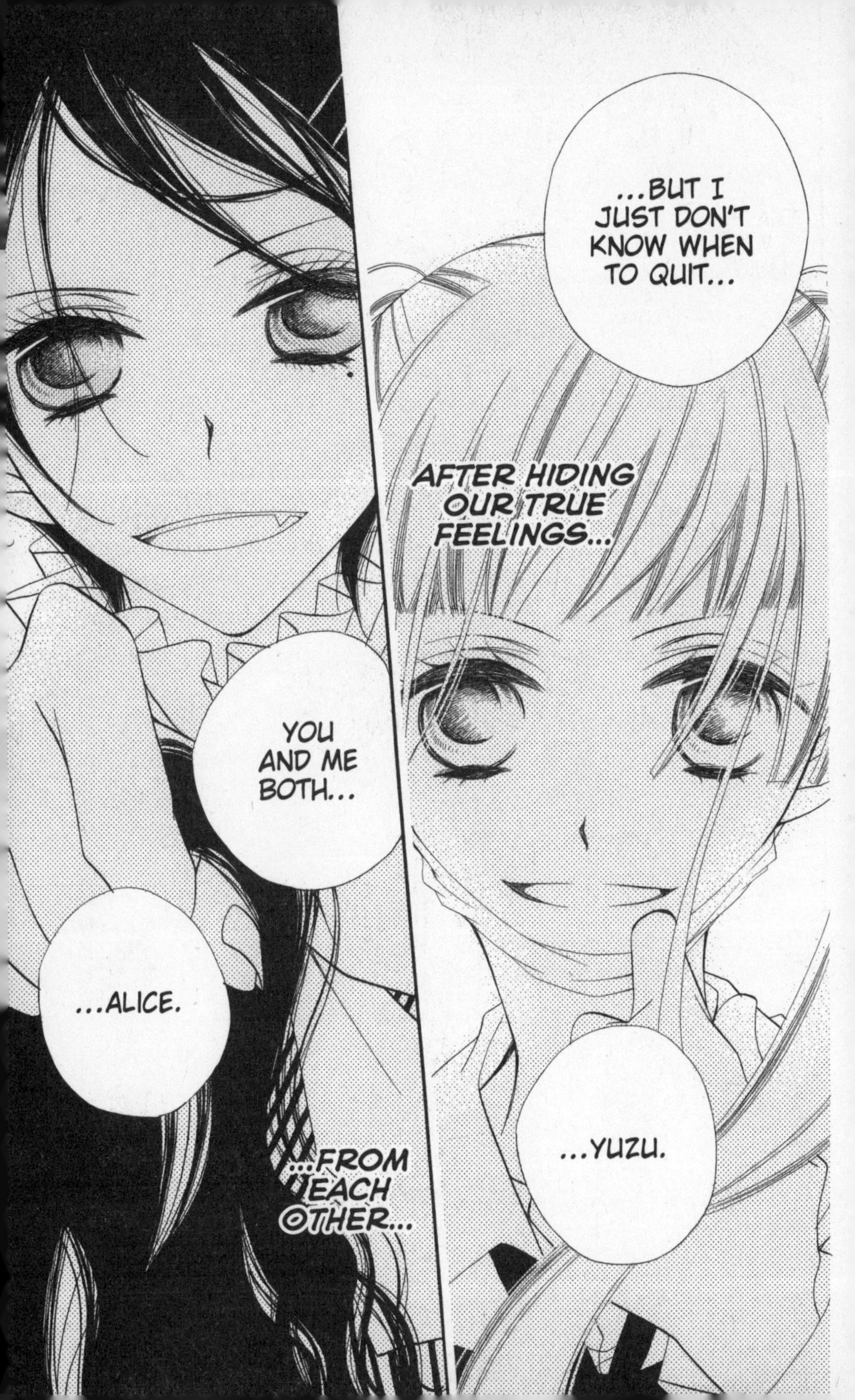
...BUT I JUST DON'T KNOW WHEN TO QUIT...
AFTER HIDING OUR TRUE FEELINGS...
YOU AND ME BOTH...
...YUZU.
...FROM EACH OTHER...
...ALICE.

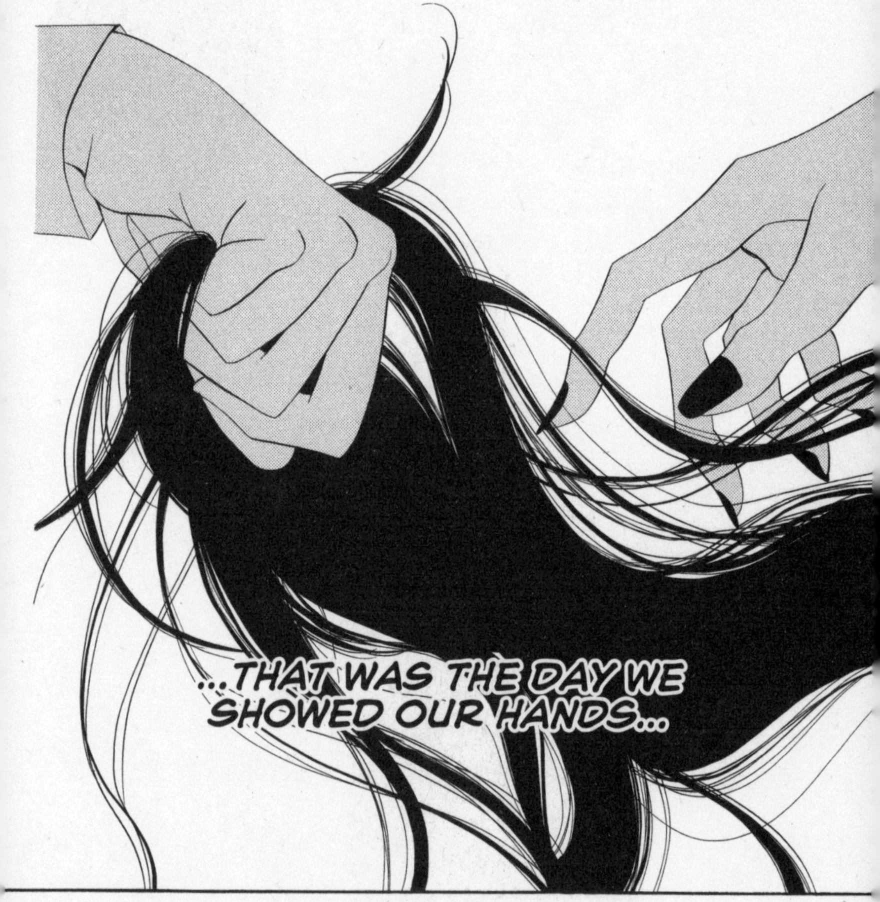
...THAT WAS THE DAY WE SHOWED OUR HANDS...

...AND JOINED THEM TOGETHER.

SONG 10

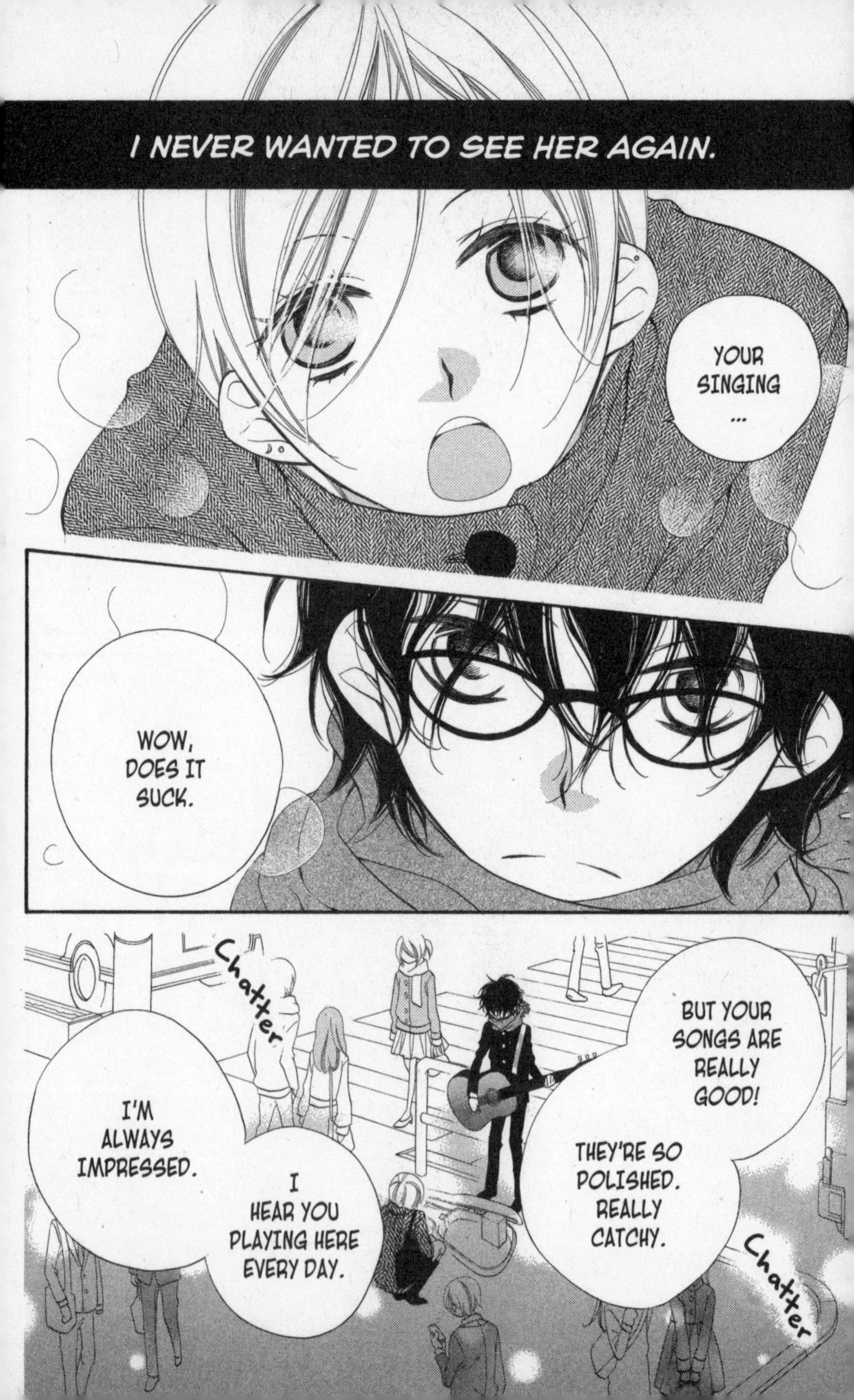
I NEVER WANTED TO SEE HER AGAIN.
YOUR SINGING...
WOW, DOES IT SUCK.
BUT YOUR SONGS ARE REALLY GOOD!
THEY'RE SO POLISHED. REALLY CATCHY.
Chatter
Chatter
I HEAR YOU PLAYING HERE EVERY DAY.
I'M ALWAYS IMPRESSED.

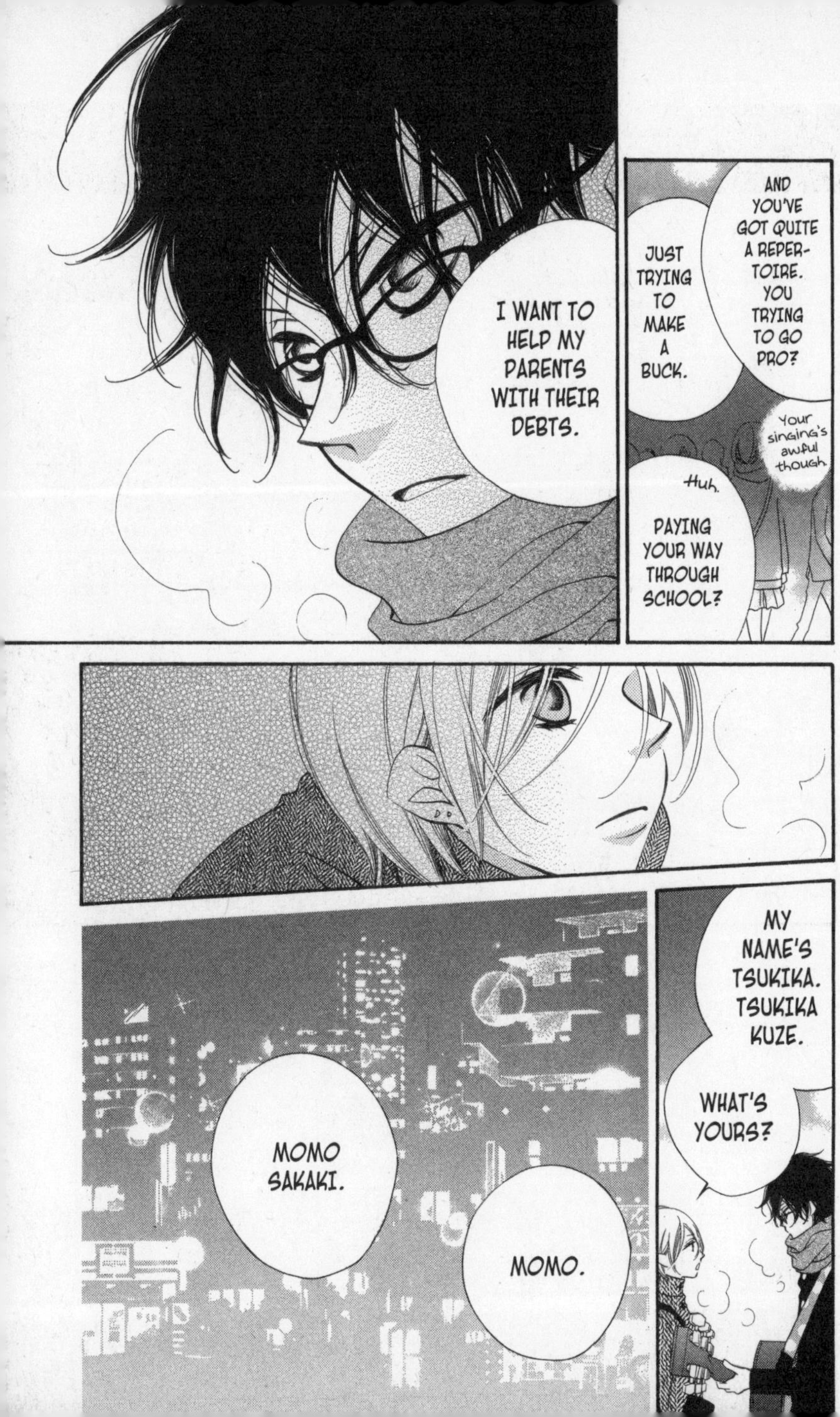
AND YOU'VE GOT QUITE A REPERTOIRE. YOU TRYING TO GO PRO?
JUST TRYING TO MAKE A BUCK.
Your singing's awful though.
Huh.
PAYING YOUR WAY THROUGH SCHOOL?
I WANT TO HELP MY PARENTS WITH THEIR DEBTS.
MY NAME'S TSUKIKA. TSUKIKA KUZE.
WHAT'S YOURS?
MOMO SAKAKI.
MOMO.

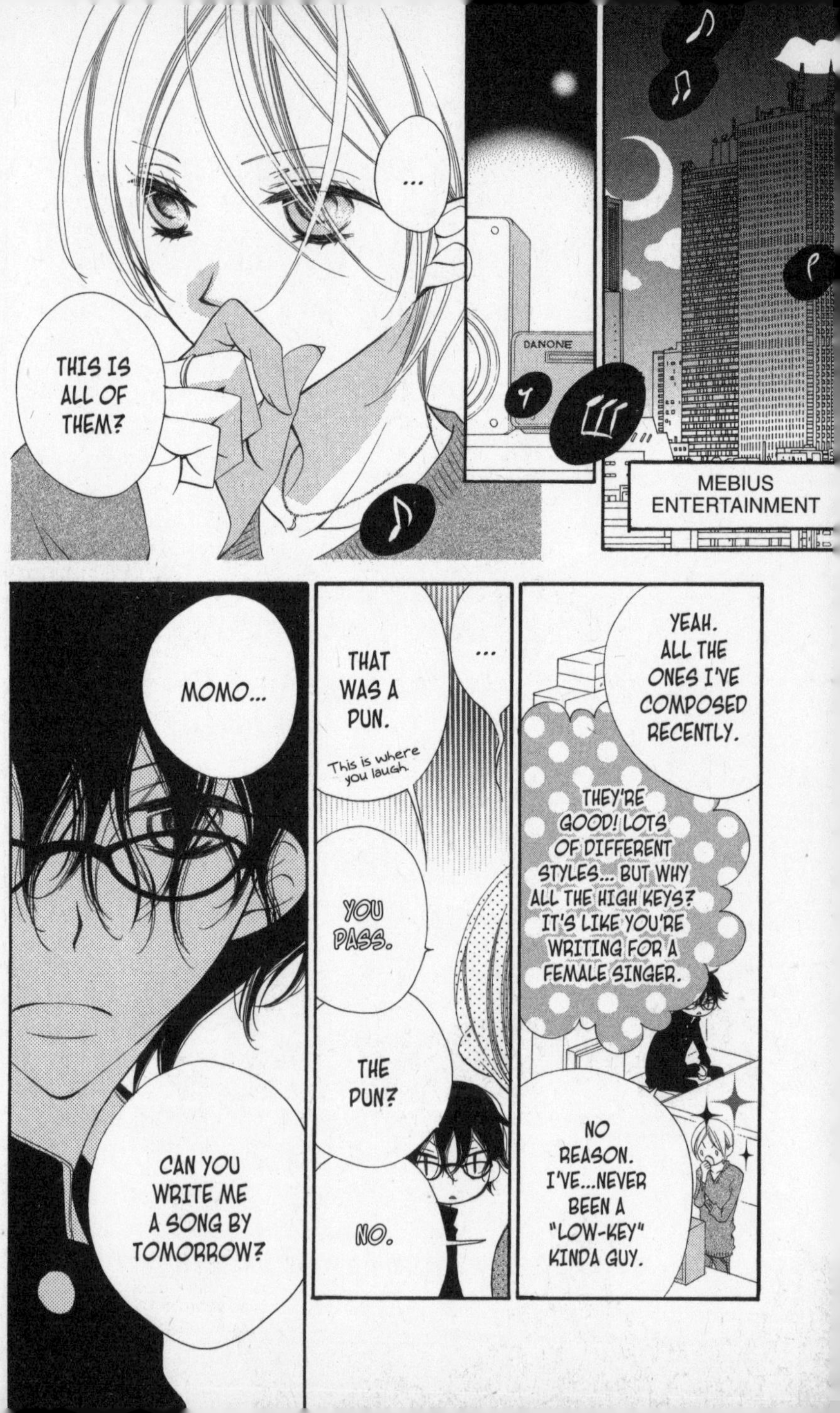
MEBIUS ENTERTAINMENT
DANONE
...
THIS IS ALL OF THEM?
YEAH. ALL THE ONES I'VE COMPOSED RECENTLY.
THEY'RE GOOD! LOTS OF DIFFERENT STYLES... BUT WHY ALL THE HIGH KEYS? IT'S LIKE YOU'RE WRITING FOR A FEMALE SINGER.
NO REASON. I'VE...NEVER BEEN A "LOW-KEY" KINDA GUY.
...
THAT WAS A PUN.
This is where you laugh.
YOU PASS.
THE PUN?
NO.
MOMO...
CAN YOU WRITE ME A SONG BY TOMORROW?

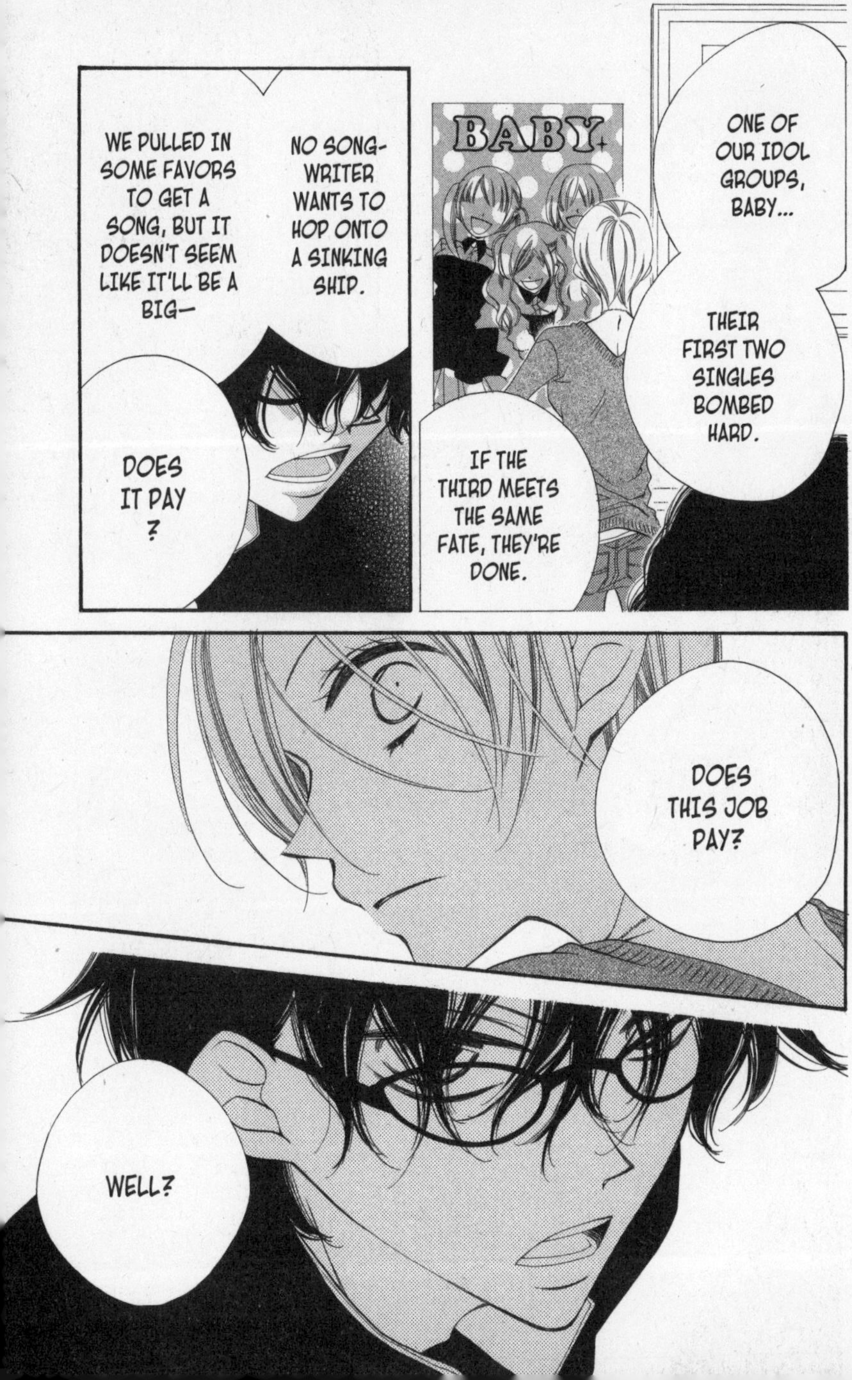
BABY
ONE OF OUR IDOL GROUPS, BABY...
THEIR FIRST TWO SINGLES BOMBED HARD.
IF THE THIRD MEETS THE SAME FATE, THEY'RE DONE.
NO SONG-WRITER WANTS TO HOP ONTO A SINKING SHIP.
WE PULLED IN SOME FAVORS TO GET A SONG, BUT IT DOESN'T SEEM LIKE IT'LL BE A BIG—
DOES IT PAY?
DOES THIS JOB PAY?
WELL?

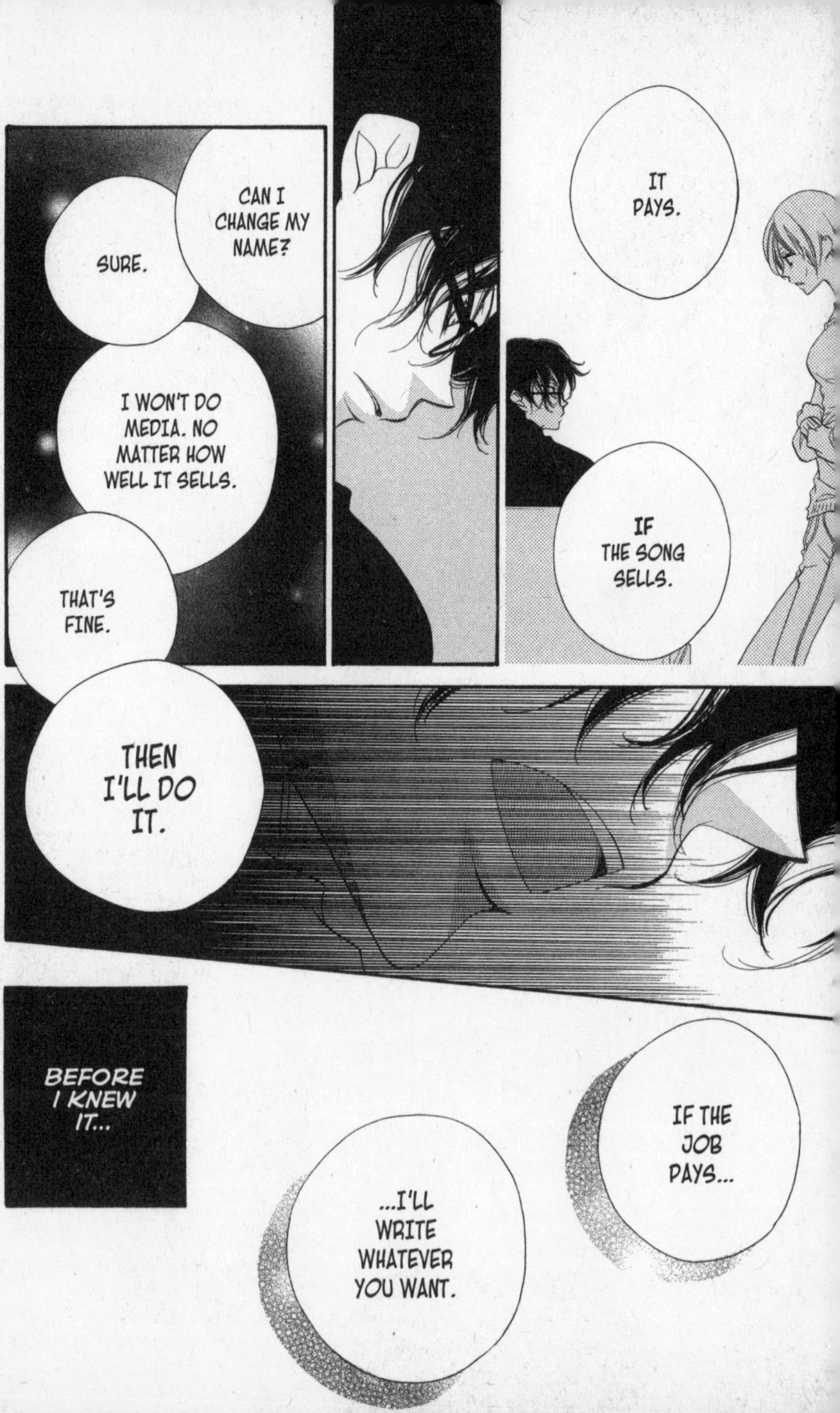
IT PAYS.
IF THE SONG SELLS.
CAN I CHANGE MY NAME?
SURE.
I WON'T DO MEDIA. NO MATTER HOW WELL IT SELLS.
THAT'S FINE.
THEN I'LL DO IT.
BEFORE I KNEW IT...
IF THE JOB PAYS...
...I'LL WRITE WHATEVER YOU WANT.

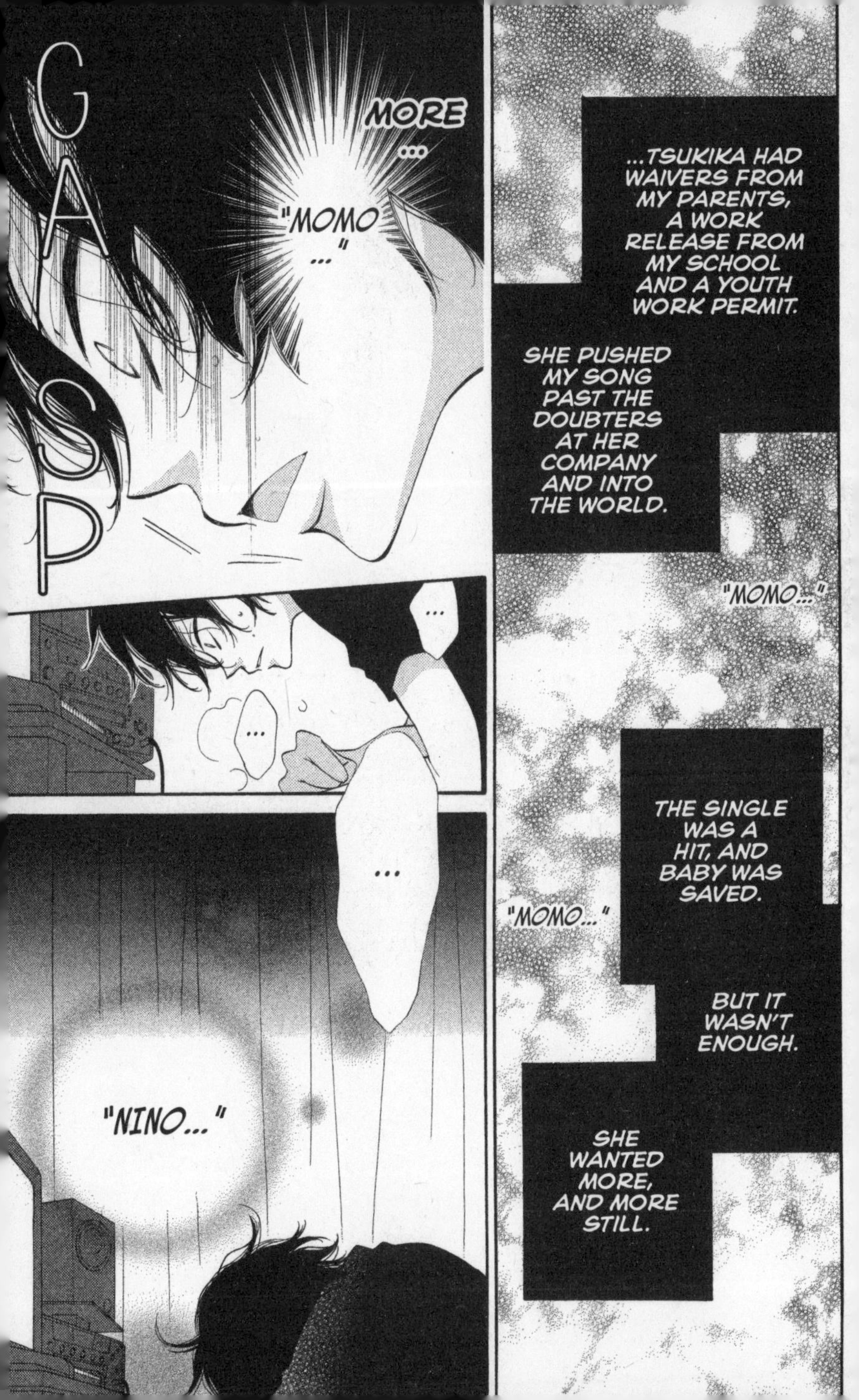
...TSUKIKA HAD WAIVERS FROM MY PARENTS, A WORK RELEASE FROM MY SCHOOL AND A YOUTH WORK PERMIT.
SHE PUSHED MY SONG PAST THE DOUBTERS AT HER COMPANY AND INTO THE WORLD.
"MOMO..."
THE SINGLE WAS A HIT, AND BABY WAS SAVED.
"MOMO..."
BUT IT WASN'T ENOUGH.
SHE WANTED MORE, AND MORE STILL.
MORE...
"MOMO"...
GASP
...
...
...
"NINO..."

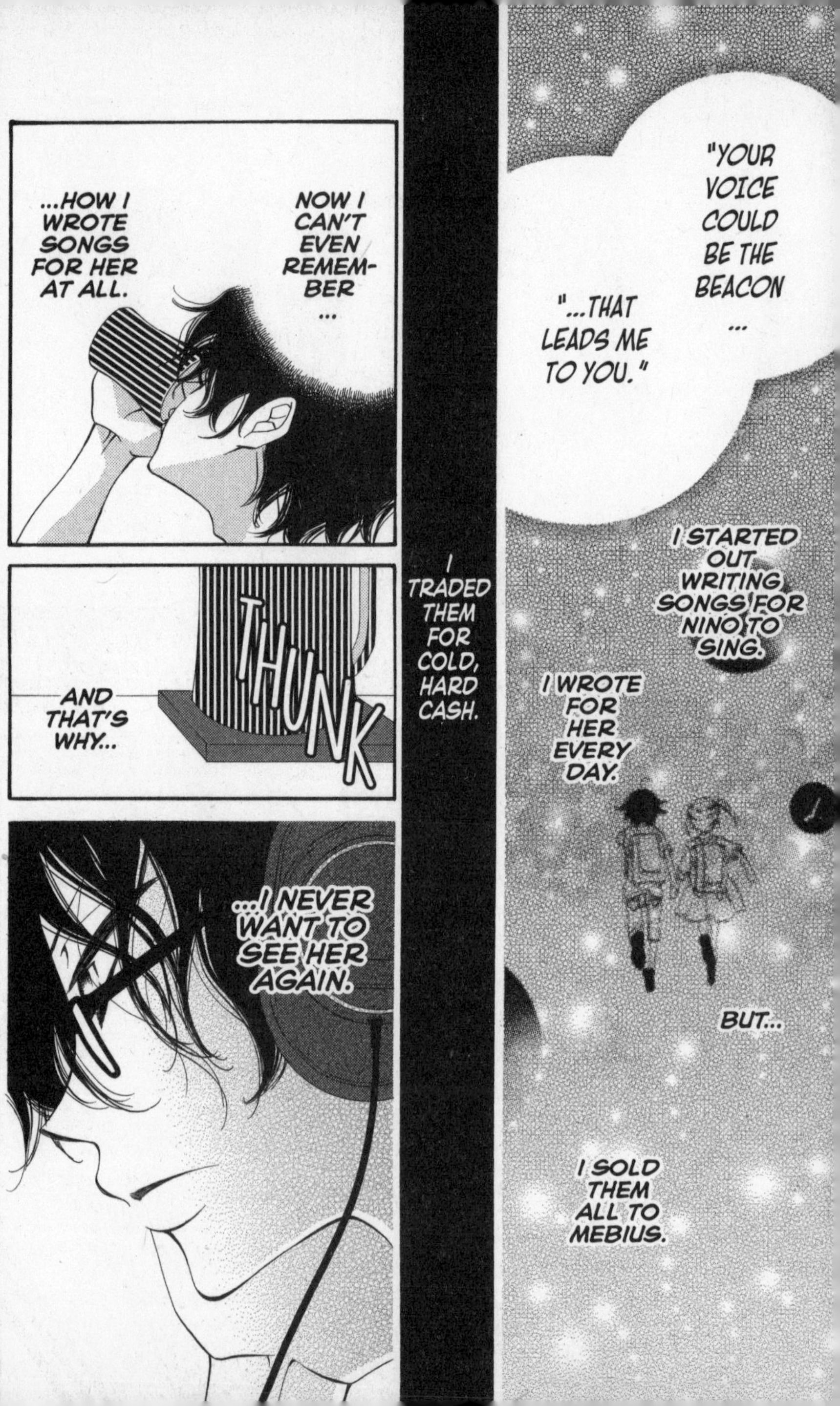
"YOUR VOICE COULD BE THE BEACON ...
"...THAT LEADS ME TO YOU."
I STARTED OUT WRITING SONGS FOR NINO TO SING.
I WROTE FOR HER EVERY DAY.
BUT...
I SOLD THEM ALL TO MEBIUS.
I TRADED THEM FOR COLD, HARD CASH.
NOW I CAN'T EVEN REMEMBER ...
...HOW I WROTE SONGS FOR HER AT ALL.
AND THAT'S WHY...
THUNK
...I NEVER WANT TO SEE HER AGAIN.

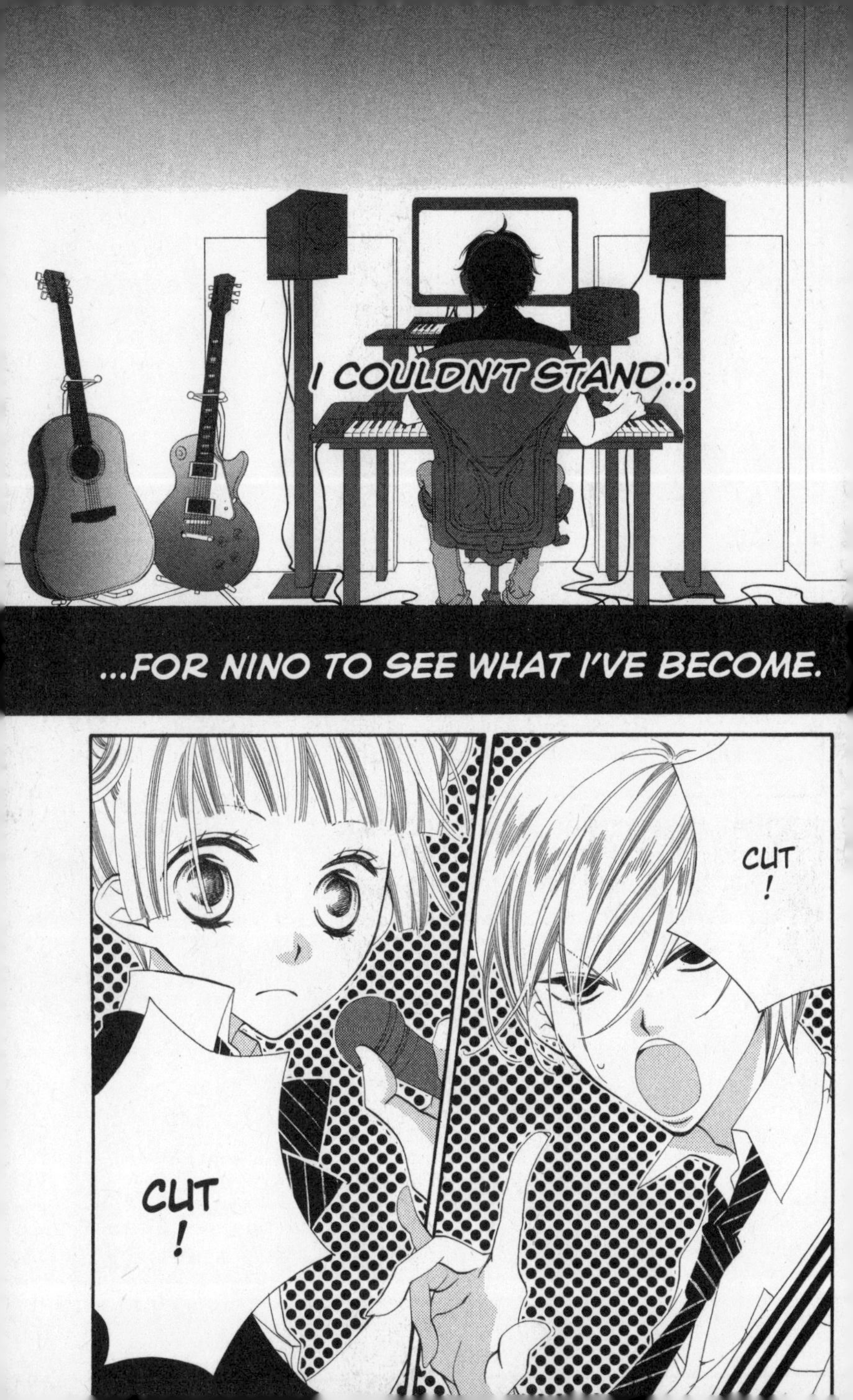
I COULDN'T STAND...
...FOR NINO TO SEE WHAT I'VE BECOME.
CUT!
CUT!

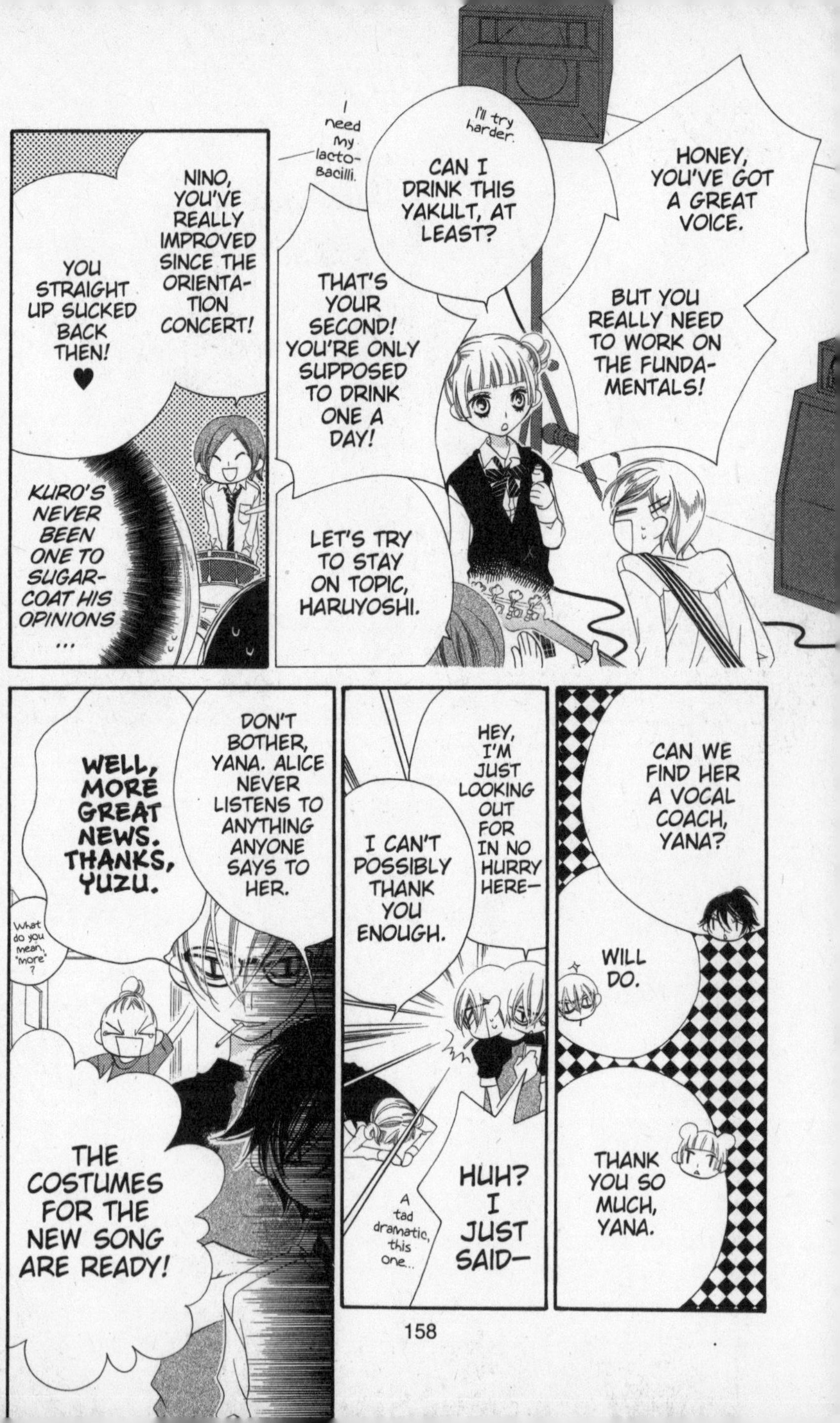
HONEY, YOU'VE GOT A GREAT VOICE.
BUT YOU REALLY NEED TO WORK ON THE FUNDAMENTALS!
I'll try harder.
CAN I DRINK THIS YAKULT, AT LEAST?
I need my lacto-bacilli.
THAT'S YOUR SECOND! YOU'RE ONLY SUPPOSED TO DRINK ONE A DAY!
LET'S TRY TO STAY ON TOPIC, HARUYOSHI.
NINO, YOU'VE REALLY IMPROVED SINCE THE ORIENTATION CONCERT!
YOU STRAIGHT UP SUCKED BACK THEN! ♥
KURO'S NEVER BEEN ONE TO SUGAR-COAT HIS OPINIONS...
CAN WE FIND HER A VOCAL COACH, YANA?
WILL DO.
THANK YOU SO MUCH, YANA.
HEY, I'M JUST LOOKING OUT FOR IN NO HURRY HERE—
I CAN'T POSSIBLY THANK YOU ENOUGH.
HUH? I JUST SAID—
A tad dramatic, this one...
DON'T BOTHER, YANA. ALICE NEVER LISTENS TO ANYTHING ANYONE SAYS TO HER.
WELL, MORE GREAT NEWS. THANKS, YUZU.
What do you mean, "more"?
THE COSTUMES FOR THE NEW SONG ARE READY!

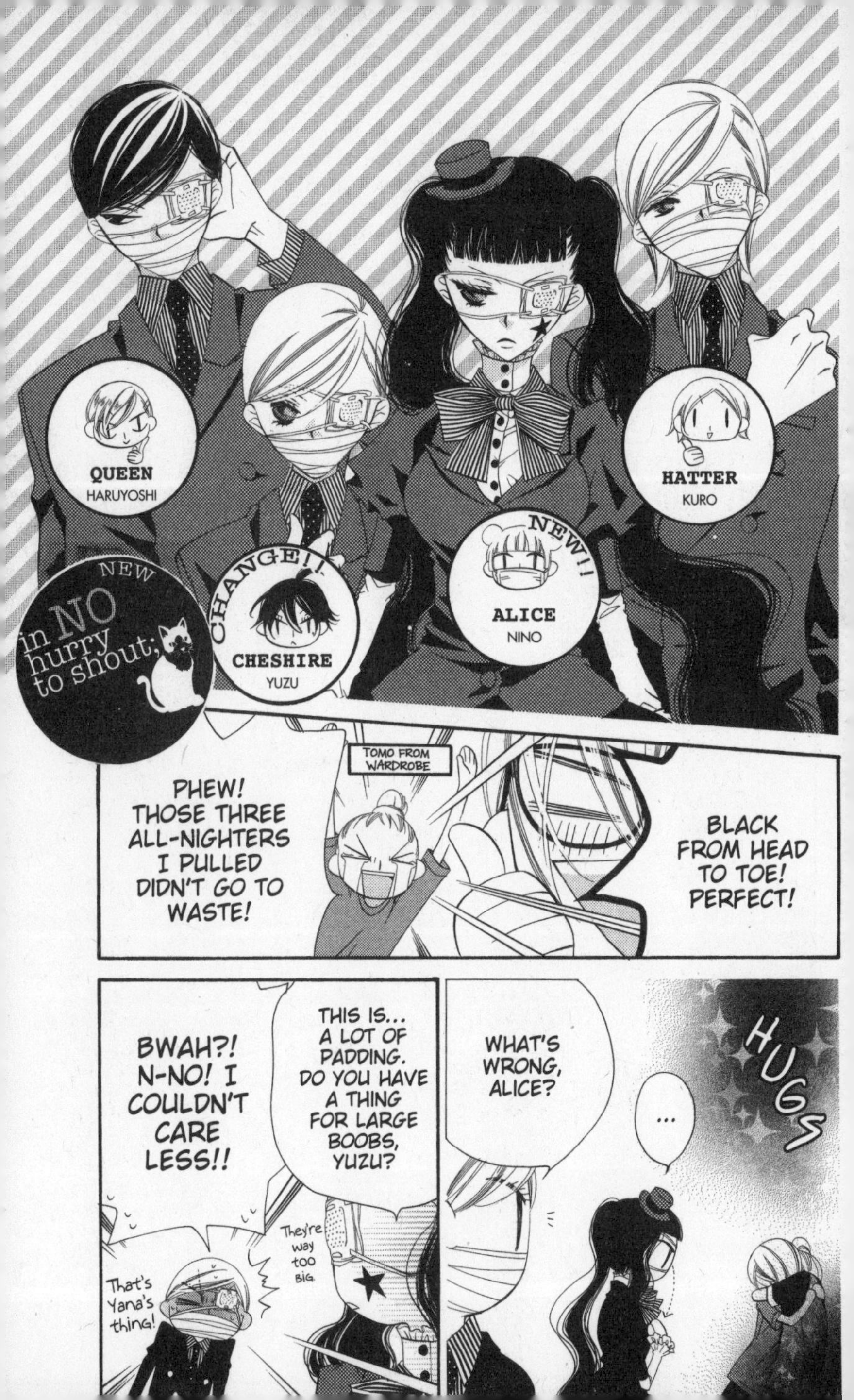
HATTER
KURO
QUEEN
HARUYOSHI
NEW!!
ALICE
NINO
CHANGE!!
CHESHIRE
YUZU
NEW
in NO hurry to shout;
TOMO FROM WARDROBE
BLACK FROM HEAD TO TOE! PERFECT!
PHEW! THOSE THREE ALL-NIGHTERS I PULLED DIDN'T GO TO WASTE!
HUGS
...
WHAT'S WRONG, ALICE?
THIS IS... A LOT OF PADDING. DO YOU HAVE A THING FOR LARGE BOOBS, YUZU?
They're way too big.
BWAH?! N-NO! I COULDN'T CARE LESS!!
That's Yana's thing!

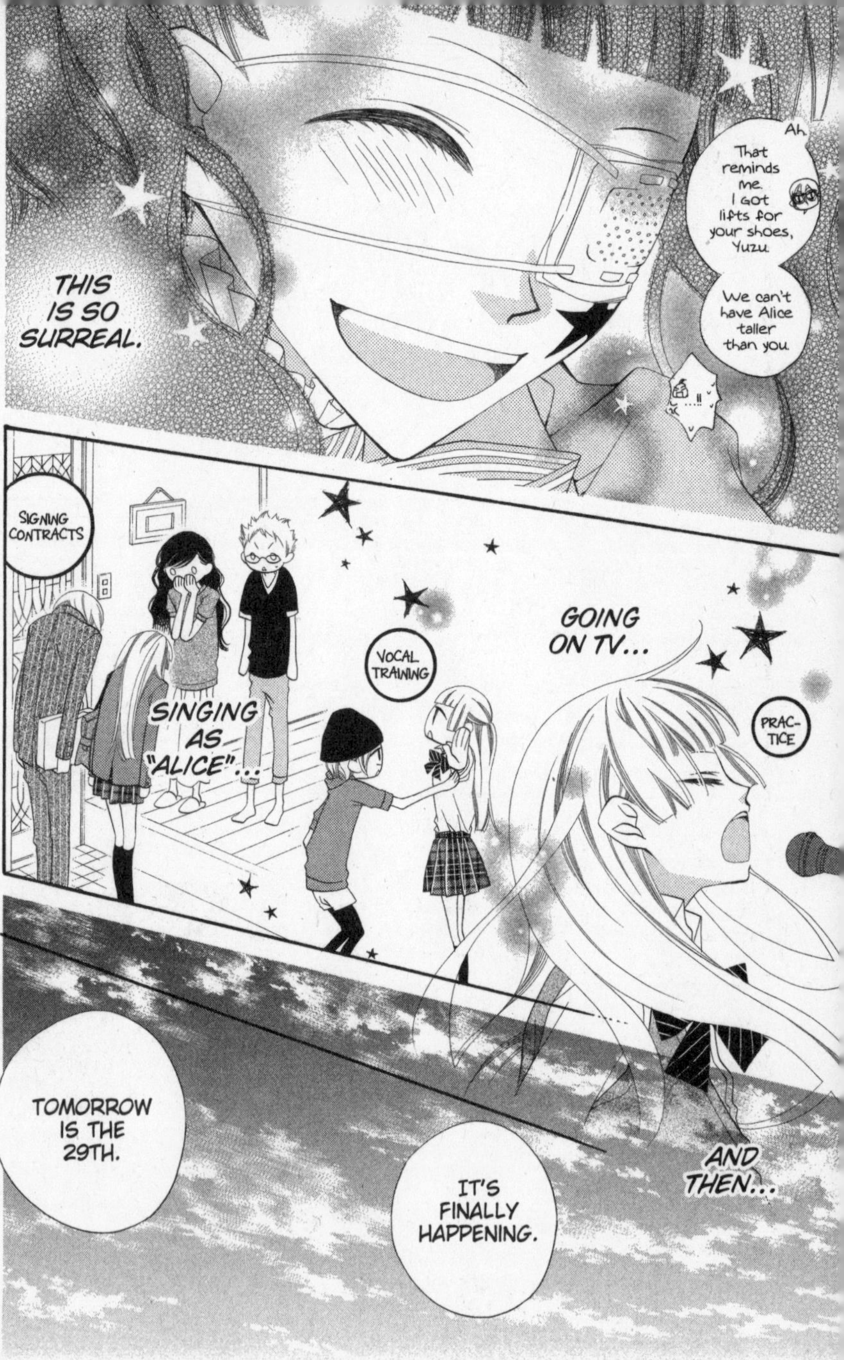
Ah.
That reminds me. I got lifts for your shoes, Yuzu.
We can't have Alice taller than you.
THIS IS SO SURREAL.
PRAC-TICE
GOING ON TV...
VOCAL TRAINING
SINGING AS "ALICE"...
SIGNING CONTRACTS
AND THEN...
IT'S FINALLY HAPPENING.
TOMORROW IS THE 29TH.

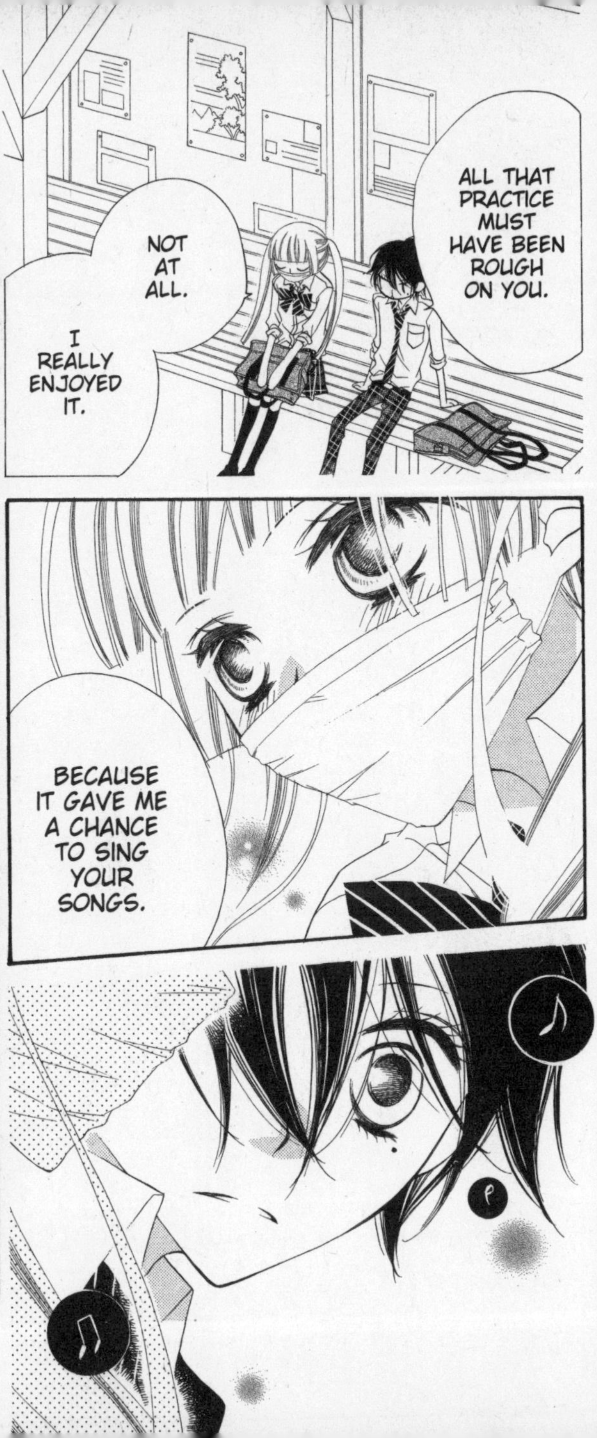
ALL THAT PRACTICE MUST HAVE BEEN ROUGH ON YOU.
NOT AT ALL.
I REALLY ENJOYED IT.
BECAUSE IT GAVE ME A CHANCE TO SING YOUR SONGS.

5

Here it is—my last column! What did you think of Anonymous Noise volume 2? I hope you've been enjoying it!

Just like with volume 1, writing this has been a deeply enjoyable experience for me. I will strive to maintain that feeling as I continue this series! I hope we have a chance to meet again in volume 3! Until then! Ryoko Fukuyama

[special thanks]

KYOKO INOUE
IZUMI HIOU
MINI KOMATSU
TAKAYUKI NAGASHIMA
KENJU NORO
MY FAMILY
MY FRIENDS
AND YOU!!

Ryoko Fukuyama
c/o Anonymous Noise Editor
VIZ Media
P.O. Box 77010
San Francisco, CA 94107

http://ryoco.net/

@ryocoryocoryoco

http://facebook.com/ryocoryocoryoco

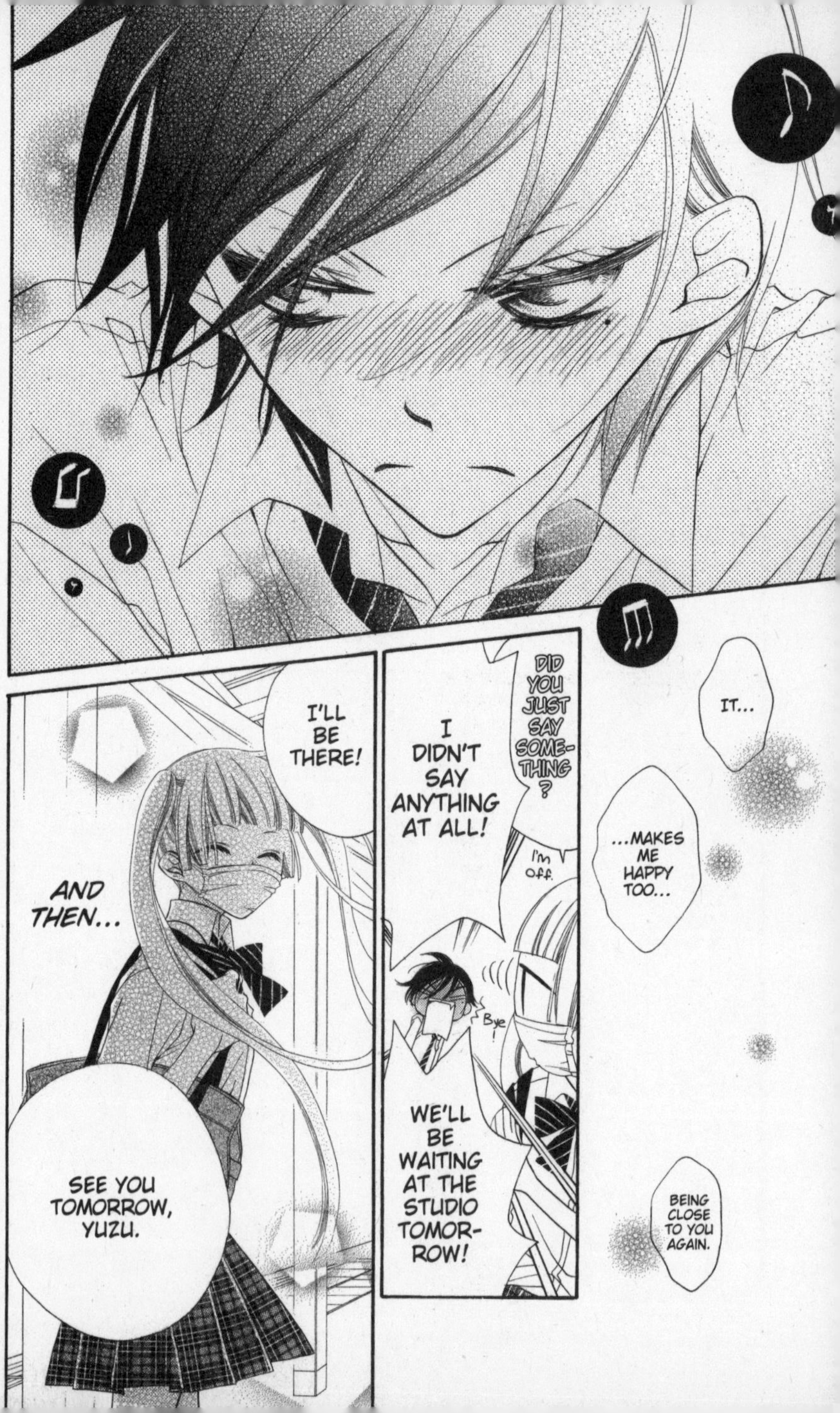
IT...
...MAKES ME HAPPY TOO...
BEING CLOSE TO YOU AGAIN.
DID YOU JUST SAY SOME-THING?
I DIDN'T SAY ANYTHING AT ALL!
I'm off.
Bye
WE'LL BE WAITING AT THE STUDIO TOMOR-ROW!
I'LL BE THERE!
AND THEN...
SEE YOU TOMORROW, YUZU.

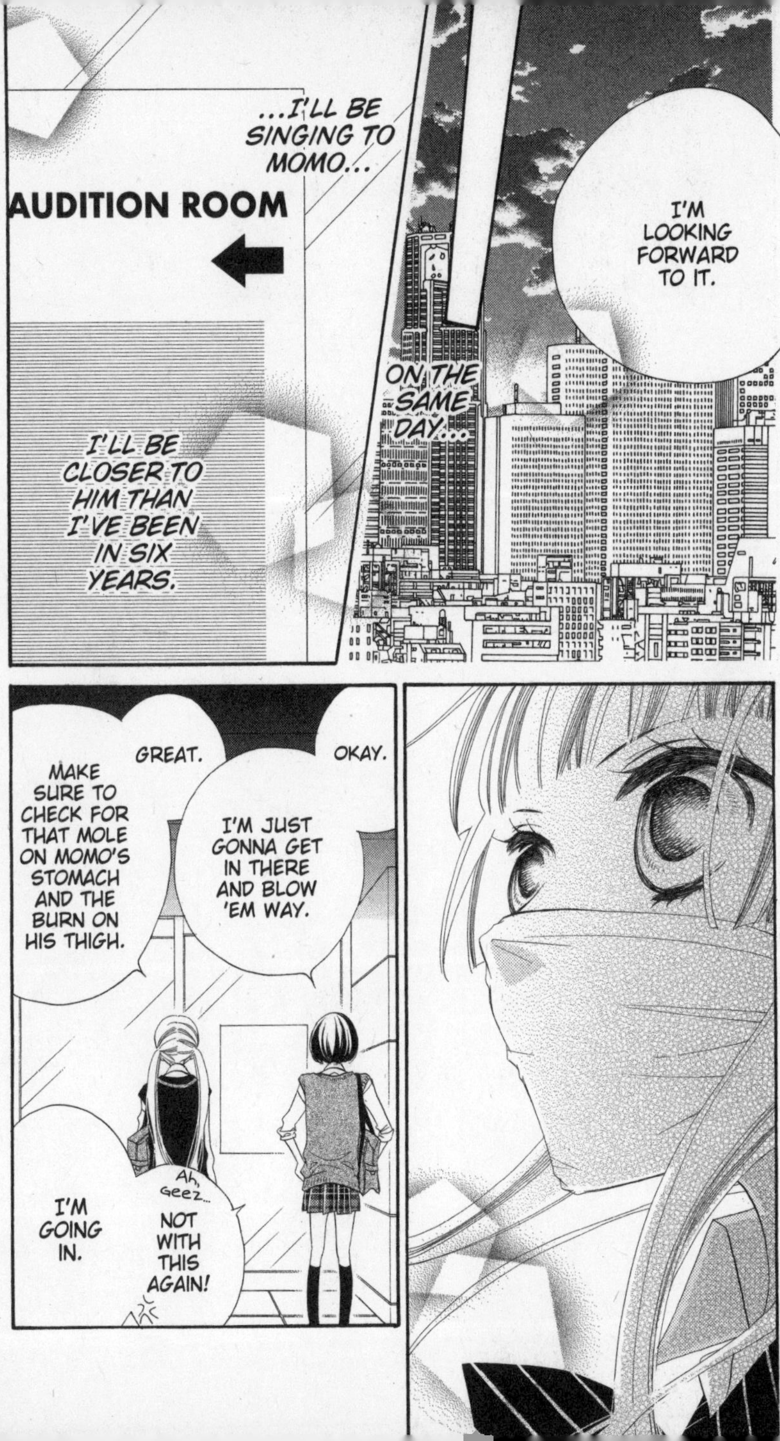
I'M LOOKING FORWARD TO IT.
ON THE SAME DAY...
...I'LL BE SINGING TO MOMO...
AUDITION ROOM
I'LL BE CLOSER TO HIM THAN I'VE BEEN IN SIX YEARS.
OKAY.
I'M JUST GONNA GET IN THERE AND BLOW 'EM WAY.
GREAT.
MAKE SURE TO CHECK FOR THAT MOLE ON MOMO'S STOMACH AND THE BURN ON HIS THIGH.
Ah, Geez...
NOT WITH THIS AGAIN!
I'M GOING IN.

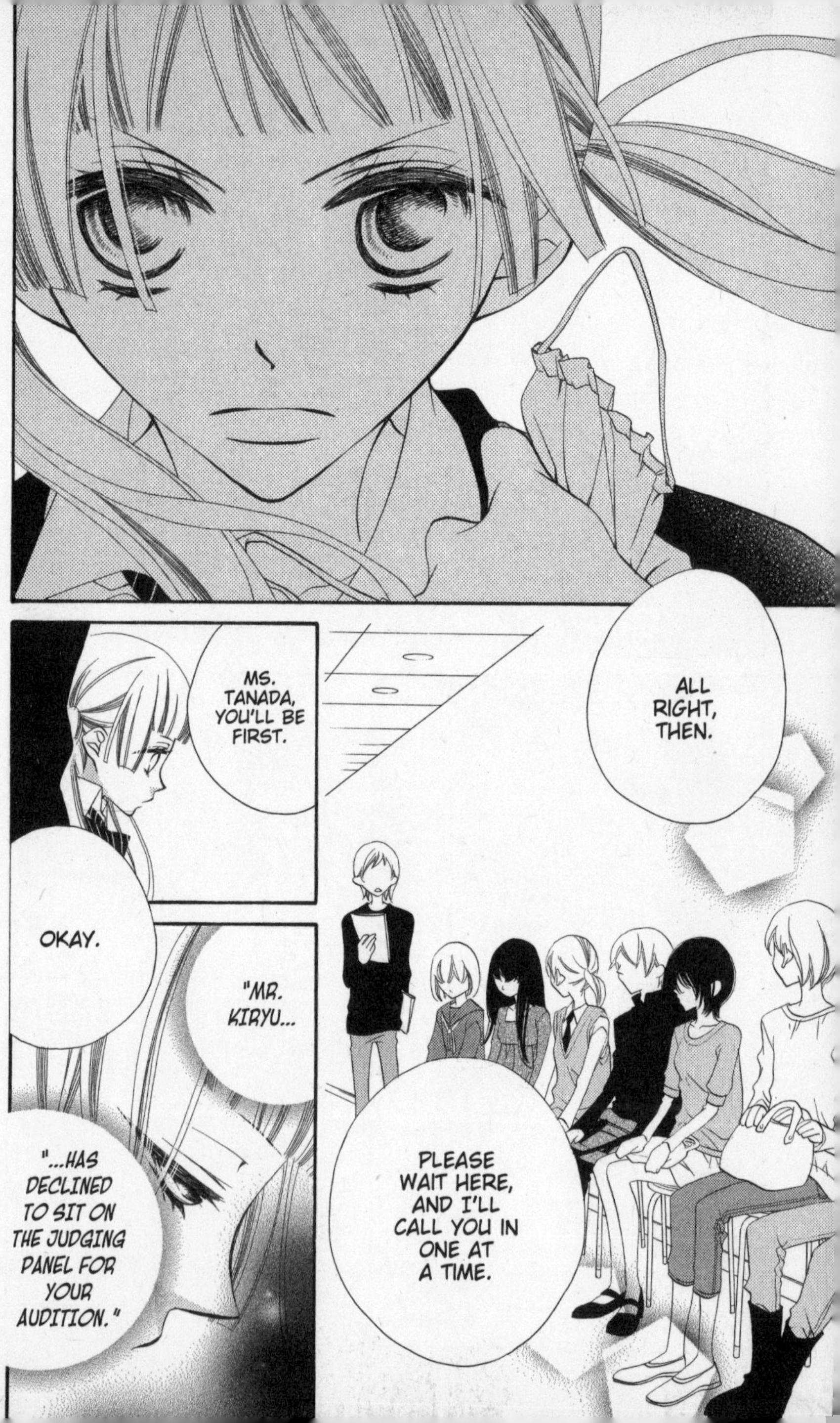
ALL RIGHT, THEN.
PLEASE WAIT HERE, AND I'LL CALL YOU IN ONE AT A TIME.
MS. TANADA, YOU'LL BE FIRST.
OKAY.
"MR. KIRYU...
"...HAS DECLINED TO SIT ON THE JUDGING PANEL FOR YOUR AUDITION."

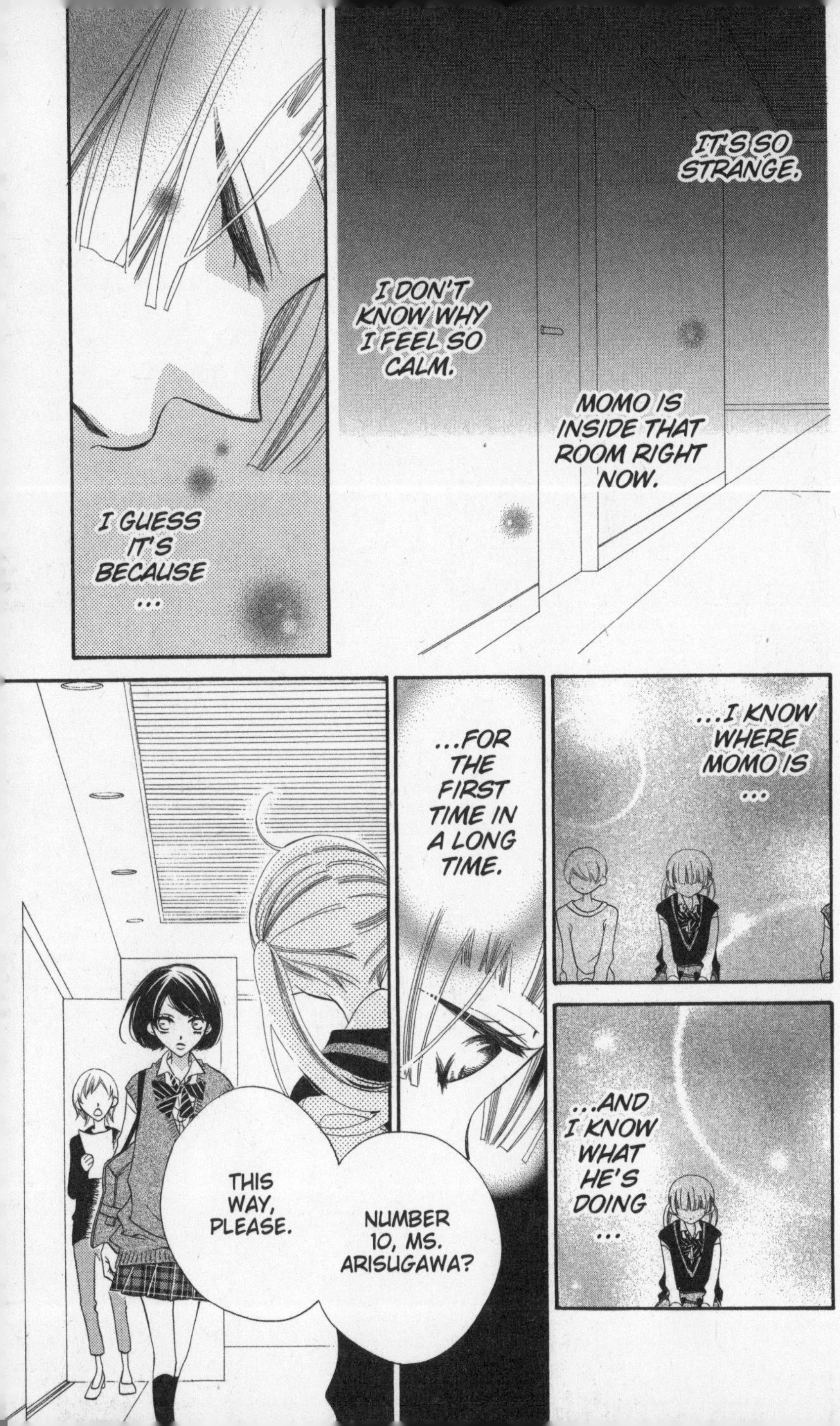
IT'S SO STRANGE.
I DON'T KNOW WHY I FEEL SO CALM.
MOMO IS INSIDE THAT ROOM RIGHT NOW.
I GUESS IT'S BECAUSE ...
...I KNOW WHERE MOMO IS ...
...AND I KNOW WHAT HE'S DOING ...
...FOR THE FIRST TIME IN A LONG TIME.
NUMBER 10, MS. ARISUGAWA?
THIS WAY, PLEASE.

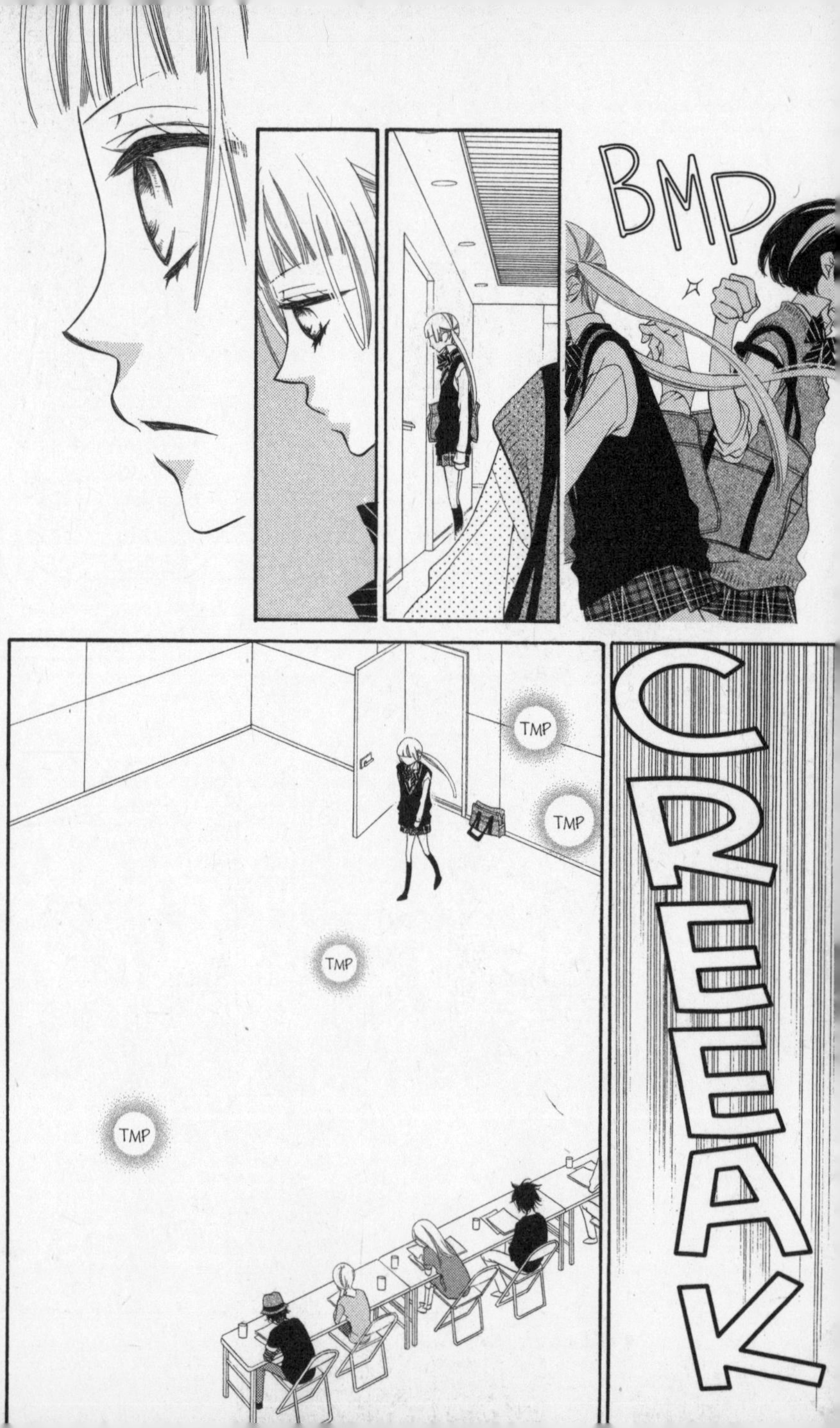
BMP
CREAK
TMP
TMP
TMP
TMP

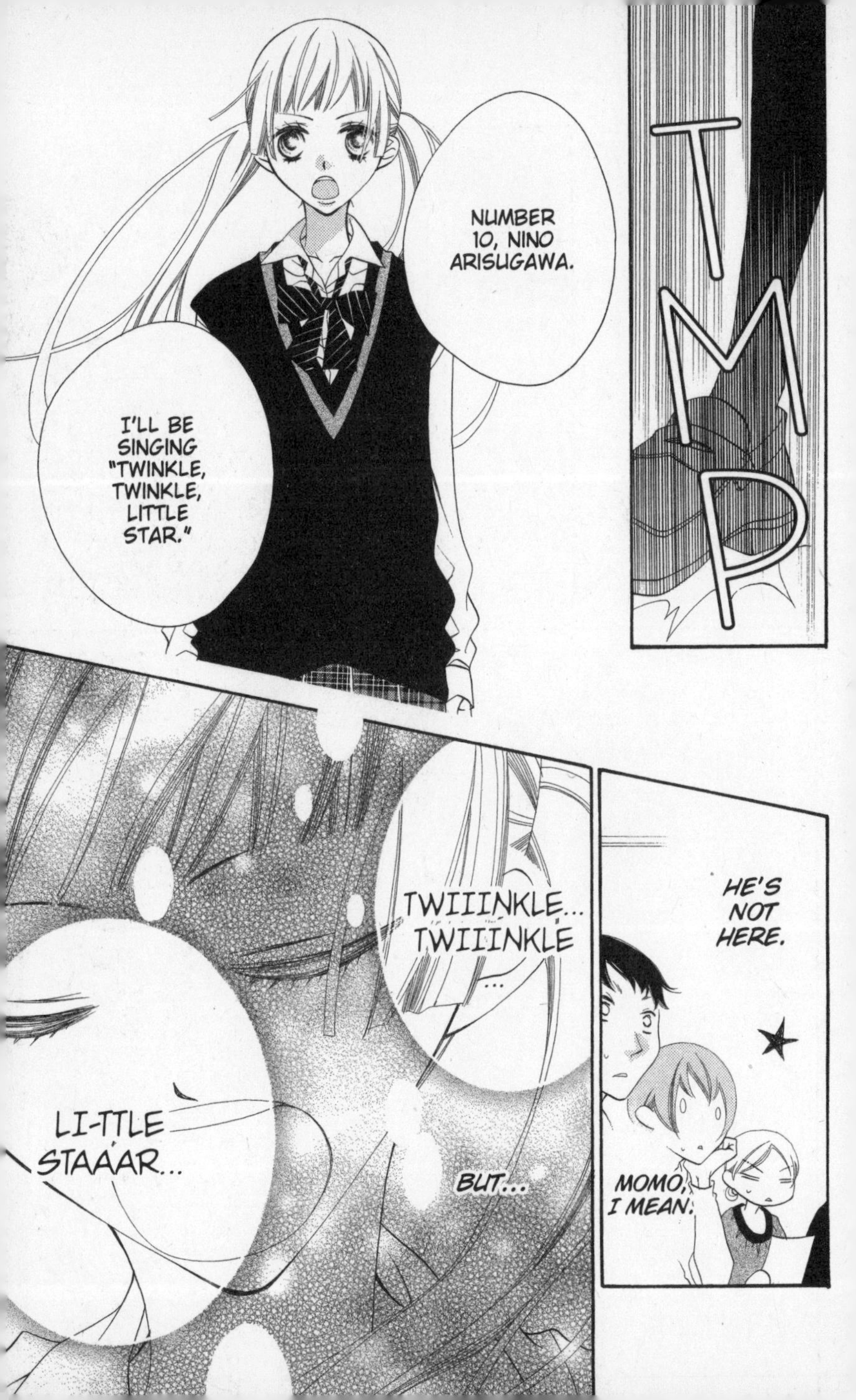
TMP
NUMBER 10, NINO ARISUGAWA.
I'LL BE SINGING "TWINKLE, TWINKLE, LITTLE STAR."
HE'S NOT HERE.
MOMO, I MEAN.
TWIIINKLE... TWIIINKLE...
LI-TTLE STAAAR...
BUT...

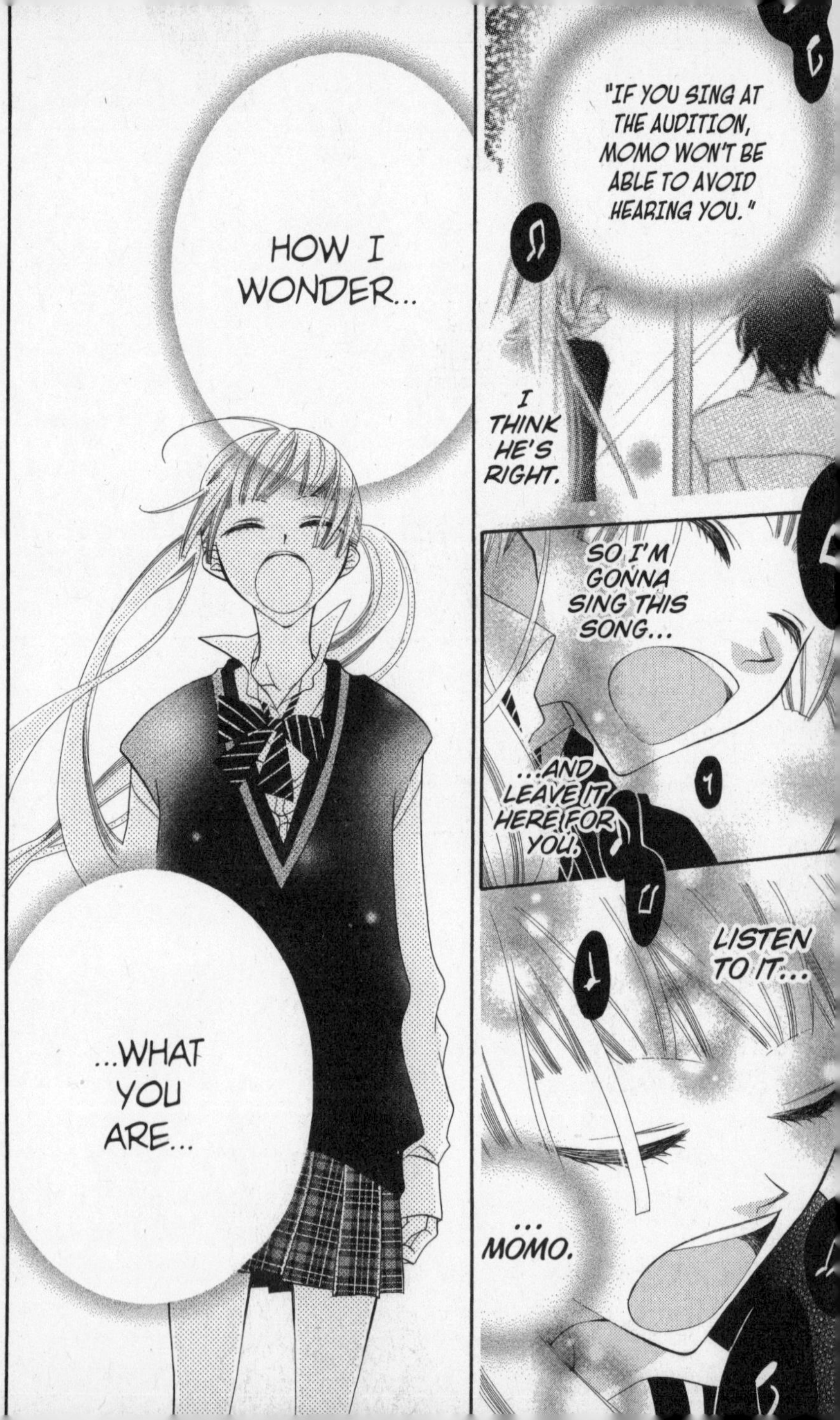
"IF YOU SING AT THE AUDITION, MOMO WON'T BE ABLE TO AVOID HEARING YOU."
I THINK HE'S RIGHT.
SO I'M GONNA SING THIS SONG...
...AND LEAVE IT HERE FOR YOU.
LISTEN TO IT...
...MOMO.
HOW I WONDER...
...WHAT YOU ARE...

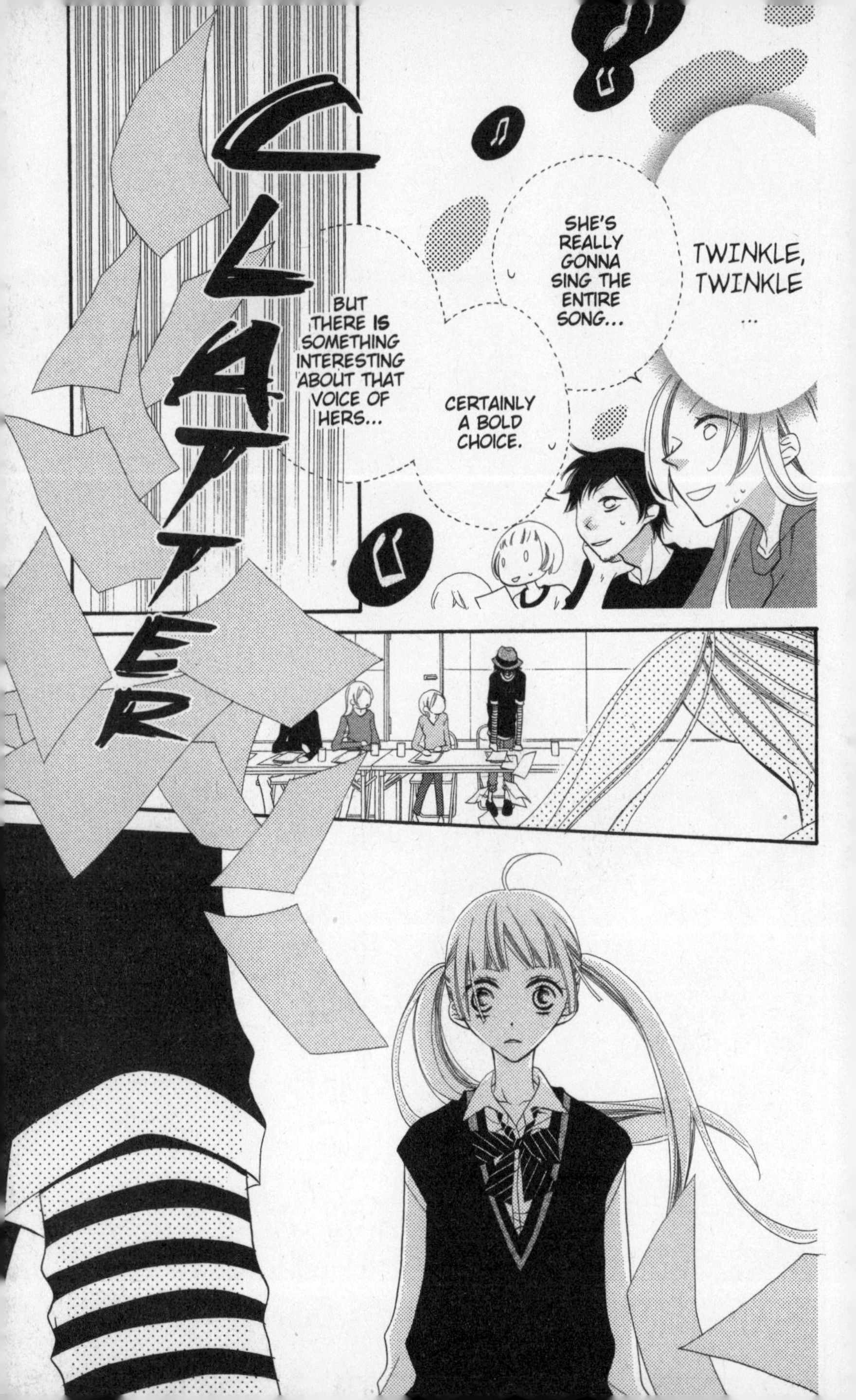
TWINKLE, TWINKLE ...
SHE'S REALLY GONNA SING THE ENTIRE SONG...
CERTAINLY A BOLD CHOICE.
BUT THERE IS SOMETHING INTERESTING ABOUT THAT VOICE OF HERS...
CLATTER

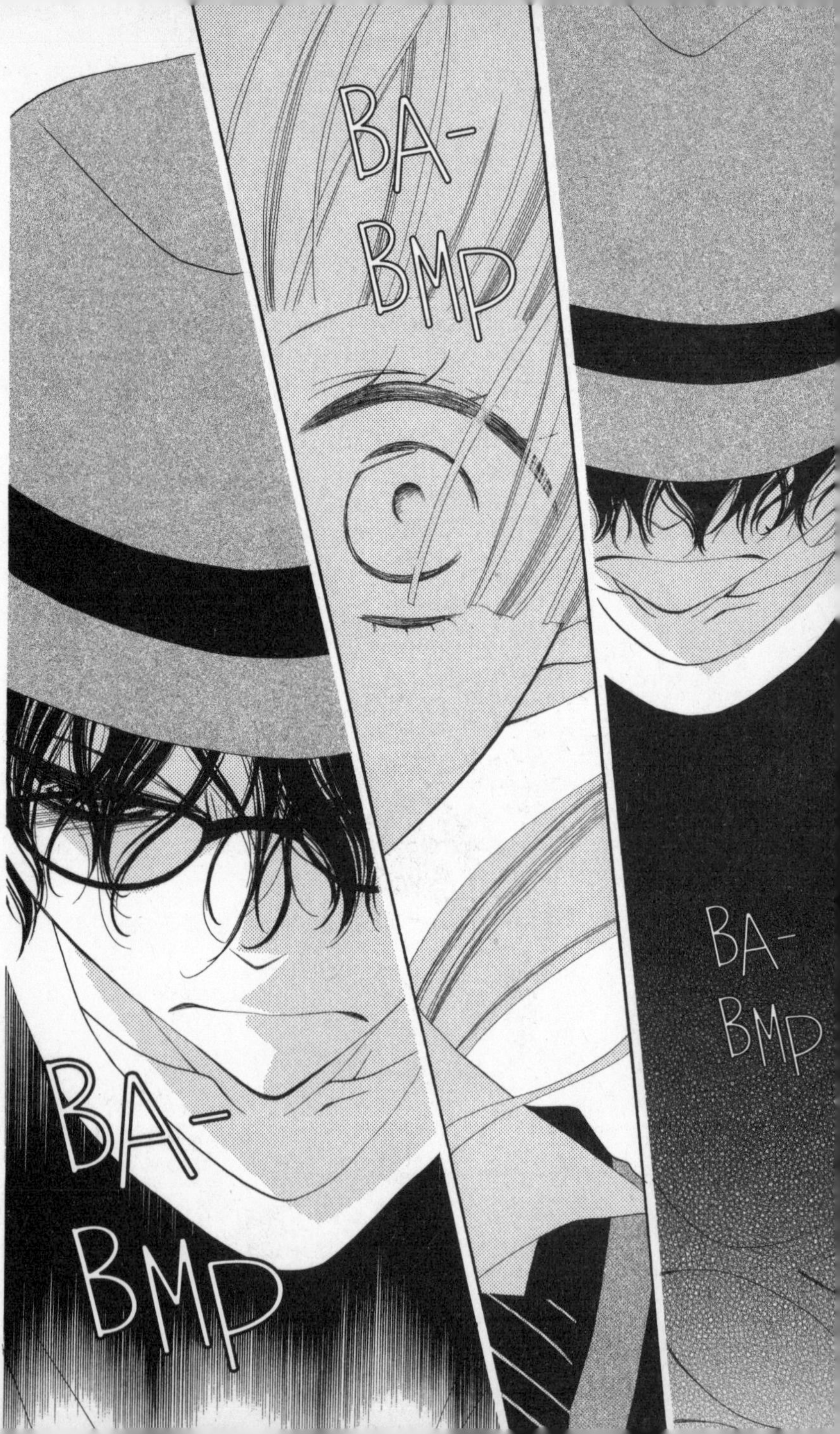
BA-
BMP
BA-
BMP
BA-
BMP

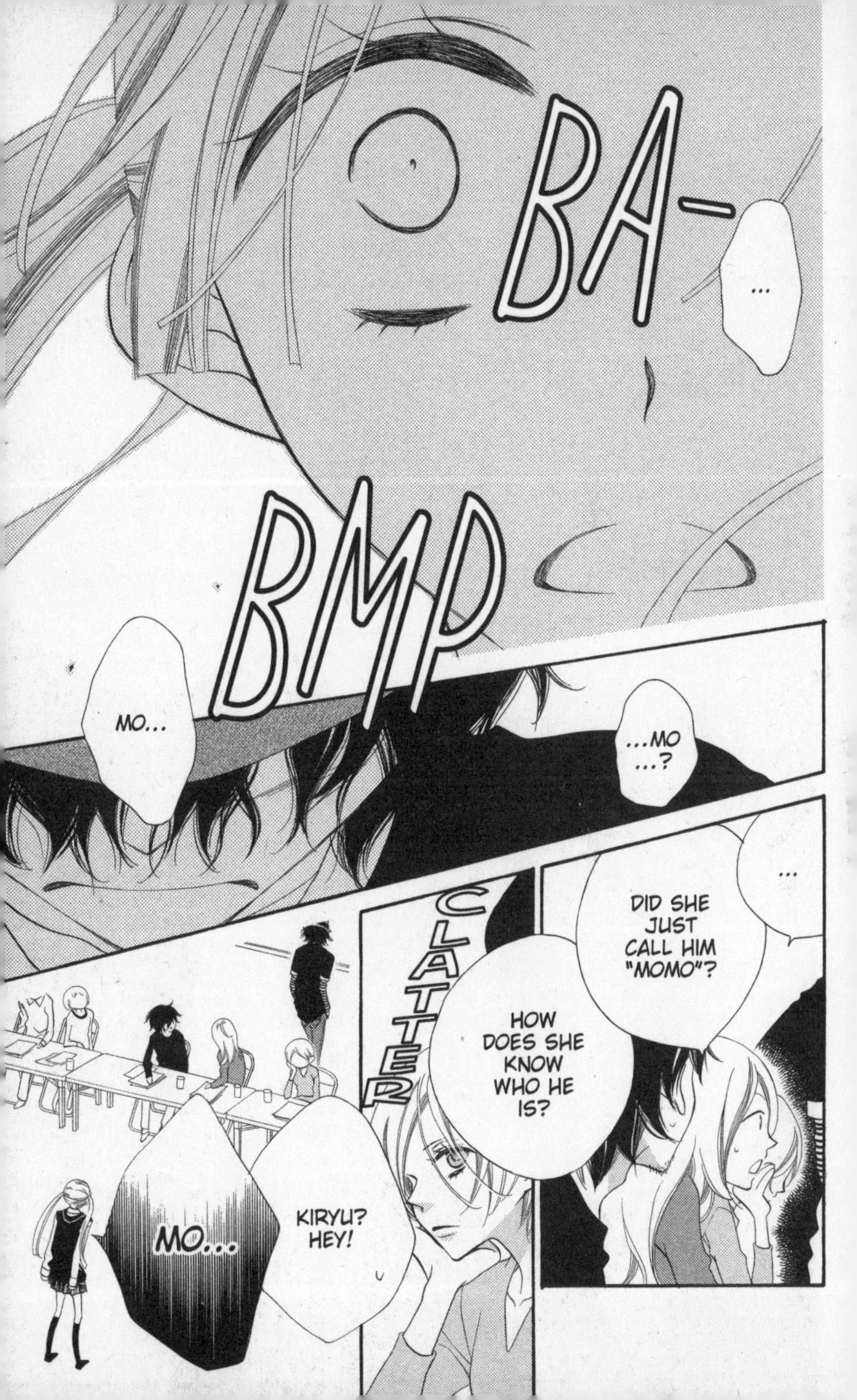
BA-
...
BMP
...MO
...?
MO...
...
DID SHE JUST CALL HIM "MOMO"?
CLATTER
HOW DOES SHE KNOW WHO HE IS?
KIRYU? HEY!
MO...

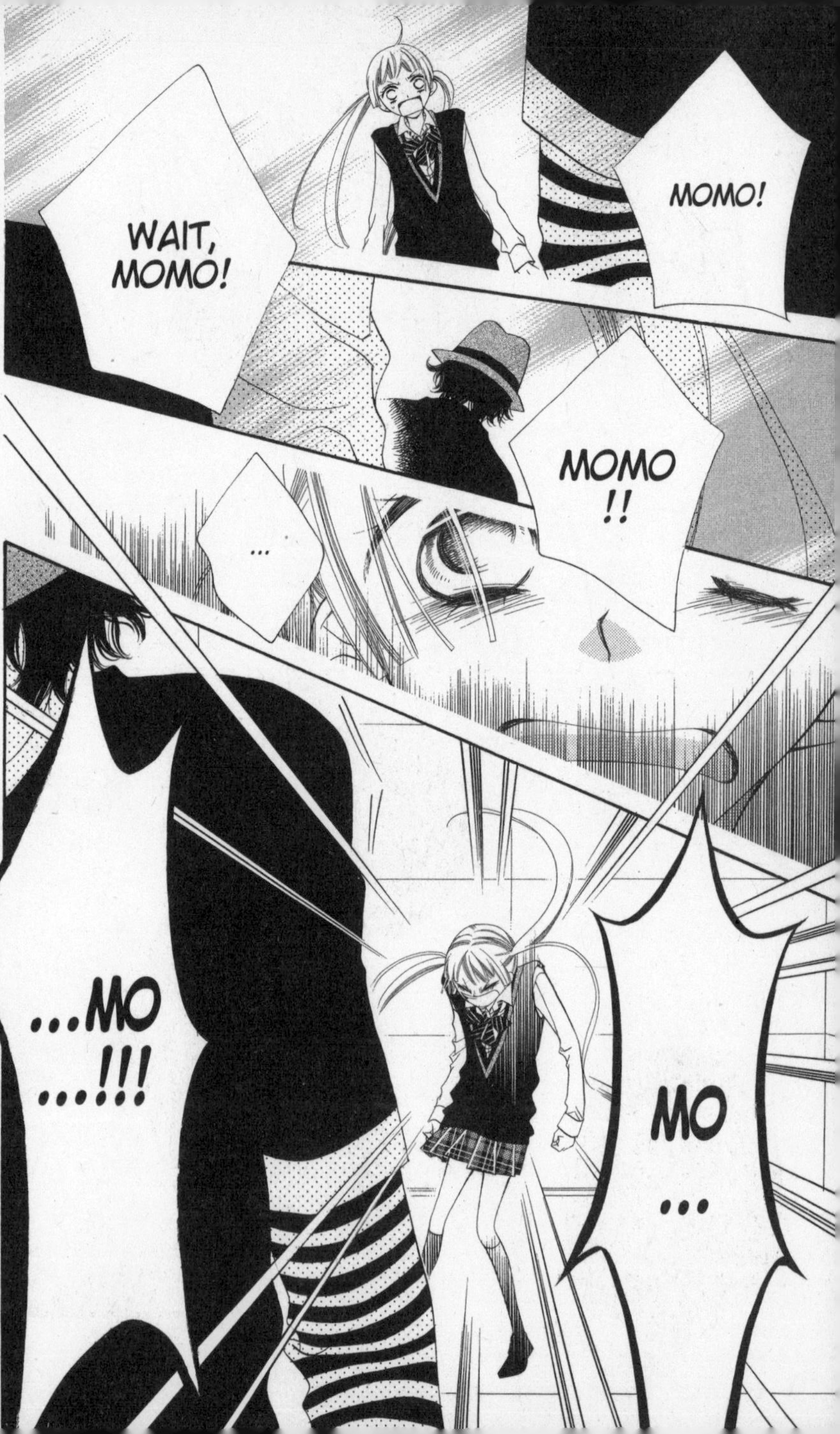
MOMO!
WAIT, MOMO!
MOMO !!
...
MO ...
...MO ...!!!

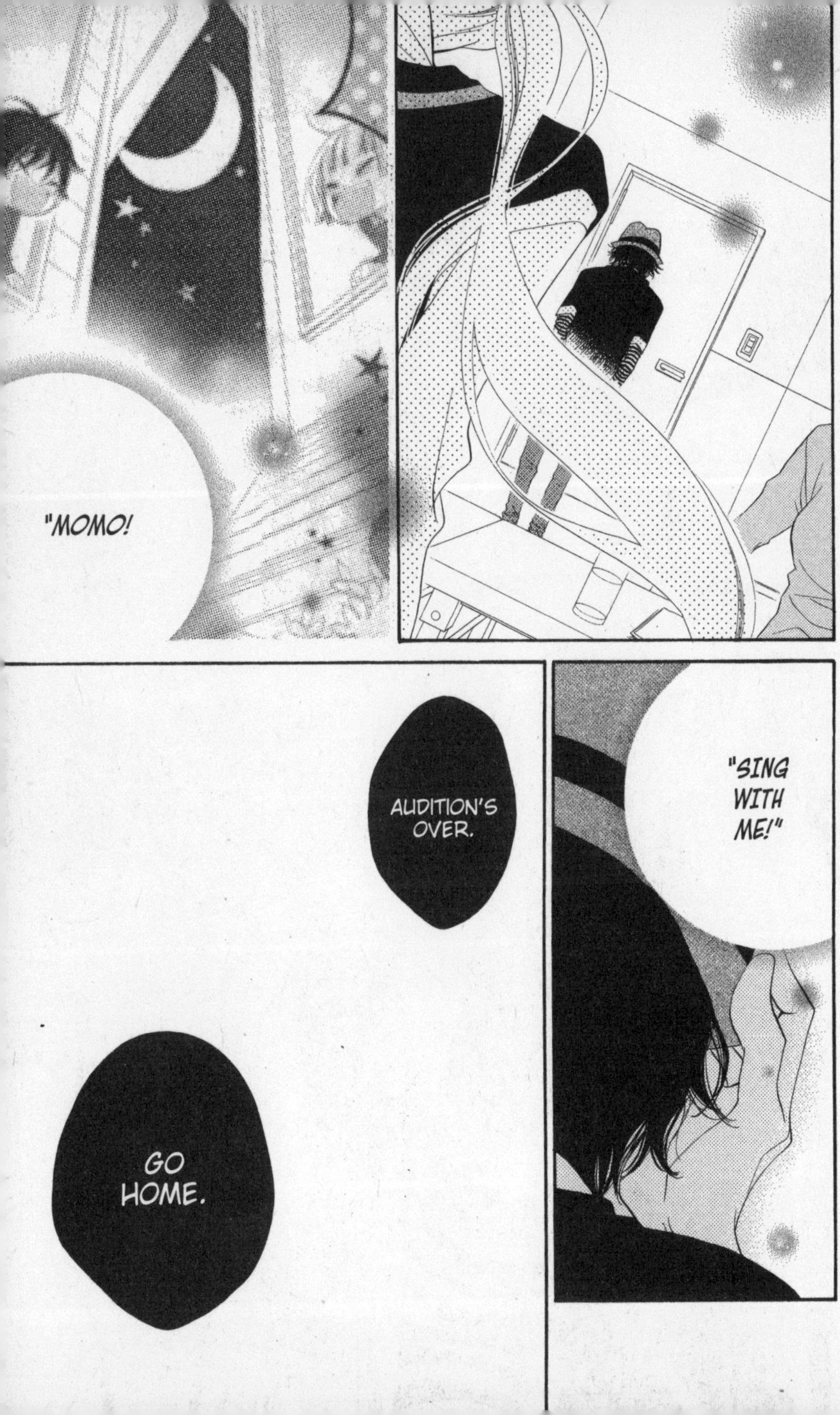
"MOMO!
"SING WITH ME!"
AUDITION'S OVER.
GO HOME.

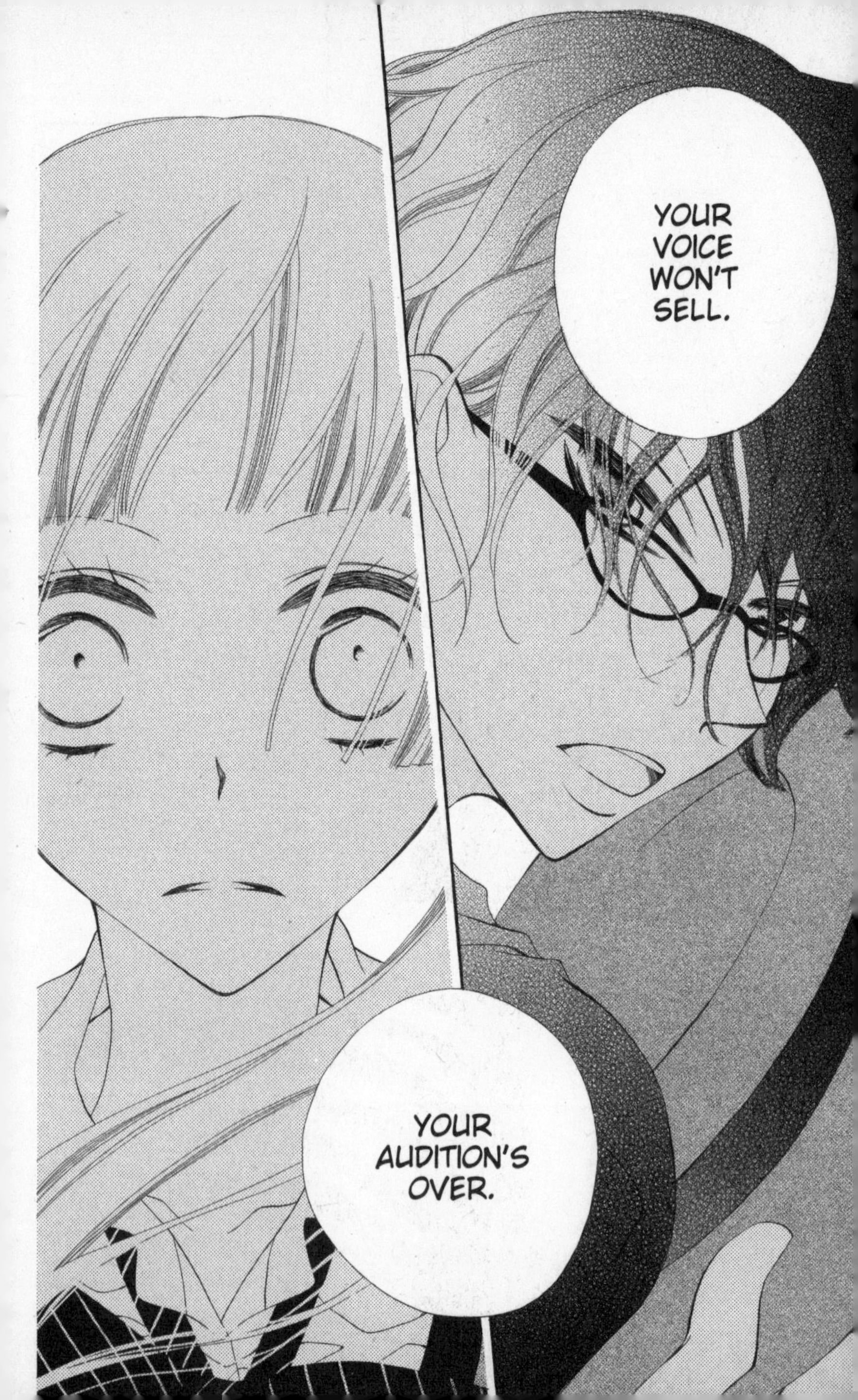
YOUR VOICE WON'T SELL.
YOUR AUDITION'S OVER.

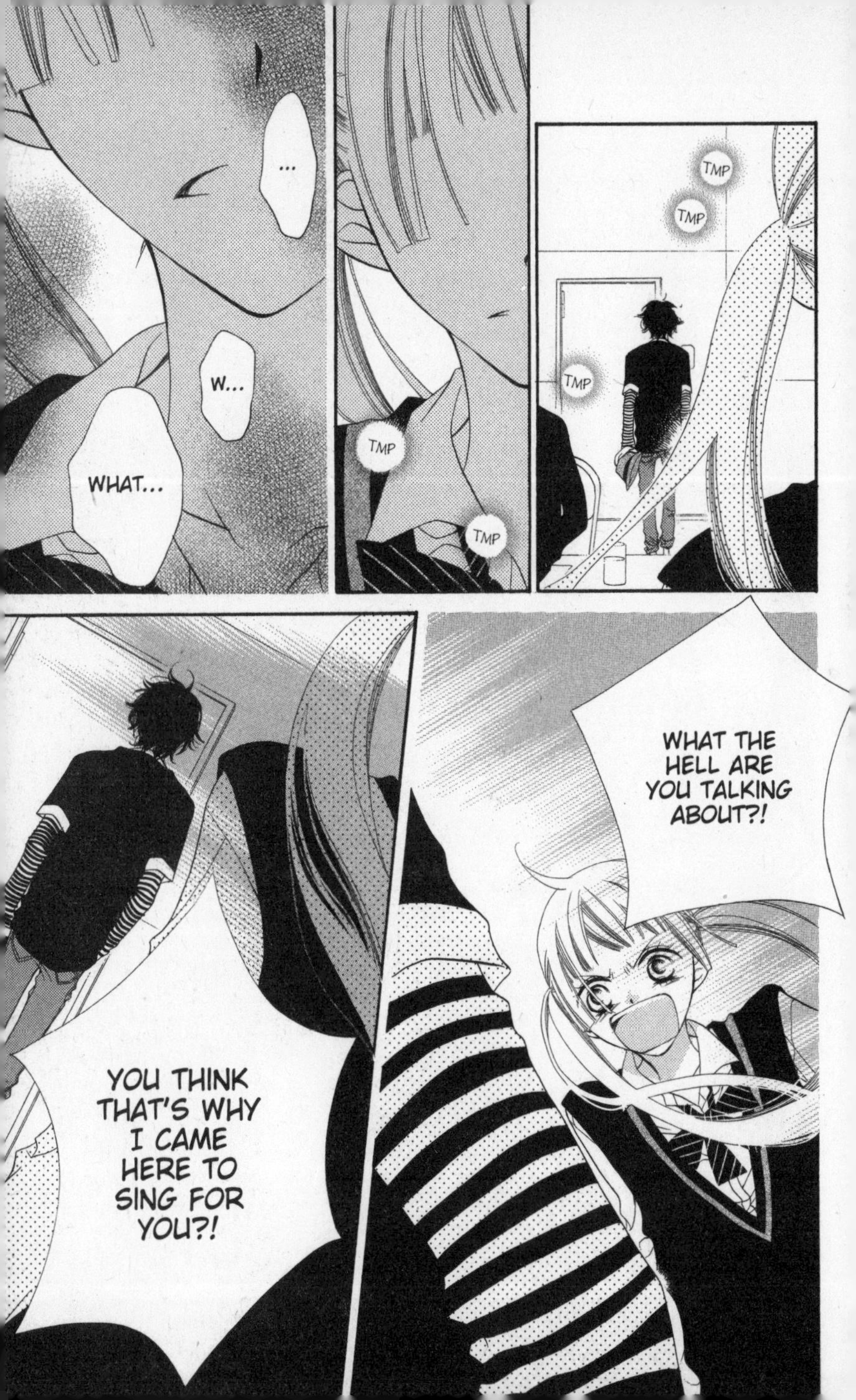
TMP
TMP
TMP
TMP
TMP
...
W...
WHAT...
WHAT THE HELL ARE YOU TALKING ABOUT?!
YOU THINK THAT'S WHY I CAME HERE TO SING FOR YOU?!

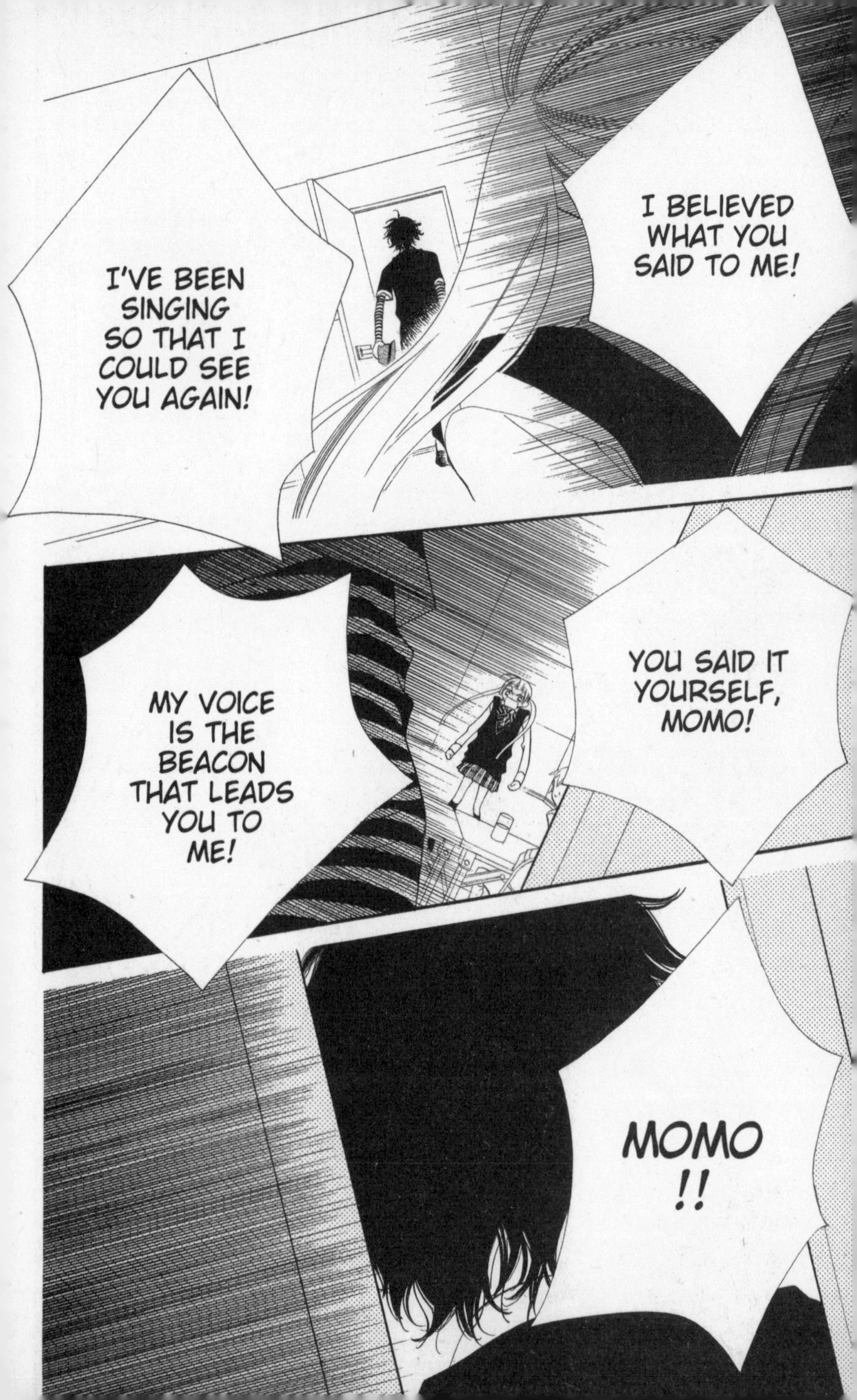
I BELIEVED WHAT YOU SAID TO ME!
I'VE BEEN SINGING SO THAT I COULD SEE YOU AGAIN!
YOU SAID IT YOURSELF, MOMO!
MY VOICE IS THE BEACON THAT LEADS YOU TO ME!
MOMO !!

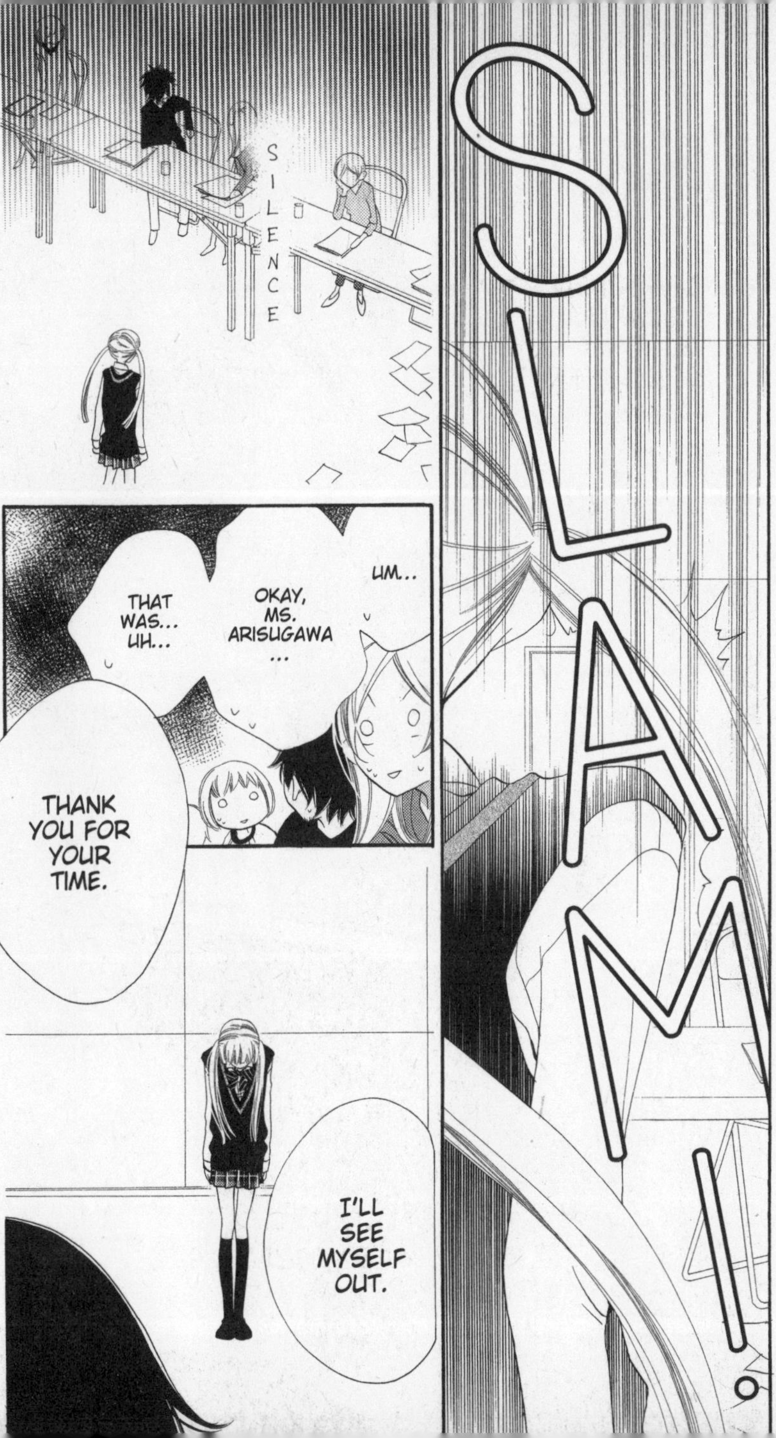
SLAM!
SILENCE
UM...
OKAY, MS. ARISUGAWA...
THAT WAS... UH...
THANK YOU FOR YOUR TIME.
I'LL SEE MYSELF OUT.

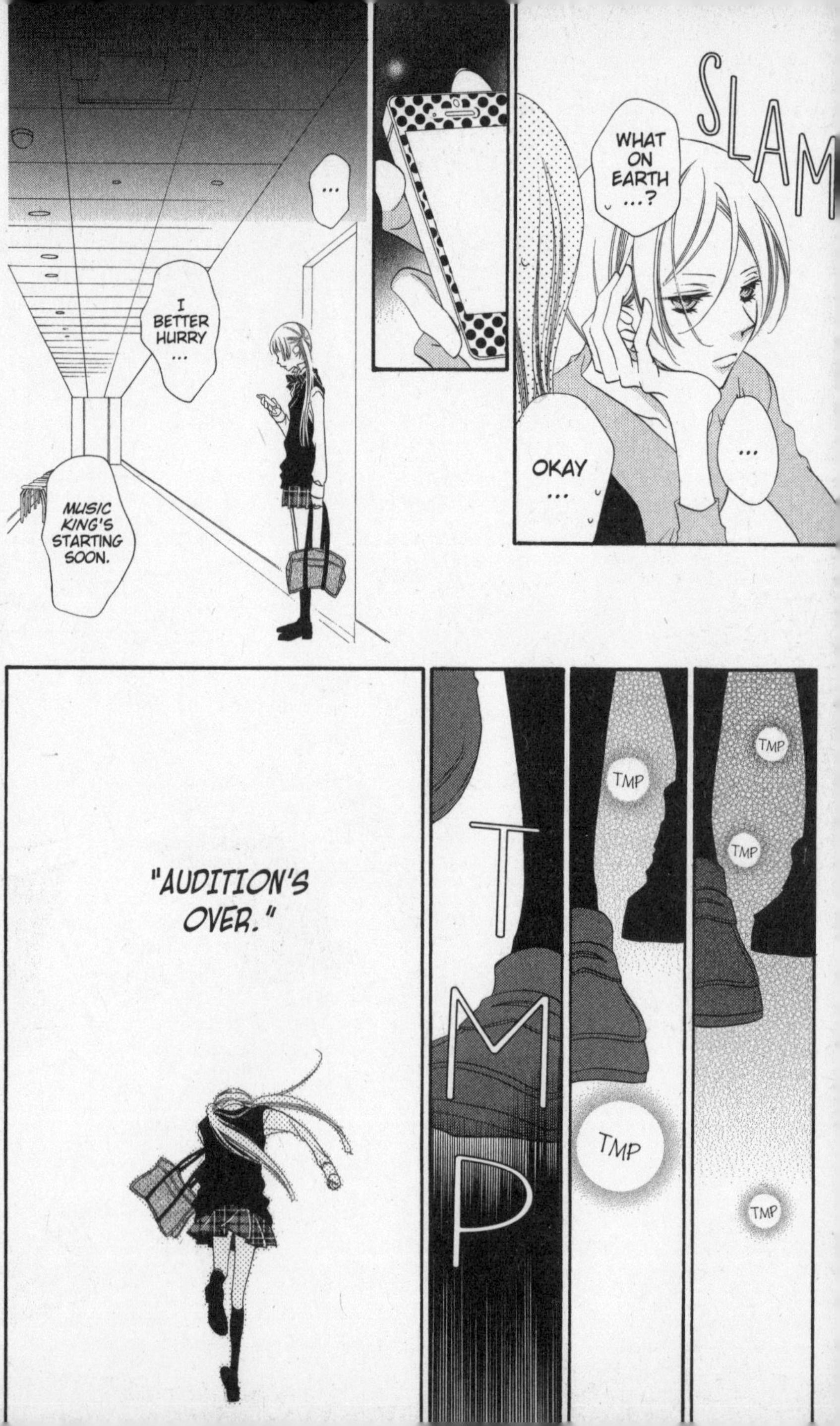
SLAM
WHAT ON EARTH ...?
...
OKAY ...
...
I BETTER HURRY ...
MUSIC KING'S STARTING SOON.
TMP
TMP
TMP
TMP
TMP
TMP
"AUDITION'S OVER."

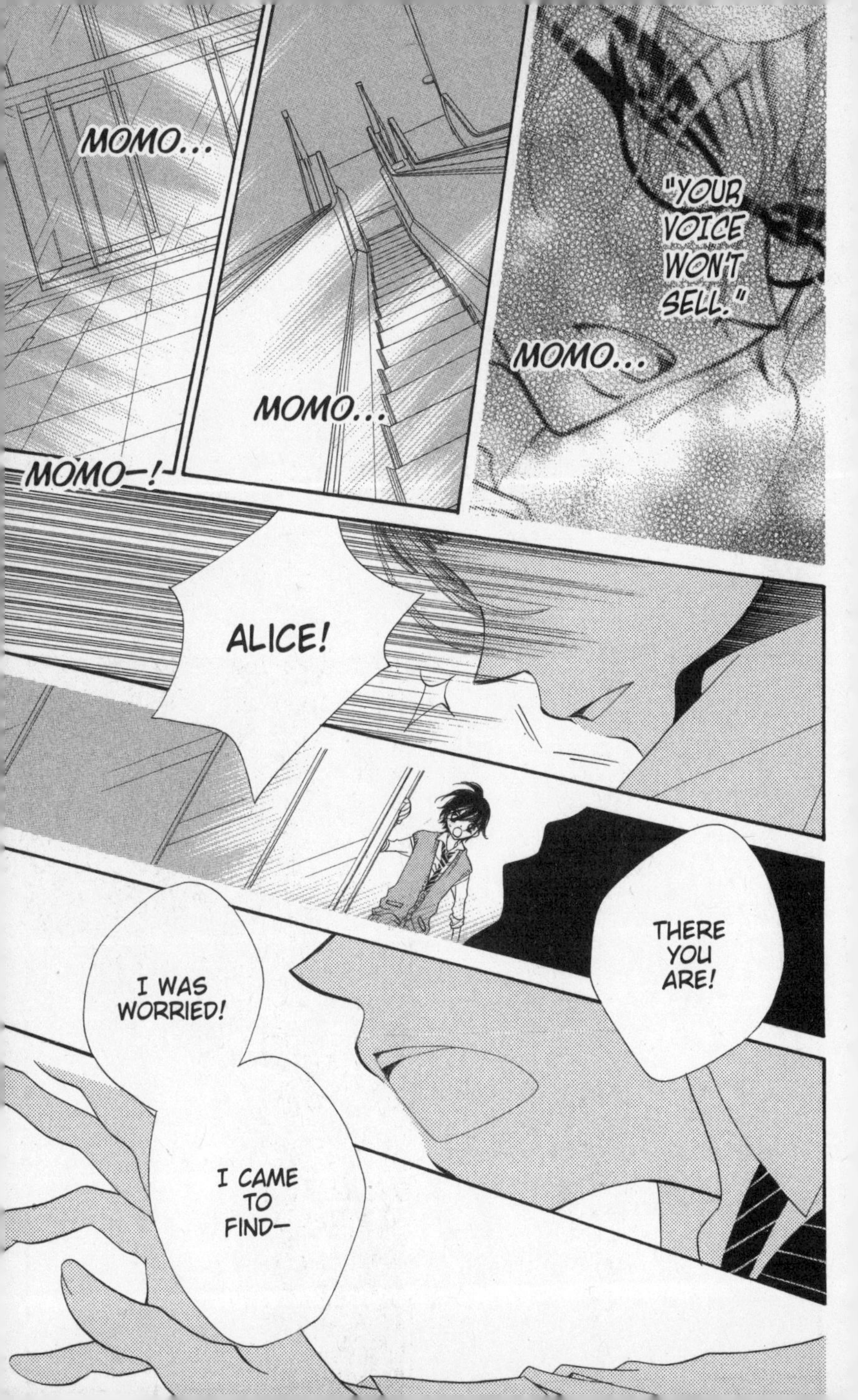
"YOUR VOICE WON'T SELL."
MOMO...
MOMO...
MOMO...
MOMO—!
ALICE!
THERE YOU ARE!
I WAS WORRIED!
I CAME TO FIND—

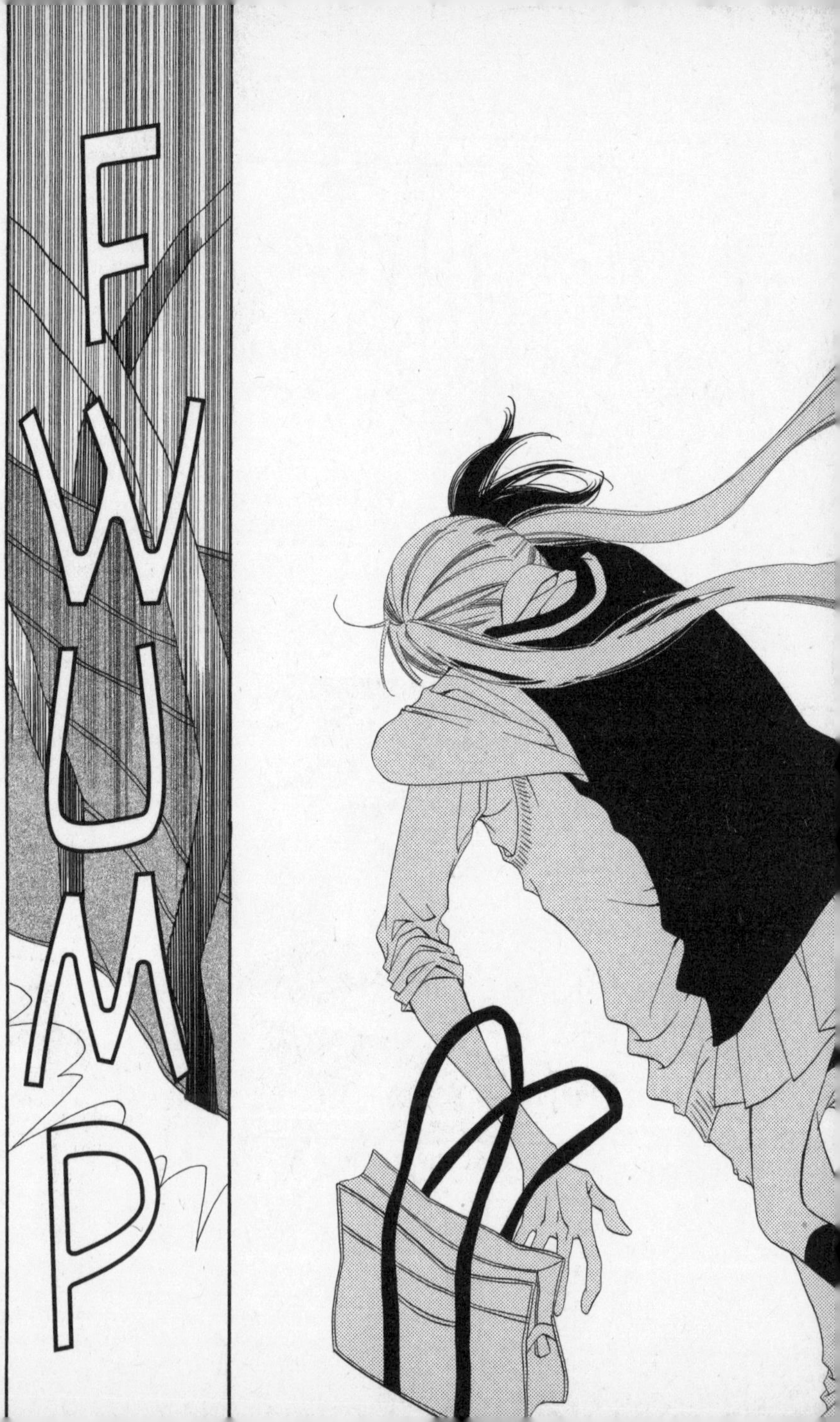
FWUMP

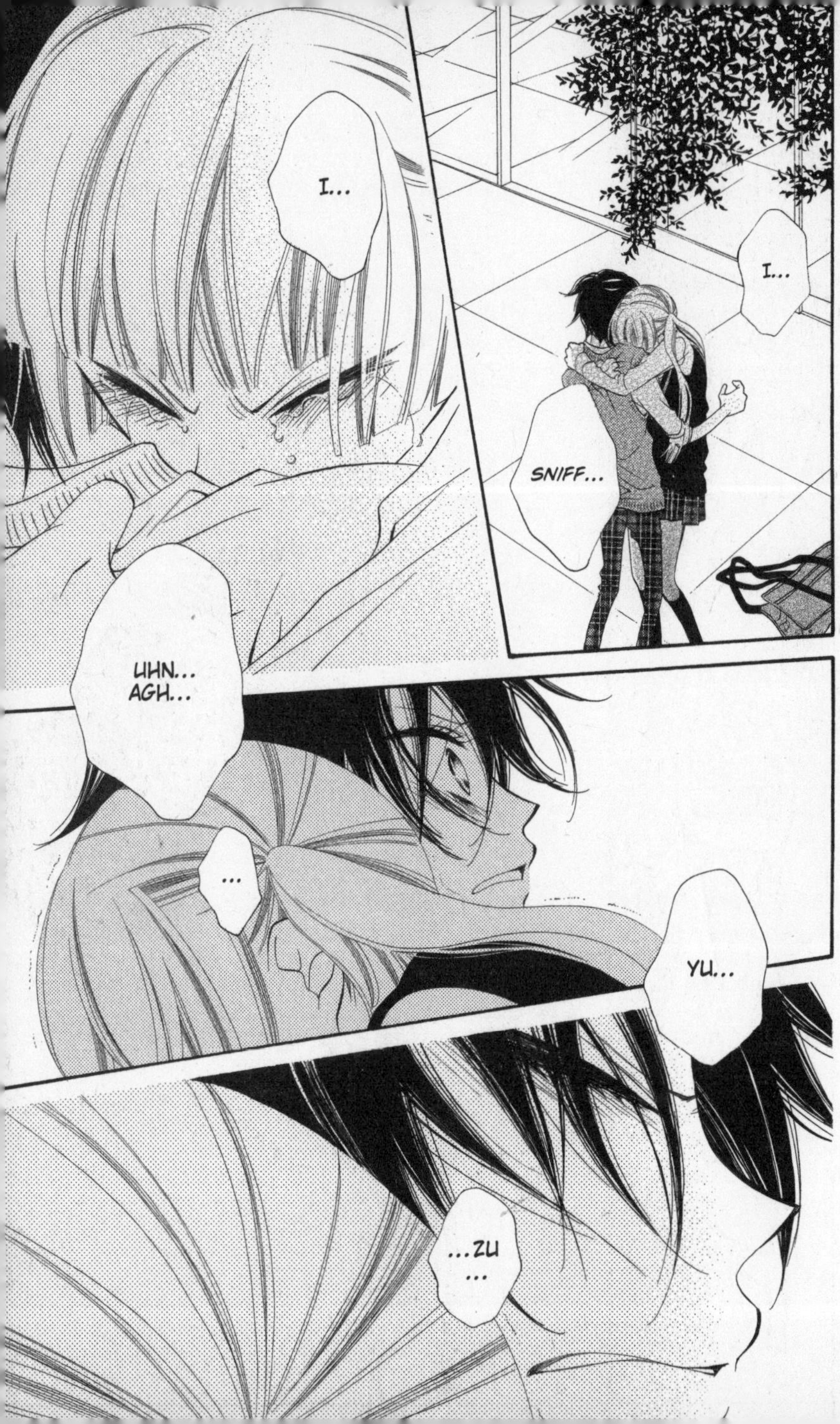
I...
SNIFF...
I...
UHN... AGH...
...
YU...
...ZU ...

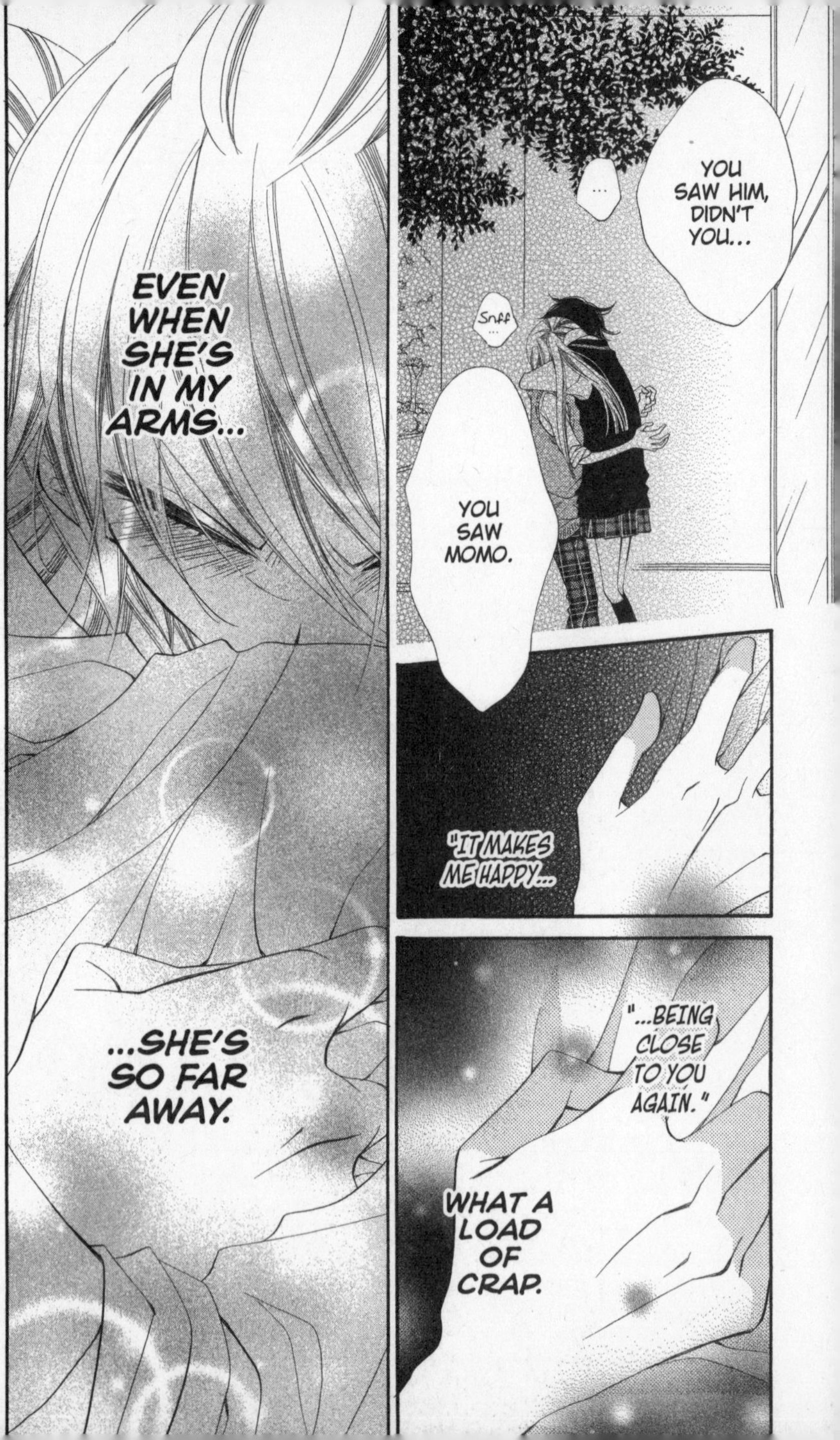
YOU SAW HIM, DIDN'T YOU...
...
Snff...
YOU SAW MOMO.
"IT MAKES ME HAPPY...
"...BEING CLOSE TO YOU AGAIN."
WHAT A LOAD OF CRAP.
EVEN WHEN SHE'S IN MY ARMS...
...SHE'S SO FAR AWAY.

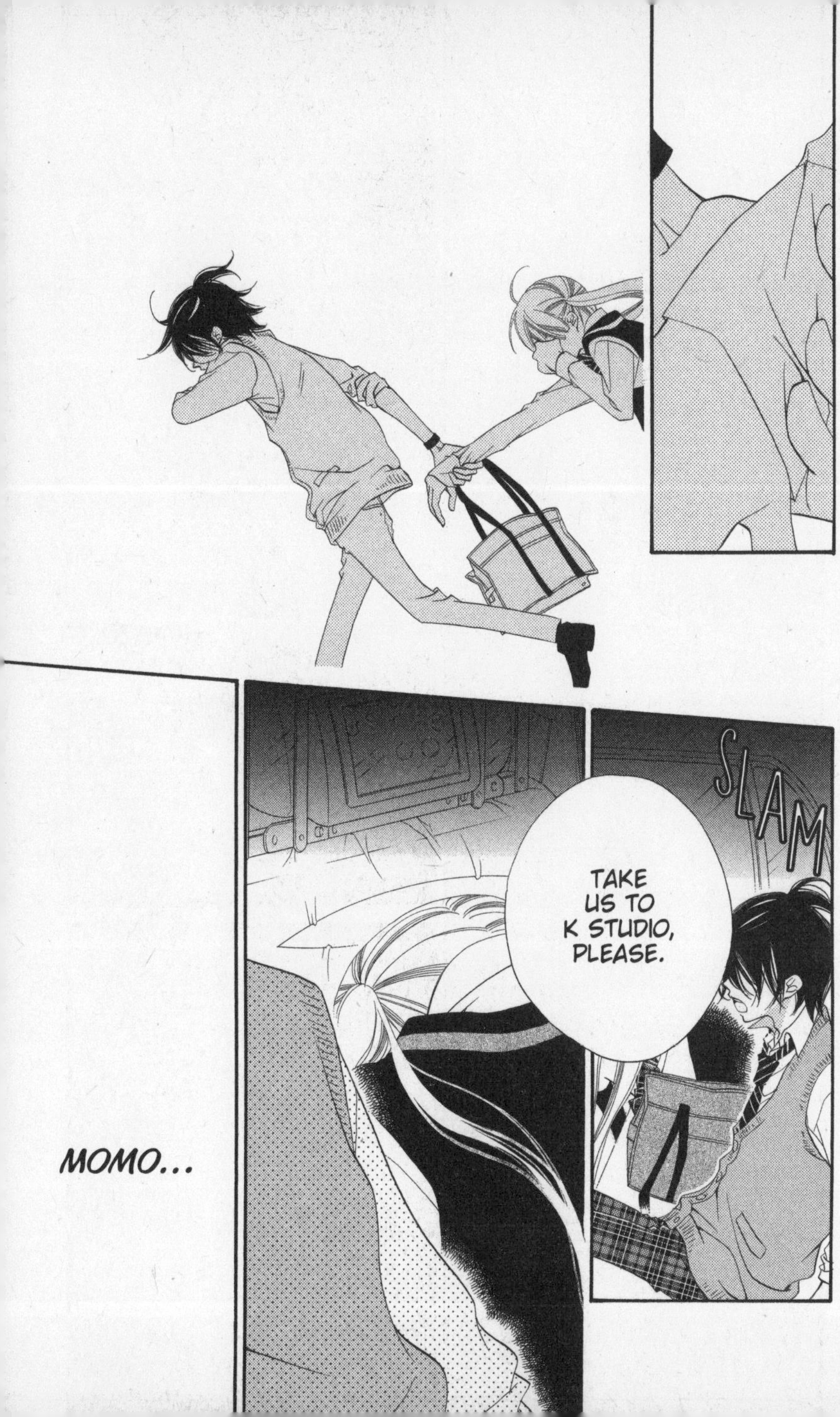
SLAM
TAKE US TO K STUDIO, PLEASE.
MOMO...

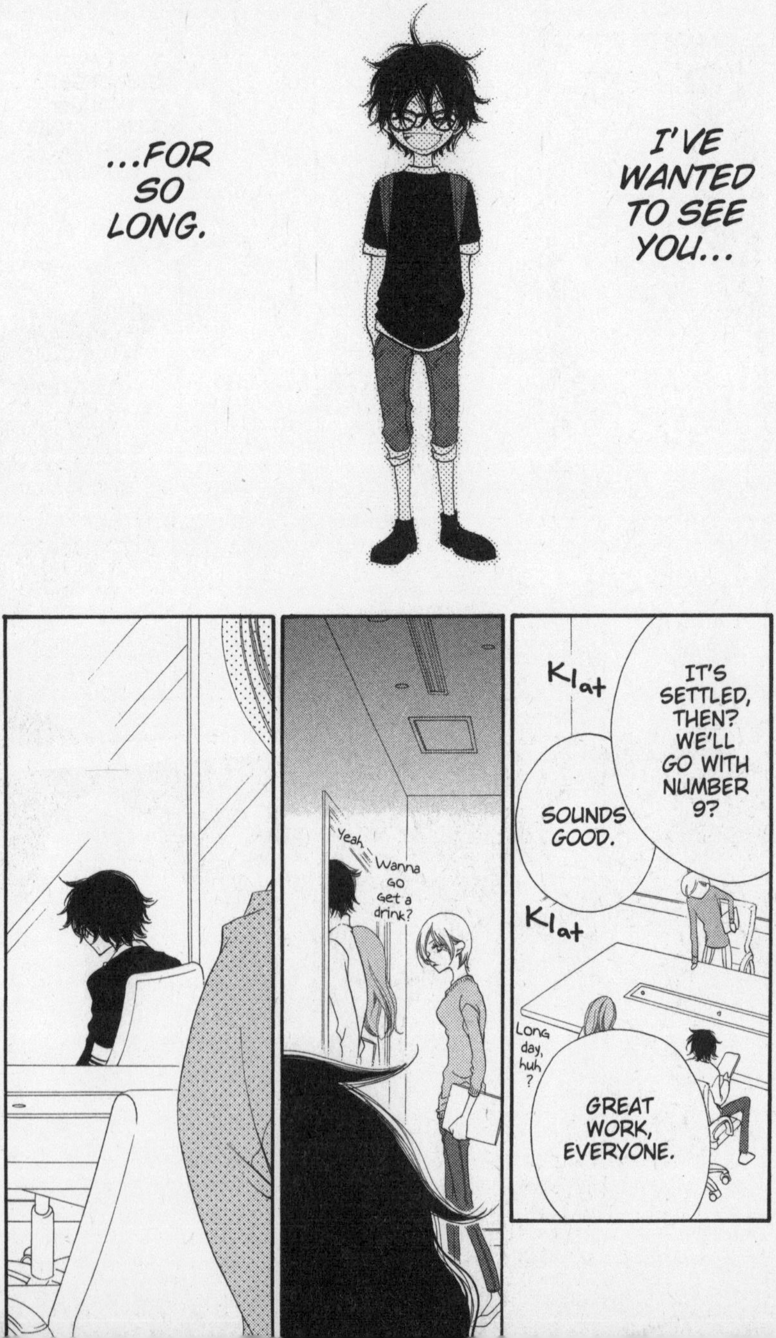
I'VE WANTED TO SEE YOU...
...FOR SO LONG.
IT'S SETTLED, THEN? WE'LL GO WITH NUMBER 9?
Klat
SOUNDS GOOD.
Klat
GREAT WORK, EVERYONE.
Long day, huh?
Wanna go get a drink?
Yeah

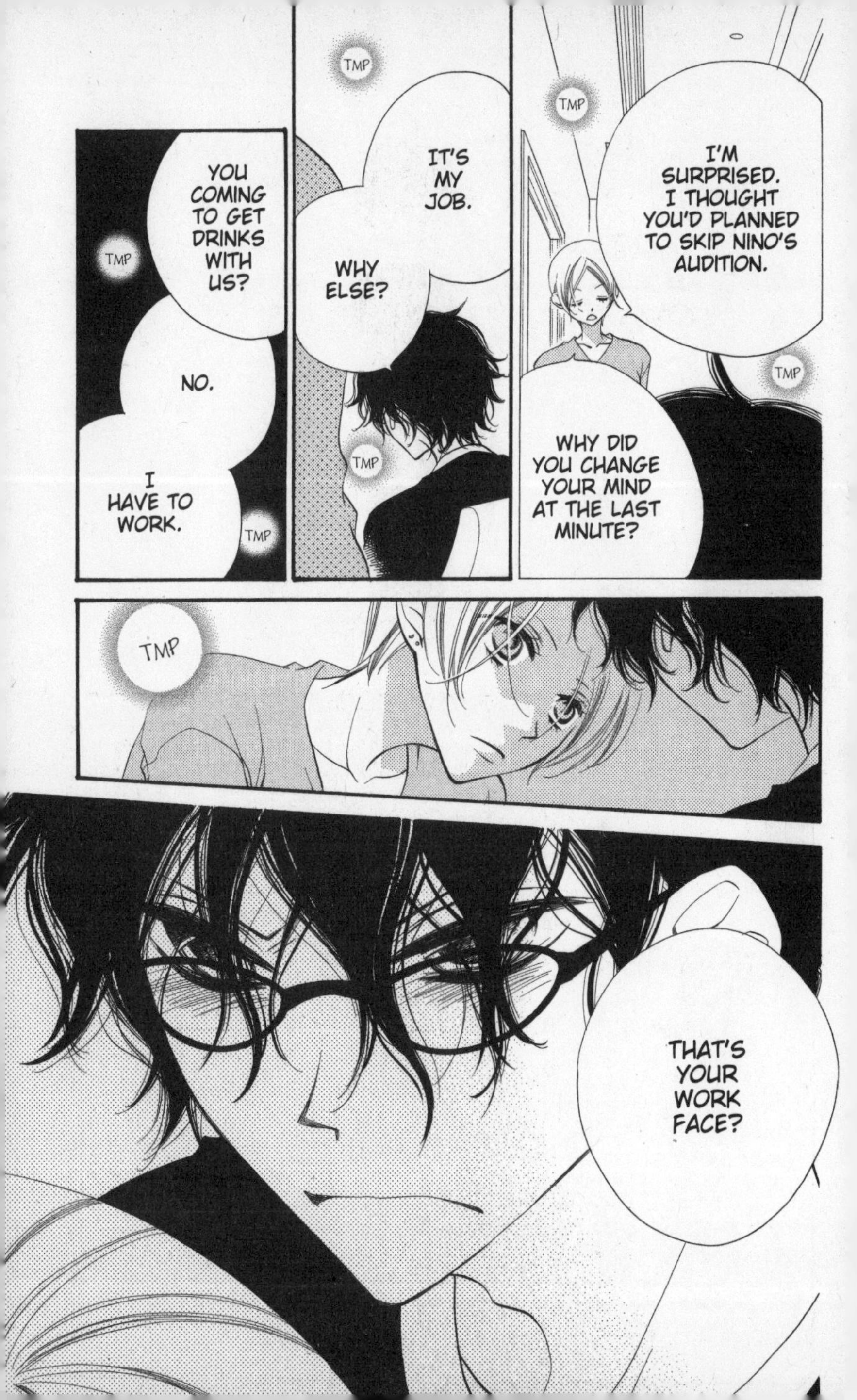

TMP
I'M SURPRISED. I THOUGHT YOU'D PLANNED TO SKIP NINO'S AUDITION.
TMP
WHY DID YOU CHANGE YOUR MIND AT THE LAST MINUTE?
TMP
IT'S MY JOB.
WHY ELSE?
TMP
YOU COMING TO GET DRINKS WITH US?
TMP
NO.
I HAVE TO WORK.
TMP
TMP
THAT'S YOUR WORK FACE?

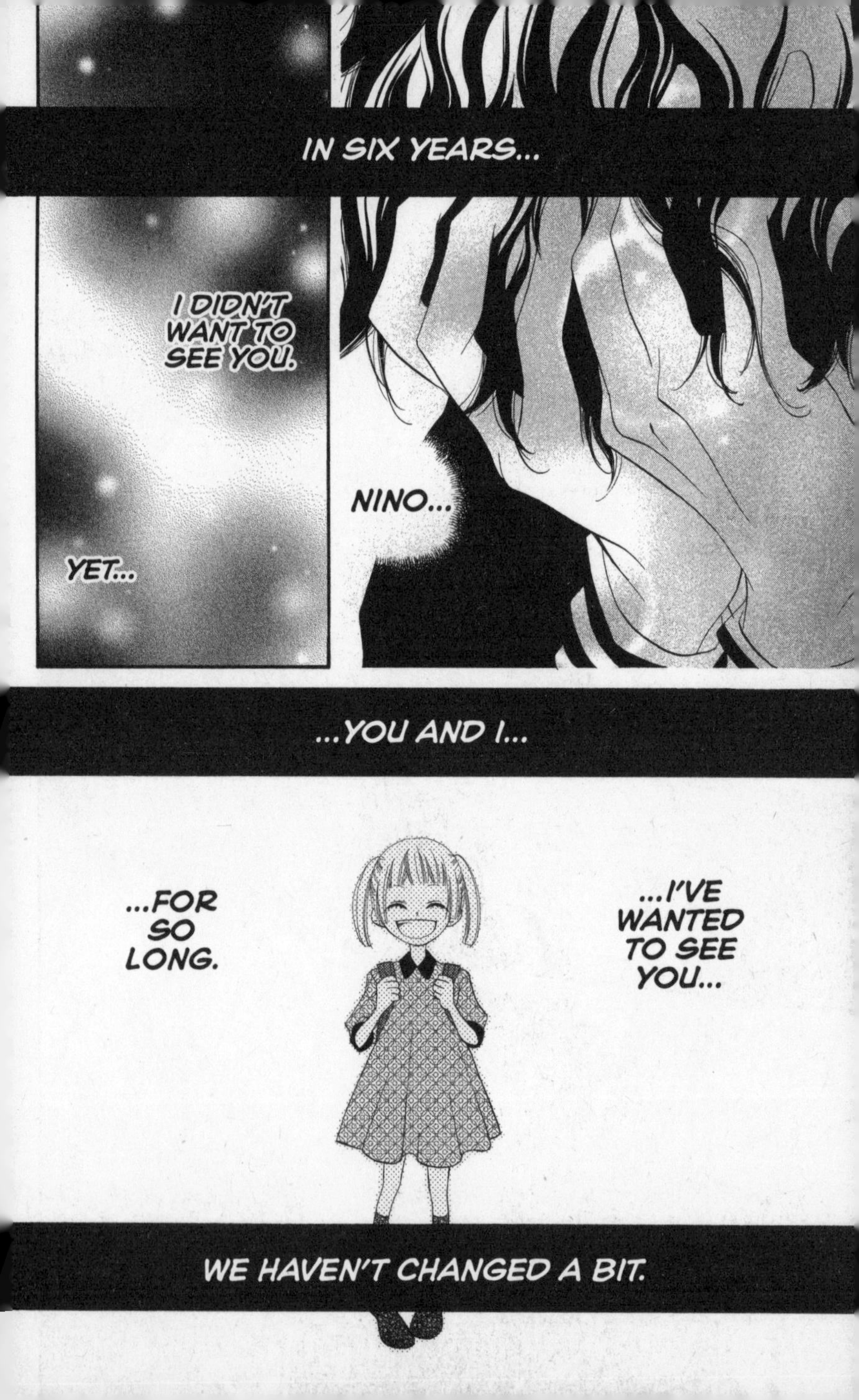
IN SIX YEARS...
NINO...
I DIDN'T WANT TO SEE YOU.
YET...
...YOU AND I...
...I'VE WANTED TO SEE YOU...
...FOR SO LONG.
WE HAVEN'T CHANGED A BIT.

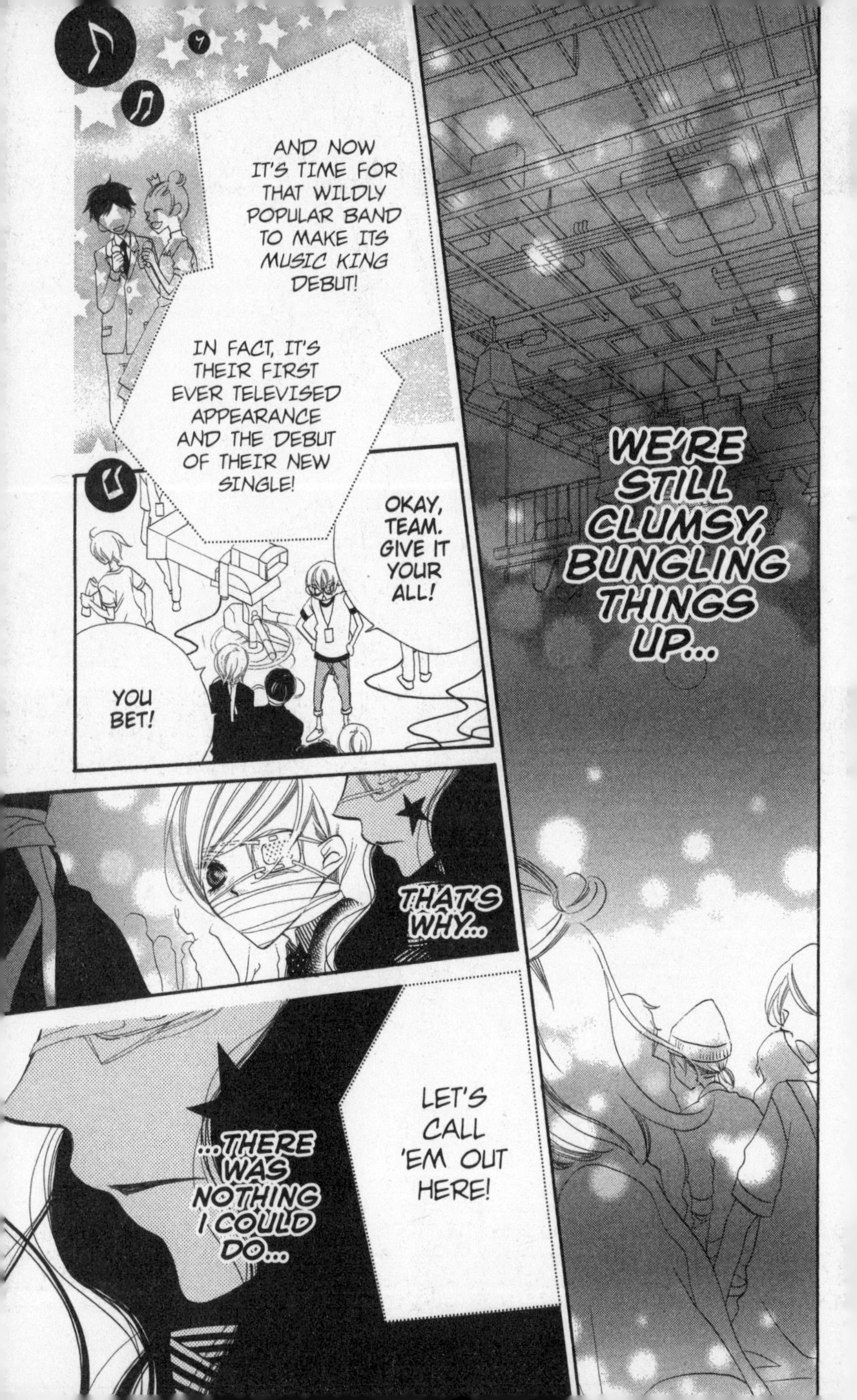
WE'RE STILL CLUMSY, BUNGLING THINGS UP...
AND NOW IT'S TIME FOR THAT WILDLY POPULAR BAND TO MAKE ITS MUSIC KING DEBUT!
IN FACT, IT'S THEIR FIRST EVER TELEVISED APPEARANCE AND THE DEBUT OF THEIR NEW SINGLE!
OKAY, TEAM. GIVE IT YOUR ALL!
YOU BET!
THAT'S WHY...
LET'S CALL 'EM OUT HERE!
...THERE WAS NOTHING I COULD DO...

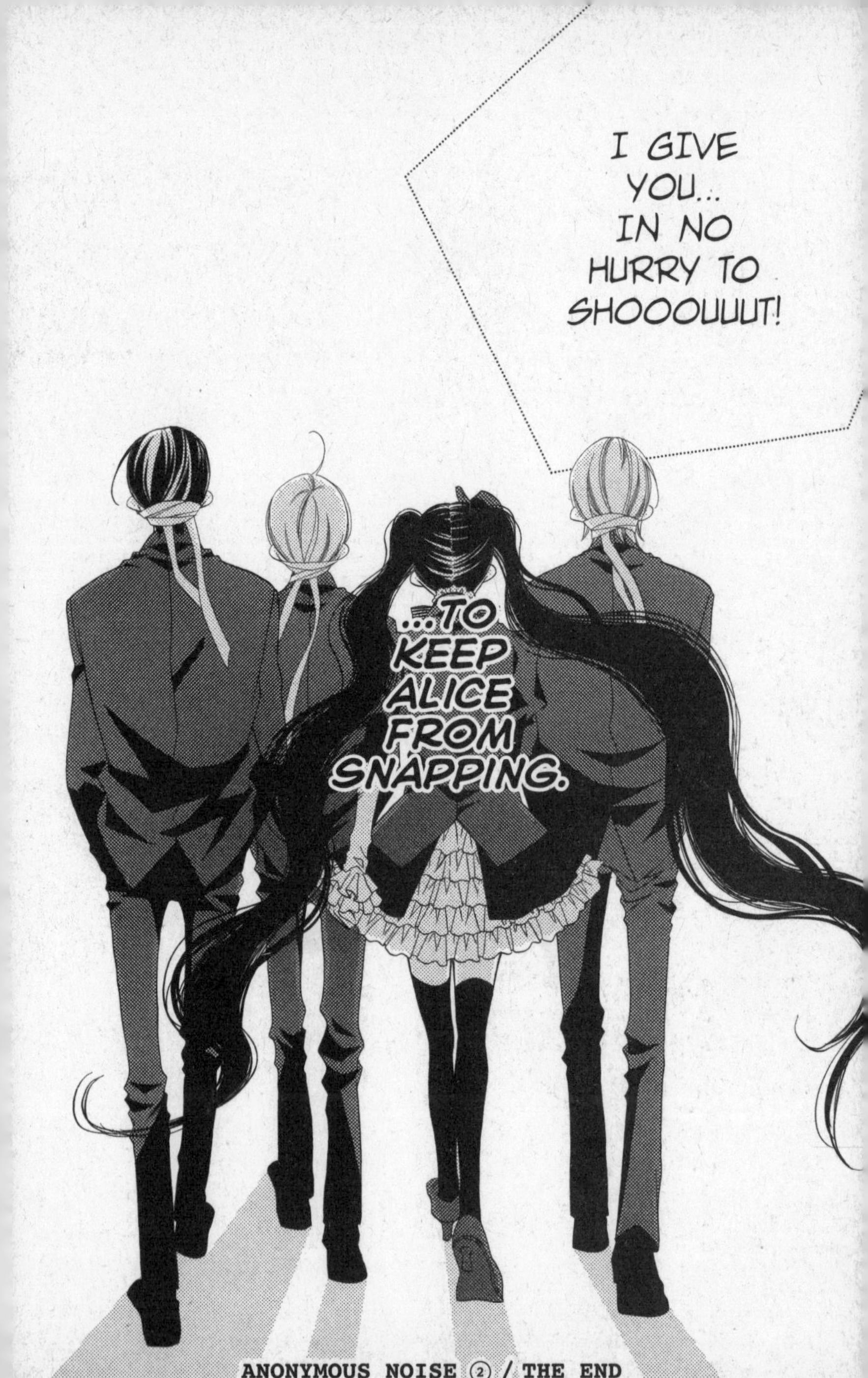
I GIVE YOU... IN NO HURRY TO SHOOOUUUT!
...TO KEEP ALICE FROM SNAPPING.

ANONYMOUS NOISE ② / THE END

TO BE CONTINUED IN ANONYMOUS NOISE 3

I'd never thought that Nino and I had much in common, so it shook me in a variety of ways when my editor recently remarked, "You're just like Nino, Fukuyama-san!"

- Ryoko Fukuyama

Born on January 5 in Wakayama Prefecture in Japan, Ryoko Fukuyama debuted as a manga artist after winning the Hakusensha Athena Shinjin Taisho Prize from Hakusensha's *Hana to Yume* magazine. She is also the author of *Nosatsu Junkie*. *Anonymous Noise* was adapted into an anime in 2017.

ANONYMOUS NOISE
Vol. 2
Shojo Beat Edition

STORY AND ART BY
RYOKO FUKUYAMA

English Translation & Adaptation/Casey Loe
Touch-Up Art & Lettering/Joanna Estep
Design/Yukiko Whitley
Editor/Amy Yu

Fukumenkei Noise by Ryoko Fukuyama
© Ryoko Fukuyama 2014
All rights reserved.
First published in Japan in 2014 by HAKUSENSHA, Inc., Tokyo.
English language translation rights arranged with HAKUSENSHA, Inc., Tokyo.

Printed in Canada

Published by VIZ Media, LLC
P.O. Box 77010
San Francisco, CA 94107

10 9 8 7 6 5 4 3 2 1
First printing, May 2017

www.viz.com

www.shojobeat.com

Surprise!

You may be reading
the wrong way!

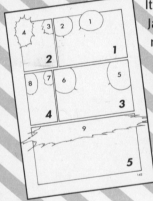

It's true: In keeping with the original
Japanese comic format, this book
reads from right to left—so action,
sound effects and word balloons are
completely reversed. This preserves
the orientation of the original
artwork—plus, it's fun! Check out the
diagram shown here to get the hang of
things, and then turn to the other side
of the book to get started!